STERNE: THE CRITICAL HERITAGE

THE CRITICAL HERITAGE SERIES

GENERAL EDITOR: B. C. SOUTHAM, M.A., B. LITT. (OXON.)
Formerly Department of English, Westfield College, University of London

For a list of books in the series see the back end paper

STERNE

THE CRITICAL HERITAGE

Edited by
ALAN B. HOWES
Professor of English
University of Michigan

ROUTLEDGE & KEGAN PAUL : LONDON AND BOSTON

First published in 1974
by Routledge & Kegan Paul Ltd
Broadway House, 68–74 Carter Lane,
London EC4V 5EL and
9 Park Street,
Boston, Mass. 02108, U.S.A.
ISBN 0 7100 7788 2
Library of Congress Catalog Card No. 73-89196

Printed in Great Britain by
Richard Clay (The Chaucer Press) Ltd
Bungay, Suffolk

General Editor's Preface

The reception given to a writer by his contemporaries and near-contemporaries is evidence of considerable value to the student of literature. On one side we learn a great deal about the state of criticism at large and in particular about the development of critical attitudes towards a single writer; at the same time, through private comments in letters, journals or marginalia, we gain an insight upon the tastes and literary thought of individual readers of the period. Evidence of this kind helps us to understand the writer's historical situation, the nature of his immediate reading-public, and his response to these pressures.

The separate volumes in the *Critical Heritage Series* present a record of this early criticism. Clearly, for many of the highly productive and lengthily reviewed nineteenth- and twentieth-century writers, there exists an enormous body of material; and in these cases the volume editors have made a selection of the most important views, significant for their intrinsic critical worth or for their representative quality – perhaps even registering incomprehension!

For earlier writers, notably pre-eighteenth century, the materials are much scarcer and the historical period has been extended, sometimes far beyond the writer's lifetime, in order to show the inception and growth of critical views which were initially slow to appear.

In each volume the documents are headed by an Introduction, discussing the material assembled and relating the early stages of the author's reception to what we have come to identify as the critical tradition. The volumes will make available much material which would otherwise be difficult of access and it is hoped that the modern reader will be thereby helped towards an informed understanding of the ways in which literature has been read and judged.

B.C.S.

Contents

CONTENTS

CONTENTS

CONTENTS

The 1780s: anthologies and complete works

CONTENTS

The Netherlands

Russia

Italy

Preface

'Shall we for ever make new books, as apothecaries make new mixtures, by pouring only out of one vessel into another?' Laurence Sterne asks in a passage in volume V of *Tristram Shandy* deploring plagiaries, which is itself plagiarized from Robert Burton's *Anatomy of Melancholy*. I cannot plead Sterne's witty excuse for pouring from many vessels into this present one, though I hope the mixture will be sufficiently new to make the undertaking worthwhile. A close look at the criticism of Sterne in England and America, as well as on the Continent, during the seventy years following the initial appearance of *Tristram Shandy* in 1760 provides more than one kind of insight. First and foremost, it contributes to an understanding of the special quality of Sterne's work and hence to a richer reading of that work by the twentieth-century reader. But it also illuminates the critical attitudes and practices of the late eighteenth and early nineteenth centuries.

A few words of explanation are in order. I have printed extensive passages from Sterne's own works because his entire literary career consisted of a long dialogue with his readers, real or imaginary, sensitive or insensitive, serious or bantering. I have tried to suggest something of the range of response among Sterne's readers by letting individual voices be heard even if they are not in any way typical. Much of the criticism of Sterne centered more on biographical and moral assessments than on literary ones, and although I have in general excluded criticism that is purely biographical, I have included some discussions in which conclusions about Sterne's work are drawn from biographical or moral considerations. I have included only a very limited amount of criticism of Sterne's *Sermons*, although some critics of Sterne's time would have seen these as his major work. I have tried to indicate the extent of Sterne's impact on the Continent with selections drawn from several countries where Sterne was revered and where he exerted an important influence.

Finally, the question of a terminal date for showing Sterne's contemporary reception was troublesome. One could find justification for stopping as early as Sterne's death in 1768 or as late as Sterne's first full-length biographer, Percy Fitzgerald, whose *Life of Sterne* appeared nearly a hundred years later in 1864. In a sense both dates reflect something of the contemporary reception, since Fitzgerald brings together some of the accumulated attitudes that begin even during Sterne's lifetime. The date of 1830 is a compromise, based on my feeling that after various ups and downs Sterne's reputation was securely established by the Romantic critics. They are both the first critics since his own time to come as close to a genuine appreciation as some of Sterne's contemporaries did, and probably the last critics to grow up with Sterne as an inevitable, as well as an important and loved part of their literary educations. After them Sterne gradually becomes a less frequently read though (in our own time, at least) more frequently respected classic. I have included a few selections dated after 1830 when they represented attitudes formed by a critic before that date or served to round out earlier comments by the same critic.

The following short titles have been used throughout; the full bibliographical information for each will be found in the Bibliography: *Life* for Cross's 3rd edition; *Letters* for Curtis's edition. The selections from *Tristram Shandy* and the *Sentimental Journey* reproduce the text of the first edition in each case, with page numbers from that edition appearing in square brackets at the end of each selection. For the convenience of the modern reader, the corresponding pages in Work's edition of *Tristram Shandy* (referred to as Work) and Stout's edition of the *Sentimental Journey* (referred to as Stout) appear at the beginning of each selection. All page references in other citations of Sterne's two works are to these editions.

I am especially grateful to my translators who have helped to provide background as well as undertaking the actual translations: for the French selections, to Isabel B. Howes, who collaborated with me; for the German selections, to Professor Valentine C. Hubbs of the Department of Germanic Languages and Literatures of the University of Michigan; for the Dutch selections, to Jelle Atema; for the Russian selections (except as otherwise noted), to Patricia Due; for the Italian selections, to William Paden Jr. Finally, unlike Sterne, I do not 'hate to praise my wife,' Lidie M. Howes. She has served as typist, editor, critic, and—most important—as lifter of spirits whenever I needed to be restored to a state of true Shandeism.

Acknowledgments

I wish to thank the following publishers and individuals for permission to reprint extracts from the sources listed below. All possible care has been taken to trace ownership of the selections included and to make full acknowledgment for their use.

Cambridge University Press for *The Correspondence of Richard Hurd and William Mason*, ed. E. H. Pearce and Leonard Whibley; the Clarendon Press, Oxford, for *Boswell's Life of Johnson*, ed. George B. Hill and L. F. Powell; *Collected Works of Oliver Goldsmith*, ed. Arthur Friedman; *Correspondence of Thomas Gray*, ed. Paget Toynbee and Leonard Whibley; *Letters of David Hume*, ed. J. Y. T. Greig; *Letters of Robert Burns*, ed. J. DeLancey Ferguson; *The Poetical Works of Charles Churchill*, ed. Douglas Grant; and *Selected Letters of Samuel Richardson*, ed. John Carroll; Columbia University Press for Nikolai Karamzin, *Letters of a Russian Traveler 1789–90*, trans. Florence Jonas; Constable and Co. Ltd for *Unpublished Letters of Samuel Taylor Coleridge*, ed. Earl Leslie Griggs; Curtis Brown Ltd for *Mrs. Montagu*, ed. Reginald Blunt; J. M. Dent & Sons Ltd for *Coleridge's Shakespearean Criticism*, ed. Thomas M. Raysor, also published by E. P. Dutton & Co. Inc. in Everyman's Library Edition and used with their permission; Harvard University Press for Ernest J. Simmons, *English Literature and Culture in Russia (1553–1840)*; William Heinemann Ltd, McGraw-Hill Book Co. and Yale University for *Private Papers of James Boswell from Malahide Castle*, ed. Geoffrey Scott and Frederick A. Pottle; Hodder & Stoughton Ltd for *Correspondence of William Cowper*, ed. Thomas Wright; Indiana University Press for *The Critical Prose of Alexander Pushkin*, ed. and trans. Carl R. Proffer; the Johns Hopkins University Press for L. P. Curtis, 'New light on Sterne,' *Modern Language Notes* (lxxvi), 1961; Methuen & Co. Ltd for *The Letters of Charles Lamb*, ed. E. V. Lucas; J. B. Metzlersche for Friedrich von Blanckenburg, *Versuch über den Roman* (in translation); Oliver & Boyd Ltd for Henry Mackenzie, *Letters to Elizabeth Rose of Kilravock*, ed. Horst W. Drescher; Oxford University Press for *Table Talk and Omniana of Samuel Taylor Coleridge*; Prof. Thomas M. Raysor for his edition of *Coleridge's Miscellaneous Criticism*; Princeton University Press

ACKNOWLEDGMENTS

for *The Papers of Thomas Jefferson*, ed. Julian P. Boyd; Stanford University Press for James Boswell, *The Hypochondriack*, ed. Margery Bailey; Marian C. Thompson for *Anecdotes and Egotisms of Henry Mackenzie*, ed. Harold W. Thompson; University of North Carolina Press for Alexander Cowie, *John Trumbull, Connecticut Wit*; and Alan Dugald McKillop, *Samuel Richardson, Printer and Novelist*; University of Texas Press for *The Satiric Poems of John Trumbull*, ed. Edwin T. Bowden; Prof. J. Thomas Shaw for his edition of *Letters of Alexander Pushkin*; Yale University Press for *Horace Walpole's Correspondence with George Montagu*, ed. W. S. Lewis and Ralph S. Brown Jr.; *Horace Walpole's Correspondence . . . with Henry Zouch*, ed. W. S. Lewis and Ralph M. Williams; *Horace Walpole's Correspondence with Sir David Dalrymple*, ed. W. S. Lewis, Charles H. Bennett, and Andrew G. Hoover; *Horace Walpole's Correspondence with Sir Horace Mann*, ed. W. S. Lewis, Warren Hunting Smith, and George L. Lam; and *Horace Walpole's Correspondence with Thomas Gray*, ed. W. S. Lewis, George L. Lam, and Charles H. Bennett. I am also most grateful to the Bodleian Library, Oxford, for permission to print James Boswell's 'A Poetical Epistle to Doctor Sterne, Parson Yorick, and Tristram Shandy' from Manuscript Douce 193.

Introduction

I. MORE HANDLES THAN ONE

A few weeks before Laurence Sterne's death an American admirer sent him an odd walking stick, 'a *shandean* piece of sculpture' with '*more handles than one.*' In his letter of thanks Sterne lamented that in reading *Tristram Shandy* readers chose 'the handle . . . which suits their passions, their ignorance or sensibility. There is so little true feeling in the *herd* of the *world,*' he continued, 'that I wish I could have got an act of parliament, when the books first appear'd, "that none but wise men should look into them." It is too much to write books and find heads to understand them,' he concluded (No. 55b).

The reader who traces the criticism of Sterne during the seventy years after the appearance of the initial volumes of *Tristram Shandy* might well share this view, for Sterne has suffered more critical vagaries than most major writers. The reader is likely to tire, as Sterne did during his lifetime, of the bantering attacks (designed mainly to earn their Grub Street authors a pittance), of the importance placed upon secondary or extraneous issues (centered on Sterne's clerical character and his personal life), and of the general failure of critics to come to grips with Sterne's essential method (exemplified by the tendency to see his work as merely a collection of fragments). The reader likewise tires, as Sterne would have, of many of the controversies that continued after his death: the disputes about the moral effect of his books, the sincerity of his feelings, and the relationship of his character to his works; and the endless discussion of the nature and extent of his borrowings from other writers. Much of the criticism of Sterne centers on a few major themes; but there are variations; for if Sterne's work invited clichés, it also invited very personal responses. The personal responses are due in part to Sterne's manner and the relationship he attempts to establish with his readers. They are due in part to the extremely varied nature of his work, which offered, as one critic said, something for each of 'the three different classes of auditors; pit, box, and gallery' (No. 35). Finally, they are due in part to the meeting of the man and the critical philosophies of the moment, for in some ways Sterne was an artistic rebel, attracting both ardent partisans and violent opponents, and he carried on a running battle with his critics, as well as a continuing dialogue with his readers.

The nature of that battle and the subjects of that dialogue were partly determined by some of the attitudes and practices of eighteenth-century criticism. The eighteenth century conceived of the task of the critic somewhat differently than we do, and some of its critical practices seem strange to modern critical sensibilities. First of all, the critic thought of his task in evaluating a work as automatically including the evaluation of the character of the writer as well, and many critics regarded the two as inseparable. The critic also felt obliged to give his readers a notion of the range of a work through a fairly large amount of summary, often letting summary substitute for analysis. Most important, the 'court of criticism' was no empty metaphor. The critic tried to judge the 'beauties' and 'defects' of a book, and his series of judgments would often add up to an overall positive or negative view; but there was seldom any attempt to give a full-scale interpretation of a work as a whole or to see it through the lens of a single critical perspective, and often the contradictory evidence pro and con was left unreconciled.

Standards for criticism centered around the concept of decorum, a concept which applied in several different contexts. It applied first of all to the character of the writer, with the result that a book considered appropriate for a young wit or man about town to have written was not necessarily considered appropriate for a clergyman. When Mrs Montagu suggested that her cousin Laurence Sterne's *Sentimental Journey* would 'not have misbecome a young Ensign' (No. 58f), she also meant to imply that it did not become a clergyman. Decorum applied also to the accepted conventions of what remained within the bounds of good taste and morality for any writer. It applied as well to the notion of what patterns and forms were appropriate to a particular genre. Thus decorum had to do with professional character, morality and aesthetics.

In the continuing battle with his critics and the continuing dialogue with his readers, Sterne challenged the notion of decorum in all of these applications. To a friend who had warned that 'some gross allusions' in *Tristram Shandy* 'would betray a forgetfulness of his character,' Sterne replied 'that an attention to his character would damp his fire, and check the flow of his humour; and that if he . . . hoped to be read,

he must not look at his band or cassock' (No. 9b). To Bishop Warburton, who had similarly urged caution, Sterne replied: 'I will . . . do
my best; though laugh, my lord, I will, and as loud as I can too' (No.
16b). To a *Monthly Review* reviewer who insulted Sterne's professional
character and complained that publishing the *Sermons of Mr. Yorick* in a
way which capitalized on the popularity of *Tristram Shandy* was 'the
greatest outrage against Sense and Decency . . . since the first establishment of Christianity' (No. 13c), Sterne replied that he would overlook
such annoyances from the critics 'with good temper' (No. 27a). To a
correspondent who had apparently chastized Sterne for the flood of
obscene imitations and bantering criticisms he had occasioned, Sterne
replied: ' "God forgive me, for the Volumes of Ribaldry I've been the
cause of"—now I say, god forgive them—and tis the pray'r I constantly
put up for those who use me most unhandsomely. . . .'[1]

Sterne showed similar defiance in the face of charges that his work
was immoral or obscene. Though he admitted his book was 'a little
tawdry in some places' (No. 3), he exclaimed sarcastically: 'Heaven
forbid the stock of chastity should be lessen'd by the life and opinions
of Tristram Shandy' (No. 5). And men of such different character as
Samuel Richardson (No. 29) and John Cleland (No. 69) agreed that
Sterne's work did not arouse the passions. The *Sentimental Journey*
Sterne called, probably only half jokingly, his '*Work of Redemption*'
(No. 53d); and he also said that if any readers thought it 'not . . . a
chaste book . . . they must have warm imaginations indeed!' (No. 53g)
Critics in general agreed that it was at least less indecent than *Tristram
Shandy*; but they raised other issues. Was Sterne's sentimental philosophy sincere and did it not substitute the indulgence of benevolent
emotions for right conduct and active charity? Was not this philosophy
therefore immoral? 'Merely to be struck by a sudden impulse of compassion at the view of an object of distress, is no more benevolence than
it is a fit of the gout,' wrote Elizabeth Carter to one of Sterne's friends,
adding that she had not read Sterne's book and probably never would
(No. 57d). Sterne himself did not live long enough to engage in the
debates over the *Sentimental Journey*.

In his dialogue with critics and readers Sterne took most pains of all
to justify and explain his method, though sometimes, perhaps, with
tongue in cheek. At the same time that he was relying on the value of
parody for making fun of some of the usual narrative conventions, he
was also keenly aware of the possibility that his audience, trained in the
notions of what was appropriate to a given form, might miss the point

of what he was trying to do. Especially in the early volumes of *Tristram Shandy* he is at pains to point out that his work is 'digressive, and . . . progressive too,—and **at t**he same time' (No. 2c), that 'writing . . . is but a different name for conversation' (No. 2f), that 'rules and compasses' or exact critical measurements are likely to destroy 'a work of genius' (No. 27b), and that 'to write a book is . . . like humming a song—be but in tune with your self . . . 'tis no matter how high or how low you take it' (No. 27h). Sterne also gave plentiful hints about his indebtedness to Locke (Nos 2d, e), and put his fundamental philosophy in the mouth of Walter Shandy: 'Every thing in this world . . . is big with jest,—and has wit in it, and instruction too,—if we can but find it out' (No. 33b). Many of Sterne's readers unfortunately did miss the point of some of these remarks: at best, they saw his work as a kind of dazzling chaos in which brilliant fragments jostled each other without plan; at worst, they saw only a wild farrago of discordant elements (see, for example, Nos 6b, 23, 25, 30d).

This lack of communication was not the only unfortunate element in the dialogue between Sterne and his readers. Sterne's bantering and ironic tone invited bantering responses, and much of the criticism of his work during his lifetime was only half serious at best (see, for example, Nos 11, 21, 31, 40). Often it was designed to display the critic's wit rather than contribute to an understanding of Sterne's work; and even serious critics engaged in a certain amount of banter of this sort (see, for example, Ralph Griffiths's remarks in Nos 48c and 52d). Furthermore Sterne's mannerisms and the particular kind of relationship he tried to establish between himself and his audience struck different readers very differently. Goldsmith objected to Sterne's manner as composed of 'bawdy' and 'pertness' (No. 19), while a more appreciative reader who savored Sterne's manner was willing to 'ride fifty miles to smoak a pipe with him' (No. 22a). Sterne realized that his readers would disagree—'I shall be attacked and pelted, either from cellars or garrets, write what I will,' he said. ' 'Tis enough if I divide the world;—at least I will rest contented with it' (No. 26b). At the same time he did take some account of the public's reception of his work, in particular catering in later installments of *Tristram Shandy* and in the *Sentimental Journey* to the widespread taste for 'the pathetic.' There were ups and downs in the sale of Sterne's works both during his life and later—he complained in volume VIII of *Tristram Shandy* (chapter 6) of having 'ten cart-loads of [the] fifth and sixth volumes still'—but the number of editions of his works throughout the period is ample testimony to his success in pleasing not one but many different publics (see Appendix).

II. THE PUBLICATION OF *Tristram Shandy* (1760–7)

As we try to follow and assess the dialogue between Sterne and his critics and readers from the distant vantage point of our own time, we encounter difficulties, starting with the appearance of the initial installment of *Tristram Shandy*, and resulting, in part at least, from the very personal nature of responses to Sterne. We may sometimes have to rely on speculation about the degree to which individual responses are representative or eccentric, widely shared or singly held. The reviews of the early installments of *Tristram Shandy* in the *Monthly Review* afford a good illustration of some of the difficulties. William Kenrick, reviewing the first installment of *Tristram Shandy* in the 1759 Appendix to the *Monthly* found the author 'infinitely more ingenious and entertaining than any other of the present race of novelists. His characters are striking and singular,' Kenrick continued, 'his observations shrewd and pertinent; and, making a few exceptions, his humour is easy and genuine' (No. 4). A little more than a year later Owen Ruffhead reviewed the second installment of *Tristram Shandy* for the *Monthly* in quite a different key. Centering his remarks around a lengthy quotation from Hobbes, Ruffhead read Sterne a lecture on 'discretion' and the 'flagrant impropriety of character' for a clergyman to write such a book as *Tristram Shandy*. He further charged Sterne with 'dullness,' asserting that the characters were 'no longer striking and singular' and that Sterne's 'prurient humour' was a prostitution of wit which might 'be compared to the spices which embalm a putrid carcase.' He did express the hope that Sterne would take his 'friendly admonitions in good part,' and avoid 'the misapplication of talents,' but the generally negative tone of the review was in sharp contrast to the generally positive tone of the earlier review (No. 28a).

One is tempted to account for the difference between the two reviews more by the differences between the reviewers[2] than by the differences between the two installments of Sterne's novel. Kenrick, author of the earlier review, was a volatile and controversial literary hack who quarreled with many of the leading literary men of the day, sometimes wrote anonymous pamphlets in order to answer himself in others, and 'seldom wrote without a bottle of brandy at his elbow.' He was proud of his versatility and the rapidity with which he worked. Ruffhead, in contrast, was a meticulous and careful writer. Trained as a lawyer, he brought 'the methodical industry that was habitual to him' to every task he undertook. One might expect that Kenrick would read Sterne more enthusiastically than Ruffhead.

But there are further complications. Although Sterne's name and his profession were unknown when Kenrick wrote his review, some five months later Sterne published *The Sermons of Mr. Yorick*, proclaiming his dual role as clergyman and novelist and bringing down upon his head the wrath of Ruffhead in a review of the *Sermons* in the *Monthly* for mounting the pulpit 'in a Harlequin's coat' and making 'obscenity . . . the handmaid to Religion' (No. 13c). Sterne himself had also appeared on the London scene in the meantime, and his behavior during this and subsequent London visits was at least questionable if not indiscreet (see No. 41). Since the same censures for impropriety of character are picked up by John Langhorne in his review of the third installment of *Tristram Shandy* for the *Monthly* (No. 34d), the further question occurs as to how far the policy of the magazine as such guided subsequent reviews.

Over the years the *Monthly* was likely to read Sterne lectures on the necessity for maintaining the dignity of his clerical character and to applaud his 'pathetic' passages while censuring his breaches in decorum in the humorous parts of his work (see Nos 34d, 48c, 52d). The *Critical Review*, on the other hand, thought of Sterne as the British Rabelais almost from the first and was willing to accept him on those terms (see Nos 28c, 34c, 52b). The *Critical* saw no impropriety in the manner in which Sterne had published his *Sermons of Mr. Yorick* (No. 13b), and was only perfunctory in censuring any supposed moral lapses in his work. In general, the *Critical* had less to say about Sterne than the *Monthly*: the five reviews of *Tristram Shandy* in the *Monthly* total 28,000 words, while the *Critical* devoted only 4,000 words to reviews of Sterne's novel.[3] Out of this tangle we can conclude only that Sterne called forth more critical disagreement than most writers. To some critics, knowledge of Sterne's profession made a profound difference in the way they judged his work; while to others, Sterne's violations of professional decorum were venial, if they were to be considered lapses at all. The taste and moral sense of each individual was usually the ultimate determining factor in criticism of Sterne. Periodicals, like individuals, tended to develop a consistent point of view over the years; but no views of Sterne were universally held.

But to return to the initial reception of *Tristram Shandy*. During the first few weeks of 1760 favorable reviews appeared in most of the periodicals, commending Sterne's characters and expressing good-natured bewilderment at how to characterize Sterne's work (No. 6). As the weeks passed, the novel's fame spread and Tristram became a fad with a soup, a game of cards, and a racehorse named after him. 'Who is more thought of, heard of, or talked of, by dukes, dutchesses, lords, ladies, earls, marquisses, countesses, and common whores, than Tristram Shandy?' asked one anonymous pamphleteer a year later. Not since the days of *Pamela* and *Tom Jones* had a book become so quickly fashionable.[4] Curiosity about its unknown author mounted.

Sterne himself burst upon the London scene in early March, satisfying that curiosity and adding to the fame of both his book and its author, but at the same time making it impossible henceforth for most critics to keep the man and his work separate in their judgments of either. At once lionized by fashionable London society (Nos 7, 14), Sterne began to play a public role which he did not abandon for the rest of his life. It is a role with ambiguities and unanswered questions. Was Sterne the rather odious 'professed wit' described by Charles Johnstone (No. 41), or was he the ubiquitous 'wellcome Guest' described by Boswell (No. 14)? Was Johnson's antipathy to Sterne (Nos 34a, 64) due more to his belief that Sterne failed to live up to the demands of his profession, to his opposition to Sterne's politics, or to his rejection of both Sterne's moral and aesthetic principles? Whatever the answers to questions like these, it seems clear that Sterne's conduct in London helped to swell the flood of pamphlets, imitations, and bantering attacks that capitalized upon his fame of the moment, often in bawdy or vulgar ways (No. 11). More serious attacks, of course, also came from sincere moralists who genuinely reprehended the supposed indecency of Sterne's novel and the impropriety of his conduct (No. 10).

Predictably, the famous names of the day were divided in their estimates of Sterne. Boswell wrote a warm appreciation in doggerel verse after meeting Sterne during the spring of 1760 (No. 14), but Johnson apparently avoided Sterne and remained firm in his disapproval (Nos 34a, 64). Thomas Gray thought there was 'much good fun' in *Tristram Shandy* and 'humour sometimes hit & sometimes mist' (No. 17); but Horace Walpole thought Sterne's book 'a very insipid and tedious performance' (No. 8). Samuel Richardson and his friend Lady Bradshaigh might well be expected to disapprove of Sterne: indeed they did, though—they hint—almost in spite of their inclinations as they read and enjoyed at least parts of the book (Nos 18, 29). Goldsmith, as we have seen, objected to Sterne's manner, called him a 'bawdy blockhead,' and thought *Tristram Shandy* empty of everything except false wit (No. 19). Edmund Burke, on the other hand, viewing *Tristram Shandy* primarily as satire, commended Sterne for his 'talent of catching the ridiculous in everything that comes before him' (No. 25). During the first few months after the appearance of *Tristram Shandy* most of these critical opinions had been formed, though some of the statements by major figures were not circulated until later. The battle lines had been drawn.

Sterne himself entered into the battle with some gusto, replying to his critics in the next installment of *Shandy*, which appeared in January of 1761. He chided the *Monthly Review* for its attack on the *Sermons*, but undertook to receive all criticism in good humor (No. 27a), and justified his work as providing a kind of comic catharsis by promoting healthy laughter (Nos 27g, j). Sterne was pleased with volumes III and IV, if we are to judge from statements in his letters (No. 26a), although he knew they would stir up even more controversy than the first two volumes among readers and critics (No. 26b). Ironically, the controversies were perhaps less sharp because critics were generally in agreement in the unfavorable tone of their criticism (Nos 28, 30a, 31). It became almost as much the fashion to attack the third and fourth volumes of *Tristram Shandy* as it had been to praise the first and second. The *Critical Review* alone felt that the first installment had been overvalued, the second undervalued by other critics (No. 28c). The novelty of *Tristram Shandy* had begun to wear off, and many critics thought that in the second installment Sterne had resorted to obscenity and obscurity when true wit failed him (see, for example, No. 31).

As Sterne worked on the next installment, volumes V and VI, he wrote to a friend, 'I care not a curse for the critics' (No. 32a); and as he neared the end of the two volumes he thought they were 'the best,' partly because he was 'delighted' with 'uncle Toby's imaginary character' (No. 32b). In the new volumes themselves he addressed fewer remarks to critics and readers to justify his technique, though he reiterated that he was trying to achieve the proper blend of wit and judgment, jesting and seriousness, in his book (No. 33c). The criticism of volumes V and VI was in general more favorable than that of volumes III and IV, and the story of 'Le Fever' was widely reprinted. The *Critical* found the volumes pretty much of a piece with those that had preceded them and noted again the resemblance to Rabelais but also added special praise for the story of 'Le Fever' (No. 34c). John Langhorne in the

Monthly echoed this praise and asserted that the new installment was 'in point of true humour' superior to the previous one, in spite of some remaining traces of indecency. Sterne's forte, he concluded, lay in the pathetic.

The next three years Sterne spent in pursuit of health on the Continent; he did not return to England until the summer of 1764. The story of the reception of Sterne and his works abroad will be told below. During his absence, his popularity in England continued, though with something of a lull. A false rumor of his death shortly after his departure brought tributes (No. 36) and critics continued to refer to him (Nos 37, 40, 42, 45).

Unable to complete two more volumes in the usual Shandy pattern by his deadline after his return to England, Sterne experimented in volume VII with a plan to use his travels—a plan which later came to more complete fruition in the *Sentimental Journey*. When the seventh and eighth volumes appeared in January of 1765, however, the reviewers felt that Sterne had imposed upon the public by padding this installment with extraneous materials from his travels (No. 48). Most reviewers intimated that Sterne should stop writing installments of *Shandy*, though Ralph Griffiths, in the *Monthly*, suggested that Sterne might 'strike out a new plan' and cultivate his talents in 'the pathetic' (No. 48c).

Sterne may well have taken this advice to heart as he took his second Continental tour from the fall of 1765 to the spring of 1766, traveling mainly in Italy and gathering materials which later found their way into the *Sentimental Journey*. During his absence the third and fourth volumes of the *Sermons of Mr. Yorick* appeared without the furor which had accompanied the publication of the first two volumes of sermons (No. 50).

After his return to England, Sterne's immediate concern was another installment of *Tristram Shandy* and the occasional glimpses we catch of him during the composition of the lone ninth volume show a man unchanged. Sterne wonders how he can 'keep up that just balance betwixt wisdom and folly, without which a book would not hold together a single year' (No. 52a); and to a Black admirer who has written to enlist his talents in the cause against Negro slavery, he replies that his pen is 'at the service of the afflicted' (No. 51b). Wit and judgment, sense and nonsense, humor and pathos—these are the elements out of which he will continue to blend his work. And the blend continues to puzzle critics, as they attempt to characterize volume IX of *Tristram Shandy*.

Its wit 'may be termed generical,' the *Critical Review* asserts (No. 52b); and Griffiths in the *Monthly* finds a new way to describe Sterne—as a harlequin producing 'the pantomime of literature' (No. 52d). What a pity, Griffiths concludes, 'that Nature should thus capriciously have embroidered the choicest flowers of genius, on a paultry groundwork of buffoonry!' (No. 52d). A review in the *Gentleman's Magazine* stated that there could be 'neither epitome nor extract' of Sterne's work; and concluded that 'its *bad* is an object of judgment, though its *good* is an object of taste' (No. 52c).

III. *A Sentimental Journey* (1768)

Further inspiration for *Shandy* was lacking for the moment, but Sterne was now ready to make a more extensive use of material from his travels. The *Sentimental Journey*, he wrote to his daughter Lydia, was to be 'something new, quite out of the beaten track' (No. 53a). Its purpose, he wrote several months later to a friend, was 'to teach us to love the world and our fellow creatures better than we do' (No. 53e). This book, he said, 'the women will read . . . in the parlour, and *Tristram* in the bed-chamber' (No. 53i).

Response to the *Sentimental Journey* was in the main enthusiastic. The *Monthly Review* and the *Political Register* termed it Sterne's 'best' work (No. 56c, d); of the reviews, the *Critical* alone was unfavorable (No. 56a). The harshness of this latter review was probably due to Sterne's satirical portrait of Smollett as Smelfungus (No. 53j), since although Smollett's connection with the *Critical* had long since ceased, the reviewers probably still felt loyalty to him. Private opinions likewise were not unanimous, though the general tone was highly favorable. Walpole thought that Sterne's travels were 'exceedingly good-natured and picturesque,' and 'infinitely preferable to his tiresome *Tristram Shandy*' (No. 57a, b). A year later Fanny Burney wrote in her diary, 'I am now going to *charm* myself for the third time with poor Sterne's *Sentimental Journey*.'[5] But not all the women read or enjoyed the *Sentimental Journey* in the parlor: Fanny Greville replied to Elizabeth Burney's praise of Sterne with the statement that 'when a man chooses to walk about the world with a cambrick handkerchief always in his hand, that he may always be ready to weep, either with man or beast,—he only makes me sick' (No. 57e).

Tributes on the occasion of Sterne's death followed hard upon the heels of comments on the *Sentimental Journey*—indeed, some periodicals combined reviews of Sterne's travels with eulogies (No. 56b, c); but even in death Sterne found no agreement in the final assessments of his character and works, some writers excusing his faults, while others lamented or censured his weaknesses (No. 58).

IV. 1769–79: CONTINUING CONTROVERSIES

In the years between Sterne's death and the publication of the first authoritative edition of his works in 1780, his reputation continued to grow. Johnson was indeed wrong when he asserted in 1776 that *Tristram Shandy* had not lasted (No. 64b), but no major critics treated Sterne at length. There were brief remarks, both pro and con, from other famous men on both sides of the Atlantic, leaving accounts fairly even. The disapproval expressed by American poet John Trumbull (No. 60) is balanced by the enthusiasm of Thomas Jefferson, who thought that Sterne's works 'form the best course of morality that ever was written' (No. 62b). John Wesley's contemptuous dismissal of the word 'sentimental' as 'not English' and his assertion that Sterne's 'book agrees full well with the title, for one is as queer as the other' (No. 70a), is contradicted in popular poet Samuel Jackson Pratt's rhapsodic praise of Sterne's sensibility and the 'milky and humane temperature' about his pulses (No. 67a). Lesser-known critics also tended to divide along the old familiar lines, with Sterne's defenders opposing clichés to the clichés of his detractors. In reply to the charge that Sterne's work lacked form or order, his defenders pointed to the originality of his genius and the excellence of his characters; in reply to attacks upon his philosophy as 'shallow' or 'false,' they praised his mastery of the 'pathetic' and his 'knowledge of the human heart'; in answering strictures upon his indecency they stressed the cathartic effect of his humor and the excellence of his satire (Nos 70, 72). The publication of various editions of Sterne's letters (No. 66) meant that his sentimental philosophy was frequently considered against the background of his own life and particularly his relationship with Mrs Draper (see No. 53d, 1, p. 187).

V. 1780–90: *The Beauties of Sterne*

In 1780, proof that Sterne had begun to stand the test of time came when a group of London booksellers published a 'complete edition' of Sterne's works, 'with those embellishments usually bestowed on our most distinguished authors.' As the unknown editor said, time had indeed 'fixed [Sterne's] reputation as one of the first writers in the English language . . . and advanced him to the rank of a classick' (No. 74).

During the next decade Sterne paid the price for having become a classic: he was anthologized . . . and, in the process, bowdlerized. *The Beauties of Sterne*, which purported to be 'Selected for the Heart of Sensibility' and to contain 'all his Pathetic Tales, & most distinguished Observations on Life' first appeared in 1782 (No. 78a); it had reached a seventh edition within a year, and a twelfth edition by 1793. Homer and Shakespeare, as well as most of the major literary figures of the previous fifty years, were accorded similar treatment; but in the case of Sterne, anthologizing gave an unusually distorted picture, since the editor took care to make his selections so that 'the *chaste* part of the world' could not possibly be offended. Thus Sterne's humorous side was further deprecated and the disordered or fragmentary character of his work underlined by the implication that his 'pathetic' tales and his 'sentiments' on a variety of subjects were the only worthwhile things he had written. Even though the tenth edition of the *Beauties* in 1787 attempted to redress the balance somewhat between the sentimental and humorous sides of Sterne's work (No. 78b), the overall effect of this anthology was to suggest that Sterne's works were valuable not as artistic wholes but only for particular highlights.

The Beauties of Sterne thus increased the tendency to value the *Sentimental Journey*, with its greater share of 'sentiments' and 'pathetic passages,' above the more boisterous *Tristram Shandy*. Robert Burns accorded equal praise to Sterne's two books (No. 80); but minor novelist Clara Reeve is much more typical in not knowing what she can 'say of [*Tristram Shandy*] with safety,' yet asserting with confidence that the *Sentimental Journey* is 'indisputably a work of merit' (No. 81).

Better-known figures like Mrs Piozzi (No. 82) and Henry Mackenzie (Nos 66d, 86) make only passing references to Sterne, and the man to treat Sterne's work at greatest length during the eighties was Vicesimus Knox, ordained minister and headmaster of Tonbridge School. His *Essays Moral and Literary*, in which he first commented at length on Sterne in the edition of 1782, had reached a thirteenth edition by 1793. Though 'far below Shakespeare on the scale of genius,' Knox asserts, Sterne shares with him 'the power of shaking the nerves, or of affecting the mind in the most lively manner in a few words.' Knox gives Sterne the praise of 'genius,' but he finds it impossible to 'give him the praise of morality,' and he revives the old charge, never quite thoroughly discredited, that Sterne arouses the passions. The pathetic, he concludes, was Sterne's 'chief excellence,' though even this side of Sterne's work poses dangers to morality and conduct (No. 77). Most other critics of the eighties agree that the pathetic is Sterne's major excellence, and some of them praise rather than distrust the moral tendency of his sentimental philosophy (Nos 87, 88).

From deprecating the quality and importance of Sterne's humorous side it was but a short step to suggesting that it was, in fact, not original at all but was plagiarized; and George Gregory took that step in 1787 (though he implied that Sterne was also indebted to other authors for his sentimental side as well (No. 83)). Gregory's friend Anna Seward, minor poetess known as the Swan of Lichfield, sprang to Sterne's defense (No. 84), and her battle with Gregory over Sterne's originality gave a preview of the more extensive battles which were to follow, beginning during the nineties after the fuller revelation of Sterne's borrowings. Meanwhile, there were some minority reports from critics who, rather than contributing to the tendency to fragment Sterne's work, saw it whole. Anna Seward herself called attention to the 'happy, thrice happy, mixture of the humorous and the pathetic' (No. 84a), and Leonard MacNally, imitator of Sterne and author of a dramatic adaptation of *Tristram Shandy*, felt the works of Sterne would always have a place 'in the hands, in the heads, and in the hearts of every man, ay, and every woman too, of feeling' (No. 88a).

VI. 1790–1815: PLAGIARISM AND SENTIMENT

During the next twenty-five years the preference for Sterne's pathetic side continued, reinforced by Dr John Ferriar's discoveries of Sterne's plagiarisms, which usually involved his humorous material. Ferriar read a paper entitled 'Comments on Sterne' to the Literary and Philosophical Society of Manchester in 1791 and this was subsequently published in the Society's *Memoirs* in 1793. Ferriar's avowed wish was to make Sterne more 'intelligible.' 'I do not mean to treat him as a plagiarist,' he says, and adds that any 'instances of copying . . . will detract nothing from his genius.' Though Ferriar finds borrowings particularly from Rabelais and Burton's *Anatomy of Melancholy*, he believes that his researches 'leave Sterne in possession of every praise but that of curious erudition, to which he had no great pretence, and of unparellelled originality, which ignorance only can ascribe to any polished writer' (No. 90a).

Ferriar revised his comments for a book-length publication with quite different conclusions. In the *Illustrations of Sterne*, which appeared in 1798, he stated that Sterne had a 'natural bias to the pathetic,' and in the 'serious parts of his works, he seems to have depended on his own force,' but 'in the ludicrous, he is generally a copyist.' Sterne is praised for 'the dexterity and the good taste with which he has incorporated in his work so many passages, written with very different views by their respective authors' (No. 90b), but this is faint praise compared to Ferriar's earlier remarks in the 'Comments.'

After Ferriar's disclosures, the more acute critics minimized the importance of Sterne's borrowings (Nos 102d and e, 109, 110); but minor critics with a moral bent seized on Sterne's plagiarism as a means for attacking the supposed immorality of all his work (No. 102a). The harshness of moral judgments against Sterne increased with the growth of the Evangelical movement at the turn of the century, and two of its chief spokesmen, William Wilberforce and Hannah More, condemned him in strong terms. Hannah More referred to his sentimentality as a 'disease' (No. 79), and Wilberforce attacked him for 'corrupting the national taste' and producing 'a morbid sensibility in the perception of indecency' (No. 95). Biographical misinformation added fuel to the flames, and the sincerity of Sterne's sentimental philosophy was called into further question by the charge, as Byron put it, that Sterne 'preferred whining over "a dead ass to relieving a living mother"' (see Nos 96, 98, 113). Only in the twentieth century have we begun to achieve a better perspective on Sterne's difficult relationships with his mother and his wife.

In spite of all the attacks, however, Sterne's influence continued to be felt: 'All the would-be lady writers have sprung from RICHARDSON,' wrote Charles Dibdin in 1790, 'just as all the would-be gentlemen writers have sprung from STERNE' (No. 89). Dibdin also opened up the interesting speculation that the esthetic principles which Sterne practiced, if he had developed them into full-fledged theories, could have provided lively competition for the literary dogmas that Samuel Johnson was enunciating. Sterne, if he did not wish exactly to number the streaks of the tulip, wished nonetheless to count the strokes of his pulse as it beat faster with each new experience, thus demonstrating his affinity with the coming age rather than with that which was passing. Later, as one critic suggested, Wordsworth had become 'the Sterne of poetry,' since he had 'endeavoured to extract sentiment where nobody else ever dreamt of looking for it' (No. 124).

Meanwhile, there were other critics besides Dibdin who began to take Sterne's measure more accurately, as more extended treatments of his works appeared (Nos 106–11, 115). In these lengthier studies critics make somewhat more perfunctory references to Sterne's obscenity or immorality and praise his special talents—the 'light electric touches,' as Mrs Barbauld says, 'which thrill the nerves of the reader who possesses a correspondent sensibility of frame' (No. 109), or 'the art of painting with his *pen*,' praised by Edward Mangin (No. 115). These critics also tend to make light of the charges of plagiarism. Though they may express impatience with Sterne's mannerisms, they recognize his fundamental talent in characterization. Sterne's style remains the subject of lively controversy, with personal taste the decisive factor in judgments (see Nos 94, 103, 104, in addition to the more extended treatments of Sterne mentioned above).

VII. 1815–30: THE ROMANTICS REDISCOVER *Tristram Shandy*

During the next fifteen years, between 1815 and 1830, Sterne's literary fortunes rose as three major figures, Coleridge, Hazlitt, and Scott, made significant contributions to an understanding of his work (Nos 116, 117, 123). All three preferred *Tristram Shandy* to the *Sentimental Journey*: Hazlitt gives most of his attention to Sterne's earlier work and Scott assumes that 'Sterne's reputation [is] chiefly founded on *Tristram Shandy*.' Coleridge found 'truth and reality' in *Tristram Shandy*, but 'little beyond a clever affectation' in the *Sentimental Journey*, which he characterized as 'poor sickly stuff.'

These three major figures helped to put into a better perspective some of the problematic things about Sterne which had distorted the judgments of earlier critics. Thus Scott gave a kinder biographical treatment of Sterne (though he used virtually the same facts and sources that were available to earlier writers), and Hazlitt asserted that one should not believe those people who tell you 'that Sterne was hardhearted.' These critics also see Sterne's 'indecency' as more a matter of taste than a matter of morality. Though the 'licentious humour of *Tristram Shandy*' argues 'coarseness of mind, and want of common manners,' Scott says, it is not 'the kind which applies itself to the passions, or is calculated to corrupt society.' For Coleridge, Sterne's indecency amounted to 'a sort of *knowingness* . . . a sort of dallying with the devil,' which would have little effect if society itself were innocent. It is quite separate, Coleridge insists, from Sterne's characters 'which are all *antagonists* to this wit.' These three critics likewise make light of the charges of plagiarism, either ignoring them or asserting, as Scott does, that Sterne should be pardoned 'in consideration of the exquisite talent with which the borrowed materials are wrought up into the new form.'

Even these critics still find it difficult to come to grips with the eccentricity of Sterne's form. Hazlitt suggests that Sterne's works 'consist only of *morceaux*—of brilliant passages,' and Scott describes *Tristram Shandy* as 'no narrative, but a collection of scenes, dialogues, and portraits, humorous or affecting, intermixed with much wit, and with much learning, original or borrowed.' Coleridge alone saw Sterne's 'digressive spirit' as 'the *very form* of his genius' with continuity supplied by the characters. All three agree on the excellence of the characters themselves. Hazlitt calls attention to the skill with which Sterne maintains 'consistency in absurdity' in his characterizations and describes Uncle Toby as 'one of the finest compliments ever paid to human nature.' Scott agrees that Uncle Toby and Trim are 'the most delightful characters in the work, or perhaps in any other.'

Though both Scott and Hazlitt note 'mannerism and affectation' in Sterne, both in general appreciate his style and his humor. For Hazlitt, Sterne's style is 'the most rapid, the most happy, the most idiomatic,' in short, the 'pure essence of English conversational style.' Both Hazlitt and Coleridge appreciate the comic elements in Sterne, and Coleridge describes the essence of Sterne's comedy well: 'the little is made great, and the great little, in order to destroy both, because all is equal in contrast with the infinite.'

Other prominent figures of the period knew and admired Sterne's work. Jane Austen parodied *Tristram Shandy* in her juvenilia.[6] Wordsworth was reading *Tristram Shandy* in 1791, one of his few 'incursions into the fields of modern literature,' and he spoke admiringly of Yorick as having 'a deal of the male mad-cap in him.'[7] Shelley quotes Sterne in an early essay.[8] Keats refers to Sterne in letters, showing a somewhat bewildered admiration for the Shandean (No. 118). Lamb, though he regretted that Sterne had 'put a sign post up to shew where you are to feel,' nonetheless thought of Sterne's works as among 'Great Nature's Stereotypes' (No. 104).

Finally, De Quincey and Carlyle, both in discussions of Jean Paul Richter, show a sensitive understanding of Sterne's humor and its relationship to his sentiment. Though Sterne is inferior to Richter in De Quincey's view, he believes that both have demonstrated 'the possibility of blending, or fusing . . . the elements of pathos and of humour, and composing out of their union a third metal *sui generis*' (No. 122). Carlyle states the same idea with a slight variation: 'The essence of humor is sensibility. . . . True humor springs not more from the head than from the heart; it is not contempt, its essence is love; it issues not in laughter, but in still smiles, which lie far deeper.' Shakespeare, Swift, and Ben Jonson all have their place in the annals of British humor, but Sterne is 'with all his faults, our best' (No. 125a). The major critics of the Romantic period had rescued Sterne's sliding fortunes and enshrined his work, and particularly *Tristram Shandy*, on a high pedestal indeed.

VIII. STERNE IN AMERICA

Almost from the first appearance of *Tristram Shandy*, Sterne's popularity in America mirrored that in England, and some of the same critical arguments took place on both sides of the Atlantic. Dr John Eustace, when he sent Sterne the '*shandean* piece of sculpture' in 1767, mentioned above, stated that he had admired *Tristram Shandy* 'ever since his introduction to the world' and had been 'one of his most zealous defenders against the repeated assaults of prejudice and misapprehension' (No. 55a). But all of Sterne's books had enthusiastic supporters. Four years earlier Benjamin Franklin reported that at Fort Pitt 'as they cannot yet afford to maintain both a Clergyman and a Dancing-master, the Dancingmaster reads Prayers and one of Tristram Shandy's Sermons every Sunday.'[9] Harvard students read both *Tristram Shandy* and the *Sentimental Journey* enthusiastically during the seventies,[10] and in 1774 Sterne became the first novelist to have a collected edition of his complete works published in the colonies.[11] More than a decade later, Sterne furnished material for William Dunlap's *The Father, or American Shandyism*, which was performed successfully in 1789 and became 'the first American play printed that had been performed in a regular theatre.'[12]

American diaries attest the popularity of Sterne's 'sensibility' during the seventies,[13] and it was this side of Sterne's work that drew both the warmest praise and the most violent censure over the years in America, as Sterne became 'high priest of the cult of sensibility.'[14] Sternesque fragments appeared frequently in the pages of the *Massachusetts Magazine* during its brief history from 1789 to 1796,[15] and the first American novel, *The Power of Sympathy*, which appeared in 1789, contained a warm defense of Sterne against the 'antisentimentalists' (No. 87). But at the same time that Sterne was imitated and praised, many moralists saw a danger in his sensibility (Nos 100, 105). As one writer said, 'By blending sentiments of benevolence and delicacy with immorality and looseness, he induces some people to think that debauchery may be innocent, and adultery meritorious' (No. 105a), and another writer saw him as a 'cassocked libertine' (No. 105c). There was ambivalence in the attitudes toward Sterne: it was as hard for the Americans as for Sterne's own countrymen to determine the point at which tender and benevolent emotions turned into selfish and destructive ones. The very 'sensibility' which won Sterne most praise also caused the strongest attacks against him.

In general, the *Sentimental Journey*, with ten American editions before 1800, was more popular than *Tristram Shandy*: it is significant that no separate edition of *Shandy* appears to have been published in America during the period. But some discerning critics did come closer to full-fledged appreciation of Sterne. William Wirt, later to be attorney-general of the United States, admitted that 'every body justly censures and admires alternately' *Tristram Shandy*, but was sure that it 'will continue to be read, abused and devoured, with ever fresh delight, as long as the world shall relish a joyous laugh, or a tear of the most delicious feeling.' A few years earlier Wirt had started his career with 'his whole magazine of intellectual artillery comprised [of] no other munitions than a copy of Blackstone, two volumes of *Don Quixote*, and a volume of *Tristram Shandy*.'[16] Theodosia Burr, daughter of Aaron, also found Sterne intellectually stimulating. Unlike the usual novelists who 'really furnish no occupation to the mind,' Sterne offers opportunities for discoveries: 'Half he says has no meaning, and, therefore, every time I read him I find a different one,' she says.[17]

Among other famous Americans, Sterne had both advocates and detractors. The praise of Jefferson and the censure of Trumbull have already been noted (Nos 62, 60). When Tom Paine traveled to France in 1787, he praised Sterne for being free of the usual prejudices Englishmen displayed toward France: 'Except Sterne,' he said, 'there is scarcely a traveling English author, but who, on his return home, has cherished and flattered those errors for the purpose of accommodating his work to the vulgar palates of his readers.'[18] The young Emerson felt that Goethe's enthusiasm for Sterne (No. 145) was one of the German writer's 'few blunders,'[19] but Sterne's name appeared more frequently than that of any other English author in the early journals of Washington Irving. '[I]t was largely in the mood of the literary Sterne,' Irving's biographer says, 'that Irving traveled through France and Italy.'[20] Irving in turn spawned his own imitators, and the young Whittier experimented with fiction before he became a poet, trying a style which was 'about half way between the abruptness of Laurence Sterne and the smooth gracefulness of W. Irving.'[21]

Despite these evidences that Sterne was widely read and appreciated in America, there was no major critical statement by an American to correspond with the famous pronouncements of the English Romantics, though the *Port Folio*, edited by Joseph Dennie, carried two important articles on Sterne in 1810 and 1811. The first, written by Philadelphia publisher Matthew Carey, undertook to vindicate Sterne from the charge of plagiarism (No. 110a); the second, which is unsigned, defended Sterne from the charge of hypocrisy, since the reader 'need not search farther than his own heart to find all those incongruities of character so apparent in the page and in the life of Lawrence Sterne.' This second critic then goes on to give some remarks on Sterne's style. Sterne is 'always disappointing and always delighting his reader.' In the 'whole compass of English literature' there is no other example 'of wit so uniformly sportive' and the 'opposition of character' provides 'inexpressible diversion' for the reader. Sterne's 'artless, unstudied, yet sweet and captivating pathos' is also to be commended, and he gives 'interest' to 'apparently trivial' incidents. He is 'not a profound writer' and 'skims the surface of things,' but 'if he had written more systematically,' he might have 'lost that spritely naïveté that now exhilarates and warms us in every page' (No. 110b).

IX. ON THE CONTINENT

On the Continent Sterne was in some places even more popular than he was in England or America, though sometimes even less well understood.[22] It was the *Sentimental Journey* which had primary appeal throughout Continental Europe, though its vogue often stimulated a secondary interest in *Tristram Shandy*. Partly as a result of the dominant popularity of Sterne's travels, perhaps partly as a result of the difficulty in translating Sterne's bawdier humor, there were fewer attacks upon the supposedly immoral tendency of his work and in general fewer comments on the more boisterous *Tristram Shandy*.

Sterne was not entirely fortunate in his translators, for they sometimes added or subtracted whole sections in their translations of both the *Sentimental Journey* and *Tristram Shandy*, translated spurious works as genuine, or even used the translation to satisfy personal literary grudges. It is not far from the truth to say that often foreign critics were talking about a virtually different book when they discussed Sterne's works in translation. Sterne's translators did, nonetheless, make possible the rapid and early spread of his popularity. The German translation of the *Sentimental Journey* had appeared before the close of 1768 (No. 143) and the French translation a few months later (No. 129). Zückert's German translations of *Tristram Shandy* had not lagged far behind the appearance of the separate English installments of the novel (No. 140) and Bode's competing translation of the whole novel appeared in 1774 (No. 141b). In France, parts of *Tristram Shandy* were translated during the seventies by Frénais (No. 131), and two conclusions to his translation appeared in the eighties (No. 132).

Sterne was first known elsewhere on the Continent through the original English editions or the French and German translations of his work, but as his popularity increased, his works were translated into other languages as well. Bernardus Brunius translated *Tristram Shandy* into Dutch in 1776–9 (No. 155) and Sterne's travels in 1779. Italians had to wait until 1829 for a translation of selections from the novel (No. 166), but translations of the *Sentimental Journey* into Italian appeared in 1792 and 1813, and a Spanish translation was published in 1821. Sterne's travels were translated into Polish in 1817, and at that time Poland's national poet, Adam Mickiewicz, and his friends were 'joyous young men' and 'Sternians' during their college days.[23] Selections from the *Sentimental Journey* were translated into Russian as early as 1779, though a complete translation was not made until 1793. Brief selections from *Tristram Shandy* were translated into Russian during the nineties, though a complete translation was not undertaken until 1804–7. By the end of the eighteenth century *Tristram Shandy* had appeared in Danish (1794) and the *Sentimental Journey* in both Danish (1775) and Swedish; early in the nineteenth century Sterne's travels appeared in Hungarian.[24]

France
In spite of the fact that the French lagged slightly behind the Germans in translating Sterne's works, Sterne was better known earlier in France, in part because of his two trips to that country in search of health in 1762–4 and 1765–6. Sterne was fêted in the salons of Paris on his trips to the capital, but although he wrote to Garrick that 'Tristram was almost as much known here as in London,'[25] the statement of a contemporary that 'there are not five people in Paris possess'd of a *Tristram*

Shandy, nor one of those who are, who pretends to understand it'[26] is probably much nearer the truth. The *Journal Encyclopédique* reviewed each of the English installments of the novel as it came out, at first with a certain admiration, mingled with surprise at the book's popularity in England, later with a tone of firm disapproval (No. 126). There were enthusiastic and appreciative readers, however, like Diderot (No. 127), Georges Deyverdun (No. 128), and Voltaire (No. 130), though Voltaire apparently did not fully understand the English text. Mlle de Lespinasse, we are told, was the first to have the 'patience' to 'venture to the end of *Tristram Shandy*.' She 'adored' Sterne because 'works which were uneven, imperfect, even outlandish, found favor in her eyes, if she discovered in them some strokes of genius or of sensibility.' Later it was she who 'made the *Sentimental Journey* famous in Paris.'[27]

But the *Sentimental Journey* did not need anyone to help make its reputation in France. At once more intelligible than *Tristram Shandy*, and more available to French readers in Frénais's translation (No. 129), the *Sentimental Journey* won and kept a place in French hearts by its basically sympathetic portrayal of Frenchmen and French life. The work of Rousseau, who, like Sterne, presented man as 'the creature of instinct, given over to the fluctuations of sensation and of feeling,' had also helped to pave the way for the widespread acceptance of Sterne and his sensibility in France.[28] The young Jules Michelet, later to become famous as a leading French historian, confided to his journal in 1820: 'To my shame, the story of Maria made me cry almost as much as the death of my mother.'[29]

But by no means all the French were in tune with Sterne's sensibility, though Sterne had more defenders than detractors. Mlle de Sommery thought the book was without wit, ridiculous and trivial; Sterne's pleasure 'in feeling the finger-tip of the lady with black silk gloves' made her 'die with laughter.' Mme Suard, wife of a journalist and miscellaneous writer who had known Sterne during his Paris visits, hastened to write a spirited defense of Sterne and the *Sentimental Journey*, which was first published in 1786 (No. 134). 'Sterne's merit,' she said, 'lies in having given interest to details which have no interest whatever in themselves.' Sterne 'enlarges . . . the human heart by painting his own feelings for us,' and the 'interest which he takes in recounting all his feelings, passes into the hearts of his readers.'

Though *Tristram Shandy* was slow to be translated, the task had been completed by the middle eighties, and the translations of Sterne's novel were in general enthusiastically received (Nos 131, 132, 133). A few years later Mme de Staël cited Sterne as the best example of that English humor in which there is 'moodiness . . . almost sadness' (No. 136a). Both Dominique-Joseph Garat (No. 137) and Charles Nodier (No. 139) read *Tristram Shandy* with pleasure and made perceptive comparisons between Sterne and Rabelais. Garat, writing in 1820, refers to Voltaire's two British Rabelaises, Swift and Sterne: in all three, Rabelaises 'buffoonery and philosophy are always very close to each other,' he says. 'But Rabelais and Swift make you think while making you laugh,' he continues, 'and never touch your heart.' In Sterne, 'laughter, profound thoughts, and gentle tears can be found on the same page.' Sterne is better than the other two at handling the '*imbroglio*' of his narrative and his opinions, though, Garat says, 'the story of Tristram is not really that of a man; it is that of human nature in Europe, as Sterne saw it.' Nodier believes that the 'two great mockers have blazed a trail for modern philosophic thought,' though Rabelais lived in an age of growth and Sterne in a dying age. From this difference in the times in which they lived, other differences followed: 'The gaiety of Rabelais is that of a boisterous child who breaks his most precious toys in order to lay bare their mechanisms. The gaiety of Sterne is that of a slightly moody old man who amuses himself by pulling the strings of his puppets.'

Germany

In Germany, as in France, it was the *Sentimental Journey* which first won fame and attention for Sterne, although an unsuccessful translation of parts of *Tristram Shandy* had appeared in 1763 and 1765 (No. 140). Christoph Martin Wieland, attacking this translation in a letter in 1767 but defending *Tristram Shandy* for its fund of 'genuine Socratic wisdom' (No. 141a), became an early partisan of Sterne, as did Johann Gottfried von Herder, who wrote the next year that he was 'already . . . accustomed to following [Sterne's] sentiments through their delicate threads all the way into the soft inner marrow of his humanity' (No. 142).

As Herder wrote, sometime in November 1768, he was preparing to read the *Sentimental Journey*, if his knowledge of English would 'not prove inadequate.' Actually Bode's German translation of the *Sentimental Journey* had already come out some weeks previously, with the famous statement in its preface by Gotthold Ephraim Lessing (described only as 'a well-known German scholar') that he would have given five years of his own life if Sterne could have been spared for another five years of writing (No. 143). The success of the *Sentimental Journey* in

Germany was immediate, giving a new word to the German language (No. 143); and in the spring of 1769 Johann Georg Jacobi initiated the Lorenzo cult, whose devotees carried snuff boxes like the one Father Lorenzo gave Sterne (No. 144). During the seventies, which has been called the 'great Yorick decade,' Sterne's popularity increased, and in 1774 Bode's successful translation of *Tristram Shandy* appeared (No. 141b), reaching some German readers who had not responded to Sterne's sentimental side.[30] The next year poet Charles Ramler wrote to fellow poet Tobias Gebler that 'everyone wants to jest now like Sterne.'[31] Friedrich von Blanckenburg's discussion of Sterne as a humorist both 'of the intellect' and 'of the heart' appeared the same year (No. 146). Goethe's *Werther* also was published the same year, its way prepared, as Goethe later said, by the sentimentality of Sterne (No. 145b). Imitations of Sterne began to appear in large numbers, and Sterne cults sprang up. A few years later a poetic cemetery was set up in the park at Marienwerder near Hanover with graves for all of Sterne's famous characters; and Louise von Ziegler of Darmstadt, we are told, 'so far assumed the character of Maria as to adopt as the companion of her contemplations not, indeed a goat . . . but, more hygienically, a lamb.'[32] Such extremes of sentimentality brought the inevitable satirical attacks (No. 147), and Georg Christoph Lichtenberg, professor at Göttingen who had visited England in the middle seventies, became the leader of a movement against Sterne and his sentimentality. He later characterized Sterne as 'a creeping parasite, a flatterer of the Great' and a hypocrite (No. 149).

Sterne's fame continued without serious check in Germany, however. In 1795 Ludwig Tieck noted the gentleness of Sterne's laughter (No. 148), and five years later Friedrich Schlegel compared Sterne's style to 'that clever game of paintings called arabesques' (No. 151). Critics frequently compared Sterne with Jean Paul Richter (Nos 150, 154), who likewise himself cited Sterne for his combination of humor with seriousness (No. 152). In 1825 Schopenhauer offered to undertake a translation of *Tristram Shandy*, a book which he read 'again and again,' but nothing came of the project.[33] Heinrich Heine thought Sterne 'of equal birth with Shakespeare': he 'reveals to us the remotest recesses of the soul' (No. 154).

Goethe's career corresponds almost exactly with the period under consideration, and he had a lifelong admiration for Sterne. Near the end of his life he said it 'would be impossible to reckon how much effect Goldsmith and Sterne had' on him during the 'main period' of

his development (No. 145f). Sterne was 'the most beautiful spirit that
ever lived,' a 'free soul' with whom 'sagacity and penetration are infinite.' He was 'a model in nothing,' but 'a guide . . . in everything'
(No. 145d). Goethe re-read Sterne late in his life and found that with
the years his admiration had increased and was still increasing. 'I still
have not met his equal in the broad field of literature,' he said (No. 145h).

The Netherlands
Sterne was also held in high esteem in the Netherlands. Though *Tristram
Shandy* was translated first into Dutch during the middle seventies
(No. 155), the Dutch apparently understood and appreciated the
Sentimental Journey more fully, after its translation in 1779. By 1782,
Willem Antony Ockerse, theologian, critic, and lifelong admirer of
Sterne, reported that after Sterne 'sentiment is so much in vogue that
one may assume it as a livery of the lovesick world' (No. 156a); a few
years later he called attention to another influence from Sterne, the
fact that one could strike 'literary sparks' from unlikely sources (No.
156b). Sterne was sometimes attacked for his immorality—Rhijnvis
Feith said he wrote 'sometimes for heaven and sometimes for hell'[34]—
but one critic, at least, recognized that it was only Sterne's imitators who
were guilty of evoking the passions 'too strongly'; Sterne himself knew
'how to play upon the fine strings of the nobler and more delicate
sentiments' (No. 157). As in other countries, special groups of Sterne
devotees were formed and we are told of Sterne clubs toward the end
of the century, whose members called each other by the names of
Sterne's characters and even tried to dress in a manner which would
recall Sterne.[35] Critics during the early nineteenth century praised
Sterne's 'enchanting' pen (No. 158), and his talent for catching life 'as
it appears in reality . . . always full of sympathy, always breathing love'
(No. 159).

Russia
In Russia, as elsewhere on the Continent, the *Sentimental Journey* won
acceptance for Sterne, making him the most popular and influential
English novelist during the last years of Catherine the Great's reign.
Fragments from Sterne's *Journey* were translated in Russian periodicals
as early as 1779, but a complete translation did not appear until 1793.
Meanwhile, some Russians had read Sterne in English or in the French
or German translations, and at the beginning of the nineties there were
two Russian books of travel by authors who owed something to their

reading of Sterne. One book won exile to Siberia for its author, while the other helped to place its author in the forefront of the Russian Sentimental movement. Alexander Radishchev's *A Journey from St. Petersburg to Moscow*, which derived its form from the *Sentimental Journey* and contained a savage indictment of 'tyranny in general and Russian serfdom in particular,' appeared in 1790. Catherine the Great had the 'mutinous' Radishchev placed on trial, and although he pleaded that he was merely attempting an imitation of Sterne, he was condemned to death, a sentence later commuted to exile to Siberia.[36] Nikolai Karamzin, who traveled extensively in Europe from 1789-90, published his *Letters of a Russian Traveler* between 1791 and 1801. Karamzin was hailed by critics as 'the Russian Sterne' (though later scholars have debated the extent of Sterne's influence on Karamzin). In any event, Karamzin caught something of the spirit of Sterne in his book, especially in the passage in which he visits Dessein's hotel in Calais (No. 160a). In a later statement he praised Sterne's 'secret of shaking with words the most delicate fibers of our hearts' (No. 160b). Other Russian writers during the nineties praise Sterne's sensibility and his knowledge of 'the secret recesses of the heart' (No. 161a, b). As in other countries, the extremes of a sentimental movement called forth satire, and in 1805 Prince Alexander Shakhovskoi successfully satirized both Sterne and the Sentimental movement in his play, *The New Sterne* (No. 162). Later Pushkin gave high praise to *Tristram Shandy* (No. 163a), which had been translated in full only between 1804 and 1807, finally paving the way for writers later in the century to focus on that side of Sterne. Pushkin himself predicted that Gogol would be 'a Russian Sterne,' since he 'knows how to laugh,' but at the same time 'makes us weep' (No. 163c).

Italy
Italians had to content themselves with reading Sterne's work in English or other foreign languages, particularly French, during most of the eighteenth century, but a translation of the *Sentimental Journey* by Angelo Gaetano Vianello from Frénais's French version was published at Venice in 1792 and another translation was published at Milan in 1812. The most famous translation from the English version, that by poet and scholar Ugo Foscolo, appeared at Pisa in 1813 (No. 164), with later editions in 1818 and 1825. In his 'Character of Yorick,' which serves as a preface to his translation, Foscolo points to Sterne's purpose in the *Sentimental Journey* to 'teach us to know others in ourselves.'

He pictures Sterne as 'a free mind' and 'an eccentric spirit,' who put much of himself into the *Sentimental Journey* 'with the avowed presentiment of approaching death . . . as though in abandoning the earth he wanted to leave it some perpetual memory of a soul so different from others' (No. 164). A few years later Giovanni Ferri di S. Costante discussed Sterne several times in the periodical *Lo Spettatore Italiano* (No. 165). Ferri, like Foscolo, chiefly appreciated Sterne's sentimental side. Carlo Bini, translator of other English works, at last translated selections from *Tristram Shandy* into Italian in 1829; but he too appreciated mainly Sterne's sensibility, suggesting that Sterne was almost an Italian in his thought and temperament: 'You would say his thought had been developed in the breezes of our clear skies, and, mixed with his blood, there flowed within him a flame of the Italic sun' (No. 166).

It is fitting that a consideration of Sterne's reception and impact upon the Continent should end with Bini's testimony to Sterne's chameleon-like ability to enter into the intellectual life and the hearts of the people in each country where he was read. Though Sterne's 'philosophy' may not have been exactly 'the most brilliant invention of eighteenth century anglomania' [37] since some English readers also appreciated this side of Sterne, it is nonetheless true that Sterne was often taken more seriously in other countries than in his own. Sterne's influence was perhaps greatest in Germany where, according to one critic, he 'affected in a greater or less degree, nearly every German writer from 1765 to the close of the century.' [38] Sterne's sensibility likewise found a receptive audience in the France of Rousseau as well as in the Germany of the young Goethe and the Storm and Stress movement, but his humor was also appreciated by enthusiastic individual readers with tastes as different as those of Goethe and Voltaire.

X. SINCE 1830

Sterne has remained a writer of international stature, though there have been further ups and downs in his literary fortunes, especially in England. Though the statements of major critics during the Romantic period were somewhat slow to circulate and hence had a less marked effect immediately than they had later, during the next few years Sterne's reputation remained high. The remarks of literary historian George L. Craik and literary critic Leigh Hunt during the 1840s may be cited as illustrative. Countering the assertion of other critics that

Sterne's 'beauties are but grains of gold glittering here and there in a heap of sand,' Craik believed that 'of no writer could this be said with less correctness,' since Sterne's language, descriptions, and characters are 'wrought with the utmost care, and to the highest polish and perfection.'[39] Hunt gave special praise to the character of Uncle Toby: 'as long as the character of Toby Shandy finds an echo in the heart of man,' he says, 'the heart of man is noble.' Hunt also found 'the profoundest wisdom' in *Tristram Shandy*, and described Sterne as 'Rabelais, reborn at a riper period of the world, and gifted with sentiment.' To accuse Sterne of 'cant and sentimentality,' Hunt believed, 'is itself a cant or an ignorance.'[40]

A major challenge to Sterne's reputation came only a few years later, however, from a man who was all too ready to accuse Sterne of cant and sentimentality. In his 'Lectures on the English Humourists,' delivered in 1851, Thackeray drew a dramatic but uncomplimentary and inaccurate portrait of Sterne the man and then used that portrait to give an adverse reading of Sterne the writer. Sterne was hypocritical and licentious, Thackeray charges, and 'there is not a page in Sterne's writing but has some thing that were better away, a latent corruption—a hint, as of an impure presence.' 'The foul Satyr's eyes leer out of the leaves constantly,' Thackeray says, and when he thinks of Sterne he is 'grateful for the innocent laughter and the sweet and unsullied page which the author of David Copperfield gives to my children.' Though Thackeray finds 'genuine love and kindness' in 'a hundred pages' of Sterne's books, the rest is false, for Sterne usually 'exercised the lucrative gift of weeping' only to achieve money and fame. Thackeray's final estimate of Sterne is that he is 'a great jester, not a great humourist.'[41]

Ideas of decorum had become more strict since the eighteenth century, and if some of Sterne's original readers were upset at his failure to live up to his clerical character, it is not surprising that part of Thackeray's hysterical denunciation seems to derive from the same source. At the same time, the Victorians were obviously fascinated by the 'bawdier' and 'less refined' quality of life in the eighteenth century, and some critics, taking their cue from Thackeray, intensified the drama and distorted the picture even further. John Cordy Jeaffreson, exaggerating Thackeray's already exaggerated picture, presented Sterne as 'the hero of a hundred love affairs,' 'the adroit teller of nasty stories,' and 'the vain, wicked, sensual old dandy.'[42]

But Thackeray did not speak for his age, an age in which there was as much critical disagreement about Sterne as ever. Charlotte Brontë thought that what Thackeray said about Sterne was 'true,'[43] and Anthony Trollope agreed with Thackeray's account of Sterne's 'meanness and littleness.'[44] Dickens and Bulwer, on the other hand, were enthusiastic readers of Sterne, and Bulwer imitated Sterne.[45] Bulwer also gave special praise to Sterne's style: '[H]e flings forth his jocund sentences loose and at random; now up towards the stars, now down into puddles; yet how they shine where they soar, and how lightly rebound when they fall!'[46]

Extended correctives to Thackeray's view of Sterne may be found in the Reverend Whitwell Elwin's essay in the *Quarterly Review* in 1854 and American essayist Henry T. Tuckerman's 'The Sentimentalist: Laurence Sterne,' published in his *Essays, Biographical and Critical* in 1857. Both see Sterne more as a lighthearted epicurean than a hypocrite or villain. In contrast to Thackeray, both Elwin and Tuckerman are also careful to separate literary criticism from biography, and both make light of any charges of plagiarism. Elwin thinks of *Tristram Shandy* as Sterne's masterpiece, while Tuckerman refers to the *Sentimental Journey* as Sterne's 'most finished, and most harmonious work,' but also gives an appreciative account of the earlier work:

To read Tristram Shandy is like comparing notes with a kindly, eccentric, philosophical good fellow, somewhat of a scholar, but more of a human creature, who 'loves a jest in his heart,' can rail good-naturedly at the world, and is consoled by wit and animal spirits for its neglect. We soon, therefore, accede to his purpose, honestly avowed, and let 'familiarity grow into friendship.'

In short, 'we seem to participate in the authorship, to enter into the process of the book . . . surrendering . . . the reins of imagination into [Sterne's] genial hand.'[47] Elwin is somewhat harsher than Tuckerman on Sterne's indecency and the affectation of his style, but the 'strokes with which the portraits [of the Shandy brothers] are drawn,' he believes, 'are altogether so deep and yet so delicate, so truthful and yet so novel, so simple in the outline, and yet so varied in the details, so laughable and yet so winning, that we question if, out of Shakespeare, there is a single character in English fiction depicted with greater or even equal power.'[48]

Thackeray's biographical distortions were further corrected by Percy Fitzgerald's *Life of Laurence Sterne*, the first full-length biography, which appeared in 1864. Fitzgerald presented a much more sympathetic (though still not completely accurate) picture of a man who 'had so many weaknesses but so many more redeeming features.' Fitzgerald also contributed a more accurate picture of Sterne at work, countering the concept of the careless writer that Sterne's own statements had sometimes fostered. Since he had available a corrected manuscript copy of the *Sentimental Journey*, he was able to give examples of Sterne's revisions and show him 'a master of the elegances of English.'[49]

In a review simultaneously of Fitzgerald's *Life of Sterne* and a biography of Thackeray, appearing in the *National Review* in April 1864, Walter Bagehot also gave a more sympathetic view than Thackeray's of Sterne's character. Sterne was 'an old flirt,' who 'dawdled about pretty women,' but there was 'no good reason to suspect his morals,' Bagehot said. Bagehot saw three major defects in *Tristram Shandy*—the 'fantastic disorder of the form,' the indecency, and the fact that 'it contains eccentric characters only,' lacking any 'half-commonplace personages' to mediate between the 'central group of singular persons' and the world at large. The *Sentimental Journey*, Bagehot felt, 'is simpler and better'—it 'is not the true France of the old monarchy, but is exactly what an observant quick-eyed Englishman might fancy that France to be.' Sterne's mind, 'like a pure lake of delicate water,' reflects the things in the ordinary landscape around it 'with a charm and fascination that they have not in themselves.' This is 'the highest attainment of art,' to be 'at the same time nature and something more than nature.'[50]

Toward the close of the nineteenth century, the researches of Sir Sidney Lee provided new biographical material and a more sympathetic perspective on Sterne in the *Dictionary of National Biography*. Lee sees Sterne's work whole: 'Both the indecency and the sentimentality faithfully and without artifice reflected Sterne's emotional nature.' Sterne is one of 'only three or four humorous writers, in any tongue or of any age' to so successfully delineate 'the comedy of human life.'[51] Other critics like Sir Leslie Stephen, George Saintsbury, and Thomas Seccombe, though they find a good deal to censure, also find much to praise, and leave somewhat more judicious estimates of Sterne than those of Thackeray and his adherents. Though Stephen subscribes in large part to Thackeray's picture of Sterne the man, he nonetheless calls him 'perhaps the greatest artist in the language.' At the same time he believes that 'Sterne represents a comparatively shallow vein of thought,' and displays a 'want of intellectual seriousness.' In spite of his excellences, Sterne remains only 'the best of jesters.'[52] Saintsbury,

Sterne's editor, agrees essentially with this view: 'If you want to soar into the heights or plunge into the depths of humour,' he says, 'Sterne is not for you. But if you want . . . a frisk on middle—*very* middle— earth . . . a peep into all manner of . . . behind-scenes of human nature, . . . then have with Sterne in any direction he pleases.'[53] Seccombe, however, puts Sterne 'in the van of English humourists,' and asserts that his humor, neither Cervantic nor Rabelaisian but 'Sternean,' is 'of a supreme order' and his 'Shandean group of portraits' 'stand out like *chefs-d'oeuvre* in a large gallery of uninspired replicas and other fifth-rate compositions.'[54]

Though late nineteenth-century criticism of Sterne became increasingly kind and rather more judicious, it is only in the twentieth century that materials have been available to give critics a full opportunity to make a juster and more appreciative assessment of Sterne. Wilbur Cross edited Sterne's *Works* in 1904, and his monumental biography, appearing first in 1909 and revised in 1925 and 1929, set many questions about Sterne's life and character straight. Lewis P. Curtis's definitive edition of the *Letters* in 1935 provided another important source of biographical information, and Lansing Hammond's study of the sermons in 1948 gave further insights into Sterne's clerical career. James A. Work's edition of *Tristram Shandy* in 1940, the first to reproduce accurately the text of the first editions, also provided extensive annotation to help the twentieth-century reader read Sterne with some of the same perceptions as readers in Sterne's own time. Gardner D. Stout Jr produced a similar definitive edition of the *Sentimental Journey* in 1967. Henri Fluchère's biographical and critical study, *Laurence Sterne: de l'Homme à l'Oeuvre* appeared in 1961 and was translated and abridged by Barbara Bray in 1965 as *Laurence Sterne: from Tristram to Yorick*.

Meanwhile, other critics continued to make contributions to an understanding of Sterne during the first half of the twentieth century. I have room to do little more than mention a few of their names. Paul Elmer More, just after the turn of the century, demonstrated how the 'quaint' Shandy household 'becomes a symbol of the great world with all its tangle of cross-purposes,' and placed Sterne in a line of descent from Rabelais, Cervantes, and Swift.[55] Sir Herbert Read, writing a quarter of a century later, called Sterne 'a moral preceptor, a subtle intelligence that masked beneath his humour and licentiousness the kindly philanthropy of his age.' *Tristram Shandy* is 'an epic of Yorkshire life,' and Sterne is 'the precursor of all psychological fiction . . . of all that is most significant in modern literature.'[56] A decade later W. B. C. Watkins supported Sir Herbert's general position that Sterne was a serious literary artist and explored Sterne's philosophy and his impact upon twentieth-century writing further in 'Yorick revisited.'[57]

While critics were thus beginning to see the importance of Sterne's influence upon twentieth-century literature, several novelists also made sensitive comments about Sterne. J. B. Priestley described the Shandy family appreciatively: '[W]e carry away from Shandy Hall a picture of human happiness, and so gradually realise that these odd lovable creatures, the prancing philosopher, the simple Captain, and the rest, for all their bickering and their whimsies, have somehow stumbled upon the secret of the happy life.'[58] James Joyce is said to have thought of Sterne as he tried 'to build up many planes of narrative with a single esthetic purpose.'[59] Elizabeth Bowen believed that 'Tristram Shandy bears no intellectual date. It is dementedly natural in its course,' she continued, 'surrealist in its association of images. One does not attempt to "follow" Tristram Shandy; one consigns oneself, dizzily, to it.'[60] Katherine Anne Porter underscored this vitality in the book and in its characters, 'who live and go about their affairs every instant, not just at moments chosen by the author when it suits his convenience.' Tristram Shandy, she says, 'contains more living, breathing people you can see and hear, whose garments have texture between your finger and thumb, whose flesh is knit firmly to their bones, who walk about their affairs with audible footsteps, than any other one novel in the world, I do believe.'[61]

Virginia Woolf, one of Sterne's editors, combines the analytical powers of the critic with the intuitive perception of the novelist in her comments on Sterne. Like Katherine Anne Porter, she believes that Sterne brings us 'as close to life as we can be,' largely because the 'usual ceremonies and conventions which keep reader and writer at arm's length disappear' and Sterne manages 'to speak to the reader as directly as by word of mouth. . . . No writing seems to flow more exactly into the very folds and creases of the individual mind,' she continues, 'to express its changing moods, to answer its lightest whim and impulse, and yet the result is perfectly precise and composed. The utmost fluidity exists with the utmost permanence. It is as if the tide raced over the beach hither and thither and left every ripple and eddy cut on the sand in marble.' Though Virginia Woolf was speaking specifically of the Sentimental Journey, she believed that the 'world' of Sterne's travels and the world of his novel were the same. It is Sterne's 'own mind that fascinates him, its oddities and its whims, its fancies and its sensibilities,' and Sterne himself 'is the most important character' in *Tristram Shandy*. Sterne is 'singularly of our own age' in his preference for 'the windings of his own mind,' but 'for all his interest in psychology Sterne was far more nimble and less profound than the masters of this somewhat sedentary school have since become.'[62]

Criticism of Sterne has multiplied since the middle of our century though disagreements have continued. The 'most enthusiastic reinterpretation' as Lodwick Hartley suggests, may have gone 'into the creation of a novelist who never really existed'; yet the general progression he notes in the 'evaluation of Sterne as man and author—from "foul satyr," to "mischievous faun," to joyous humanist and moralist, to subtle rhetorician and philosopher largely on the side of the angels' has surely improved our understanding of Sterne.[63] Nonsense is still written about Sterne—to cite merely one example, F. R. Leavis's dismissal in a footnote in 1948 of the works of Sterne as 'irresponsible (and nasty) trifling'[64] is fully as bad-tempered and even less perceptive than Goldsmith's similar attack of nearly two hundred years before.

But recent criticism of Sterne has managed to explore new territory, much of which had remained largely unexplored before. One may note briefly three groups of critics. First, there are those who have studied the relationship between Sterne and his audience, taking their cue from earlier critics like Tuckerman and Virginia Woolf, and concentrating on Sterne's use of rhetoric, as well as on the psychology of the relationship between reader, narrator, and author. Second, there are those critics who have tried to come to an understanding of the blending of the comic and the pathetic in Sterne and explore in greater depth his philosophy, his use of time, and the relationship of certain elements in his biography to his work. Third, there are those critics who have attempted to discover structure beneath the seeming chaos of Sterne's work and arrive at a more accurate understanding of the genre he represents. Northrop Frye's 'The Four Forms of Prose Fiction,' first published in the *Hudson Review* in 1950 and later included in the *Anatomy of Criticism* in 1957, may be mentioned as an example within the last group. Frye attempts to dispel some of the generic confusion hovering over *Tristram Shandy* and many other examples of prose fiction by suggesting that they may be viewed as combinations of rather separate subgeneric forms. Frye's analysis, itself breaking new ground, suggests further possibilities for exploration.

Throughout the history of criticism of Sterne, however, critics have often found schemes of analysis less satisfactory than metaphors for expressing their views. For Scott, *Tristram Shandy* resembled 'the irregularities of a Gothic room, built by some fanciful collector, to contain the miscellaneous remnants of antiquity which his pains have accumulated, and bearing as little proportion in its parts as there is connexion between the pieces of rusty armour with which it is decorated' (No. 123a). At about the same time, the *Port Folio*, on the other hand, thought that 'to prescribe system to Sterne' would be 'like teaching a humming-bird to fly according to mathematics; it is his delightful wildness that enables him to rifle every flower of its sweets, and to give his quivering and delicate rainbows to the sun' (No. 110b). Sterne would not have been surprised at the disagreement and might well have been pleased with the metaphors. '[I]t is not in the power of any one to taste humor,' he said, 'however he may wish it—'tis the gift of God— and besides, a true feeler always brings half the entertainment along with him. His own ideas are only call'd forth by what he reads, and the vibrations within, so entirely correspond with those excited, 'tis like reading *himself* and not the *book*' (No. 55b). Perhaps Sterne's own metaphor is the best way to end an account of the two hundred odd years of criticism of Laurence Sterne.

NOTES

1 *Letters*, p. 118.
2 Biographical information for Kenrick and Ruffhead is drawn from the DNB.
3 See Robert D. Mayo, *The English Novel in the Magazines 1740–1815* (1962), p. 207.
4 *Ways to Kill Care* (1761) as quoted in J. C. T. Oates, *Shandyism and Sentiment, 1760–1800* (1968), pp. 9–10. For further discussions of Sterne's fashionable fame, see Oates, pp. 5–10, and Alan B. Howes, *Yorick and the Critics* (1958), pp. 1–5. For the reception of *Pamela* and *Tom Jones*, see Bernard Kreissman, *Pamela-Shamela* (1960), and Frederic T. Blanchard, *Fielding the Novelist* (1926), ch. 2.
5 *Early Diary of Frances Burney*, ed. Annie Raine Ellis (1889), i. 45.
6 See Archibald B. Shepperson, *The Novel in Motley* (1936), pp. 138–9.
7 *The Letters of William and Dorothy Wordsworth*, ed. Ernest de Selincourt, 2nd ed., revised by Chester L. Shaver (1967), i. 56–7.
8 'On Love,' *The Keepsake for 1829* (1828), p. 49.

INTRODUCTION

9 Letter to Richard Jackson, 8 March 1763, *The Papers of Benjamin Franklin*, ed. Leonard W. Labaree, x. 212.

10 Albert Goodhue Jr, 'The reading of Harvard students, 1770–1781, as shown by records of the Speaking Club,' *Essex Institute Historical Collections*, lxxii (April 1937). 121.

11 See James D. Hart, *The Popular Book* (1950), p. 60.

12 Oates, *Shandyism and Sentiment*, p. 27.

13 See Roy Harvey Pearce, 'Sterne and sensibility in American diaries,' *Modern Language Notes*, lix (June 1944). 403–7.

14 See Herbert R. Brown, *The Sentimental Novel in America, 1789–1860* (1959), pp. 74–99; cf. Tremaine McDowell, 'Sensibility in the eighteenth-century American novel,' *Studies in Philology*, xxiv (1937). 383–402.

15 See Brown, op. cit., and Herbert R. Brown, 'Richardson and Sterne in the *Massachusetts Magazine*,' *New England Quarterly*, v (January 1932). no. 1. 65–82.

16 See William Wirt, *The Letters of the British Spy*, 10th ed. (1836), p. 187 (the remarks first appeared in the *Virginia Argus* in 1803); and John Pendleton Kennedy, *Memoirs of the Life of William Wirt*, new and revised ed. (1860), 2 vols in 1, i. 57.

17 Mark van Doren, ed., *Correspondence of Aaron Burr and his Daughter Theodosia* (1929), pp. 130–1. The remarks come from a letter written in 1803.

18 Alfred Owen Aldridge, *Man of Reason: the Life of Thomas Paine* (1959), p. 119.

19 *The Journals and Miscellaneous Notebooks of Ralph Waldo Emerson*, ed. Merton M. Sealts Jr (1965), v. 314.

20 George S. Hellman, *Washington Irving Esquire* (1925), pp. 30–1.

21 John A. Pollard, *John Greenleaf Whittier Friend of Man* (1949), p. 100.

22 For fuller accounts of Sterne's reception and influence in the various European countries, where he was often taken seriously as a philosopher, see the Bibliography.

23 Czeslaw Milosz, *The History of Polish Literature* (1969), p. 209.

24 See Oates, *Shandyism and Sentiment*, pp. 20–2, and Oates, 'On collecting Sterne,' *Book Collector*, vol. 1, no. 4 (winter 1952), pp. 254–8.

25 *Letters*, p. 151.

26 Arthur H. Cash, 'Some new Sterne letters,' *The Times Literary Supplement*, 8 April 1965, p. 284.

27 M. de Guibert, 'Éloge d'Éliza,' translated here from *Lettres de Mlle. de Lespinasse*, ed. Eugène Asse (1906), p. 362.

28 Joseph Texte, *Jean-Jacques Rousseau and the Cosmopolitan Spirit in Literature*, trans. J. W. Mathews (1899), p. 291. Three other translations of Sterne's travels appeared before 1830 and an additional seven versions had appeared before the end of the nineteenth century.

29 Translated here from Jules Michelet, *Mon Journal 1820–1823* (1888), p. 122.

34

30 For a discussion of the differing responses of different German literary groups to Sterne, see Gertrude J. Hallamore, *Das Bild Laurence Sternes in Deutschland von der Aufklärung bis Romantik* (Germanische Studien, Heft 172, 1936); and Peter Michelsen, *Laurence Sterne und der Deutsche Roman des Achtzehnten Jahrhunderts* (1962). For a penetrating sketch of German reactions to Sterne's 'originality,' see Bernhard Fabian, 'Tristram Shandy and Parson Yorick among some German Greats,' *The Winged Skull*, pp. 194–209.

31 Quoted in August Koberstein, *Geschichte der Deutschen Nationalliteratur* (1873), iv. 168. See also Thayer, *Sterne in Germany*, p. 90.

32 Oates, *Shandyism and Sentiment*, p. 23; see also Thayer, *Sterne in Germany*, p. 89.

33 Arthur Schopenhauer, *Mensch und Philosoph in Seinen Briefer*, ed. Arthur Hübscher (1960), p. 99.

34 Lohman, *Laurence Sterne en der Nederlandse schrijvers*, p. 117. Feith (1753–1824), poet, dramatist, and novelist, was known for his 'morbid melancholy.'

35 See William J. B. Pienaar, *English Influences in Dutch Literature and Justus Van Effen as Intermediary* (1929), p. 253.

36 See D. M. Lang, 'Sterne and Radishchev, an episode in Russian sentimentalism,' *Revue de Littérature Comparée*, xxi (1947). 254–60; cf. Jesse V. Clardy, *The Philosophical Ideas of Alexander Radishchev* (1964), pp. 44–6.

37 Texte, *Jean-Jacques Rousseau and the Cosmopolitan Spirit in Literature*, p. 282.

38 Thomas Stockham Baker, 'The influence of Laurence Sterne upon German literature,' *Americana Germanica* (1899), vol. 2, no. 4, p. 41.

39 George L. Craik, *Sketches of the History of Literature and Learning in England*, 6 vols in 3 (1844–5), v. 158–61. Craik, Professor of History and English Literature at Queen's College, Belfast, is probably the best-known literary historian of his time; his work was often reprinted.

40 Leigh Hunt, *Wit and Humour* (1846), pp. 68–72; see also pp. 11–12.

41 *English Humourists of the Eighteenth Century*, *Works of Thackeray* (Harry Furniss Centenary ed., 1911), pp. 160-73.

42 John Cordy Jeaffreson, *Novels and Novelists, from Elizabeth to Victoria* (1858), i. 180–222.

43 *The Brontës. Their Lives, Friendships and Correspondence*, ed. T. J. Wise and J. A. Symington, Shakespeare Head ed. (1932), iii. 259.

44 Anthony Trollope, *Thackeray* (English Men of Letters series, 1882), pp. 166-7.

45 See *Works of Charles Dickens: Letters*, ed. Walter Dexter (1938), ii. 52. Bulwer's best-known imitation of Sterne, *The Caxtons* (1849), was said by a reviewer to have been read 'by nearly every educated man' in England ('*Tristram Shandy* or *The Caxtons*?,' *Fraser's Magazine*, liii (March 1856). 253–67).

46 Edward Bulwer-Lytton, 'On style and diction,' *Caxtoniana* (1863), i. 126.
47 Henry T. Tuckerman, *Essays, Biographical and Critical; or, Studies of Character* (1857), pp. 315–41.
48 *Quarterly Review*, xciv (March 1854). 303–53; reprinted in Elwin's *Some Eighteenth Century Men of Letters* (1902).
49 Percy Fitzgerald, *The Life of Laurence Sterne* (1864), i. 7; ii. 432. In Fitzgerald's revised edition of Sterne's *Life* (1896), he modified some of his earlier judgments, censuring Sterne's character more harshly.
50 *Works of Walter Bagehot*, ed. Mrs Russell Barrington (1915), iv. 229–66.
51 DNB, article, 'Sterne,' pp. 1103, 1106.
52 Leslie Stephen, *Hours in a Library*, 4th ed. (1919), iii. 130–63.
53 George Saintsbury, 'Introduction (1898),' *Essays and Prefaces* (1933), p. 149; all of Saintsbury's criticism of Sterne is gathered on pp. 130–93.
54 Thomas Seccombe, *The Age of Johnson*, revised ed. (1928), pp. 179–88.
55 Paul Elmer More, 'Laurence Sterne,' *Shelburne Essays*, 3rd ser. (1905), pp. 177–212.
56 Herbert Read, 'Sterne,' *The Sense of Glory* (1929 ed.), pp. 124–51.
57 W. B. C. Watkins, 'Yorick revisited,' *Perilous Balance: the Tragic Genius of Swift, Johnson, and Sterne* (1939), pp. 99–156.
58 J. B. Priestley, 'The brothers Shandy,' *The English Comic Characters* (1931 ed.), pp. 128–57.
59 See Louis D. Rubin Jr, 'Joyce and Sterne: a study in affinity,' *Hopkins Review*, iii (winter 1950). 14–22.
60 Elizabeth Bowen, *English Novelists* (1942), p. 20.
61 Katherine Anne Porter, 'The Winged Skull,' *Nation*, clvii (17 July 1943). 72–3.
62 'The *Sentimental Journey*,' *The Common Reader, First and Second Series* (1948), series 2, pp. 80–8 (first published as introduction to World's Classics ed. of *Sentimental Journey*, 1928); 'Phases of fiction,' *Granite and Rainbow* (1958), pp. 133–5 (first published in *Bookman* in 1929).
63 Hartley, *Laurence Sterne in the Twentieth Century*, pp. 33, 30.
64 F. R. Leavis, *The Great Tradition* (1948), p. 2.

Note on the Text

Except for the silent correction of some obvious typographical errors, the materials in this volume follow the original texts in spelling, conventions of punctuation, etc., in order that the reader may get some sense of the flavor of the originals. It has been necessary in many cases either to excerpt from longer texts or to excise passages from a text, both from considerations of space and from the fact that eighteenth century reviews often contained much material that was summary and quotation rather than criticism, or was tangential to criticism. Omissions have been indicated in the text and omitted material has been summarized if a knowledge of the omission was necessary to an understanding of the remaining text.

The selections have been divided by countries: England and America, France, Germany, the Netherlands, Russia, and Italy. Within these divisions material has been arranged chronologically, except in a few cases where logic has dictated that the remarks of the same critic at different times be brought together.

1. The composition of *Tristram Shandy*, vols I, II

1759

(a) Extract from Sterne's letter, 23 May 1759, offering his manuscript to Robert Dodsley (*Letters*, p. 74)

With this You will rec^ve the Life & Opinions of Tristram Shandy, wch I choose to offer to You first—and put into your hands without any kind of Distrust both from your general good Character, & the very handsome Recommendation of Mr Hinksman. The Plan, as you will perceive, is a most extensive one,—taking in, not only, the Weak part of the Sciences, in wch the true point of Ridicule lies—but every Thing else, which I find Laugh-at-able in my way—.

(b) Extract from Sterne's letter, summer 1759, replying to an unidentified friend who had read the manuscript of *Tristram Shandy* and urged Sterne, especially since he was a clergyman, to be more prudent (*Letters*, pp. 76–7)

I will use all reasonable caution—Only with this caution along with it, not to spoil My Book;—that is the air and originality of it, which must resemble the Author—& I fear 'tis a Number of these slighter touches which Mark this resemblance & Identify it from all Others of the [same] Stamp—Which this understrapping Virtue of Prudence would Oblige Me to strike out.—A Very Able Critick & One of My Colour too—

who has Read Over tristram—Made Answer Upon My saying I Would consider the colour of My Coat, as I corrected it—That that very Idea in My head would render My Book not worth a groat—still I promise to be Cautious—but I deny I have gone as farr as Swift—He keeps a due distance from Rabelais—& I keep a due distance from him—Swift has said a hundred things I durst Not Say—Unless I was Dean of St. Patricks—

I like Your Caution of the Ambitiosa recidet ornamenta[1]—as I revise My book, I will shrive My conscience upon that sin & What ever Ornaments are of that kind shall be defac'd Without Mercy.

Ovid is justly condemn'd in being Ingenij sui Amator[2]—and it is a seasonable hint to Me, as I am Not sure I am clear of it—to Sport too Much with Your wit—or the Game that wit has pointed is surfeiting—like toying with a Mans Mistress—it may be a Very delightful Solacement to the Inamorato—tho little to the bystander.

Tho I plead guilty to a part of this Charge Yet twould greatly alleviate the Crime—If My Readers knew how Much I suppress'd of this desire—I have Burn'd More wit, then I have publish'd upon that very Acc[t]—since I began to Avoid the Very fault I fear I may have Yet given Proofs of. I will reconsider Slops fall & my too Minute Account of it[3]—but in general I am perswaded that the happiness of the Cervantic humour arises from this very thing—of describing silly and trifling Events, with the Circumstantial Pomp of great Ones—perhaps this is Overloaded—& I can soon ease it—

I have a project of getting Tristram put into the ABishops[4] hands, if he comes down this Autumn, Which will ease my conscience of all troubles Upon the Topick of Discretion—.

(c) Extract from Sterne's letter, ? October 1759, replying to Robert Dodsley's refusal to buy his manuscript (see No. 1a above), proposing to print the book at his own expense, and describing changes he has made in the manuscript (*Letters*, p. 81)

All locality is taken out of the book—the satire general; notes are added where wanted, and the whole made more saleable—about a

[1] 'Lop off superfluous ornaments' (Horace, *Ars Poetica*, ll. 447–8).
[2] 'Enamored of his own talents' (Quintilian, *Institutio Oratoria*, x. i. 88).
[3] See *Tristram Shandy*, II. 9, pp. 104–6.
[4] John Gilbert (1693–1761), Archbishop of York.

hundred and fifty pages added—and to conclude, a strong interest formed and forming in its behalf, which I hope will soon take off the few I shall print on this *coup d'essai*.[1]

2. Sterne to his readers

1759–60

(a) Extract from *Tristram Shandy*, I. 4, p. 7

I Know there are readers in the world, as well as many other good people in it, who are no readers at all,—who find themselves ill at ease, unless they are let into the whole secret from first to last, of every thing which concerns you.

It is in pure compliance with this humour of theirs, and from a backwardness in my nature to disappoint any one soul living, that I have been so very particular already. As my life and opinions are likely to make some noise in the world, and, if I conjecture right, will take in all ranks, professions, and denominations of men whatever,—be no less read than the *Pilgrim's Progress*[2] itself—and, in the end, prove the very thing which *Montaigne* dreaded his essays should turn out, that is, a book for a parlour-window;[3]—I find it necessary to consult every one a little in his turn; and therefore must beg pardon for going on a little further in the same way: For which cause, right glad I am, that I have begun the history of myself in the way I have done; and

---

[1] First attempt.

[2] John Bunyan (1628–88), *The Pilgrim's Progress from this World to that which Is to Come* (1678–84).

[3] Michel Eyquem de Montaigne (1533–92), French essayist, contributed inspiration to Sterne in both idea and style. In 'Upon Some Verses of Virgil' Montaigne said he was vexed that his essays should 'only serve the *Ladies* for . . . A Book to lye in the Parlour Window; this Chapter,' he continued, 'shall prefer me to the Closet.'

that I am able to go on tracing every thing in it, as *Horace* says, *ab Ovo*.[1]
(pp. 8–10)

(b) Extract from *Tristram Shandy*, I. 6, pp. 10–11

I have undertaken, you see, to write not only my life, but my opinions
also; hoping and expecting that your knowledge of my character, and
of what kind of a mortal I am, by the one, would give you a better
relish for the other: As you proceed further with me, the slight acquaintance which is now beginning betwixt us, will grow into familiarity;
and that, unless one of us is in fault, will terminate in friendship.—O
diem praeclarum![2]—then nothing which has touched me will be
thought trifling in its nature, or tedious in its telling. Therefore, my
dear friend and companion, if you should think me somewhat sparing
of my narrative on my first setting out,—bear with me,—and let me go
on, and tell my story my own way:—or if I should seem now and then
to trifle upon the road,—or should sometimes put on a fool's cap with a
bell to it, for a moment or two as we pass along,—don't fly off,—but
rather courteously give me credit for a little more wisdom than appears
upon my outside;—and as we jogg on, either laugh with me, or at me,
or in short, do any thing,—only keep your temper. (pp. 17–19)

(c) Extract from *Tristram Shandy*, I. 22, pp. 72–4

For in this long digression which I was accidentally led into, as in all
my digressions (one only excepted) there is a master-stroke of digressive
skill, the merit of which has all along, I fear, been overlooked by my
reader,—not for want of penetration in him,—but because 'tis an
excellence seldom looked for, or expected indeed, in a digression;—
and it is this: That tho' my digressions are all fair, as you observe,—and
that I fly off from what I am about, as far and as often too as any writer

---

[1] 'From the egg'; i.e., 'from the beginning.' In his *Ars Poetica*, ll. 146 ff., Quintus Horatius
Flaccus (65–8 BC) praises Homer for not detailing the war of Troy 'from the egg' (i.e.
from the birth of Helen), but rather hurrying his reader into the middle of events, where a
skillful blend of fact and fiction will create both interest and a sense of form.
[2] O splendid day!

in *Great-Britain*; yet I constantly take care to order affairs so, that my main business does not stand still in my absence.

I was just going, for example, to have given you the great out-lines of my uncle *Toby*'s most whimsical character;—when my aunt *Dinah* and the coachman came a-cross us, and led us a vagary some millions of miles into the very heart of the planetary system: Notwithstanding all this you perceive that the drawing of my uncle *Toby*'s character went on gently all the time;—not the great contours of it,—that was impossible,—but some familiar strokes and faint designations of it, were here and there touch'd in, as we went along, so that you are much better acquainted with my uncle *Toby* now than you was before.

By this contrivance the machinery of my work is of a species by itself; two contrary motions are introduced into it, and reconciled, which were thought to be at variance with each other. In a word, my work is digressive, and it is progressive too,—and at the same time. . . .

Digressions, incontestably, are the sunshine;—they are the life, the soul of reading;—take them out of this book for instance,—you might as well take the book along with them;—one cold eternal winter would reign in every page of it; restore them to the writer;—he steps forth like a bridegroom,—bids All hail; brings in variety, and forbids the appetite to fail.

All the dexterity is in the good cookery and management of them, so as to be not only for the advantage of the reader, but also of the author, whose distress, in this matter, is truely pitiable: For, if he begins a digression,—from that moment, I observe, his whole work stands stock-still;—and if he goes on with his main work,—then there is an end of his digression.

—This is vile work.—For which reason, from the beginning of this, you see, I have constructed the main work and the adventitious parts of it with such intersections, and have so complicated and involved the digressive and progressive movements, one wheel within another, that the whole machine, in general, has been kept a-going;—and, what's more, it shall be kept a-going these forty years, if it pleases the fountain of health to bless me so long with life and good spirits. (pp. 160–4]

(d) Extract from *Tristram Shandy*, II. 2, p. 85

Pray, Sir, in all the reading which you have ever read, did you ever read such a book as *Locke*'s Essay upon the Human Understanding?[1]— Don't answer me rashly,—because many, I know, quote the book, who have not read it,—and many have read it who understand it not:—If either of these is your case, as I write to instruct, I will tell you in three words what the book is.—It is a history.—A history! of who? what? where? when? Don't hurry yourself.—It is a history-book, Sir, (which may possibly recommend it to the world) of what passes in a man's own mind; and if you will say so much of the book, and no more, believe me, you will cut no contemptible figure in a metaphysic circle. (pp. 12–13)

(e) Extract from *Tristram Shandy*, II. 8, p. 103

It is about an hour and a half's tolerable good reading since my uncle *Toby* rung the bell, when *Obadiah* was order'd to saddle a horse, and go for Dr. *Slop* the man-midwife;—so that no one can say, with reason, that I have not allowed *Obadiah* time enough, poetically speaking, and considering the emergency too, both to go and come;—tho', morally and truly speaking, the man, perhaps, has scarce had time to get on his boots.

If the hypercritick will go upon this; and is resolved after all to take a pendulum, and measure the true distance betwixt the ringing of the bell and the rap at the door;—and, after finding it to be no more than two minutes, thirteen seconds, and three fifths,—should take upon him to insult over me for such a breach in the unity, or rather probability, of time;—I would remind him, that the idea of duration and of its simple modes, is got merely from the train and succession of our ideas,[2]—and is the true scholastick pendulum,—and by which, as a scholar, I will be tried in this matter,—abjuring and detesting the jurisdiction of all other pendulums whatever.(pp. 55–6)

[1] John Locke (1632–1704), *An Essay Concerning Human Understanding* (1690). Sterne drew specific ideas as well as inspiration for his general plan from Locke.
[2] See John Locke, *An Essay Concerning Human Understanding*, II. 14, 3–4.

(f) Extract from *Tristram Shandy*, II. 11, pp. 108–9

Writing, when properly managed, (as you may be sure I think mine is) is but a different name for conversation: As no one, who knows what he is about in good company, would venture to talk all;—so no authro, who understands the just boundaries of decorum and good breeding, would presume to think all: The truest respect which you can pay to the reader's understanding, is to halve this matter amicably, and leave him something to imagine, in his turn, as well as yourself.

For my own part, I am eternally paying him compliments of this kind, and do all that lies in my power to keep his imagination as busy as my own. (p. 68)

3. Sterne promotes his book

1 January 1760

Extract from a letter which Sterne wrote for his friend, Catherine Fourmantel, a concert singer, to copy and send to an influential London friend, probably David Garrick (*Letters*, pp. 85–6).

There are two Volumes just published here which have made a great noise, & have had a prodigious Run; for in 2 Days after they came out, the Bookseller sold two hundred—& continues selling them very fast. It is, The Life & Opinions of Tristram Shandy, which the Author told me last night at our Concert, he had sent up to London, so perhaps you have seen it; If you have not seen it, pray get it & read it, because it has a great Character as a witty smart Book, and if You think it is so, your good word in Town will do the Author; I am sure great Service; You must understand, He is a kind & generous friend of mine whom Provi-

dence has attachd to me in this part of the world where I came a stranger
—& I could not think how I could make a better return than by en-
deavouring to make you a friend to him & his Performance.—this is
all my Excuse for this Liberty, which I hope you will excuse. His name
is Sterne, a gentleman of great Preferment & a Prebendary of the
Church of York, & has a great Character in these Parts as a man of
Learning & wit.—the Graver People however say, tis not fit for young
Ladies to read his Book. so perhaps you'l think it not fit for a young
Lady to recommend it however the Nobility, & great Folks stand up
mightily for it. & say tis a good Book tho' a little tawdry in some
places.—

4. William Kenrick: the first review of *Tristram Shandy*

January 1760

Extract from William Kenrick's unsigned review in the *Monthly
Review*, Appendix to xxi (July–December 1759). 561–71. Most of
the portions not reprinted here are lengthy quotations from *Tristram Shandy*.

For a brief account of Kenrick (1725(?)–79) see the Introduction,
pp. 5–6.

Of Lives and *Adventures* the public have had enough, and, perhaps,
more than enough, long ago. A consideration that probably induced the
droll Mr. Tristram Shandy to entitle the performace before us, his
Life and *Opinions*. Perhaps also, he had, in this, a view to the design he
professes, of giving the world two such volumes every year, during the
remainder of his life. Now, adventures worth relating, are not every
day to be met with, so that, in time, his budget might be exhausted;

but his opinions will, in all probability, afford him matter enough to write about, tho' he should live to the age of Methusalem. Not but that our Author husbands his adventures with great oeconomy, and sows them so extremely thin, that, in the manner he has begun, his narrative may very well last as long as he lives; nor, if that be long, and he as good as his word, will his history make an inconsiderable figure among the numerous diminutive tomes of a modern library.

But, indeed, Mr. Shandy seems so extremely fond of digressions, and of giving his historical Readers the slip on all occasions,* that we are not a little apprehensive he may, some time or other, give them the slip in good earnest, and leave the work before his story be finished. And, to say the truth, we should, for our own parts, be sorry to lose him in that manner; as we have no reason to think that we shall not be very willing to accompany him to the end of his tale, notwithstanding all his denunciations of prolixity. For, if we were sure he would not serve us this trick, we have no objection to his telling his story his own way, tho' he went as far about to come to the point, as Sancho Pancha[1] himself. Every Author, as the present justly observes, has a way of his own, in bringing his points to bear; and every man to his own taste. . . .

But to return to our hero himself, whom we shall next consider and take leave of, as an Author; in which character we cannot help expressing, on many accounts, a particular approbation of him. The address with which he has introduced an excellent moral sermon, into a work of this nature (by which expedient, it will probably be read by many who would peruse a sermon in no other form) is masterly.

There prevails, indeed, a certain quaintness, and something like an affectation of being immoderately witty, throughout the whole work. But this is perhaps the Author's *manner*. Be that, however, as it will, it is generally attended with spirit and humour enough to render it entertaining. . . .

On the whole, we will venture to recommend Mr. Tristram Shandy, as a writer infinitely more ingenious and entertaining than any other of

* We must do Mr. Tristram the Justice, however, to confess, that he generally carries his excuse for rambling along with him; and tho' he be not always hammering at his tale, yet he is busy enough: . . . in so much that we are apt to believe him, when he protests he makes all the speed he possibly can. It would not be amiss, however, if, for the future, he paid a little more regard to going strait forward, lest the generality of his Readers, despairing of ever seeing the end of their journey, should tire, and leave him to jog on by himself.
[1] Sancho Panza, Don Quixote's squire in Miguel de Cervantes's (1547–1616) immortal novel, *Don Quixote* (1605–15), was always quoting proverbs and speaking around rather than to a point. Sterne consciously imitated Cervantes (see Nos 1b, 26a).

the present race of novelists. His characters are striking and singular, his observations shrewd and pertinent; and, making a few exceptions, his humour is easy and genuine.

5. Sterne defends *Tristram Shandy*

30 January 1760

Sterne's letter to an unidentified physician, perhaps Dr Noah Thomas of Scarborough, who had apparently criticized Sterne for his satirical attacks upon individuals and especially upon Dr Richard Mead (1673–1754), the eminent London physician who was the original for Kunastrokius. Sterne may well have intended the letter as a public defense (see the penultimate sentence) (*Letters*, pp. 88–91).

Dear Sir,

—*De mortuis nil nisi bonum*, is a maxim which you have so often of late urged in conversation, and in your letters, (but in your last especially) with such seriousness, and severity against me, as the supposed transgressor of the rule;—that you have made me at length as serious and severe as yourself:—but that the humours you have stirred up might not work too potently within me, I have waited four days to cool myself, before I would set pen to paper to answer you, '*de mortuis nil nisi bonum*.' I declare I have considered the wisdom, and foundation of it over and over again, as dispassionately and charitably as a good Christian can, and, after all, I can find nothing in it, or make more of it, than a nonsensical lullaby of some nurse, put into Latin by some pedant, to be chanted by some hypocrite to the end of the world, for the consolation of departing lechers.—'Tis, I own, Latin; and I think that is all the weight it has—for, in plain English, 'tis a loose and futile position below a dispute—'*you are not to speak any thing of the dead, but what is good.*'

Why so?—Who says so? neither reason or scripture.—Inspired authors
have done otherwise—and reason and common sense tell me, that if
the characters of past ages and men are to be drawn at all, they are to be
drawn like themselves; that is, with their excellencies, and with their
foibles—and it is as much a piece of justice to the world, and to virtue too,
to do the one, as the other.—The ruleing passion *et les egarements du
coeur*,[1] are the very things which mark, and distinguish a man's character;—in which I would as soon leave out a man's head as his hobby-
horse.—However, if like the poor devil of a painter, we must conform
to this pious canon, *de mortuis, &c.* which I own has a spice of piety in
the *sound* of it, and be obliged to paint both our angels and our devils
out of the same pot—I then infer that our Sydenhams, and Sangrados,[2]
our Lucretias,—and Massalinas, our Sommers, and our Bolingbrokes—
are alike entitled to statues, and all the historians, or satirists who have
said otherwise since they departed this life, from Sallust,[3] to S[tern]e,
are guilty of the crimes you charge me with, 'cowardice and injustice.'

But why cowardice? 'because 'tis not courage to attack a dead man
who can't defend himself.'—But why do you doctors of the faculty
attack such a one with your incision knife? Oh! for the good of the
living.—'Tis my plea.—But I have something more to say in my behalf—and it is this—I am not guilty of the charge—tho' defensible. I
have not cut up Doctor Kunastrokius at all—I have just scratch'd him—
and that scarce skin-deep.—I do him first all honour—speak of Kunastrokius as a great man—(be he who he will) and then most distantly
hint at a drole foible in his character[4]—and that not first reported (to
the few who can even understand the hint) by me—but known before
by every chamber-maid and footman within the bills of mortality—
but Kunastrokius, you say, was a great man—'tis that very circumstance which makes the pleasantry—for I could name at this instant a

---

[1] 'The wanderings of the heart.' The allusion is to C. P. Jolyot de Crébillon's *Les Égare-
ments du coeur et de l'esprit* (1736–8). See No. 72d, n. 2.
[2] Sterne pairs some 'angels' with some 'devils': Thomas Sydenham (1624–89), a distinguished physician, with Sangrado, the quack doctor of Alain René Lesage's *Gil Blas* (1715–
35); Lucretia, the virtuous wife of Collatinus Tarquinius, with Valeria Messalina, the dis-
solute and scheming wife of the Emperor Claudius; John Somers (1651–1716), Baron
Somers and Lord Chancellor, the Whig statesman instrumental in achieving the union of
Scotland and England, with Henry St John (1678–1751), Viscount Bolingbroke, the controversial Tory statesman who was convicted of treason in 1715 for his part in attempting
to restore the Pretender to the British throne.
[3] Gaius Sallustius Crispus (86–34 BC), Roman historian, was morally rigorous in his writing,
though not in his personal life.
[4] See *Tristram Shandy*, I. 7.

score of honest gentlemen who might have done the very thing which Kunastrokius did, and seen no joke in it at all—as to the failing of Kun[a]strokius, which you say can only be imputed to his friends as a misfortune—I see nothing like a misfortune in it to any friend or relation of Kunastrokius—that Kunastrokius upon occasions should sit with ******* and *******—I have put these stars not *to hurt your worship's delicacy*—If Kunastrokius after all is too sacred a character to be even smiled at, (which is all I have done) he has had better luck than his betters:—In the same page (without imputations of cowardice) I have said as much of a man of twice his wisdom—and that is Solomon, of whom I have made the same remark 'That they were both great men—and like all mortal men had each their ruling passion.'

—The consolation you give me, 'That my book however will be read enough to answer my design of raising a tax upon the public'—is very unconsolatory—to say nothing how very mortifying! by h[eave]n! an author is worse treated than a common ***** at this rate—'*You will get a penny by your sins, and that's enough.*' Upon this chapter let me comment.—That I proposed laying the world under contribution when I set pen to paper—is what I own, and I suppose I may be allow'd to have that view in my head in common with every other writer, to make my labour of advantage to myself.

Do not you do the same? but I beg I may add, that whatever views I had of that kind, I had other views—the first of which was, the hopes of doing the world good by ridiculing what I thought deserving of it— or of disservice to sound learning, &c.—how I have succeeded my book must shew—and this I leave entirely to the world—but not to that little world *of your acquaintance*, whose opinion, and sentiments you call the general opinion of the best judges *without exception*, who all affirm (you say) that my book cannot be put into the hands of any woman of *character*. (I hope you except widows, doctor—for they are not *all* so squeamish—but I am told they are all really of my party in return for some good offices done their interests in the 176th page of my second volume.[1] But for the chaste married, and chaste unmarried part of the sex—they must not read my book! Heaven forbid the stock of chastity should be lessen'd by the life and opinions of Tristram Shandy—yes, his opinions—it would certainly debauch 'em! God take them under his

[1] The page alluded to in the first edition (Work, p. 151, last paragraph, to p. 152, middle of second line) does not contain any specific reference to widows, but presents the idea that subsequent children are borne more easily and with less chance of damage to the child than the first.

protection in this fiery trial, and send us plenty of Duenas to watch the workings of their humours, 'till they have safely got thro' the whole work.—If this will not be sufficient, may we have plenty of Sangrados to pour in plenty of cold water, till this terrible fermentation is over— as for the *nummum in loculo*,[1] which you mention to me a second time, I fear you think me very poor, or in debt—I thank God tho' I don't abound—that I have enough for a clean shirt every day—and a mutton chop—and my contentment with this, has thus far (and I hope ever will) put me above stooping an inch for it, for—estate.—Curse on it, I like it not to that degree, nor envy (*you may be sure*) any man who kneels in the dirt for it—so that howsoever I may fall short of the ends proposed in commencing author—I enter this *protest*, first that my end was *honest*, and secondly, that I wrote not [to] be *fed*, but to be *famous*.[2] I am much obliged to Mr. Garrick for his very favourable opinion—but why, dear Sir, had he done better in finding fault with it than in commending it? to humble me? an author is not so soon humbled as you imagine—no, but to make the book better by castrations—that is still *sub judice*,[3] and I can assure you upon this chapter, that the very passages, and descriptions you propose, that I should sacrifice in my second edition, are what are best relish'd by men of wit, and some others whom I esteem as sound criticks—so that upon the whole, I am still kept up, if not above fear, at least above despair, and have seen enough to shew me the folly of an attempt of castrating my book to the prudish humours of particulars. I believe the short cut would be to publish this letter at the beginning of the third volume, as an apology for the first and second. I was sorry to find a censure upon the insincerity of some of my friends —I have no reason myself to reproach any one man—my friends have continued in the same opinions of my books which they first gave me of it—many indeed have thought better of 'em, by considering them more; few worse.

I am, Sir,

Your humble servant,

LAURENCE STERNE

[1] 'Pocket the money' (see Horace, *Epistolae*, 2. i. 175).
[2] In *A Letter from Mr. Cibber to Mr. Pope* (London, 1742), Colley Cibber (1671–1757), the English actor frequently satirized for his lack of literary talent, had written: 'I wrote more to be Fed, than to be Famous.'
[3] 'Before the judge,' i.e. 'still unjudged' (Horace, *Ars Poetica*, l. 78).

6. Reviews in the magazines

January–February 1760

(a) Unsigned notice in the *Critical Review*, ix (January 1760). 73–4

This is a humorous performance, of which we are unable to convey any distinct ideas to our readers. The whole is composed of digressions, divertingly enough introduced, and characters which we think well supported. For instance, uncle *Toby*, corporal *Trim*, and Dr. *Slop*, are excellent imitations of certain characters in a modern truly Cervantic performance, which we avoid naming, out of regard to the author's delicacy.[1] Nothing can be more ridiculous than uncle *Toby*'s embarrassment in describing the siege of Namur, *Trim*'s attitude reading aloud a sermon, and Dr. *Slop*'s overthrow in the rencounter with Obadiah the coachman. To those, however, who have perused this performance, specifying particulars will be unnecessary, and to those readers who have not, it would be unentertaining. We therefore refer them to the work itself, desiring they will suspend their judgment till they have dipt into the second volume.

(b) Extract from an unsigned notice in the *London Magazine*, xxix (February 1760). 111

Oh rare Tristram Shandy!—Thou very sensible—humorous—pathetick—humane—unaccountable!—what shall we call thee?—Rabelais, Cervantes, What?—Thou hast afforded us so much real pleasure in perusing thy life,—we can't call it thy life neither, since thy mother is still in labour of thee,—as demands our gratitude for the entertainment. Thy uncle Toby—Thy Yorick—thy father—Dr. Slop—corporal Trim; all thy characters are excellent, and thy opinions amiable! If thou pub-

[1] The allusion is probably to Smollett's *Peregrine Pickle*. Smollett was editor of the *Critical Review* at this time.

lishest fifty volumes, all abounding with the profitable and pleasant, like these, we will venture to say thou wilt be read and admir'd,—Admir'd! by whom? Why, Sir, by the best, if not the most numerous class of mankind.

(c) Extract from an unsigned notice in the *Royal Female Magazine*, i (February 1760). 56

THE LIFE AND OPINIONS OF TRISTRAM SHANDY ... affects (and not unsuccessfully) to please, by a contempt of all the rules observed in other writings, and therefore cannot justly have its merit measured by them. It were to be wished though, that the wantonness of the author's wit had been tempered with a little more regard to delicacy, throughout the greatest part of his work.

7. Lord Bathurst praises Sterne

Spring 1760

Extract from a letter from Sterne to Mrs Daniel Draper, his Eliza (see No. 53d, p. 187, n. 1), probably written in March of 1767, describing his meeting with Allen, Baron Bathurst (1684–1775), during his London visit in the spring of 1760 (*Letters*, pp. 304–5).

I got thy letter last night, Eliza, on my return from Lord Bathurst's, where I dined. ... This nobleman is an old friend of mine.—You know he was always the protector of men of wit and genius; and has had those of the last century, Addison, Steele, Pope, Swift, Prior, &c. &c. always at his table.—The manner in which his notice began of me, was as singular as it was polite.—He came up to me, one day, as I was at the Princess of Wales's[1] court. 'I want to know you, Mr. Sterne; but it is fit you should know, also, who it is that wishes this pleasure. You have heard, continued he, of an old Lord Bathurst, of whom your Popes, and Swifts, have sung and spoken so much: I have lived my life with geniuses of that cast; but have survived them; and, despairing ever to find their equals, it is some years since I have closed my accounts, and shut up my books, with thoughts of never opening them again: but you have kindled a desire in me of opening them once more before I die; which I now do; so go home and dine with me.'

[1] Augusta (1719–72), widow of Frederick Louis (1707–51), Prince of Wales, and mother of George III.

8. Horace Walpole on *Tristram Shandy*

4 April 1760

Extract from a letter to Sir David Dalrymple, *Horace Walpole's Correspondence with Sir David Dalrymple*, ed. W.S. Lewis, Charles H. Bennett, and Andrew G. Hoover (1951), pp. 66-7.

Walpole (1717-97) in a letter to Henry Zouch, the antiquary and social reformer, dated 7 March 1761, was even more critical of the second installment of *Tristram Shandy*: 'The second and third [i.e. third and fourth] volumes of *Tristram Shandy*, the dregs of nonsense, have universally met the contempt they deserved. Genius may be exhausted—I see that Folly's invention may be so too.' (*Horace Walpole's Correspondence . . . with Henry Zouch*, ed. W. S. Lewis and Ralph M. Williams (1951), p. 44.) For Walpole's later, more favorable view of *A Sentimental Journey*, see No. 57 a, b.

At present nothing is talked of, nothing admired, but what I cannot help calling a very insipid and tedious performance: it is a kind of novel called, *The Life and Opinions of Tristram Shandy*; the great humour of which consists in the whole narration always going backwards. I can conceive a man saying that it would be droll to write a book in that manner, but have no notion of his persevering in executing it. It makes one smile two or three times at the beginning, but in recompense makes one yawn for two hours. The characters are tolerably kept up; but the humour is forever attempted and missed. The best thing in it is a sermon —oddly coupled with a good deal of bawdy, and both the composition of a clergyman. The man's head indeed was a little turned before, now topsyturvy with his success and fame. Dodsley has given him £650 for the second edition and two more volumes (which I suppose will reach backwards to his great-grandfather); Lord Falconberg[1] a donative of £160 a year; and Bishop Warburton[2] gave him a purse of gold and

---

[1] Thomas Belasyse (1699-1774), first Earl Fauconberg of Newburgh, presented Sterne to the perpetual curacy of Coxwold in late March 1760.
[2] For Warburton's relations with Sterne, see No. 16.

this compliment (which happened to be a contradiction) *that it was quite an original composition, and in the true Cervantic vein*—the only copy that ever was an original except in painting, where they all pretend to be so. Warburton, however, not content with this, recommended the book to the bench of bishops and told them Mr Sterne, the author, was the English Rabelais—they had never heard of such a writer.

9. The design of *Tristram Shandy*

March–April 1760

Though Sterne may well have had the general plan for *Tristram Shandy* in mind from the beginning, he also appears to have improvised a good bit from installment to installment, responding to his public and taking as grist for his mill whatever came his way from his reading and his experience. In the spring of 1760 rumors went around that Sterne was going to satirize Bishop Warburton (see No. 16) as Tristram's tutor in the next installment of *Shandy*. If this was Sterne's intention, he changed his mind after he had come to London and sensed the imprudence of such a plan. The authenticity of the letter in (b) below cannot be proved, but it contains nothing at variance with known facts (cf., e.g., No. 1b). For further background see a letter in the *European Magazine* for October 1792 (xxii. 255–6).

(a) Extract from a letter, 4 March 1760, from Dr Thomas Newton, York precentor and later Bishop of Bristol, to the Reverend John Dealtary, Yorkshire pluralist (L. P. Curtis, 'New Light on Sterne,' *Modern Language Notes* (1961), lxxvi. 501.

I wish Laury Sterne may have more comfort of his wife than he has had, but he has, and happy for him it is that he has, such a spring of good spirits in himself, and I suppose the success of *Tristram Shandy* has pleased him not a little. Many people are pleased even with the oddness and wildness of it, and no body more than the new Bishop of Glouces-ter, who says that it is wrote, in the very spirit of Rabelais, and has spoke to me highly of it several times, and inquired much after the author, and last Saturday made very honorable mention of it at the Bishop of Durham's [Richard Trevor] before six or seven of the Bishops, some of whom were rather offended with the levity of it, thinking it not in character for a clergyman. I hope therefore that there is no foundation of truth in the report I have heard, that Tristram is to have his education under the tutorage of Dr. Warburton. He may be as severe as he pleases upon impertinent fools and blockheads, but I do not love to see diamond cut diamond.

(b) Letter, 15 April 1760, supposedly from an (unidentified) acquaintance of Sterne to a friend, first published in *St James Chronicle* in April 1788 and reprinted here from the *European Magazine*, xxi (March 1792). 169–70

Indeed, my dear Sir, your letter was quite a surprise to me. I had heard that Mr. Shandy had engaged the attention of the gay part of the world; but when a gentleman of your active and useful turn can find time for so many enquiries about him, I see it is not only by the idle and the gay that he is read and admired, but by the busy and the serious; nay, Common Fame says, but Common Fame is a great liar, that it is not only a Duke and an Earl, and a new-made Bishop,[1] who are contending for the honour of being god-father to his dear child Tristram, but that men and women too, of all ranks and denomina-tions, are caressing the father, and providing slavering-bibs for the bantling.

In answer to your enquiries, I have sat down to write a longer letter than usual, to tell you all I know about him and the design of his book. I think it was some time in June last that he shewed me his papers, more than would make four such volumes as those two he has published; and we sat up a whole night together reading them. I thought I discovered a vein of humour which must take with readers of taste, but I took the liberty to point out some gross allusions, which

[1] Warburton became Bishop of Gloucester in 1759. See Nos 12, 16.

I apprehended would be matter of just offence, especially when coming from a clergyman, as they would betray a forgetfulness of his character. —He observed, that an attention to his character would damp his fire, and check the flow of his humour; and that if he went on and hoped to be read, he must not look at his band or cassock. I told him, that an over-attention to his character might perhaps have that effect; but that there was no occasion for him to think all the time he was writing his book, that he was writing sermons; that it was no difficult matter to avoid the dirtiness of Swift on the one hand, and the looseness of Rabelais on the other; and that if he steered in the middle course, he might not only make it a very entertaining, but a very instructive and useful book! and on that plan I said all I could to encourage him to come out with a volume or two in the winter.

At this time he was haunted with doubts and fears of its not taking. He did not, however, think fit to follow my advice; yet when the two volumes came out, I wrote a paper or two by way of recommending them, and particularly pointed to Yorick, Trim reading the sermon, and such parts as I was most pleased with myself.

If any apology can be made for his gross allusions and *double entendres*, it is, that his design is to take in all ranks and professions, and to laugh them out of their absurdities. If you should ask him, why he begins his hero nine months before he was born, his answer would be, that he might exhibit some character inimitably ridiculous, without going out of his way, and which he could not introduce with propriety had he begun him later. But as he intends to produce him somewhere in the third or fourth volume, we will hope, if he does not keep him too long in the nursery, his future scenes will be less offensive. Old women, indeed, there are of both sexes, whom even Uncle Toby can neither entertain nor instruct, and yet we all have hobby-horses of our own. The misfortune is, we are not content to ride them quietly ourselves, but are forcing everybody that comes in our way to get up behind. Is not intolerance the worst part of Popery? What pity it is, that many a zealous Protestant should be a staunch Papist without knowing it!

The design, as I have said, is to take in all ranks and professions. A system of education is to be exhibited, and thoroughly discussed. For forming his future hero, I have recommended a private tutor, and named no less a person than the great and learned Dr. W[arburton]:[1] Polemical Divines are to come in for a slap. An allegory has been run

[1] See n. 1, p. 57.

upon the writers on the Book of Job. The Doctor is the Devil who smote him from head to foot, and G[re]y, P[ete]rs and Ch[appel]ow[1] his miserable comforters. A group of mighty champions in literature is convened at Shandy-hall. Uncle Toby and the Corporal are thorns in the private tutor's side, and operate upon him as they did on Dr. Slop at reading the sermon; all this for poor Job's sake; whilst an Irish Bishop, a quondam acquaintance of Sterne's, who has written on the same subject, and loves dearly to be in a crowd, is to come uninvited and introduce himself.

So much for the book, now for the man. I have some reason to think that he meant to sketch out his own character in that of Yorick; and indeed, in some part of it, I think there is a striking likeness, but I do not know so much of him as to be able to say how far it is kept up. The gentlemen in and about York will not allow of any likeness at all in the best parts of it: whether his jokes and his jibes may not be felt by many of his neighbours, and make them unwilling to acknowledge a likeness, would be hard to say; certain, however, it is, that he has never, as far as I can find, been very acceptable to the grave and serious. It is probable too, he might give offence to a very numerous party when he was a curate, and just setting out; for he told me, that he wrote a weekly paper in support of the Whigs during the long canvass for the great contested election for this county, and that he owed his preferment to that paper—so acceptable was it to the then Archbishop.[2]

From that time, he says, he has hardly written anything till about two years ago; when a squabble breaking out at York, about opening a patent and putting in a new life, he sided with the Dean and his friends, and tried to throw the laugh on the other party, by writing The History of an Old Watchcoat; but the affair being compromised, he was desired not to publish it. About 500 copies were printed off, and all committed to the flames but three or four, he said; one of which I read, and, having some little knowledge of his *Dramatis Personae*, was highly entertained by seeing them in the light he had put them. This was a real disappointment to him; he felt it, and it was to this disappointment

[1] Zachary Grey (1688–1766), Yorkshire churchman and antiquary who was related to Sterne's wife's cousin, Mrs Edward Montagu, carried on a running literary battle with Warburton. Charles Peters (1690–1774), churchman and Hebrew scholar, likewise had a literary battle with Warburton over interpretation of the book of Job. Leonard Chappelow (1683–1768), orientalist and professor of Arabic at Cambridge, published a 'Commentary on the Book of Job' (1752), claiming that it was originally an Arabic poem.
[2] For a complete account of Sterne's political activities and his journalistic career, see Lewis P. Curtis, *The Politicks of Laurence Sterne* (1929).

that the world is indebted for Tristram Shandy. For till he had finished his Watchcoat, he says, he hardly knew that he could write at all, much less with humour, so as to make his reader laugh. But it is my own opinion, that he is yet a stranger to his own genius, or at least that he mistakes his forte. He is ambitious of appearing in his fool's coat; but he is more himself, and his powers are much stronger, I think, in describing the tender passions, as in Yorick, Uncle Toby, and the Fly, and in making up the quarrel between old Mr. Shandy and Uncle Toby.

I can say nothing to the report you have heard about Mrs. Sterne; the few times I have seen her she was all life and spirits; too much so, I thought. He told me, in a letter last Christmas, that his wife had lost her senses by a stroke of the palsy; that the sight of the mother in that condition had thrown his poor child into a fever; and that in the midst of these afflictions it was a strange incident that his ludicrous book should be printed off; but that there was a stranger still behind, which was, that every sentence of it had been conceived and written under the greatest heaviness of heart, arising from some hints the poor creature had dropped of her apprehensions; and that in her illness he had found in her pocket-book—

Jan. 1st, Le dernier de ma vie, helas![1]

Thus, my dear Sir, I have been as particular as I well can, and have given you as ample an account both of the man and the design of his book, as you can reasonably expect from a person who, bating a few letters, has not conversed more than three or four days with this very eccentric genius.

[1] January first, the last of my life, alas!

10. The serious attacks

Spring 1760

(a) Extracts from two letters from Mary Granville Delany, wife of Dr Patrick Delany, Dean of Down (referred to as 'Dean' and 'D.D.'), to her sister Anne Granville Dewes

24 April 1760 (*The Autobiography and Correspondence of Mary Granville, Mrs. Delany*, ed. Augusta Waddington Hall, Lady Llanover, 1st ser., (1861), iii. 588):

The Dean is indeed very angry with the author of Tristram, etc. and those who do not condemn the work as it deserves; it *has not* and *will not* enter this house, especially now your account is added to a very bad one we had heard before. We were upon the brink of having it read among us; Mr. Sandford heard Faulkner, the printer, cry it up so much, and say it had had a great run in England, and he would have brought it had we not been engaged in another book, and no one would have been more distressed at reading it than himself.

14 May 1760 (ibid., iii. 593):

D.D. is not a little offended with Mr. Sterne; his book is read here as in London, and seems to divert more than it offends, but as neither I nor any of my particular set have read it, or shall read it, I know nothing of it more than what you have said about it. Mrs. Clayton[1] and I had a furious argument about reading books of a bad tendency; I stood up for preserving a purity of mind, and discouraging works of *that kind—she* for trusting to her *own strength* and *reason*, and bidding defiance to any injury such books could do her; but as I *cannot presume* to depend on my own strength of mind, I think it safest and best to *avoid* whatever may prejudice it.

[1] Widow of Dr Robert Clayton (1695–1758), Bishop of Cork and Ross.

(b) Extract from an unsigned review of *Explanatory Remarks upon the Life and Opinions of Tristram Shandy . . . by Jeremiah Kunastrokius*, one of the numerous pamphlets spawned by *Tristram Shandy* (see No. 11b), in the *Critical Review*, ix (April 1760). 319

We must own we are tired with the encomiums bestowed on *Tristram Shandy* by those half-witted critics, who echo public report from coffee-house to coffee-house, and suspend their own opinion till the signal is made by a wit of superior rank. We would caution the author and his friends against raising the public expectation of the subsequent part, too high. Every thing in this country is directed by caprice; we praise and depreciate in extremes, and a new writer must either be at the top or the bottom of his profession, for a season. To own the truth, we harbour some suspicions that the author himself is here giving breath to the trumpet of fame; and, under the form of explanatory notes, pointing the finger at some of those latent strokes of wit in Tristram's life and opinions, which may perchance have escaped the eye of the less discerning reader.

(c) Extract from an unidentified correspondent's letter to the *Universal Magazine of Knowledge and Pleasure*, xxvi (April 1760). 189–90

Immodest Words admit of no Defence,
For Want of Decency is Want of Sense.
—POPE[1]

Whether the using immodest words, and the want of decency, always imply want of sense; according to the motto; or whether, on the contrary, such freedom, may not, on certain occasions, be the result of good sense; I will not take upon me absolutely to determine. I know very well that a skilful physician can manage and compound some of the rankest and most deadly poisons in such a manner, that they shall

[1] The quotation is actually from the *Essay on Translated Verse* (1684), ll. 113–14, by Wentworth Dillon, Earl of Roscommon (1633–85).

answer very salutary purposes. Perhaps a writer, in compliance with a public corruption of taste, may be able so to blend and intermix the broad hint, and double entendre, with the moral and useful part of his work, as to engage the attention of such readers as would not otherwise look into his book; and by this means he insensibly leads them on, and agreeably deceives them at last, by leaving their hearts better than he found them. When this is the aim of an author, it is truly laudable; but it requires so much art and skill in the execution of this design, that very few, if any, meet with the desired success. If the author is a person whose character and influence may be of some weight, his using liberties of this kind, unless under proper restrictions, may be attended with pernicious consequences on the morals of his readers; for the world is very apt to use the sanction of such a person's authority, who, though contrary to his intention, is thus made to patronise and promote the reigning practice of immodest conversation, and the evil spreads in proportion as his works gain credit and acceptance.

I have been led into these reflections by the perusal of a book lately published, which meets with abundance of admirers, I mean *Tristram Shandy*. Far be it from me to detract from the credit of an author, who has discovered such original and uncommon abilities in that manner of writing. I shall only beg leave to observe, that it were greatly to be wished, he had been more sparing in the use of indecent expressions. Indecent! did I say? Nay, even downright gross and obscene expressions are frequently to be met with throughout the book. . . . It is generally observable that the playhouses are most crouded, when any thing smutty is to be brought on the stage; and the reverend author of this ingenious performance has no doubt used this method as the most effectual, by making it as universally acceptable as possible. But how far it is excusable in any author, especially one who wears the gown, to gratify and promote a prevailing corrupted taste, either directly or indirectly, let himself and the world judge. I again repeat that it is really great pity he has not shewn more delicacy in this particular, for otherwise the book is truly excellent in its kind.

11. The bantering attacks

Spring 1760

(a) Extract from 'Animadversions on *Tristram Shandy*' in a letter from an unidentified correspondent to the *Grand Magazine*, iii (April 1760). 194–8

I have the pleasure to acquaint you that I am one of the jolly sons of Comus, and that we are all in raptures with his facetious disciple, that paragon of mirth and humour, *Tristram Shandy*. We are firmly persuaded, with friend *Tristy*, that every time a man smiles, but more so when he laughs, it adds something to this fragment of life.[1] This being the case, we pronounce *Tristy* the best physician [in] the world, for there is no reading him without laughing; nay the very sight of him is reviving—for his long sharp nose, and his droll look altogether, affect our risible faculties so strongly, that there is no looking at him without laughing.

But the best of all is—may be you do not know it—*Tristy*'s a clergyman of the church of *England*—smoke the parson!—Did you ever know such a jolly dog of a divine?—He has the finest knack at talking bawdy!—And then he makes such a joke of religion!—What do you think of his introducing a sermon in the midst of a smutty tale, and making the preacher curse and swear by way of parenthesis?—('D—n them all, quoth *Trim*.') There's divinity for you—There is nothing STERN in this doctrine—*Nomini nulla fides*.[2]

There are some stupid drones however, who do not enter into the spirit of the thing, and who charge *Tristy* with the want of *decorum*, sentiment and design.—Pox on their decorums, their sentiments, their connections, their systems, and their ratiocinations—*Tristy* speaks to the senses, and—

The senses always reason well.[3]

[1] See Sterne's dedication to William Pitt of the second edition of vols I and II of *Tristram Shandy*.
[2] No faith in the Name [of God].
[3] Cf. Lucretius, *De Rerum Natura*, I. 699–700.

By all that's luscious, *Aristotle* and *Rochester*[1] were mere Puritans compared to *Shandy*. . . .

Here I must not forget to do justice to *Tristy*'s obstetrical knowledge —By the bye, I suspect him to be the author of Mrs. NIHELL'S *practice of midwifery*.—But be that as it may—No man or woman of warm imagination, can read his dissertation on this subject, without feeling a violent itching and propensity, to make work for the sons and daughters of *Pilumnus* and *Lucina*. . . .[2]

Would you believe, after all, that as I was running on t'other day in high encomiums on dear *Shandy*, that I was reprehended by a solemn coxcomb, who made a humdrum moral harangue, in the following words, as near as I can recollect.—

'Sir,' said Mr. *Cynicus*, with an air of authority, 'You don't know what it is that you are so highly extolling—I blush for you, and for the age I live in—It argues a total depravation of taste and corruption of manners, when light, trifling, or obscene trash is perused with avidity. Literature must be in a declining taste, when they who ought to be patrons of the learned, and promote useful knowledge, are so lost in dissipation, that nothing but what is ludicrous, incoherent, and incon-sistent, will engage their attention. . . . What then shall be said of one in sacred orders, a dignitary of the Church; who turns pander to the public, and tickles their sensuality with the feather of buffoonry and obscenity? —O what a reproach to public taste and understanding!—That a studied and affected extravagance, should pass for wit, of which it is but the counterfeit—That two or three strokes of ribaldry should attone for a score of dull pages—And that a smatterer, who is only acquainted with the outlines of science, and by the help of a dictionary has acquired the cant of the learned professions, which he often ridiculously misapplies, should be admired for his knowledge, and applauded for his humour!— Hence-forward, let no man toil in quest of truth, or in pursuit of useful knowledge!—Let him laugh at all the sciences, without knowing any one.—Then he may rival the *reverend romancer*.—Then the great will caress him; invite him to their tables; and hail him master of the jest. —When their patronage is to be so cheaply purchased, who would not be a *Tristram Shandy*? . . .'

Did you ever hear such rantum, tantum, tarum[3] stuff, in all your life?

[1] John Wilmot, second Earl of Rochester (1647–80) is referred to because of the indecency of his poetry; Aristotle is mentioned probably because of his authorship of works de-scribing animal reproduction.

[2] Deities connected with childbirth in classical mythology.

[3] An obscure expression, probably derived from 'ranting.'

—Who does not see that this is envy, rank envy at *Shandy*'s success?—But as I could not answer *Cynicus* in his own Buckram stile, I chose to expose him through the channel of your Magazine—I am sure this formal pedant does not know *Tristy*—if he had ever been in his company, he would make him laugh, as gloomy as he is—Did you ever see *Shandy*?—Why, if he does but twist his nose on one side, there's humour in the distortion—and one cannot help laughing at his joke, even before he opens his mouth.—I only wish he was fatter—He looks as meagre as if he had pored over the metaphysical lamp, and made sermons, in good earnest.—This made an ill-natur'd fellow say, that *Tristy*'s humour was more in his head than his heart—But if he makes us laugh heartily, what is it to us whether his humour is in his pericranium, or in his toe-nails? It is of no more consequence, than to know whether the soul is seated in the *cellulae* of the *occiput*, or in the *medulla oblongata*.—In short, let the moral blockheads rant and cant as much as they please—*Vive la bagattelle,*[1] still say I—that is, in plain English—TRISTRAM SHANDY *for ever*!

(b) Extract from anonymous *Explanatory Remarks on the Life and Opinions of Tristram Shandy by Jeremiah Kunastrokius*, published 23 April 1760, pp. 44–5. Profound is speaking

---

I tell you, gentlemen, *Tristram Shandy* is one compleat system of modern politics, and that to understand him, there is as much occasion for a key, as there is for a catalogue to the Harleian library: I own, that I should not myself have penetrated so far as I have, notwithstanding my great reading in works of this nature, if I had not had the opportunity of supping the other evening with the author, who let me into the whole affair. I advised him to publish a key, but he told me it was too dangerous.—What is the Siege of *Namur*, which he often mentions, but the Siege of Fort St. Philip's in Minorca?[2]—or, the wound his uncle Toby

[1] Long live trifles.
[2] In 1756 Admiral John Byng (1704–57) was ordered to relieve the garrison of Fort St Philip, which was being besieged by the French; but Byng, judging that he could not effectively do so, sailed away, and Minorca fell to the French. He was subsequently court-martialed, condemned to death and shot. There was a later movement of public opinion in Byng's favor, although he had been convicted under a law which made the death penalty mandatory for anyone who did not do his utmost against the enemy in battle or in pursuit.

received there but the distress the nation was thrown into thereupon? His application to the study of fortification, and the knowledge he therein gained, means nothing else but the rectitude and clear sightedness of the administration which afterwards took up the reins of government. This is a master piece of allegory, beyond all the poets of this or any period whatever. There is but one fault to be found with Mr. *Tristram Shandy* as a politician—that is making *Yorick*'s horse so lean—but then he *is armed at all points*—I think too he should have told us the horse was white, to have made the symbolical application:—but he did not dare declare himself so openly upon this head—he told me so.

(c) Extracts from *The Clockmakers Outcry Against the Author of The Life and Opinions of Tristram Shandy*, published 9 May 1760. All the clockmakers of the kingdom have assembled to comment on and condemn Sterne's work

---

The drift of all Authors is, or ought to be, either to usefully instruct, or innocently amuse. In the works of the one and the other a plan is to be laid, and some main point had in view throughout the performance.

Where design and method are neglected, be the manner of writing ever so sprightly and elegant, the whole turns out but a mere wild-goose chace, that tends only to bewilder, but conducts to no profitable end: it is an *ignis fatuus*, whose twinkling leads us astray, but yields no serviceable light.

To this doctrine some people will perhaps object; Is then such strict regard to plan and method to be required from the hands of merely humorous authors? No, surely.

We have never read any of the truly excellent humorists that neglected it: *Swift*'s facetious works are a strong proof of what we have advanced: he has always some great point in view.

Consult his *Tale of a Tub*: see with what art he steals you along: how complete, apposite, and instructive are his digressions! not like the late flimsy imitations of them. . . .

The hue and cry was raised by church dignitaries, and the mistakenly pious of the laity, against the inimitable author of *The Tale of a Tub*. The now tagger[1] of a really contemptible *farrago* has met with a

---

[1] From 'tag' in the meaning of 'join, string, or tack together.'

profusion and wantonness of success (a discouragement to real merit) from church dignitaries and noble peers.

Wherefore, to expose such *Pseudo-Mecenases*[1] by laying open the Turpitude of their admired book is the scheme proposed by the writers of this pamplet, and the dictate of a just indignation for what we and our brethren the clockmakers suffer through the heretical and damnable Opinions of TRISTRAM SHANDY. (pp. vii–viii)

The injured have a right to complain, and to expose either the wantonness or concealed wickedness of those who have basely done them wrong.

Wickedness exerts itself in a two-fold manner; the one less, the other more formidable: the one less so, is when it appears bareface, and manifesting its sinister dispositions, alarms and puts all it approaches on their guard against any attack from its ferocity: the more so, is when under an affected mask of folly or insanity of mind, and as it were in a frolicksome mood, it endeavours to sap, undermine, and blow up all that is sacred in our moral, religious, and political system.

That the latter is the light in which this forerunner of *Antichrist* (pray heaven that he may not be the real one, of which there is not a little room to suspect when we contemplate his figure, and penetrate into his real sentiments!) the pernicious author of *The Life and Opinions of Tristram Shandy, Gent.* is to be looked at with horror and detestation; will appear from our subsequent remarks: which with a heart full of sorrow, and in the midst of the sighs and lamentations of our trade, we here pen down for publication; in order to lay our undeserved grievances and cruel persecution before the world in hopes of some redress. Otherwise we and our miserable families are entirely devoted to ruin, and must consequently become a burden to the community.

But now to begin, and follow this infernal emissary (that has assumed a human form) in all his abominable vagaries. . . . (pp. 9–10)

[The pamphlet then proceeds to comment on various passages in vol. I of *Tristram Shandy*, capitalizing on any suggestions of bawdiness and purporting to give serious criticism of Sterne's morals, his supposedly materialistic philosophy, and his ignorance of physiology. Much is made of the business of winding up the clock in the first four chapters of vol. I. There is also comment on Sterne and his style:]

[1] The name of Gaius Cilnius Maecenas (*c.* 70–8 BC), Roman statesman and patron of Vergil and Horace, has come to mean any literary patron.

P. 55.[1] *Tristram*, if he meant it, has not mistypified himself and works; 'an heteroclite creature in all his declensions—With all his sail poor *Yorick* carried not one ounce of ballast.'—Without the ballast of good Sense, Judgment holding the helm, and Decency directing what course to steer, all attempts at wit or humour must prove ineffectual, though for a while they may excite an ideot gaze: yet ultimately they will expose such adventurers to the slight and derision of those whom it would be a happiness and honour to please.

P. 57. What he descants upon Gravity is far from new, and therefore no way interesting: it helps to eke out the two volumes, as do an hundred other adventitious articles not naturally arising from the subject, and may therefore be called the superfluous labours of a rantipole[2] brain.

P. 60. There may be humour and great pleasantry concealed under 'the mortgager and mortgagee differ the one from the other not more in length of *purse*, than the *jester* and *jestee* do in that of memory, &c.' but our dull knobs cannot reach it; nor can we find any of those who laugh so inconsiderately at this and many other equally brilliant strokes, able to give us a reason why. Their applausive acclaim is, *Eo melius, nihil intelligo*, O the charming book, although I do not understand it! it is so odd! and so whimsical! and so out of the way! and so absurd! and so all that—

Now the plain maxim of us grave adherents to common sense, concerning authors who wrap themselves up from the ken of our comprehension in rhapsodical obscurity, is, *Non vis intelligi, nec ego intelligere*, Author, since thou dost not choose to be understood, I will take no pains to understand thee.

In consequence of this declaration we are resignedly prepared to be called heavy blockheads, vile tasteless wretches, stupid dolts: they should never read books of wit and humour: cruel sentence! However we can relish the works of Fielding, Swift, Le Sage, Cervantes, Lucian, &c. that is some comfort to us.

The account of *Yorick* and his *Exit*, which stretches to p. 71, is well imagined and pathetically written. It has not a little contributed to provoke our indignation against the author, for mispending his time on ridiculous and immoral bagatelles, who seems to be possessed of talents, that, properly employed, cannot fail of penetrating the heart: for, *si sic omnia dixisset*, if he had written all his book on a par with this,

[1] The page references to the first edition which follow correspond to the following pages in Work: 25, 26, 27, 32.
[2] Wild, disorderly, rakish.

he would have found us among his warmest advocates, instead of being assailants. . . . (pp. 25–7)

Ned Paradox, who had listened demurely hitherto, and was more over blessed with the happy knack of discovering in all transactions what no mortal besides himself had ever dreamt of, thrice shook his head, and thus observed to the company:

'The ludicrous manner in which this sermon is introduced, and many other previous instances, but too obviously prove the design of this Antichristian author; which is to disgrace, revile, and overthrow our holy religion. . . .' (p. 38)

Harry Love-Glee, the wag of the club, who had much ado to refrain from a laugh during his brother *Ned*'s profound speculation, thus attempted to introduce mirth:

'Why really, Gentlemen, I fear we look at, in too serious a light, a man and his writings, that are only the cause of jollity in most other companies.

'Our manners and speech at present are all *be-Tristram'd*. Nobody speaks now but in the *Shandean* style. The modish phraseology is all taken from him, and his equally intelligible imitators, especially in love affairs. The common and approved salute in *high life* for a lover to his fair-one now is, "My dear, if you are desirous of being *inflated*, pray grant me the favour of *homunculating*[1] you. . . ." ' (pp. 40–1)

All the company broke into a fit of laughter, except contemplative *Ned Paradox*, and the zealous member who took the lead in this work: 'Why, Gentlemen (quoth this latter) this is very ill-tim'd pleasantry. Did you know but all, you have reason to wail and weep instead of *giggling*; for this *Tristram*, as I have learned by letters from the country, is like to ruin our trade.'—At this they all looked grave.

The directions I had for making several clocks for the country are countermanded; because no modest lady now dares to mention a word about *winding-up a clock*, without exposing herself to the sly leers and jokes of the family, to her frequent confusion. Nay, the common expression of street-walkers is, 'Sir, will you have your clock wound-up?' Alas, reputable, hoary clocks, that have flourished for ages, are ordered to be taken down by virtuous matrons, and be disposed of as obscene lumber, exciting to acts of carnality!

[1] The italicized words are quoted from *Two Lyric Epistles: one to my Cousin Shandy . . . the other To the Grown Gentlewomen, The Misses of ★★★★*, bawdy poems published on 17 April 1760 by Sterne's friend, John Hall-Stevenson (1718–85), the Eugenius of *Tristram Shandy*. See *Tristram Shandy*, I. 1–4. See also No. 54.

Nay, hitherto harmless watches are degraded into agents of debauchery. If a gentleman wind-up his watch in company, and looks affectionately at any particular lady, that is as much as to say that he prefers her to all the rest, and is in love with her: if she wind hers immediately after, and reciprocates a look of fondness to him, it is as much as to say, on her side, that she approves his passion.—That I should live to see the unhappy day, when sober and well-regulated clocks are treated as the alarms of lust, as veteran bawds; and jemmy[1] watches dwindled into pimps! . . .

All this hath been occasioned by that type of Antichrist, that foe to every thing that is good. His infernal scheme is to overturn church and state: for clocks and watches being brought into contempt and disuse, nobody will know how the time goes, nor which is the hour of prayer, the hour of levee, the hour of mounting guard, &c. &c. &c. consequently an universal confusion in church, senate, playhouse, &c. must ensue and we be prepared for the reign of that dreadful being so long foretold; and of which SHANDY is the undoubted fore-runner.—Ah, woful period for the sons and daughters of Man!

> Time's out of rule; no Clock is now *wound-up*:
> TRISTRAM the *lewd* has *knock'd* Clock-making up. (pp. 42–4)

(d) Extract from *Tristram Shandy's Bon Mots, Repartees, odd Adventures, and Humorous Stories . . . and a New Dialogue of the Dead, between Dean Swift, and Henry Fielding, Esq*, published 12 June 1760, pp. 67–71. After a pastiche of anecdotes about Sterne, scraps of biography, and vulgar jokes having nothing to do with Sterne, there follows an imaginary dialogue between Swift and Fielding discussing *Tristram Shandy*. Swift has just said that 'nothing but a yahoo, both in taste and principles, could endure, much less admire such a paltry performance,' and has hinted the book's popularity won't last

---

Swift.

In a few words—it is a hotch potch of technical terms—broken sentences—trite satir—obscenity—low buffoonery, without wit—humour —or design.

[1] Smart, fashionable, or neatly made.

71

Fielding.

I beg pardon for interrupting you—but that word low is often given by the sons of dullness to humour the most exquisite—is there no humour in the book?

Swift.

Would you think there was humour—if a blackguard in the street should pull down his breeches and shew you his dirty—If you would, then there is humour in Tristram Shandy.

Fielding.

How the devil can the town be so absurd then, as to put this man in competition with you and me?

Swift.

Because they are a pack of asses—but do not imagine that all do so— a player that pretends to a taste, perhaps, when he has none—or a rabble of fashionable people may make a noise about him—as a mob often will do about nothing—but the few good judges, Mercury[1] assures me, hold his book in the contemptible light it deserves.

Fielding.

I fancy he owes the success of it to its not being understood.

Swift.

He does most certainly—the majority of the world are ignorant— and ignorance, whatever face it may put upon it outwardly, is always conscious—these, therefore, place to their own account—what should be put to that of the author—true, they do not understand him—but they never consider that he is not to be understood—in my opinion, any man who should sit down to write—if, at the same time, he was not absolutely void of what is called the funny stile, might produce as good a work—only going upon the simple principle, of putting down whatever came into his head.

[1] Mercury, as conductor of souls to the Underworld, was the intermediary between the living and the dead.

12. The first biography of Sterne

1 May 1760

Extract from Dr John Hill, 'A Letter to the Ladies Magazine,' *Royal Female Magazine* (April 1760); reprinted here from *The Works of Laurence Sterne*, ed. Wilbur L. Cross (1904), vi. 40–6.

Hill (1716(?)–75), literary hack and manufacturer of herb medicines, was Sterne's first biographer. Since he did not know Sterne personally, there are inaccuracies in his account, which was copied by most of the London newspapers. Though Hill is sympathetic to Sterne, the article nettled Sterne considerably, in part because the example of his generosity (in the last paragraph of the excerpt below) was both untrue and beyond his means to accomplish. The portions of the essay not excerpted here contain an outline of Sterne's life and various anecdotes.

The publication of his book, obtained him . . . by really deserving it, . . . [a] high reputation in town. Here were none of the common arts of making a reputation practised: no friend before hand told people how excellent a book it was:[1] no bookseller, a proprietor, whose interest should lead him to cry it up, and bid his authors do the same. A parcel of the books were sent up out of the country; they were unknown, and scarce advertised; but thus friendless they made their own way, and their author's. They have been resembled to Swift's, and equalled to Rabelais's, by those who are considered as judges; and they have made their author's way to the tables of the first people in the kingdom, and to the friendship of Mr. Garrick.

Fools tremble at the allusions that may be made from the present volumes, and authors dread the next: forty people have assumed to themselves the ridiculous titles in these volumes: and it is scarce to be credited whose liberal purse has bought off the dread of a tutor's character, in those which are to come.[2]

[1] Hill did not know about No. 3 above.
[2] The reference is to William Warburton, Bishop of Gloucester. See Nos 8, 9, 16.

As to the author himself, his view was general—He is too good, and too good-natur'd a man, to have levell'd a syllable at any private person: nay, where one character seemed possible of an application which he had never intended, he alter'd it, new-dress'd it, and even sent it to the person who might be supposed, by the malicious, to be intended by it; nor would suffer the page to be published, till he was assured by that gentleman it gave him no offence. . . .

Resentment, therefore, has been able to do the author of *Tristram Shandy* not the least harm; but the spirit of the performance has been of infinite service to him. Every body is curious to see the author; and, when they see him, every body loves the man. There is a pleasantry in his conversation that always pleases; and a goodness in his heart, which adds the greater tribute of esteem.

Many have wit; but there is a peculiar merit in giving variety. This most agreeable joker can raise it from any subject; for he seems to have studied all; and can suit it to his company; the depth of whose understandings he very quickly fathoms. . . .

We are talking of the singularities of Yorick; 'tis fit we name one more, which is the extreme candour and modesty of his temper. A vain man would be exalted extremely, at the attention that is paid to him; the compliments, invitations, civilities, and applauses: he sees them in another light, attributing that to novelty, which perhaps few could more justly place to the account of merit. He says he is now just like a fashionable mistress, whom every body solicits, because 'tis the fashion, but who may walk the street a fortnight, and in vain solicit corporal Stare for a dinner.

To sum up all, we must recount the last and newest incident of all. Lord Falconberg has given Yorick a benefice;[1] and the incumbent, whose death has made the vacancy, has left a widow destitute of all, but the country parson's certain legacy, a family of children. Yorick, when he entered upon the living, gave her, 'tis said, a hundred pounds, and proposes to take annual care of her. If anything can add to doing this, it is the modesty of concealing it. Others would take care it should be known; but on the contrary, this singular creature, when a friend was complimenting him upon this act of goodness, cut him short, and answered, 'I'm an odd fellow; but if you hear any good of me, don't believe it.'

[1] See No. 8, p. 55, n. 1.

13. *The Sermons of Mr. Yorick*, vols I and II

Spring and summer 1760

(a) Extract from Sterne's preface to his sermons, published 22 May 1760, pp. v–xi

---

The Sermon which gave rise to the publication of these, having been offer'd to the world as a sermon of *Yorick's*, I hope the most serious reader will find nothing to offend him, in my continuing these two volumes under the same title: lest it should be otherwise, I have added a second title page with the real name of the author:—the first will serve the bookseller's purpose, as *Yorick's* name is possibly of the two the more known;—and the second will ease the minds of those who see a jest, and the danger which lurks under it, where no jest was meant.

   I suppose it is needless to inform the publick, that the reason of printing these sermons, arises altogether from the favourable reception which the sermon given as a sample of them in TRISTRAM SHANDY, met with from the world. . . . As the sermons turn chiefly upon philanthropy, and those kindred virtues to it, upon which hang all the law and the prophets, I trust they will be no less felt, or worse received, for the evidence they bear, of proceeding more from the heart than the head. I have nothing to add, but that the reader, upon old and beaten subjects, must not look for many new thoughts,—'tis well if he has new language; in three or four passages, where he has neither the one or the other, I have quoted the author I made free with—there are some other passages, where I suspect I may have taken the same liberty,—but 'tis only suspicion, for I do not remember it is so, otherwise I should have restored them to their proper owners, so that I put it in here more as a general saving, than from a consciousness of having much to answer for upon that score: in this however, and every thing else, which I offer, or shall offer to the world, I rest, with a heart much at ease, upon the protection of the humane and candid, from whom I have received many favours, for which I beg leave to return them thanks—thanks.

(b) Extract from an unsigned review of the sermons in the *Critical Review*, ix (May 1760). 405-7

It is with pleasure that we behold this son of Comus descending from the chair of mirth and frolick, to inspire sentiments of piety, and read lectures in morality, to that very audience whose hearts he has captivated with good-natured wit, and facetious humour. Let the narrow-minded bigot persuade himself that religion consists in a grave forbidding exterior and austere conversation; let him wear the garb of sorrow, rail at innocent festivity, and make himself disagreeable to become righteous; we, for our parts, will laugh and sing, and lighten the unavoidable cares of life by every harmless recreation: we will lay siege to Namur with uncle *Toby* and *Trim*, in the morning, and moralize at night with Sterne and Yorick; in one word, we will ever esteem religion when smoothed with good humour, and believe that piety alone to be genuine, which flows from a heart, warm, gay, and social. . . .

The reverend Mr. Sterne aims at mending the heart, without paying any great regard to the instruction of the head; inculcating every moral virtue by precepts, deduced from reason and the sacred oracles. Would to God his example were more generally followed by our clergy, too many of whom delight in an ostentatious display of their own abilities, and vain unedifying pomp of theological learning. Most of the discourses before us are penned in a plain and artless strain, elegant without the affectation of appearing so, and familiar without meanness, at least, in general. . . .

We could almost venture to pronounce, concerning the goodness of the author's heart, by his choice of subjects, most of which must have occasioned serious reflections in every man who has felt the distresses of his fellow-creatures.

(c) Extract from an unsigned review of the first volume of the sermons in the *Monthly Review*, xxii (May 1760). 422–5, by Owen Ruffhead and William Rose (the latter of whom is responsible for only the last two sentences. For Ruffhead see the Introduction. Rose (1719(?)–86) was a co-founder of the *Monthly*, a dissenting clergyman, and a friend of Johnson)

Before we proceed to the matter of these sermons, we think it becomes us to make some animadversions on the manner of their publication, which we consider as the greatest outrage against Sense and Decency, that has been offered since the first establishment of Christianity—an outrage which would scarce have been tolerated even in the days of paganism.

Had these Discourses been sent into the world, as the Sermons of Mr. *Yorick*, pursuant to the *first* title-page, every serious and sober Reader must have been offended at the indecency of such an assumed character. For who is this *Yorick*? We have heard of one of that name who was a *Jester*—we have read of a *Yorick* likewise, in an obscene Romance.[1]—But are the solemn dictates of religion fit to be conveyed from the mouths of Buffoons and ludicrous Romancers? Would any man believe that a Preacher was in earnest, who should mount the pulpit in a *Harlequin's coat*? . . .[2]

Must obscenity then be the handmaid to Religion—and must the exordium to a sermon, be a smutty tale? Tillotson, Clarke, and Foster[3] found other means of raising attention to divine truths; and their names will be respected, when those of YORICK and TRISTRAM SHANDY will be forgotten or despised. . . .

Perhaps the Reverend Writer, inflated with vanity, and intoxicated with applause, will affect to smile at our strictures, which ought to awaken him to serious reflection—Perhaps he will be forward to persuade himself and others, that we reprehend his indecencies, because we *envy* his success. But in this he is more likely to impose upon himself, than to deceive others.

The wanton Harlot affects to laugh at the indignant scorn of Chas-

[1] Presumably a reference to *Tristram Shandy*.
[2] Harlequin, the hero of pantomimes, was both clown and successful lover.
[3] John Tillotson (1630–94), Archbishop of Canterbury; Samuel Clarke (1675–1729); and James Foster (1697–1753) all published sermons which were widely read in the eighteenth century and from which Sterne borrowed in composing his own *Sermons of Mr. Yorick*.

tity—she calls virtue prudery; and would persuade herself and the world, that the contempt and reproach to which she is hourly subject, arise from *envy* of her superior charms and endowments. In short, this is the common affectation of every Libertine and Prostitute, from K— F—[1] down to TRISTRAM SHANDY.

But we are so far from envying the success of the Reverend Author's writings, that we should have rejoiced to see such a numerous and noble appearance of Subscribers, had the *manner* of publication been as unexceptionable as the *matter* of his Sermons, which, in our judgment, may serve as models for many of his brethren to copy from. They abound with moral and religious precepts, clearly and forcibly expressed: though we here and there meet with an affectation of archness, which is insuitable to Discourses of this nature. . . .

We know of no compositions of this kind in the English language, that are written with more ease, purity, and elegance; and tho' there is not much of the pathetic or devotional to be found in them, yet there are many fine and delicate touches of the human heart and passions, which, abstractedly considered, shew marks of great benevolence and sensibility of mind. If we consider them as moral Essays, they are, indeed, highly commendable, and equally calculated for the entertainment and instruction of the attentive Reader.

(d) Extract from an unsigned review of the sermons in the *Royal Female Magazine*, i (May 1760). 238

The dissipated taste of the age, leaves little room to hope for much advantage from works, under this serious title; but the expectation, which has been *however improperly*, raised of these, may perhaps gain them a reading; and their familiar style, and insinuating manner of address, improve the favour, to a success, denied to more regular and argumentative performances. I would not be thought to mean, that this is the only merit, of these sermons: they really have much, so much as will bear witness against the abuse of such abilities, to improper ends, in that day, *when every idle word shall be accounted for*,[2] how much soever present applause may intoxicate a man to pursue the bent of a licentious turn to wit and pleasantry.

[1] Kitty Fisher, the noted courtesan.
[2] See Matthew, 12:36.

(e) Extract from a letter of the Reverend Henry Venn (1724–97), evangelistic clergyman, to his friend Mrs Knipe, 20 June 1760 (*Life and Letters of Henry Venn*, ed. Henry Venn, 4th ed. (1836), pp. 80–1)

The most plausible way that I know, and by far the most successful, of supplanting the Gospel, is, by a pretended or real zeal for the practice of moral duties. . . . Certainly the crying abomination of our age is, contempt of Christ. In proof of this, you may hear sermons and religious books much extolled, where there is not so much as any mention of the Prince of Peace, in whom God was manifest, to reconcile the world into Himself. Mr. Lawrence Sterne, prebendary of York, published, a few weeks since, two volumes of sermons. They are much commended by the Critical Reviewers. I have read them; and, excepting a single phrase or two, they might be preached in a synagogue or a mosque without offence.

(f) Extract from a letter of Georgina, Countess Cowper, to Anne Granville Dewes (see No. 10a), 3 September 1760 (*Autobiography and Correspondence of Mary Granville, Mrs. Delany*, 1st ser, iii. 602)

Pray read *Yorick's* sermons, (though *you would not read Tristram Shandy*). They are more like Essays. I like them extremely, and I think he must be a good man.

14. Boswell on Sterne

Spring 1760

Extracts from 'A Poetical Epistle to Doctor Sterne, Parson Yorick, and Tristram Shandy,' reprinted here from the manuscript in the Bodleian Library, Douce 193. (Some portions of the text below have previously appeared in Frederick A. Pottle, 'Bozzy and Yorick,' *Blackwood's Magazine*, ccxvii (March 1925). 297–313; and in Alan B. Howes, *Yorick and the Critics* (1958), pp. 6, 11–12.) Boswell's intended order for this text is partly conjectural.

The young Boswell, as this manuscript shows, met Sterne in London in the spring of 1760 and then or soon afterwards started to compose a 'Poetical Epistle' to the older man. Boswell never finished the poem and its existence was unknown until the present century. He also attempted to imitate Sterne in his *Observations, Good or Bad, Stupid or Clever, Serious or Jocular, on Squire Foote's Dramatic Entertainment, intitled The Minor*, in his poem 'The Cub at Newmarket,' and in some of his writing exercises, which were composed, he says, following 'the example of Rabelais, *Tristram Shandy*, and all those people of unbridled imagination who write their books as I write my themes—at random, without trying to have any order or method' (*Boswell in Holland 1763–1764*, ed. Frederick A. Pottle (1952), p. 67). Boswell continues to refer to Sterne appreciatively throughout his literary career, although in *The Hypochondriack* he attacks Sterne (see No. 68a). The paths of the two men never crossed again after the spring of 1760.

> *In nova fert animus mutatas dicere formas*
> *Corpora: Di coeptis, nam vos mutastis et illas,*
> *Favete.* —OVID.[1]

[1] The opening lines of Book I of Ovid's *Metamorphoses*, with one minor variation. John Dryden translated the lines as follows:

> Of bodies chang'd to various forms, I sing:
> Ye gods, from whom these miracles did spring,
> Inspire my numbers with celestial heat. . . .

Dear Sir! if you're in mood to whistle
As Prologue to my poor Epistle—
I beg your audience for a minute,
In favour of the stuff that's in it.
    'What does the Dog by whistle mean?'
Methinks you say—good future Dean
My meaning Sir is very plain;
I mean if you've a vacant brain.
    For without question it would be
Just downright sacriledge in me
To interrupt one single thought
Of your's with—we shall call it nought.

    Permitt me, Doctor, then, to show
A certain Genius whom you know,
A mortal enemy to strife,[1]
At different periods of his life.
    To Country Curacy confin'd,
Ah! how unlike his soaring mind,
Poor Yorick stuck for many a day,
Like David in the miry clay.
    There for his constant occupation
He had the duties of his station;
Sundays and Holidays to Him
Were times on which he was in trim;
When with Ecclesiastic Gown
Of colour dubious, black or brown,
And wig centauric, form'd with care
From human & equestrian hair,
Thro' shades of which appear'd the caul;
Nay, some affirm his pate & all,
And band well starch'd by faithfull John,
For, to be sure, Maids he had none,
He solemn walk'd in grand Procession,
Like Justice to a Country Session,
To Church—'You'll step in there, I hope?'
No, Sir, excuse me—there I stop.[2]

---

[1] Boswell originally wrote 'Not old enough to have a Wife,' evidence not of the slightness
of their acquaintance but rather of Sterne's characteristic behavior in London.
[2] Boswell originally wrote, 'No, Sir—that's sacred, there I stop.'

In his retirement time was spent
So calm he knew not how it went
To murm'ring envy quite a Stranger
Nor of the spleen in the least danger.
For ease he would his head enwrap
In party-colour'd woolen Cap;
A threadbare Coat with sleeves full wide
A formal nightgown's place supply'd.
He wore, his new ones not t'abuse,
A pair of ancient, downheel'd shoes;
He roll'd his stockings 'bove his knees,
And was as *dégagé*'s you please.

Now, God of love or God of wine,
Or muse, whichever of the nine
That erst blithe Ovid's tunefull tongue
Touch'd till he fancifully sung
Of Transformation's wondrous Power,
Such as Jove turn'd to Golden Shower,
O! to my Supplication list!
I will describe, if you assist,
As strange a metamorphosis,
I'm sure, as any one of his.
Who has not *Tristram Shandy* read?
Is any mortal so ill bred?
If so, don't dare your birth to boast,
Nor give fam'd C[hu]dl[eig]h[1] for your toast.
This much about the time of lent,
His Harbinger to town he sent;
Procur'd Bob Dodsley[2] for his friend,
Dodsley, who lives at the Court end—
A Circumstance which, Sir, I say't,
Must be allow'd to have some weight.
So soon as its reception kind
Was known, on swiftest wings of wind,
To reap a crop of fame and Pelf
Up comes th' original himself.

[1] The notorious Elizabeth Chudleigh, at this time mistress of the Duke of Kingston, whom she later married.
[2] See No. 1a, c.

By Fashion's hands compleatly drest,
He's everywhere a wellcome Guest:
He runs about from place to place,
Now with my Lord, then with his Grace,
And, mixing with the brilliant throng,
He straight commences *Beau Garcon.*[1]
In Ranelagh's[2] delightfull round
Squire Tristram oft is flaunting found;
A buzzing whisper flys about;
Where'er he comes they point him out;
Each Waiter with an eager eye
Observes him as he passes by;
'That there is he, do, Thomas! look,
Who's wrote such a damn'd clever book.'

Next from the press there issues forth
A sage divine fresh from the north;
On Sterne's discourses we grew mad,
Sermons! where are they to be had?
Then with the fashionable Guards
The Psalms supply the place of Cards
A strange enthusiastic rage
For sacred text now seis'd the age;
Arround S.t Jamess[3] every table
Was partly gay & partly sable,
The manners by old Noll[4] defended
Were with our modern chitte chat blended.
'Give me some maccaroni pray,'
'Be wise while it is call'd today;'
'Heavns! how Mingotti[5] sung last Monday'
'—Alas how we profane the Sunday.'
'My Lady Betty! hob or nob!—'[6]
'Great was the patience of old Job,'
Sir Smart breaks out & one & all
Adore S.t Peter & S.t Paul.

[1] 'Good-looking fellow' or 'man of fashion'.
[2] A fashionable resort area by the Thames with gardens and a concert hall.
[3] A park near Buckingham Palace, recreation area for fashionable society.
[4] The reference is to Oliver Cromwell.
[5] Regina Mingotti (1722–1808), Italian opera singer who helped to re-establish the popularity of opera in England during the several years she spent in London.
[6] A drinking salutation.

Now Sir! when I am in the cue
I wou'd not worship but praise you.
You need not try to shake your head
Or with Hawks eye strike me wth dread;
For as your uncle Toby stout,
What I incline I will have out.
Truth with a look of Approbation
Calls him t'encrease our Admiration:
This Sovreign's fav'rite, Edward's frien[d],[1]
Could Sycophants him more commend?
Sweet Sentiment, the certain test;
Of Goodness, commendation best!

I will admire and will pretend
To taste while I your works commend.

Yes, Sir, from partial motives free,
Which while I live I hope to be—
Your various meri[t]s sollid light:
Judgment, Imagination bright,
Great erudition, polish'd taste,
Pure language tho' you write in haste,
Sweet sentiments on Human life—
This I am sure, tis not for gain—
I firmly promise to maintain
Altho the public voice should fail
And envious Grubs[2] should half prevail,
Who swear like Shuttlecock they'll bandy
This upstart Willing Tristram Shandy.

O thou! whose quick-discerning eye
The nicest strokes of wit can spy;
Whose sterling jests, a sportive strain,
How warmly-genuine from the brain
And with bright poignancy appear,
Original to ev'ry ear!
Whose heart is all Benevolence;
Whose constant leader is good sense,

---

[1] The reference is to Edward Augustus (1739–67), Duke of York and Albany. It was probably in his company that Boswell met Sterne.
[2] Hack writers of Grub Street.

84

Who very seldom makes a real slip,
Altho at times he take[s] a trip
To frolic's lightsom regions where
Mirth dissipates the dregs of care.
    To hear a fellow talk away
Who has not got a Word to say
Is of all things the most provoking:
Don't you think so too without joking?
Such now am I who can [no] more,
Having exhausted all my Store;
Therefore to shun your smarting Scoff
I without more ado break off.

15. Sterne as Juvenilian satirist

1 June 1760

Letter from an unidentified correspondent to *Lloyd's Evening Post*,
vi (4–6 June 1760). 539

Sir,

So great an out cry is there in the world against the performance of
the Author of *Tristram Shandy*, that, tho' I have only just looked into it,
I am entirely convinced 'tis a smart satyrical piece on the vices of the
age, particularly of that part of the Creation, which were designed for
the pleasure and happiness of man. But this is not an age for wit and
humour: arms and military atchievements engross the attention of one
part of the public; pleasure and luxury occupy the minds of the other:
So that neither Gentlemen nor Ladies have leisure to inspect their own
conduct. But, notwithstanding all the clamours against this excellent
production of *Tristram Shandy*, I would only beg leave to observe, that
the Author has made use of a very proper expedient to put vice to the

blush, and to restore to the Belle-monde, that innocency and virtue which can be their only ornaments. Perhaps, in some particular passages, he may seem to savour too much of the Libertine and Infidel; but let me recommend such nice and delicate Critics to the perusal of the sixth satyr of Juvenal,[1] which, if they be able to read and understand it, they will find was wrote with the same virtuous view, as the most abused *Tristram Shandy* is, and will be applauded as long as literature exists.

Your's,
W. K.

16. Sterne and Bishop Warburton

June 1760

William Warburton (1698–1779), Bishop of Gloucester, was introduced to Sterne by David Garrick in March of 1760. Warburton had been worried by a rumor that Sterne was planning to satirize him as Tristram's tutor in the next installment of *Shandy*, and indeed Sterne may have had some such vague plan (see No. 9). Sterne assured Garrick, however, that he had no intention of satirizing Warburton and Garrick brought the two men together. Warburton recommended *Tristram Shandy* to his friends and presented Sterne with a purse of guineas and some books 'to improve his style' (see *Letters*, p. 103). After Sterne's return to York in late May, Warburton apparently became increasingly embarrassed by his patronage of Sterne and increasingly uneasy over some of Sterne's indiscretions and the notoriety that the scribblers and pamphleteers were bringing to Sterne. The day after he wrote the first letter excerpted below, Warburton was writing to Garrick to thank him for 'the hints . . . concerning our heteroclite Parson. I heard enough of his conduct in town since I left it,' Warburton continued, 'to make me think he would soon lose the fruits of all the

---

[1] Satire VI of Decimus Junius Juvenalis (AD 60(?)–140(?)) is a savage attack upon women.

advantage he had gained by a successful effort, and would disable me from appearing as his friend or well-wisher' (*Private Correspondence of David Garrick* (1831–2), i. 117). The second installment of *Tristram Shandy* contained an uncomplimentary allusion to the bishop (see No. 27f); Warburton then wrote to a friend that 'Tristram Shandy is falling apace from his height of glory' (A. W. Evans, *Warburton and the Warburtonians* (1932), p. 231). The fifth and sixth volumes of *Shandy* Warburton thought 'wrote pretty much like the first and second; but whether they will restore his reputation as a writer,' he continued, 'is another question.—The fellow himself is an irrecoverable scoundrel' (*Letters from a Late Eminent Prelate to One of his Friends*, 1st American ed. (1809), p. 249). For Sterne's parting thrust at Warburton, see *Tristram Shandy*, IX. 8, p. 610; for Warburton's comments at the time of Sterne's death, see No. 58b.

(a) Extract from Warburton's letter to Sterne, 15 June 1760 (*Letters*, pp. 112–13)

I . . . am glad to understand, you are got safe home, and employ'd again in your proper studies and amusements. You have it in your power to make that, which is an amusement to yourself and others, useful to both: at least, you should above all things, beware of its becoming hurtful to either, by any violations of decency and good manners; but I have already taken such repeated liberties of advising you on that head, that to say more would be needless, or perhaps unacceptable. . . .

But of all these things, I dare say Mr. Garrick, whose prudence is equal to his honesty or his talents, has remonstrated to you with the freedom of a friend. He knows the inconstancy of what is called the Public, towards all, even the best intentioned, of those who contribute to its pleasure, or amusement. He (as every man of honour and discretion would) has availed himself of the public favour, to regulate the taste, and, in his proper station, to reform the manners of the fashionable world. . . .'

(b) Extract from Sterne's reply to Warburton, 19 June 1760
(*Letters*, p. 115)

Be assured, my lord, that willingly and knowingly I will give no
offence to any mortal by anything which I think can look like the least
violation either of decency or good manners; and yet, with all the
caution of a heart void of offence or intention of giving it, I may find it
very hard, in writing such a book as *Tristram Shandy*, to mutilate everything in it down to the prudish humour of every particular. I will,
however, do my best; though laugh, my lord, I will, and as loud as I
can too.

(c) Extract from Warburton's reply to Sterne, 26 June 1760
(*Letters*, pp. 118–19)

It gives me real pleasure . . . that you are resolved to do justice to your
genius, and to borrow no aids to support it, but what are of the party
of honour, virtue, and religion.

You say you will continue to laugh aloud. In good time. But one
who was no more than even a man of spirit would wish to laugh in
good company, where priests and virgins may be present. . . .

I would recommend a maxim to you which Bishop Sherlock formerly told me Dr. Bentley recommended to him,[1] that a man was never
writ out of the reputation he had once fairly won, but by himself.

[1] Warburton had told the same anecdote in a note to his edition of Pope's works (1751; iv,
159 n.).

17. Thomas Gray on Sterne

c. 20 June 1760

Excerpt from a letter from the poet Thomas Gray (1716–71) to his friend Thomas Warton the Younger (1728–90), *Correspondence of Thomas Gray*, ed. Paget Toynbee and Leonard Whibley (1935), ii. 681.

Gray had written in April to Warton, Professor of Poetry at Oxford, describing Sterne's popularity in London society (see ibid., ii. 670), but did not comment on Sterne's work until June.

If I did not mention *Tristram* to you, it was because I thought I had done so before. there is much good fun in it, & humour sometimes hit & sometimes mist. I agree with your opinion of it, & shall see the two future volumes with pleasure. have you read his Sermons (with his own comic figure at the head of them)?[1] they are in the style I think most proper for the Pulpit, & shew a very strong imagination & a sensible heart: but you see him often tottering on the verge of laughter, & ready to throw his perriwig in the face of his audience.

[1] The frontispiece for the *Sermons* was an engraving of the portrait of Sterne by Sir Joshua Reynolds painted during March and April 1760.

18. Lady Bradshaigh on Sterne

June 1760

Extract from a letter from Lady Dorothy Bradshaigh to Samuel Richardson, printed in Alan Dugald McKillop, *Samuel Richardson, Printer and Novelist* (1936), pp. 181–2, from Forster MS XI, f. 274. Lady Bradshaigh (*c.* 1706–85), wife of Sir Roger, fourth baronet of Haigh, was Richardson's correspondent and admirer from the time when *Clarissa* was being published. The remarks below are in answer to Richardson's question whether she knew the word 'Shandy.' For Richardson's own view of Sterne, see No. 29.

The word *Shandy* having been re'd by all the world, no wonder that I am not Ignorant of it. I did read the short vol^{mes} thro, . . . and to say the truth, it some times made me laugh. It is pity a man of so much humour, cou'd not contain himself within the bounds of decency. Upon the whole, I think the performance, mean, *dirty Wit*. I may add *scandelous*, considering the *Man*. But what shall we say, that the writing such a Book, shou'd recomend the author to the great favour of a R^t. Rev^d.[1] It will not be improper, here, to add another *scandelous*, and that *Tristram Shandy* shou'd clear the way for a large Edition of Yorick's Sermons. In my opinion, the worst that ever appear'd in print, if they are all answerable to the three first, for I look'd no farther. But why shou'd I tire you with this man, who is, I dare say, as unworthy as man can be.

[1] I.e. William Warburton; see No. 16.

19. Goldsmith attacks Sterne

30 June 1760

Oliver Goldsmith's *The Citizen of the World* appeared serially in the *Public Ledger* during 1760–1. Letter liii, given complete below, had Sterne as its major target, although *Tristram Shandy* is mentioned only in the table of contents added to the collected edition of 1762. The text below, which has minor variations from that of the *Public Ledger*, is taken from *Collected Works of Oliver Goldsmith*, ed. Arthur Friedman (1966), ii. 221–5. (Friedman gives the *Public Ledger* variants in footnotes.)

Elsewhere in the *Citizen of the World* Goldsmith may be attacking Sterne obliquely: see especially letters li (referring to 'strokes of wit and satire' that consist merely in 'dashes' and to the fact that the criticisms on a certain book sold better than the book itself), lxxv (referring to 'a bawdy blockhead' who cannot escape censure 'even though he should fly to nobility for shelter'), and xcvii (referring to an author who 'promises his own face neatly engraved on copper' in his book; see below and No. 17, n.1).

From Lien Chi Altangi, to Fum Hoam, first president of the Ceremonial Academy at Pekin, in China.[1]

How often have we admired the eloquence of Europe! That strength of thinking, that delicacy of imagination, even beyond the efforts of the Chinese themselves. How were we enraptured with those bold figures which sent every sentiment with force to the heart. How have we spent whole days together in learning those arts by which European writers got within the passions, and led the reader as if by enchantment.

But though we have learned most of the rhetorical figures of the last age, yet there seems to be one or two of great use here, which have not yet travelled to China. The figures I mean are called *Bawdy* and *Pertness*; none are more fashionable; none so sure of admirers;

---

[1] Goldsmith uses the device of a Chinese visitor to England describing his impressions to a friend back in China.

they are of such a nature, that the merest blockhead, by a proper use of them, shall have the reputation of a wit; they lie level to the meanest capacities, and address those passions which all have, or would be ashamed to disown.

It has been observed, and I believe with some truth, that it is very difficult for a dunce to obtain the reputation of a wit; yet by the assistance of the figure *Baudy*, this may be easily effected, and a bawdy blockhead often passes for a fellow of smart parts and pretensions. Every object in nature helps the jokes forward, without scarce any effort of the imagination. If a lady stands, something very good may be said upon that, if she happens to fall, with the help of a little fashionable Pruriency, there are forty sly things ready on the occasion. But a prurient jest has always been found to give most pleasure to a few very old gentlemen, who being in some measure dead to other sensations, feel the force of the allusion with double violence on the organs of risibility.

An author who writes in this manner is generally sure therefore of having the very old and the impotent among his admirers; for these he may properly be said to write, and from these he ought to expect his reward, his works being often a very proper succedaneum to cantharides, or an assa foetida pill. His pen should be considered in the same light as the squirt of an apothecary, both being directed to the same generous end.

But though this manner of writing be perfectly adapted to the taste of gentlemen and ladies of fashion here, yet still it deserves greater praise in being equally suited to the most vulgar apprehensions. The very ladies and gentlemen of Benin, or Cafraria,[1] are in this respect tolerably polite, and might relish a prurient joke of this kind with critical propriety; probably too with higher gust, as they wear neither breeches nor petticoats to intercept the application.

It is certain I never could have expected the ladies here, biassed as they are by education, capable at once of bravely throwing off their prejudices, and not only applauding books in which this figure makes the only merit, but even adopting it in their own conversation. Yet so it is, the pretty innocents now carry those books openly in their hands, which formerly were hid under the cushion; they now lisp their double meanings with so much grace, and talk over the raptures they bestow with such little reserve, that I am sometimes reminded of a custom among the entertainers in China, who think it a piece of necessary breeding to

[1] Goldsmith mentions Benin, a province in Southern Nigeria, and Kaffraria, a portion of the present South Africa, to represent primitive or savage societies.

whet the appetites of their guests, by letting them smell dinner in the kitchen before it is served up to table.

The veneration we have for many things, entirely proceeds from their being carefully concealed. Were the idolatrous Tartar permitted to lift the veil which keeps his idol from view, it might be a certain method to cure his future superstition; with what a noble spirit of freedom therefore must that writer be possessed, who bravely paints things as they are, who lifts the veil of modesty, who displays the most hidden recesses of the temple, and shews the erring people that the object of their vows is either perhaps a mouse, or a monkey.

However, though this figure be at present so much in fashion; though the professors of it are so much caressed by the great, those perfect judges of literary excellence; yet it is confessed to be only a revival of what was once fashionable here before. There was a time, when by this very manner of writing, the gentle Tom. Durfey, as I read in English authors, acquired his great reputation, and became the favourite of a King.[1] The works of this original genius, tho' they never travelled abroad to China, and scarce have reach'd posterity at home, were once found upon every fashionable toilet, and made the subject of polite, I mean very polite conversation. '*Has your Grace seen Mr. Durfey's last new thing, the Oylet Hole. A most facetious piece?*' '*Sure, my Lord, all the world must have seen it; Durfey is certainly the most comical creature alive. It is impossible to read his things and live. Was there ever any thing so natural and pretty, as when the Squire and Bridget meet in the cellar. And then the difficulties they both find in broaching the beer barrel, are so arch and so ingenious, we have certainly nothing of this kind in the language.*' In this manner they spoke then, and in this manner they speak now; for though the successor of Durfey does not excel him in wit, the world must confess he out-does him in obscenity.

There are several very dull fellows, who, by a few mechanical helps, sometimes learn to become extremely brilliant and pleasing; with a little dexterity in the management of the eye-brows, fingers, and nose. By imitating a cat, a sow and pigs; by a loud laugh, and a slap on the shoulder, the most ignorant are furnished out for conversation. But the writer finds it impossible to throw his winks, his shrugs, or his attitudes upon paper; he may borrow some assistance indeed, by printing his face at the title page;[2] but without wit to pass for a man of ingenuity,

[1] Thomas D'Urfey (1653–1723), writer of comedies and ballads noted for their wit, was a favorite of Charles II.
[2] See No.17, n.1.

93

no other mechanical help but downright obscenity will suffice. By speaking to some peculiar sensations, we are always sure of exciting laughter; for the jest does not lie in the writer, but in the subject.

But Bawdry is often helped on by another figure, called Pertness: and few indeed are found to excell in one that are not possessed of the other.

As in common conversation, the best way to make the audience laugh, is by first laughing yourself; so in writing, the properest manner is to shew an attempt at humour, which will pass upon most for humour in reality. To effect this, readers must be treated with the most perfect familiarity: in one page the author is to make them a low bow, and in the next to pull them by the nose: he must talk in riddles and then send them to bed in order to dream for the solution. He must speak of himself and his chapters, and his manner, and what he would be at, and his own importance, and his mother's importance with the most unpitying prolixity, now and then testifying his contempt for all but himself, smiling without a jest, and without wit possessing vivacity.

Adieu.

20. Sterne and the *Monthly* reviewers

June 1760

Extract from 'An Account of the Rev. Mr. ST★★★★, and his Writings,' *Grand Magazine*, iii (June 1760). 308–11.

This article, in the form of a dialogue, is unsigned, but Ralph Griffiths, founder and editor of the *Monthly Review*, also published the *Grand Magazine*. For extracts of the *Monthly*'s reviews of *Tristram Shandy* and Sterne's *Sermons*, referred to here, see Nos 4 and 13c.

Sir JOHN.

Sir Patrick, your most obedient. You are welcome to England.

Sir PATRICK.

Sir John, I am heartily glad to see you. Pray, what news in the learned world? It is but a few hours since I have trodden on English ground, and I am impatient to know the state of literature in a country which has always been famous for producing men of bold genius and correct judgment.

Sir JOHN.

Give me leave to tell you, Sir Patrick, that you seem to form a very false estimate of literary merit, according to the present standard. Our modern men of talents know better than to trouble themselves about correctness of judgement. All that kind of dull wisdom is exploded as stiff and pedantic. An extravagance of imagination, and a vein of ludicrous humour is what pleases the more elegant taste of these times. Read *Tristram Shandy*, Sir Patrick. That is the only model of fine, easy, modish writing. In short, it engrosses all the literary attention of the age.

Sir PATRICK.

Do me the favour, Sir John, to give me some account of this work, and its author.

Sir JOHN.

I will very readily, Sir, oblige you with the best information I am able. To begin therefore in proper biographical form, I must acquaint you that *Tristram Shandy*, alias *Yorick*, alias the Rev. Mr. *St****, was born—No—I beg pardon—*Tristram Shandy* is not born yet:—*Yorick* is dead, buried, and resuscitated—and the Reverend Mr. *St**** is just beginning to live in the fiftieth year of his age, or thereabouts. The hour of his first birth is not material, but the time of his second was in the year of our Lord one thousand seven hundred and fifty-nine; and, paradoxical as it may seem, the unborn *Tristram Shandy* was mid-wife to the second birth of his own parent, having ushered into light this motley phaenomenon, who is lawyer, engineer, man-midwife, parson, and buffoon: In short, who is every thing and nothing. . . . He has discovered a new method of talking bawdy astronomically; and has made *four stars* (which, perhaps, may stand for the four Satellites of *Jupiter*) convey ideas which have set all the maidens a madding, have tickled the whole bench of bishops, and put all his readers in good humour. . . . In few words, Sir, and without a figure, *Tristram Shandy* is an obscene novel, the reverend author is a *prebend* of the church of England; and both are at present in the highest estimation.

Sir PATRICK.

Is it possible, Sir John, that a work of this obscene nature, written by one in holy orders, can be esteemed or countenanced by a judicious, discerning, and virtuous people? . . .

Doctor GALENICUS.

Your observations, Sir, are extremely just: . . . this literary de-pravity is a certain leading symptom of national corruption and decay. O shame to the public taste! . . . [Sterne] has hashed up the most rich and luscious morsel that ever was digested since the days of Rochester[1]—nay, he has almost out-rochestered Rochester himself.

Sir JOHN.

Me thinks, however, this is a proof of the Reverend's extraordinary talents. Surely his merit must be superlative, who could make a tit bit so universally palatable, by larding it skillfully with the fat of obscenity. . . .

The Rev. Mr. VICARIUS.

Pardon me for interrupting you, Sir, but you seem to treat this subject too ludicrously. . . . For my own part, I think the *reverend*

[1] See No. 11a, p. 65, n. 1.

writer, if I may venture to call him so, deserves serious reprehension. *Pudet me fratres.*[1] His loose writings are a disgrace to his holy function: And I cannot sufficiently applaud the very sensible, spirited and masterly stricture on his indecency, in the last *Monthly Review*, under the article of *Yorick's Sermons*. They are such as do great honour to the Reviewers, and cannot fail of gaining approbation from every judicious and discreet reader.

Sir JOHN.

I must confess, Sir, that I differ from you greatly with respect to the Reviewer's merit in that article: I look upon their strictures to be extremely harsh, malicious, and ill-placed. They evidently appear to be dictated by spleen, and envy of the reverend writer's success, rather than by a regard for decency and morality. You may recollect, Sir, that, in their account of *Tristram Shandy*, when the author was unknown, not a word was said of the indecency or obscenity of this novel: but when *Yorick's Sermons* appeared, when Mr. *St****'s* merit and good fortune were the standing topics, then forsooth these godly Reviewers found out that *Tristram Shandy* was an obscene novel, and that for a *clergyman* openly to avow such a performance, was an outrage against christianity, and a mockery on religion. But their having made this discovery so late, is a proof of the inconsistency of their criticisms, and the malice of their intentions.

Here a gentleman who sate by unobserved, addressed himself to the company with great composure in the following terms of apology.

'I beg pardon (said he) gentlemen, for breaking into a discourse, with which it may be thought, perhaps, I have no right to interfere, but as the conversation turns on the merit of a public performance, I hope I may be excused the liberty of obtruding my sentiments. You appear to me, Sir, said he (turning to Sir John) in your remarks on the Review with regard to the article in question, to overlook the most obvious distinctions. What you call an inconsistency of criticism in the Reviewers, is a mark of good sense, moderation, and lenity. You are to consider that qualities vary their nature, according to the different characters in which they reside. What is only levity in one man, in another may, not unjustly, be stiled obscenity. Nay qualities may vary in the same subject. What is only levity within doors, may, tho' in the same man, if it passes in public, deserve an harsher appellation. But to apply these propositions. When *Tristram Shandy* appeared, the author,

[1] I am ashamed, brothers.

as you have intimated, was unknown. It might have been the production of some youthful imagination, and as the work is not destitute of wit and humour, it might justly have been deemed too rigid and cynical, to have given hard names, to the indelicacies with which it is interspersed. They therefore very properly considered it as a *lusus ingenii*,[1] and treated it accordingly. But when *Yorick's Sermons* made their appearance under the real name of the reverend author, when he thought proper to claim Tristram Shandy as his own, in his preface to his *religious discourses*, then circumstances varied, and the *Reviewers* preserved a consistency of character, in reprehending such indecency, and in appropriating proper epithets to that indelicate novel; which, though not *malam vel obscenum in se*,[2] might be justly deemed both *malam & obscenum quoad hunc*.[3] The declaring himself the author of this novel, is not the only circumstance of indecency complained of by the *Reviewers*. They very properly consider his making his declaration in his *sacerdotal* character, and using it as a recommendation to his *sermons*, as an aggravation of the indecency. This they justly deem a mockery on religion, and they are by no means late in making this discovery; for they could not deem it such till the reverend writer had published his name, and indiscreetly confounded the loose novelist with the divine. Since this is the circumstance which constitutes the mockery. With respect to the charge of malice and envy, there is not the least ground for such imputation. The Reviewers have candidly spoken of his *sermons* in the highest terms of praise; and, in my opinion, have rather overrated their merit; for they can only, as they admit, be considered as *moral essays*; and, as such, are greatly excelled by *Addison*'s, and others. In short, they have in express terms declared that they have no exceptions to the *matter* of his Sermons, which they stile *excellent*, but to the *manner* of their publication: And certainly these are not the concessions of envy. Had they been personal in their strictures, had they attacked his private character, they might have been accused of malice. To write against the *man* looks like envy, and may be deemed defamation. But to censure a vice, a folly, or publickly impropriety of character, is just correction. The chastisement of an indecency of this kind cannot be too severe, as the consequences of such bad examples are most pernicious. Had the author of *Tristram Shandy* remained unknown, the work perhaps would have had few, if

[1] Sporting of genius.
[2] Improper or obscene in itself.
[3] Improper and obscene as far as he was concerned.

any, imitators: But the extraordinary circumstances of its being avowed by a *clergyman*, and, what is stranger still, of its being patronized by the *Bishops*,[1] has encouraged every scribler to mimic the reverend writer's manner. . . . Where the reverend romancer is ludicrous, they are licentious: Where he is obscene, they are filthy. In short, if this taste prevails, we need not wonder to see, in some future novel, the words which are chalked out on church walls, boldly printed in *Italicks*.'

. . . A stranger, who came in during the harangue, whisper'd the knight, and inform'd him, that the gentleman who spoke last was himself one of the *Reviewers*. This intelligence silenced Sir John, who did not think it prudent, perhaps, to contend with one who was a critic by profession.

Sir John's silence put an end to the debate. The whole company, however, appeared to be very well satisfied with the unknown critic's observations; and all agreed that it was impossible to invalidate such powerful and irrefragable arguments, as he urged in vindication of the *Review* of the article under consideration.

[1] See Nos 8, 16.

21. Attack on Sterne and the Methodists

July 1760

Extracts from *A Letter from the Rev. George Whitefield, M.A. to the Rev. Laurence Sterne, M.A.* (1760).

This pamphlet by an unknown literary hack, which had two editions in 1760, one under a different title, attacks both Sterne and the Methodists, two very different targets. George Whitefield (1714–70), the ostensible but not the real author, was a prominent evangelist and leader of the Calvinistic branch of the Methodists.

'Tis an old proverb but a very true one, that 'one scabby sheep spoils a whole flock;' but alas! how dreadful must the condition of the flock be, when the shepherd himself is scabby.

Oh *Sterne*! thou art scabby, and such is the leprosy of thy mind that it is not to be cured like the leprosy of the body, by dipping nine times in the river Jordan.[1] Thy prophane history of *Tristram Shandy* is as it were anti-gospel, and seems to have been penned by the hand of Antichrist himself; it tends to excite laughter, but you should remember that the wisest man that ever was, that the great king Solomon himself said of laughter 'it is mad,' and of mirth 'what doth it?'[2] *Sterne*! (for brother I can no longer call thee, though I look upon the clergy of the Church of England as my brethren, when they discharge conscientiously the duties of their function) *Sterne*, apostate *Sterne*! if Solomon was now alive, he would not put the question, 'What doth mirth.' Thy book would fully shew him, that mirth is nearly akin to wickedness, and that the tickling of laughter is occasioned by the obscene Devil. . . . (pp. 2–3)

Come, I'll tell you a story, but it shan't be a story in the *Shandy* taste, it shall be a story of righteousness.

Once upon a time a graceless author took it into his head to write

[1] See II Kings, 5: 10–14.
[2] Ecclesiastes, 2: 2.

several tracts against Christianity, but being soon taken desperately ill, he sent for a clergyman, and expressed himself as follows. 'Alas! I fear my works have perverted half mankind; I have done my utmost to propagate infidelity, and though I have acquired a great reputation, it avails me nothing, since I run a risque of losing my own soul.' Hereupon the man of God desired him not to be uneasy upon that account; 'For, says he, your books are all so weakly written, that no man of common sense can give them a reading, without, at the same time, discovering their futility.'

Such was his answer, and really I think your writings might be answered much in the same manner; for, though the town has been taken in by them, the criticks, I mean the judicious criticks, will always look upon them as the productions of a crazy head and a depraved heart. . . . (pp. 17–18)

Sterne, Sterne! if thou hadst been full of the Holy Ghost, thou would'st never have written that prophane book, *The Life and Opinions of Tristram Shandy*, to judge of which, by the hand that wrote it, one would think the author had a cloven foot.

Thou art puffed up with spiritual pride, and the vanity of human learning has led thee aside into the paths of prophaneness.

Thou hast even been so far elated as to give the likeness of thyself before thy sermons,[1] but, though it is the likeness of something upon earth, I shrewdly doubt that it will never be the likeness of any thing in heaven.

Return therefore to grace before it is too late; throw aside Shakespear, and take up the word of God. . . . (p. 20)

[1] See No. 17, n. 1.

22. Sterne and an appreciative reader

Summer 1760

(a) Sterne's copy in his Letter Book of a letter from the Reverend Robert Brown, dated at Geneva, 25 July 1760, to Sterne's friend, John Hall-Stevenson. Brown was a Scottish Presbyterian who was minister of the Scottish church at Utrecht (*Letters*, pp. 432–3)

—Tristram Shandy has at last made his way here. never did I read any thing with more delectation. What a comical Fellow the author must be! & I may add also what a Connoisseur in Mankind! Perhaps if the Book has any fault at all, it is, that some of his touches are too refined to be perceived in their full force & extent by every Reader. We have been told here he is a Brother of the cloath; pray is it really so? or in what part of the Vineyard does he labour? I'd ride fifty miles to smoak a pipe with him, for I could lay any wager that so much humour has not been hatch'd or concocted in his pericrainium without the genial fumes of celestial Tobacco: but perhaps like one of the same Trade, tho' his Letters be strong and powerful, his speech is mean and his bodily presence contemptible—Yet I can hardly think it. He must be a queer dog, if not sooner, at least after supper; I would lay too, that he is no stranger to Montaigne;[1] nay that he is full as well acquainted with him, as with the book of common prayer, or the Bishop of London's pastoral Letters; tho at the same time I would be far from insinuating, either on one hand, that his Reverence is not as good a Tradesman in his way as any of his neighbours,—or on the other, That this celebrated Performance of his, is not perfectly an Original. The Character of Uncle Toby, his conversations with his Brother, who is also a very drole and excellent personage, & I protest such Characters I have known—his Acc[ts] of the Campaign &c &c are inimitable. I have been much diverted wth some people here who have read it. they torture their brains to find out some hidden meaning in it, & will per force have all the Starts—Digressions—& Ecarts[2] which

[1] See No. 2a, n. 3.
[2] Swervings aside, digressions.

the Author runs out into, & which are surely the Excellencies of his Piece, to be the constituent Members of a close connected Story. is it not provoking to meet with such wise acres who, tho' there be no trace of any consistent plan in the whole of their insipid Life, & tho their Conversation if continued for half a quarter of an hour has neither head or tail, yet will pretend to seek for connection in a Work of this Nature.

(b) Extract from Sterne's reply, 9 September 1760, after Hall-Stevenson had shown him Brown's letter (*Letters*, pp. 121–2)

My good friend Mr Hall knowing how happy it would make me, to hear that Tristram Shandy had found his way to Geneva, and had met with so kind a reception from a person of your Character, was so obliging as to send me y^r letter to him. I return you Sir, all due thanks and desire you will suffer me to place the many civilities done to this ungracious whelp of mine, to my own account, and accept of my best acknowledgements thereupon.

You are absolutely right in most of your conjectures about me (unless what are excessively panygerical)—1st That I am 'a queer dog'— only that you must not wait for my being so, till supper, much less till an hour after—for I am so before I breakfast. 2^d 'for my conning Montaigne as much as my pray'r book'—there you are right again,— but mark, a 2^d time, I have not said I admire him as much;—tho' had he been alive, I would certainly have gone twice as far to have smoakd a pipe with him, as with Arch-Bishop Laud or his Chaplains, (tho' one of 'em by the bye, was my grandfather).[1] As for the meaness of my speech, and contemptibility of my bodily presence—I'm the worst Judge in the world of 'em—Hall is ten times better acquainted with those particulars of me, & will write you word. In y^r Conjecture of smoaking Tobacco—there you are sadly out—not that the con-jecture was bad but that my brain is so—it will not bear Tobacco, inasmuch as the fumes thereof do concoct my conceits too fast so that they would be all done to rags before they could be well served up— the heat however at 2^d hand, does very well with them, so that you may

---

[1] William Laud (1573–1645), Archbishop of Canterbury and advisor to King Charles I, was an authoritarian in church matters and vigorously opposed the Puritans. Richard Sterne (1596(?)–1683), great-grandfather of Laurence, was Archbishop of York.

rely upon it, that for every mile You go to meet me for this end, I will go twain. . . .

The Wise heads I see on the continent are made up of the same materials, & cast in the same Moulds; with the Wise heads of this Island,—they philosophize upon *Tristram Shandy* alike to a T—they all look to high—tis ever the fate of low minds.

23. Horace Mann on Sterne's 'humbugging'

1 November 1760

Extract from a letter to Horace Walpole, written from Florence, in *Horace Walpole's Correspondence with Sir Horace Mann*, ed. W. S. Lewis, Warren Hunting Smith, and George L. Lam (1960), p. 446.

Sir Horace Mann (1701–86) was the British envoy at Florence for many years and corresponded regularly with Walpole. Walpole had sent Mann 'a fashionable thing called *Tristram Shandy*' in May; when Mann later saw volumes III and IV, he wrote to Walpole on 1 August 1761: '[N]onsense pushed too far becomes insupportable' (ibid., p. 521).

You will laugh at me, I suppose, when I say I don't understand *Tristram Shandy*, because it was probably the intention of the author that nobody should. It seems to me *humbugging*, if I have a right notion of an art of talking or writing that has been invented since I left England. It diverted me, however, extremely, and I beg to have as soon as possible the two other volumes which I see advertised in the papers for next Christmas.

24. *Tristram Shandy* as satire

1760

Extract from 'On the Present State of Literature in England' by an unidentified critic signing himself 'D.', *Imperial Magazine*, i (Sup. 1760). 687.

I shall finish this paper with a few observations on Mr. Sterne's celebrated performance, concerning which the generality of opinions are so much divided. *Tristram Shandy* has certainly acquired its author great fame for that peculiar vein of wit and humour which runs through it; Mr. Sterne doubtless possesses in the highest degree the art of ridiculing the ruling passions, or hobby horses, as well as the vices and follies of mankind. No man is equal to him in the 'ridentem dicere verum,'[1] and, I think, he and his work may both justly be styled originals.

[1] Speaking the truth while laughing. See Horace, *Satires*, I. i. 24.

25. Edmund Burke on *Tristram Shandy*

1760

Extract from a review of *Tristram Shandy*, *Annual Register*, iii (1760). 247.

Burke (1729–97) began a literary career before going on to his brilliant career in politics. Though Burke never admitted publicly to being editor of the *Annual Register*, Thomas W. Copeland has established his authorship for this review with near certainty ('Edmund Burke and the Book Reviews in Dodsley's *Annual Register*,' PMLA, lvii (June 1942). 448, 468).

It is almost needless to observe of a book so universally read, that the story of the hero's life is the smallest part of the author's concern. The story is in reality made nothing more than a vehicle for satire on a great variety of subjects. Most of these satirical strokes are introduced with little regard to any connexion, either with the principal story or with each other. The author perpetually digresses; or rather having no determined end in view, he runs from object to object, as they happen to strike a very lively and very irregular imagination. These digressions so frequently repeated, instead of relieving the reader, become at length tiresome. The book is a perpetual series of disappointments. However, with this, and some other blemishes, the life of *Tristram Shandy* has uncommon merit. The faults of an original work are always pardoned; and it is not surprizing, that at a time, when a tame imitation makes almost the whole merit of so many books, so happy an attempt at novelty should have been so well received.

The satire with which this work abounds, though not always happily introduced, is spirited, poignant, and often extremely just. The characters, though somewhat overcharged, are lively, and in nature. The author possesses in an high degree, the talent of catching the ridiculous in every thing that comes before him. The principal figure, old Shandy, is an humourist; full of good nature; full of whims; full of learning, which for want of being ballanced by good sense, runs him into an

innumerable multitude of absurdities, in all affairs of life, and disquisitions of science. A character well imagined; and not uncommon in
the world. The character of Yorick is supposed to be that of the author
himself. There is none in which he has succeeded better; it is indeed
conceived and executed with great skill and happiness.

26. The composition of *Tristram Shandy*, vols III, IV

1760

(a) Extract from Sterne's letter, 3 August 1760, to his 'witty widow', Mrs [Jane?] F[enton] (*Letters*, pp. 120–1)

I have just finished one volume of *Shandy*, and I want to read it to some one who I know can taste and rellish humour—this by the way, is a little impudent in me—for I take the thing for granted, which their high Mightinesses the World have yet to determine—but I mean no such thing—I could wish only to have your opinion—shall I, in truth, give you mine?—I dare not—but I will; provided you keep it to yourself—know then, that I think there is more laughable humour,—with equal degree of Cervantik Satyr—if not more than in the last—but we are bad Judges of the merit of our Children.

(b) Extract from Sterne's letter, dated 25 December 1760, to his friend Stephen Croft (*Letters*, p. 126)

I am not much in pain upon what gives my kind friends at Stillington so much on the chapter of *Noses*[1]—because, as the principal satire throughout that part is levelled at those learned blockheads who, in all ages, have wasted their time and much learning upon points as foolish

[1] The Croft family, who lived at Stillington, had obviously seen vols III and IV in manuscript.

—it shifts off the idea of what you fear, to another point—and 'tis thought here very good—'twill pass muster—I mean not with all—no—no! I shall be attacked and pelted, either from cellars or garrets, write what I will—and besides, must expect to have a party against me of many hundreds—who either do not—or will not laugh.—'Tis enough if I divide the world;—at least I will rest contented with it.

27. Sterne to his critics and his readers: *Tristram Shandy*, vols III and IV

1760–1

In the second installment of *Tristram Shandy*, published 28 January 1761, Sterne continued his dialogue with his imagined readers, justifying his style of writing, and also felt impelled to extend the dialogue to his critics and especially to the *Monthly* reviewers who had attacked the *Sermons of Mr. Yorick* (see Nos 13c, 20).

(a) Extract from *Tristram Shandy*, III. 4, pp. 160–2

A Man's body and his mind, with the utmost reverence to both I speak it, are exactly like a jerkin, and a jerkin's lining;—rumple the one—you rumple the other. There is one certain exception however in this case, and that is, when you are so fortunate a fellow, as to have had your jerkin made of a gum-taffeta, and the body-lining to it, of a sarcenet or thin persian. . . .[1]

I believe in my conscience that mine is made up somewhat after

[1] 'Persian' and 'sarcenet' are soft silks used for linings; 'gum-taffeta' is a fabric, usually silk, stiffened with gum and hence, Sterne implies below, more easily damaged than the pure silk of the lining. Since 'taffeta' was used figuratively to mean 'florid or bombastic language,' Sterne may also be hinting that the attacks of the reviewers did not penetrate below the surface of his language to the 'lining' or core of his book.

this sort:—for never poor jerkin has been tickled off, at such a rate as it has been these last nine months together,—and yet I declare the lining to it,—as far as I am a judge of the matter, it is not a three-penny piece the worse;—pell mell, helter skelter, ding dong, cut and thrust, back stroke and fore stroke, side way and long way, have they been trimming it for me:—had there been the least gumminess in my lining,—by heaven! it had all of it long ago been fray'd and fretted to a thread.

—You Messrs. the monthly Reviewers!—how could you cut and slash my jerkin as you did?—how did you know, but you would cut my lining too?

Heartily and from my soul, to the protection of that Being who will injure none of us, do I recommend you and your affairs,—so God bless you;—only next month, if any one of you should gnash his teeth, and storm and rage at me, as some of you did last MAY, (in which I remember the weather was very hot)—don't be exasperated, if I pass it by again with good temper,—being determined as long as I live or write (which in my case means the same thing) never to give the honest gentleman a worse word or a worse wish, than my uncle *Toby* gave the fly which buzz'd about his nose all *dinner time*,—'Go,—go poor devil,' quoth he, '—get thee gone,—why should I hurt thee? This world is surely wide enough to hold both thee and me.' (pp. 13–17)

(b) Extract from *Tristram Shandy*, III. 12, pp. 180–2

I'll undertake this moment to prove it to any man in the world, except to a connoisseur; ... the whole set of 'em are so hung round and *befetish'd* with the bobs and trinkets of criticism,—or to drop my metaphor, which by the bye is a pity,—for I have fetch'd it as far as from the coast of *Guinea*;—their heads, Sir, are stuck so full of rules and compasses, and have that eternal propensity to apply them upon all occasions, that a work of genius had better go to the devil at once, than stand to be prick'd and tortured to death by 'em.

—And how did *Garrick*[1] speak the soliloquy last night?—Oh,

---

[1] David Garrick (1717–79), the famous actor and theatrical manager, was one of Sterne's close and influential friends. (See No. 3.) Garrick was known for the versatility of his acting style; his eye, one of his contemporaries says, 'was surely equal to Argus's hundred' (DNB).

against all rule, my Lord,—most ungrammatically! betwixt the substantive and the adjective, which should agree together in *number*,
case and *gender*, he made a breach thus,—stopping, as if the point
wanted settling;—and betwixt the nominative case, which your lordship knows should govern the verb, he suspended his voice in the
epilogue a dozen times, three seconds and three fifths by a stop-watch,
my Lord, each time.—Admirable grammarian!—But in suspending his
voice—was the sense suspended likewise? Did no expression of attitude
or countenance fill up the chasm?—Was the eye silent? Did you
narrowly look?—I look'd only at the stop-watch, my Lord.—Excellent observer!

And what of this new book the whole world makes such a rout
about?—Oh! 'tis out of all plumb, my Lord,—quite an irregular
thing!—not one of the angles at the four corners was a right angle.—I
had my rule and compasses, &c. my Lord, in my pocket.—Excellent
critic! . . .

I would go fifty miles on foot, for I have not a horse worth riding
on, to kiss the hand of that man whose generous heart will give up the
reins of his imagination into his author's hands,—be pleased he knows
not why, and cares not wherefore.

Great Apollo! if thou art in a giving humour,—give me,—I ask no
more, but one stroke of native humour, with a single spark of thy
own fire along with it—and send *Mercury*, with the *rules and compasses*,
if he can be spared,[1] with my compliments to—no matter. (pp. 57–61)

(c) Extract from *Tristram Shandy*, III. 20,[2] pp. 192–203

All I know of the matter is,—when I sat down, my intent was to write
a good book; and as far as the tenuity of my understanding would
hold out,—a wise, aye, and a discreet,—taking care only, as I went
along, to put into it all the wit and the judgment (be it more or less)
which the great author and bestower of them had thought fit originally
to give me,—so that, as your worships see,—'tis just as God pleases.
. . . [Sterne continues by contradicting Locke's assertion in *An Essay*

[1] Apollo, god of light, music, and poetry, was brother to Mercury (Greek name, Hermes),
who was the messenger of the gods and conductor of the dead and later came to be regarded
as the inventor of letters, figures, mathematics, and astronomy.
[2] This chapter contains Sterne's 'preface' for vols III and IV.

Concerning Human Understanding, 2.11.2, that wit and judgment are incompatible operations of the mind.]

Now, my dear Anti-Shandeans, and thrice able critics, and fellow-labourers, (for to you I write this Preface)[1]—and to you, most subtle statesmen and discreet doctors (do—pull off your beards) renowned for gravity and wisdom;—*Monopolos* my politician,—*Didius*, my counsel; *Kysarcius*, my friend; *Phutatorius*, my guide;—*Gastripheres*, the preserver of my life; *Somnolentius*, the balm and repose of it,—not forgetting all others as well sleeping as waking,—ecclesiastical as civil, whom for brevity, but out of no resentment to you, I lump all together.—Believe me, right worthy,

My most zealous wish and fervent prayer in your behalf, and in my own too, in case the thing is not done already for us,—is, that the great gifts and endowments both of wit and judgment, with every thing which usually goes along with them,—such as memory, fancy, genius, eloquence, quick parts, and what not, may this precious moment without stint or measure, let or hinderance, be poured down warm as each of us could bear it,—scum and sediment an' all; (for I would not have a drop lost) into the several receptacles, cells, cellules, domiciles, dormitories, refectories, and spare places of our brains,—in such sort, that they might continue to be injected and tunn'd into, according to the true intent and meaning of my wish, until every vessel of them, both great and small, be so replenished, saturated and fill'd up therewith, that no more, would it save a man's life, could possibly be got either in or out.

Bless us!—what noble work we should make!—how should I tickle it off!—and what spirits should I find myself in, to be writing away for such readers!—and you,—just heaven!—with what raptures would you sit and read,—but oh!—'tis too much,—I am sick,—I faint away deliciously at the thoughts of it!—'tis more than nature can bear! —lay hold of me,—I am giddy,—I am stone blind,—I'm dying,—I am gone.—Help! Help! Help!—But hold,—I grow something better again, for I am beginning to foresee, when this is over, that as we shall

---

[1] Sterne echoes the manner of Rabelais in his prefaces. The characters he mentions, presumably satirical representations of local figures, can mostly no longer be identified. *Monopolos* is 'a monopolist'; *Didius* is Sterne's satirical portrait of Dr Francis Topham, an able Yorkshire lawyer who frequently opposed Sterne in ecclesiastical squabbles and had been the object of Sterne's ridicule in *A Political Romance*; *Kysarcius* is a portmanteau-word, probably Sterne's translation of *Baise-cul* or Kissbreech (Rabelais, bk. II, chs 10–13); *Phutatorius* means 'copulator, lecher'; *Gastripheres* is another portmanteau-word meaning 'paunch-carrier' or 'big-belly'; *Somnolentius* means 'sleeper.'

all of us continue to be great wits,—we should never agree amongst ourselves, one day to an end:—there would be so much satire and sarcasm,—scoffing and flouting, with raillying and reparteeing of it,—thrusting and parrying in one corner or another,—there would be nothing but mischief amongst us.—Chaste stars! what biting and scratching, and what a racket and a clatter we should make, what with breaking of heads, and rapping of knuckles, and hitting of sore places, —there would be no such thing as living for us.

But then again, as we should all of us be men of great judgment, we should make up matters as fast as ever they went wrong; and though we should abominate each other, ten times worse than so many devils or devilesses, we should nevertheless, my dear creatures, be all courtesy and kindness,—milk and honey,—'twould be a second land of promise, —a paradise upon earth, if there was such a thing to be had,—so that upon the whole we should have done well enough. . . .

Will you give me leave to illustrate this affair of wit and judgment, by the two knobs on the top of the back of [a cane chair]—they are fasten'd on, you see, with two pegs stuck slightly into two gimlet-holes, and will place what I have to say in so clear a light, as to let you see through the drift and meaning of my whole preface, as plainly as if every point and particle of it was made up of sun beams.

I enter now directly upon the point.

—Here stands *wit*,—and there stands *judgment*, close beside it, just like the two knobbs I'm speaking of, upon the back of this self same chair on which I am sitting.

—You see, they are the highest and most ornamental parts of its *frame*,—as wit and judgment are of *ours*,—and like them too, indubitably both made and fitted to go together, in order as we say in all such cases of duplicated embellishments,—*to answer one another*.

Now for the sake of an experiment, and for the clearer illustrating this matter,—let us for a moment, take off one of these two curious ornaments (I care not which) from the point or pinacle of the chair it now stands on; nay, don't laugh at it.—But did you ever see in the whole course of your lives such a ridiculous business as this has made of it?—Why, 'tis as miserable a sight as a sow with one ear; and there is just as much sense and symmetry in the one, as in the other:—do,— pray, get off your seats, only to take a view of it.—Now would any man who valued his character a straw, have turned a piece of work out of his hand in such a condition?—nay, lay your hands upon your hearts, and answer this plain question, Whether this one single knobb which now stands here like a blockhead by itself, can serve any purpose upon earth, but to put one in mind of the want of the other;—and let me further ask, in case the chair was your own, if you would not in your consciences think, rather than be as it is, that it would be ten times better without any knobb at all. . . .

Now your graver gentry having little or no kind of chance in aiming at the one,—unless they laid hold of the other,—pray what do you think would become of them?—Why, Sirs, in spight of all their *gravities*, they must e'en have been contented to have gone with their insides naked:—this was not to be borne, but by an effort of philosophy not to be supposed in the case we are upon,—so that no one could well have been angry with them, had they been satisfied with what little they could have snatched up and secreted under their cloaks and great perrywigs, had they not raised a *hue* and *cry* at the same time against the lawful owners.

I need not tell your worships, that this was done with so much cunning and artifice,—that the great *Locke*, who was seldom outwitted by false sounds,—was nevertheless bubbled here. The cry, it seems, was so deep and solemn a one, and what with the help of great wigs, grave faces, and other implements of deceit, was rendered so general a one against the *poor wits* in this matter, that the philosopher himself was deceived by it,—it was his glory to free the world from the lumber of a thousand vulgar errors;—but this was not of the number; so that instead of sitting down cooly, as such a philosopher should have done, to have examined the matter of fact before he philosophised upon it; —on the contrary, he took the fact for granted, and so joined in with the cry, and halloo'd it as boisterously as the rest. . . .

As for great wigs, upon which I may be thought to have spoken my mind too freely,—I beg leave to qualify whatever has been unguardedly said to their dispraise or prejudice, by one general declaration—That I have no abhorrence whatever, nor do I detest and abjure either great wigs or long beards,—any further than when I see they are bespoke and let grow on purpose to carry on this self-same imposture— for any purpose,—peace be with them;—☞ mark only,—I write not for them. (pp. 85–109)

(d) Extract from *Tristram Shandy*, IV. 10, p. 281

Is it not a shame to make two chapters of what passed in going down one pair of stairs? for we are got no farther yet than to the first landing, and there are fifteen more steps down to the bottom; and for aught I know, as my father and my uncle *Toby* are in a talking humour, there may be as many chapters as steps;—let that be as it will, Sir, I can no more help it than my destiny:—A sudden impulse comes across me— drop the curtain, *Shandy*—I drop it—Strike a line here across the paper, *Tristram*—I strike it—and hey for a new chapter?

The duce of any other rule have I to govern myself by in this affair— and if I had one—as I do all things out of all rule—I would twist it and tear it to pieces, and throw it into the fire when I had done—Am I warm? I am, and the cause demands it—a pretty story! is a man to follow rules—or rules to follow him? (pp. 96–7)

(e) Extract from *Tristram Shandy*, IV. 13, pp. 285–6

Was every day of my life to be as busy a day as this,—and to take up,— truce—

I will not finish that sentence till I have made an observation upon the strange state of affairs between the reader and myself, just as things stand at present—an observation never applicable before to any one biographical writer since the creation of the world, but to myself— and I believe will never hold good to any other, until its final destruc- tion—and therefore, for the very novelty of it alone, it must be worth your worships attending to.

I am this month one whole year older than I was this time twelve- month; and having got, as you perceive, almost into the middle of my fourth volume—and no farther than to my first day's life—'tis demon- strative that I have three hundred and sixty-four days more life to write just now, than when I first set out; so that instead of advancing, as a common writer, in my work with what I have been doing at it—on the contrary, I am just thrown so many volumes back—was every day of my life to be as busy a day as this—And why not?—and the trans-

actions and opinions of it to take up as much description—And for
what reason should they be cut short? as at this rate I should just live
364 times faster than I should write—It must follow, an' please your
worships, that the more I write, the more I shall have to write—and
consequently, the more your worships read, the more your worships
will have to read. (pp. 105–7)

(f) Extract from *Tristram Shandy*, IV. 20, pp. 298–9

What a rate have I gone on at, curvetting and frisking it away, two up
and two down[1] for four volumes together, without looking once
behind, or even on one side of me, to see whom I trod upon!—I'll
tread upon no one,—quoth I to myself when I mounted—I'll take a
good rattling gallop; but I'll not hurt the poorest jack-ass upon the
road—So off I set—up one lane—down another, through this turn-
pike—over that, as if the arch-jockey of jockeys had got behind me.

Now ride at this rate with what good intention and resolution you
may,—'tis a million to one you'll do some one a mischief, if not
yourself—He's flung—he's off—he's lost his seat—he's down—he'll
break his neck—see!—if he has not galloped full amongst the scaffold-
ing of the undertaking[2] criticks!—he'll knock his brains out against
some of their posts—he's bounced out!—look—he's now riding like
a madcap full tilt through a whole crowd of painters, fiddlers, poets,
biographers, physicians, lawyers, logicians, players, schoolmen,
churchmen, statesmen, soldiers, casuists, connoisseurs, prelates, popes,
and engineers—Don't fear, said I—I'll not hurt the poorest jack-ass upon
the king's high-way—But your horse throws dirt; see you've splash'd
a bishop[3]—I hope in God, 'twas only *Ernulphus*,[4] said I—But you
have squirted full in the faces of Mess. *Le Moyne, De Romigny*, and
De Marcilly, doctors of the Sorbonne[5]—That was last year, replied I—
But you have trod this moment upon a king.—Kings have bad times
on't, said I, to be trod upon by such people as me. (pp. 136–8)

[1] The metaphor is that of a prancing or leaping horse.
[2] Engaged in a literary work. A pun involving the meaning 'conducting funeral arrange-
ments' may also be suspected.
[3] See No. 16.
[4] See *Tristram Shandy*, III. 10.
[5] See *Tristram Shandy*, I. 20.

(g) Extract from *Tristram Shandy*, IV. 22, pp. 301-2

Albeit, gentle reader, I have lusted earnestly, and endeavoured carefully (according to the measure of such slender skill as God has vouchsafed me, and as convenient leisure from other occasions of needful profit and healthful pastime have permitted) that these little books, which I here put into thy hands, might stand instead of many bigger books—yet have I carried myself towards thee in such fanciful guise of careless disport, that right sore am I ashamed now to entreat thy lenity seriously —in beseeching thee to believe it of me, that in the story of my father and his christen-names,—I had no thoughts of treading upon *Francis* the First—nor in the affair of the nose—upon *Francis* the Ninth[1]—nor in the character of my uncle *Toby*—of characterizing the militiating spirits of my country—the wound upon his groin, is a wound to every comparison of that kind,—nor by *Trim*,—that I meant the duke of *Ormond*[2]—or that my book is wrote against predestination, or free will, or taxes—If 'tis wrote against any thing,—'tis wrote, an' please your worships, against the spleen; in order, by a more frequent and a more convulsive elevation and depression of the diaphragm, and the succussations of the intercostal and abdominal muscles in laughter, to drive the *gall* and other *bitter juices* from the gall bladder, liver and sweet-bread of his majesty's subjects, with all the inimicitious[3] passions which belong to them, down into their duodenums. (pp. 142-4)

(h) Extract from *Tristram Shandy*, IV. 25, p. 315

Now the chapter I was obliged to tear out, was the description of this cavalcade, in which Corporal *Trim* and *Obadiah*, upon two coach-horses a-breast, led the way as slow as a patrole—whilst my uncle *Toby*, in his laced regimentals and tye-wig, kept his rank with my father, in

[1] There was no Francis IX, though Francis I of France had an extremely large nose. For other Francises who may be relevant see Work, p. 301, n. 1.
[2] James Butler (which was, indeed, Trim's name; see *Tristram Shandy*, II. 5) (1665-1745), second Duke of Ormonde, an Irish statesman and soldier who fought in some of the same campaigns as Uncle Toby and Trim did and was held prisoner at Namur; he was later appointed to succeed Marlborough as captain-general and was involved in the conduct of the campaign in Flanders in 1712.
[3] Unfriendly, or hostile.

deep roads and dissertations alternately upon the advantage of learning and arms, as each could get the start.

—But the painting of this journey, upon reviewing it, appears to be so much above the stile and manner of any thing else I have been able to paint in this book, that it could not have remained in it, without depreciating every other scene; and destroying at the same time that necessary equipoise and balance, (whether of good or bad) betwixt chapter and chapter, from whence the just proportions and harmony of the whole work results. For my own part, I am but just set up in the business, so know little about it—but, in my opinion, to write a book is for all the world like humming a song—be but in tune with yourself, madam, 'tis no matter how high or how low you take it.—(pp. 161–2)

(i) Extract from *Tristram Shandy*, IV. 26, p. 317

I have undergone such unspeakable torments, in bringing forth this sermon, quoth *Yorick*,[1] upon this occasion,—that I declare, *Didius*,[2] I would suffer martyrdom—and if it was possible my horse with me, a thousand times over, before I would sit down and make such another: I was delivered of it at the wrong end of me—it came from my head instead of my heart—and it is for the pain it gave me, both in the writing and preaching of it, that I revenge myself of it, in this manner.— To preach, to shew the extent of our reading, or the subtleties of our wit—to parade it in the eyes of the vulgar with the beggarly accounts of a little learning, tinseled over with a few words which glitter, but convey little light and less warmth—is a dishonest use of the poor single half hour in a week which is put into our hands—'Tis not preaching the gospel—but ourselves—For my own part, continued *Yorick*, I had rather direct five words point blank to the heart—(pp. 166–7)

(j) Extract from *Tristram Shandy*, IV. 32, pp. 337–8

And now that you have just got to the end of these four volumes— the thing I have to *ask* is, how you feel your heads? my own akes dis-

---

[1] Sterne is speaking autobiographically in the character of Yorick.
[2] See No. 27c, p. 112, n. 1.

mally—as for your healths, I know, they are much better—True *Shandeism*, think what you will against it, opens the heart and lungs, and like all those affections which partake of its nature, it forces the blood and other vital fluids of the body to run freely thro' its channels, and makes the wheel of life run long and chearfully round. (pp. 218–19)

28. Reviews of *Tristram Shandy*, vols III, IV

February–April 1761

Volumes III and IV of *Tristram Shandy* were published on 28 January 1761. Though Sterne wrote to his friend Stephen Croft in mid-February that 'one half of the town abuse my book as bitterly, as the other half cry it up to the skies' and that a second edition was planned (*Letters*, pp. 129–30), the general tone of criticism was not as favorable as it had been for the first installment.

(a) Extract from Owen Ruffhead's unsigned review in the *Monthly Review*, xxiv (February 1761). 101–16

In our Review of the first two volumes of this whimsical and extravagant work,[1] we ventured to recommend Mr. Tristram Shandy as a Writer infinitely more ingenious and entertaining than any other of the present race of Novelists: and, indeed, amidst all the things of that kind, which we are condemned to peruse, we were glad to find one which merited distinction. His characters, as we took notice, were striking and *singular*, his observations shrewd and pertinent; and, *allowing a few exceptions*, his humour easy and genuine. As the work had confessedly, merit upon the whole, we forbore any strictures on the

[1] See No. 4. William Kenrick had reviewed the first two volumes, although Ruffhead had written part of the review of Sterne's *Sermons* (No. 13c).

indelicacies with which it was interspersed, and which we attributed
to the warm imagination of some *young Genius* in Romance.

Little did we imagine, that the diminutive volumes then before us,
would swell into such importance with the public: much less could we
suppose, that a work of so light a nature, could be the production of a
Dignitary of the Church of England, had not the wanton brat been
publicly owned by its reverend Parent.

It is true, that in some degree, it is our duty, as Reviewers, to examine
books, abstracted from any regard to their Author. But this rule is
not without exception: for where a Writer is publicly known, by his
own acknowledgement, it then becomes a part of our duty, to anim-
advert on any flagrant impropriety of character. What would be
venial in the farcical Author of the Minor,[1] would be highly reprehensible from the pen of a Divine. In short, there is a certain faculty
called *Discretion*, which reasonable men will ever esteem; tho' you,
the arch *Prebend* Mr. *Yorick*, alias *Tristram Shandy*, have done all in your
power to laugh it out of fashion.

A celebrated Philosopher, of as much eminence as any in the Shandean family, treating of the intellectual virtues, gives the following
account of Discretion.[2] 'In the succession,' says he, 'of men's thoughts,
there is nothing to observe in the things they think on, but either in
what they be *like one another*, or in what they be *unlike*, or *what they
serve for*, or *how they serve to such a purpose*; they who observe their
similitudes, in case they be such as are but rarely observed by others,
are said to have a *good Wit*; by which, in this respect, is meant a good
Fancy. But they who observe their differences and dissimilitudes, which
is called *distinguishing* and *discerning*, and *judging* between thing and
thing; in case such discerning be not easy, are said to have a good
Judgment; and particularly in matter of conversation, &c. wherein
times, places, and *persons*, are to be discerned, this virtue is called
Discretion. The former, that is Fancy, without the help of Judgment, is
not commended as a virtue; but the latter, which is Judgment and
Discretion, is commended for itself, without the help of Fancy.' He
adds, 'that in some poems, and other pieces, both Judgment and Fancy
are required; but the Fancy must be more eminent, because they please

---

[1] Samuel Foote (1720–77), comic actor and dramatist, sometimes known as 'the English
Aristophanes,' first presented *The Minor* in 1760. The play satirized Whitefield and the
Methodists (see No. 21).
[2] Ruffhead quotes and paraphrases from chapter 8 of *Leviathan* by English philosopher
Thomas Hobbes (1588–1679). For the passage in *Tristram Shandy* which probably helped
to trigger Ruffhead's discussion, see No. 27c.

by their *Extravagancy*; yet (he continues) they ought not to *displease by their Indiscretion*: and, in any discourse whatever, if the *defect of Discretion be apparent*, how extravagant soever the Fancy be, the whole Discourse will be taken for *want of Wit*; but so it never will when the Discretion is manifest, though the Fancy be ever so ordinary.

'The secret thoughts of a man,' our Philosopher proceeds, 'run over all things holy, profane, clean, obscene, grave, and light, without shame or blame; which Discourse cannot do, farther than the Judgment shall approve of the time, place, and *persons*. An *Anatomist*, or a *Physician*, may speak or write his judgment of unclean things; because it is not to please, but to profit; but for *another man to write his extravagant and pleasant Fancies of the same*, is, as if a man, from being tumbled into the dirt, should come and present himself before good company. And it is the want of *Discretion* that makes the difference. Again, in professed remissness of mind, and familiar company, a man may play with the sounds and equivocal significations of words, and that many times with encounters of extraordinary Fancy; but in a *Sermon*, or in *public*, or before persons unknown, or whom we ought to reverence, there is no jingling of words, which will not be accounted Folly; and the difference is only in the want of *Discretion*. So that where Wit is wanting, it is not Fancy that is wanting, but Discretion. Judgment, therefore, without Fancy, is Wit: but Fancy without Judgment, is not.'

We shall make no apology for the length of this quotation, because, tho' written in the last century, it is as applicable to *Tristram* and his works, as if it had been penned yesterday, purposely to rebuke this Author. The illustrations are all as apposite, and as evident as the Stranger's *great nose* at Strasburg. For instance,—Hast not thou, O Tristram! run over things holy, profane, clean, obscene, grave, and light, without regard to time, place, thy *own person*, or the persons of *thy Readers*? Hast thou not written thy extravagant and pleasant Fancies about unclean things, about *Forceps*, *Tire Tete*,[1] and *Squirts*, which became none but an Anatomist, a Physician, or the obstetrical Doctor Slop? Hast thou not tumbled into the dirt, and after being worse beluted and bemired than the aforesaid squab Doctor, hast thou not indecently presented thyself before good, nay before the best company? Hast thou not played with sounds, and equivocal significations of words, ay, and with *Stars* and *Dashes*, before those whom thou oughtest to reverence—for whom should'st thou reverence more than the

[1] Head-drawer, or forceps.

Public? Will not these things be accounted unto thee as *Folly?* Do they
not most manifestly prove, what the Philosopher has most justly
concluded, that *Fancy without Judgment,* is *not Wit.*

But your Indiscretion, good Mr. Tristram, is not all we complain
of in the volumes now before us. We must tax you with what you will
dread above the most terrible of all imputations—nothing less than
DULLNESS. Yes, indeed, Mr. Tristram, you are dull, *very dull.*
Your jaded Fancy seems to have been exhausted by two pigmy octavos,
which scarce contained the substance of a twelve-penny pamphlet;
and we now find nothing new to entertain us.

Your characters are no longer striking and singular. We are sick of
your uncle Toby's wound in his groin; we have had enough of his
ravelines and breastworks: in short, we are quite tired with his *hobby
horses;* and we can no longer bear with Corporal Trim's insipidity:
and as to your wise father, his passion for Trismegistus, and all his
whimsical notions, are worn threadbare. The novelty and extravagance of your manner, pleased at first; but Discretion, Shandy, would
have taught you, that a continued affectation of extravagance, soon
becomes insipid. What we prophesied in our Review of the first two
volumes, will be soon accomplished to your cost and confusion.
We there told you, that—'If you did not pay a little more regard to
going strait forward, the generality of your Readers, despairing of ever
seeing the end of their journey, would tire, and leave you to jog on by
yourself.' In short, *Polly Honeycomb,*[1] or any of Mr. *Noble's* fair Cus-
tomers,[2] would have told you, that novelty is the very soul of Romance;
and when you are continually chiming on one set of ideas, let them be
ever so extravagant and luscious, they soon become stupid and un-
affecting.

But you will tell us, that you have introduced a new character.
Who is he? What! the Stranger from the Promontary, with his great
nose, and his fringed—? No, absolutely we will not stain our paper with
so gross an epithet.—It would ill become us to transcribe what you,
Mr. Shandy, do not blush to write at full length. But after all, what does
this Stranger do or say? Why he brandishes his naked scymetar,
swears no body shall touch his nose, figh[t]s for his Julia, and then
leaves us in the lurch.

There may be some ingenious or deep allusion in this nasonic

[1] Heroine of a play of the same name by George Colman the Elder, first produced in
December 1760.
[2] Edward Noble (*d.* 1784) was a bookseller.

Rhodomontade; but we confess, that we have not capacity enough to fathom it. Whether it is religious, political, or lascivious, is difficult to determine; and, in truth, not worth a scrutiny. Much may be said on all sides, but on which side soever the allusion lies, we will venture to observe, it is so far fetched, that it loses its zest before it comes home.

We hope that Mr. Shandy will not be offended at our freedom; for, in truth, we set down nought in malice. Nevertheless, we wish, and that without any degree of malevolence, that we could rumple the *lining of his jerkin*,[1] as it is the best expedient we know of, to make the owner ashamed of exposing it: for though he assures us, that it is not yet frayed, yet all the world may see that it is in a filthy pickle.

Our former animadversions on the Reverend *Yorick*,[2] were intended as a warning to Mr. *Shandy*, to hide his dirty lining: but though our counsel was lost on a giddy mortal, who has no sense of decency, yet we cannot but admire the good humour with which he received it. It will be necessary to transcribe his own words, that our Readers may understand this *jerkin* gibberish. [Quotes *Tristram Shandy*, III. 4; see No. 27a.]

Very right, Mr. Shandy! the world to be sure is wide enough to hold us all. Yet was it ten times as wide as it is, we should never walk without interruption, when we deviate from the paths of Discretion. When once we leave the track, we shall infallibly meet with some indignant spirits, who will think it meritorious to jostle us.

But after all, if this gumtaffeta jerkin has been a kind of heir-loom in the Shandean family, yet only imagine to yourself, what an antic figure it must cut upon a prunella gown and cassock! As well might a grave Judge wear a Jockey's cap on his full-bottomed periwig, or a right reverend Bishop clap a grenadier's cap over his mitre. Do, for shame, Mr. Shandy, hide your jerkin, or, at least, send the lining to the Scowerer's. Believe us, when it is once thoroughly cleaned, you will find it as apt to fray and fret as other people's, but at present it is covered with such a thick scale of nastiness, that there is no coming at a single thread of it. We know that you hate gravity, but you must pardon us one dull reflection. If, to drop your whimsical metaphor, your mind is really as callous as you describe it, you should have kept the secret to yourself. For we will not scruple to affirm, that where sensibility is wanting, every virtue is deficient. . . .

This topic [of noses], as might be supposed, affords the wanton

[1] See No. 27a.
[2] See No. 13c.

Tristram an opportunity of indulging his prurient humour, in a variety of indelicate and sensual allusions. But had he been master of true wit, he might have been entertaining without having recourse to obscenity. Wit thus prostituted, may be compared to the spices which embalm a putrid carcase. . . .

In short, all Mr. Shandy's ideas center *circa cingulum*. . . .[1]

Having thus endeavoured to give our Readers a general idea of this whimsical romance, we will add, that we have done Mr. Shandy the justice to select the most curious and entertaining parts of these little volumes, which, *upon the whole* are not only scandalously indecent, but absolutely DULL. So far from being a remedy against the spleen, as he vainly presumes, the work is rather a dose of *diacodium*, which would lull us to sleep, was it not seasonably dashed with a little tincture of *canthar*[2]—In short, if the Author cannot infuse more spirit, and preserve more decency in the *continuation*, we advise him to remain where he is, in his *swadling cloaths*, without insulting the public any farther. We hope he will take our friendly admonitions in good part, for if he goes on at the rate of the two volumes before us, he will unavoidably sink into that contempt, which, sooner or later, ever attends the misapplication of talents.

(b) Unsigned notice in the *British Magazine*, ii (February 1761). 98

Alas, poor Yorick! was it the nose or the cerebellum that those unlucky forceps compressed?—My service to your mother's—I'll tell you what I mean in the next chapter: but it had been well for the father, and perhaps for the public, that she had remained all her life un— You'll find the sequel in Slawkenbergius.—O, my dear *Rabelais*! and my yet dearer *Cervantes*! *Ah, mon cher Ciceron! je le connois bien; c'est le meme que Marc Tulle!*[3] Mr. Shandy, here's a cup of fresh caudle at your honour's service.

[1] Around the belt.
[2] Diacodium is an opiate, canthar an aphrodisiac.
[3] 'Oh, my dear Cicero! I know him well; he is the same as Marcus Tullius.' Marcus Tullius Cicero (106–43 BC), the famous Roman orator and statesman, was also called Tully.

(c) Extract from an unsigned review in the *Critical Review*, xi (April 1761). 314–17

A man who possesses the faculty of exciting mirth, without exposing himself as the subject of it, is said to have humour, and this humour appears in a thousand different forms, according to the variety of attitudes in which folly is exhibited; but all these attitudes must be in themselves ridiculous; for humour is no more than the power of holding up and displaying the ridiculous side of every object with which it is concerned. Every body has heard of the different species of humour; grave humour and gay humour, genteel humour and low humour, natural humour and extravagant humour, grotesque and buffoonery. Perhaps these two last may be more properly stiled the bastards of humour than the power itself, although they have been acknowledged and adopted by the two arch priests of laughter *Lucian* and *Rabelais*. They deserve to be held illegitimate, because they either desert nature altogether, in their exhibitions, or represent her in a state of distortion. Lucian and Rabelais, in some of their writings, seem to have no moral purpose in view, unless the design of raising laughter may in some cases be thought a moral aim. It must be owned, that there is abundance of just satire in both; but at the same time they abound with extravagances, which have no foundation in nature, or in reason. Lucian . . . expressly says, that his writings were no more than figures of clay, set up to amuse the people on a shew day. His *true history*, indeed, the most extravagant of all his works, he tells us he intended as a satire upon the ancient poets and historians. . . .[1]

As for Rabelais, notwithstanding the insinuation in his preface, in which he applies to his own writings the comparison of Alcibiades in Plato, who likens Socrates to the gally-pots of druggists or apothecaries, painted on the outside with ridiculous figures, but containing within the most precious balsams:[2] notwithstanding the pains which

[1] See Lucian's 'A Literary Prometheus' and the introduction to *The True History*.
[2] In his preface to bk. I (*Gargantua*), Rabelais compares his work to the Sileni, statues or little wooden boxes or vases with comic and distorted figures painted on the outside, which nonetheless were used to store precious drugs, gems, or carvings of gods. Rabelais alludes to Alcibiades's contention in Plato's *Symposium* that Socrates likewise had a comic or ridiculous exterior and manner but also divine knowledge, and claims for his book the same combination of outer comedy and frivolity with inner wisdom. Silenus, associated with Bacchus, was a satyr with a grotesque figure. Sterne, though he does not allude speci-

have been taken by many ingenious commentators, to wrest the words
and strain the meaning of Rabelais, in order to prove the whole a
political satire on the times in which he wrote, we are of opinion, that
the book was intended, as well as written, merely *pour la refection
corporelle—a l'aise du corps et au profit du rains*.[1] We the rather take
notice of Rabelais on this occasion, as we are persuaded that he is the
pattern and prototype of Tristram Shandy, notwithstanding the
declaration of our modern author, when he exclaims in a transport,
'My dear Rabelais, and my dearer Cervantes!'[2] There is no more
resemblance between his manner and that of Cervantes, than there is
between the solemnity of a Foppington and the grimace of a Jack
Pudding.[3] On the other hand, we see in Tristram Shandy the most
evident traces of Rabelais, in the address, the manner, and colouring,
tho' he has generally rejected the extravagancies of his plan. We find
in both the same sort of apostrophes to the reader, breaking in upon
the narrative, not unfrequently with an air of petulant impertinence;
the same *sales Plautini*;[4] the *immunda—ignominiosaq; dicta*;[5] the same
whimsical digressions; and the same parade of learning. . . . Perhaps
it would be no difficult matter to point out a much closer affinity
between the works of the French and English author; but we have not
leisure to be more particular. Nor will it be necessary to explain the
conduct of the performance now before us, as it is no more than a
continuation of the first two volumes, which were published last year,
and received with such avidity by the public, as boded no good to the
sequel; for that avidity was not a natural appetite, but a sort of *fames
canina*,[6] that must have ended in *nausea* and *indigestion*. Accordingly all
novel readers, from the stale maiden of quality to the snuff-taking
chambermaid, devoured the first part with a most voracious swallow,
and rejected the last with marks of loathing and aversion. We must
not look for the reason of this difference in the medicine, but in the
patient to which it was administered. While the two first volumes of

---

fically to this metaphor, expresses the same idea in the first volume of *Tristram Shandy* (see
No. 2b), and other critics, among them Voltaire, utilized the comparison to describe
Sterne's work (see Nos 130a, 131d, 137).

[1] For bodily nourishment—for the pleasure of the flesh and the profit of the loins. See
Rabelais's preface to bk. I.
[2] See *Tristram Shandy*, III. 19, p. 191.
[3] Foppington is a character derived from 'fop,' a conceited pretender to wit and fashion;
Jack Pudding is a buffoon or clown, often the assistant of a mountebank.
[4] Jokes of Plautus.
[5] Impurities and shameful words.
[6] Dog-like voraciousness.

Tristram Shandy lay half-buried in obscurity, we, the Critical Reviewers, recommended it to the public as a work of humour and
ingenuity, and, in return, were publickly reviled with the most dull
and indelicate abuse: but neither that ungrateful insult, nor the maukish
disgust so generally manifested towards the second part of Tristram
Shandy, shall warp our judgment or integrity so far, as to join the cry
in condemning it as unworthy of the first. One had merit, but was
extolled above its value; the other has defects, but is too severely
decried. The reader will not expect that we should pretend to give a
detail of a work, which seems to have been written without any plan,
or any other design than that of shewing the author's wit, humour,
and learning, in an unconnected effusion of sentiments and remarks,
thrown out indiscriminately as they rose in his imagination. Nevertheless, incoherent and digressive as it is, the book certainly abounds
with pertinent observations on life and characters, humourous incidents, poignant ridicule, and marks of taste and erudition. We will
venture also to say, that the characters of the father and uncle are
interesting and well sustained, and that corporal Trim is an amiable
picture of low life. . . .

Having pointed out the beauties of this performance, we cannot,
in justice to the public, but take some notice also of its defects. We
frequently see the author failing in his endeavours to make the reader
laugh; a circumstance which throws him into a very aukward attitude,
so as even to excite contempt, like an unfortunate *relator*, who says,
'O! I'll tell you a merry story, gentlemen, that will make you burst
your sides with laughing;' and begins with a ha! ha! ha! to recite a
very dull narrative, which ends in a general groan of the audience.
Most of his apostrophes and digressions are mere tittle-tattle, that
species which the French distinguish by the word *caqueter*,[1] fitter for the
nursery than the closet. A spirit of petulance, an air of self-conceit, and
an affectation of learning, are diffused through the whole performance,
which is likewise blameable for some gross expressions, impure ideas,
and a general want of decorum. If we thought our opinion could
have any weight with a gentleman who seems to stand so high in his
own opinion, we should advise him to postpone the history of Tristram's childhood and youth, until the world shall have forgot the
misfortune he received in his birth: by that time he may pass for a new
man, and once more enjoy that advantage which novelty never fails
to have with the public.

[1] To chatter.

29. Samuel Richardson on Sterne

January–February 1761

Extract from a letter to Mark Hildesley, *Selected Letters of Samuel Richardson*, ed. John Carroll (1964), pp. 341–2.

Hildesley (1698–1772), Bishop of Sodor and Man, had asked Richardson for information about Sterne and his compositions. Internal evidence in other parts of Richardson's letter (as printed in Mrs Barbauld's edition of Richardson's *Correspondence*) dates it in late January or early February of 1761. For Hildesley's reply, see No. 30c.

Who is this Yorick? you are pleased to ask me. You cannot, I imagine have looked into his books: execrable I cannot but call them; for I am told that the third and fourth volumes are worse, if possible, than the two first; which, only, I have had the patience to run through. One extenuating circumstance attends his works, that they are too gross to be inflaming.

My daughter shall transcribe for me the sentiments of a young lady, as written to another lady, her friend in the country, on the publication of the two first volumes only.

'Happy are you in your retirement, where you read what books you choose, either for instruction or entertainment; but in this foolish town, we are obliged to read every foolish book that fashion renders prevalent in conversation; and I am horribly out of humour with the present taste, which makes people ashamed to own they have not read, what if fashion did not authorise, they would with more reason blush to say they had read! Perhaps some polite person from London, may have forced this piece into your hands, but give it not a place in your library; let not Tristram Shandy be ranked among the well chosen authors there. It is, indeed, a little book, and little is its merit, though great has been the writer's reward! Unaccountable wildness; whimsical digressions; comical incoherencies; uncommon indecencies; all with an air of novelty, has catched the reader's attention, and applause has flown from one to another, till it is almost singular to disapprove: even the bishops admire, and recompense his wit,[1] though his own character as a clergyman seems much impeached by printing such gross and vulgar tales, as no decent mind can endure without extreme disgust! Yet I will do him justice; and, if forced by friends, or led by curiosity, you have read, and laughed, and almost cried at Tristram, I will agree with you that there is subject for mirth, and some affecting strokes; Yorick, Uncle Toby, and Trim are admirably characterised, and very interesting, and an excellent sermon of a peculiar kind, on conscience, is introduced; and I most admire the author for his judgment in seeing the town's folly in the extravagant praises and favours heaped on him; for he says, he passed unnoticed by the world till he put on a fool's coat, and since that every body admires him!

But mark my prophecy, that by another season, this performance will be as much decryed, as it is now extolled; for it has not intrinsic merit sufficient to prevent its sinking, when no longer upheld by the short-lived breath of fashion: and yet another prophecy I utter, that this ridiculous compound will be the cause of many more productions, witless and humourless, perhaps, but indecent and absurd; till the town will be punished for undue encouragement, by being poisoned with disgustful nonsense.'

[1] See Nos 8, 16, 20.

30. Some private opinions

February–June 1761

(a) Extract from a letter, 26 February 1761, from Dr Thomas Newton to the Reverend John Dealtary (see No. 9a) (L. P. Curtis, 'New Light on Sterne,' *Modern Language Notes*, lxxvi (1961). 501)

The two last volumes of *Tristram Shandy* have had quite contrary success to the two former. It is almost as much the fashion to run these down, as it was to cry up the others. Not that I think there is that great difference between them, but certainly these are inferior in wit and humor, and in other respects are more gross and offensive. . . . All the Bishops and Clergy cry out shame upon him. All the graver part of the world are highly offended; all the light and trifling are not pleased; and the Bishop of Glocester[1] and I and all his friends are sorry for him. He has not come near us, and I believe is almost ashamed to see us. Garrick's advice to him was very good 'Mr. St[erne] you are in a very bad state of health; I would advise you to go into the country, to keep quiet upon your living, to take care of your health, and if you write any more of these things, be sure to mend your hand.'

(b) Extract from a letter from Richard Hurd, Bishop of Worcester, to the Reverend William Mason, Precentor of York, 30 March 1761 (*Correspondence of Richard Hurd and William Mason*, ed. Ernest Harold Pearce and Leonard Whibley (1932), p. 53)

It is as violent a transition as any in your Odes to pass at once from *Rousseau*, to *Stern*. Yet in speaking of Romances, I must tell you my mind of his. The 3^d Vol. is insufferably dull and even stupid. The 4th is full as humorous as either of the other two. But this broad humour,

---

[1] I.e. William Warburton (see No. 16).

even at its best, can never be endured in a work of length. And he does not seem capable of following the advice which one gave him—*of laughing in such a manner, as that Virgins and Priests might laugh with him.*[1]

(c) Extract from a letter from Mark Hildesley, Bishop of Sodor and Man, to Samuel Richardson, 1 April 1761, replying to No. 29, as quoted from Morgan MSS in Sterne's *Letters*, p. 131

Your Strictures, Good Sir, upon the indelicately witty Yorric,—From that little I accidentally Read of Shameless-Shandy—(for that little was enough to forbid me to read more) I believe to be very just. . . . That Spiritual Men, & ecclesiastical Dignitaries Shoud Countenance & Encourage Such—a Production, & such—an Author, is hardly Capable of any sort of Defence.

(d) Extract from a letter from Dr James Grainger to the Reverend Thomas Percy, 5 June 1761 (John Nichols, *Illustrations of the Literary History of the Eighteenth Century*, vii (1848). 276). Grainger (1721?–66) was a physician and poet and for a while the friend of Smollett, with whom he later quarreled. Percy (1729–1811) was the editor of the famous *Reliques of Ancient English Poetry*

Sterne's ravings I have read, and have as often swore as smiled at them. I never relished Rabelais, it was ever too highly relished for me. I cannot therefore admire his shatter-brained successor.

[1] See No. 16c.

31. A mock funeral discourse

October 1761

Extract from *Alas! Poor YORICK! or, a FUNERAL DIS-COURSE*, an anonymous pamphlet written under the pen name of Christopher Flagellan, commended for its wit by the *Monthly* and the *Critical* in October 1761.

The pamphleteer, arguing that Yorick was still-born morally and that the third and fourth volumes of *Tristram Shandy* prove that the intellectual part of him has died, asserts that 'only the animal part' is left and hence he may be called dead.

We lament the death of YORICK'S better part, that part which was the vehicle of judgment and wit. That this *part* was not *still-born* is manifest from the excellent sermons that appeared to the world under his name, and that it is now totally dead appears as evidently from the Book entitled, *the Life and opinions of Tristram Shandy*, and more especially from the III and IV Volumes, we may say the *last* of that wonderful performance. In the two first Volumes of this work, YORICK appeared sick and declining, yet certain sparks of intellectual fire flew out here and there, which prevented our looking upon his wit, as utterly evaporated; nay, there seemed to be some hopes of its recovery, notwithstanding the long fits of absence, perplexity and delirium into which it had fallen. But no sooner did the two last Volumes appear, than all the sons of drollery yawned over the witless, senseless, lifeless page, and striking their pensive bosoms, said within themselves, YORICK is no more what he was, and of his recovery there is no hope. They saw his wit labouring, tugging, striving for life, but all to no purpose. They saw it sinking under every effort to keep it alive, and observed that the *History of Noses*, or SLAWKENBER-GIUS'S *tale*, instead of raising it above the water, made it sink much deeper, and presented to the reader the most amazing, unintelligible jumble of words, that perhaps has been penned or pronounced either in ancient or modern times. They lamented the total extinction of poor

YORICK'S judgment and the absolute annihilation of his wit; succeeded by dreadful fits of raving in which he evacuated many incoherent and obscure words and sentences. These sentences multiplied prodigiously the number of head-aches among the good people of England, who strained the fibres of their anxious brains to find wit among the excrements of a dying genius. . . .

[The pamphlet continues with an imaginary scene of Sterne on his deathbed. One of Sterne's friends mentions the name of his publisher, Dodsley.]

At the name of *Dodsley*, YORICK lifted a feeble eye, resumed strength, recollected all his fire to express his indignation, looked aghast for some moments—and uttered in broken accents the words which follow:

'Dodsley—name fatal to YORICK—and ominous to the Shandean race—Dodsley has been my ruin.—It is to him I owe my death—the approaching annihilation of my thinking substance. It is owing to him, that I am soon to be no more than a material mass, moved by *animal spirits*, whose fermentation will be called life; and accompanied with *memory*, which metaphysicians look upon as *corporal*. *Dodsley* has been my ruin—he has forced *wit*, which will not be forced, and has cracked the strings of my intellect by drawing them too violently. I gave him two Volumes of pretty good stuff, and the unexpected sale of them made him yawn after twenty. Twenty, said I,—Mr. *Dodsley*—that cannot be.—It is impossible to hold out so long in the strain, upon which I began. It is too extraordinary to be.—"No matter what strain you write in, *replied the judicious bookseller*; it is now become the *mode* to admire you;—the giddy part of the nation are your zealous patrons, and the public voice is in your favour;—therefore whatever you disgorge, were your productions nothing more than the wretched crudities of a disturbed brain, they will be swallowed with avidity; provided—" aye, *said I*, I understand you, provided they be larded with a little bawdy, nicely gawzed over, and seasoned with a proper mixture of impiety and profaneness.—"That is not all, Sir,"—*replied the man-midwife of the republick of letters*, "I add another proviso, that you continue to follow a rule, which you have tolerably well observed in your two first volumes. That rule is, that when *wit* does not flow, you must become *unintelligible* rather than continue *insipid*.—Obscurity, Sir, is an admirable thing; it excites respect, and many of your readers will admire you in proportion as they cease to understand you. By the specimens they have had of your wit they will conclude that where the wit does not strike them, as for example in your intended *chapter of noses*, it must be their fault, and not yours, they will suppose that this same wit lies like truth in a well, and they will laugh with a foolish [face] of praise at every thing you say, provided it be thrown with a happy air of ease and impudence. *Obscurity*, Sir, I repeat it, is an admirable thing, and it has given reputation to many an author.—Pray Master YORICK are you so much deceived with respect to the truth of things, as to imagine that your two first Volumes were admired only for their wit?—Wit indeed there was in them more or less—some striking images of a ludicrous kind; and though you had no principal figures that made a true composition, yet the corners of your picture presented here and there entertaining decorations. But after all, Sir, wit was not the only thing that drew applause. ODDITY was the bait that hooked in the gaping multitude.—Oddity in the author who united the two most contradictory characters:[1] *Oddity* in the book, which, certainly resembles nothing that ever was, or ever will be, which is without any design moral or immoral, and is no more, indeed, than a combination of notions, facts, and circumstances, that terminate in—*nothing*. So then, Sir, give me twenty Volumes more of this same brilliant *nothing*." '

[The pamphleteer next undertakes in a witty strain to prove that Sterne was not obscene and then concludes with a tongue-in-cheek '*improper* application of what has been said':]

Let us learn, from the annihilation of YORICK, that licentious wit is a bubble, and that ill-got fame is a capricious strumpet, whose uncertain and transitory smiles portend future infamy and contempt, while decency and virtue are the surest paths to true honour, will, sooner or later captivate the reluctant applause of the most worthless, and be perfectly happy, without it, in the esteem of the wise and good.

[1] At the beginning of the pamphlet, the author has discussed whether Sterne was 'a clergyman converted into a buffoon, or rather remained both one and the other.'

TRISTRAM SHANDY
vols V, VI (1761)

32. The composition of *Tristram Shandy*, vols V, VI

Summer 1761

(a) Extract from Sterne's letter to his friend John Hall-Stevenson, June 1761 (*Letters*, p. 140)

To-morrow morning, (if Heaven permit) I begin the fifth volume of Shandy—I care not a curse for the critics—I'll load my vehicle with what goods *he* sends me, and they may take 'em off my hands, or let them alone—I am very valourous—and 'tis in proportion as we retire from the world and see it in its true dimensions, that we despise it— no bad rant!

(b) Extract from Sterne's letter, probably to Lady Anna Dacre, dated 21 September 1761 (*Letters*, p. 143)

I am scribbling away at my Tristram. These two volumes are, I think, the best.—I shall write as long as I live, 'tis, in fact, my hobby-horse: and so much am I delighted with my uncle Toby's imaginary character, that I am become an enthusiast.

33. Sterne to his readers: *Tristram Shandy*, vols V and VI

1761

(a) Extract from *Tristram Shandy*, V. 25, p. 382

'Tis a point settled,—and I mention it for the comfort of *Confucius*,*
who is apt to get entangled in telling a plain story—that provided he
keeps along the line of his story,—he may go backwards and forwards
as he will,—'tis still held to be no digression. (p. 93)

(b) Extract from *Tristram Shandy*, V. 32, p. 393

Every thing in this world, said my father, is big with jest,—and has
wit in it, and instruction too,—if we can but find it out. (p. 115)

(c) Extract from *Tristram Shandy*, VI. 1, p. 408

—We'll not stop two moments, my dear Sir,—only, as we have got
thro' these five volumes, (do, Sir, sit down upon a set—they are better
than nothing) let us just look back upon the country we have pass'd
through.—
    —What a wilderness has it been! and what a mercy that we have
not both of us been lost, or devoured by wild beasts in it.
    Did you think the world itself, Sir, had contained such a number of
Jack Asses?—How they view'd and review'd us as we passed over the
rivulet at the bottom of that little valley!—and when we climbed over

* Mr. *Shandy* is supposed to mean ***** *** ***, Esq; member for ******,—and
not the *Chinese* Legislator.

136

that hill, and were just getting out of sight—good God! what a braying did they all set up together!

—Prithee, shepherd! who keeps all those Jack Asses?★★★

—Heaven be their comforter—What! are they never curried? —Are they never taken in in winter?—Bray bray—bray. Bray, on,—the world is deeply your debtor;—louder still—that's nothing;—in good sooth, you are ill-used:—Was I a Jack Asse, I solemnly declare, I would bray in G-sol-re-ut from morning, even unto night. (pp. 1–3)

(d) Extract from *Tristram Shandy*, VI. 17, p. 436

In all nice and ticklish discussions,—(of which, heaven knows, there are but too many in my book)—where I find I cannot take a step without the danger of having either their worships or their reverences[1] upon my back—I write one half *full*,—and t'other *fasting*;—or write it all full,—and correct it fasting;—or write it fasting,—and correct it full, for they all come to the same thing. . . . These different and almost irreconcileable effects, flow uniformly from the wise and wonderful mechanism of nature,—of which,—be her's the honour.—All that we can do, is to turn and work the machine to the improvement and better manufactory of the arts and sciences.—

Now, when I write full,—I write as if I was never to write fasting again as long as I live;—that is, I write free from the cares, as well as the terrors of the world.—I count not the number of my scars,—nor does my fancy go forth into dark entries and bye corners to antedate my stabs.—In a word, my pen takes its course; and I write on as much from the fullness of my heart, as my stomach.—

But when, an' please your honours, I indite fasting, 'tis a different history.—I pay the world all possible attention and respect,—and have as great a share (whilst it lasts) of that understrapping virtue of discretion, as the best of you.—So that betwixt both, I write a careless kind of a civil, nonsensical, good humoured *Shandean* book, which will do all your hearts good—

—And all your heads too,—provided you understand it. (pp. 69–71)

[1] That is, either the fashionable world or the clergy.

34. Assessments of *Tristram Shandy*, vols V and VI

1761–2

(a) Extract from the Reverend Baptist Noel Turner, 'Account of Dr. Johnson's Visit to Cambridge, in 1765,' *New Monthly Magazine*, x (1 December 1818). 389

A question was then asked him respecting Sterne. Johnson: 'In a company where I lately was,[1] Tristram Shandy introduced himself; and Tristram Shandy had scarcely sat down, when he informed us that he had been writing a Dedication to Lord Spencer; and sponte suâ, he pulled it out of his pocket; and sponte suâ, for nobody desired him, he began to read it; and before he had read half a dozen lines, sponte meâ, sir, I told him it was not English, sir.'

(b) Unsigned brief notice in the *British Magazine*, iii (January 1762). 44

Agreeably whimsical and characteristic, interspersed with many pathetick touches of nature.

(c) Extract from an unsigned review in the *Critical Review*, xiii (January 1762). 66–9

Mr. S—might have saved himself the trouble of signing his name to each volume of this performance; a precaution first used (if we mistake

[1] Turner may well have been recalling an earlier conversation with Johnson since the dedication to Lord Spencer of volumes V and VI of *Tristram Shandy* was published in December 1761. Despite the slight discrepancy in dates and the fact that there is no corroborating evidence, the remarks have a ring of authenticity. This occasion was probably Johnson's only meeting with Sterne. For Johnson's later remarks, see No. 64.

not) by the ingenious Mrs. Constantia Philips,[1] as it would be impossible for any reader, even of the least discernment, not to see in the perusal of half a page, that these volumes can be the production of no other than the original author of Tristram Shandy. Here we find the same unconnected rhapsody, the same rambling digression, the eccentric humour, the peculiar wit, petulance, pruriency and ostentation of learning, by which the former part was so happily distinguished. With respect to the moral tendency of the work, and the decency of the execution, we shall refer the reader to the observations of other critics, who have taken the trouble to discuss these particulars: our business shall be to consider how far the performance conduces to the entertainment or information of the reader. Common justice obliges us to own that it contains much good satire on the follies of life; many pertinent remarks on characters and things; and some pathetic touches of nature, which compels us to wish the author had never stooped to the exhibition of buffoonery. The incidents upon which these two volumes turn, are these: a ridiculous disaster which happened to Tristram Shandy in his infancy, and which we think rather too impure to be repeated; the death of lieutenant le Fever; and the memoirs of uncle Toby. All these incidents, however, are comprehended in a very few pages. The rest of the book is filled with fine things to make the reader laugh and stare, and wonder with a foolish face of praise, at the witty conceits and immense erudition of the author. But the author of *Tristram Shandy*, with all his merit, is not so much of an original as he is commonly imagined. Rabelais dealt in the same kind of haberdashery. His wit was as bright, his satire as keen, and his humour as powerful as any we have yet seen in *Tristram Shandy*. He had his extravagant rhapsodies, his abrupt transitions, his flux of matter, his familiar apostrophes, his disquisitions on arts and sciences, theology and ethics; his Hebrew, Greek, Latin, Italian, Spanish, High Dutch, Low Dutch, Lanternois, &c. his decent allusions to the work of generation, and the parts that distinguish the sexes; and his cleanly comments upon intestinal exoneration. . . . [The reviewer continues with some sarcastic pleasantries on the blank page in VI. 38, and the passage imitating the tuning of a fiddle in V. 15, concluding:]

If the work should be continued, we expect to see the reader entertained with the sounds uttered by the winding of a jack, the filing of a

[1] Teresia Constantia Phillips (1709–65), notorious courtesan, published her memoirs in 1748.

saw, and the grinding of a pair of scizzars; and who will deny the passages are affecting?

Of a very different stile are some touches of character relating to Toby and to Trim, that we meet with in this volume, by which it appears, that if our author has sometimes lost sight of Rabelais, he has directed his eye to a still greater original, even nature herself. The episode of Le Fever is beautifully pathetic, and exhibits the character of Toby and his corporal in such a point of view, as must endear them to every reader of sensibility. The author has contrived to make us laugh at the ludicrous peculiarity of Toby, even while we are weeping with tender approbation at his goodness of heart. . . .

[Quotes from the Le Fever episode, VI. 8.]

We know not whether most to censure the impertinence, or commend the excellencies of this strange, incongruous, whimsical performance.

(d) Extract from an unsigned review by John Langhorne in the *Monthly Review*, xxvi (January 1762). 31–41. Langhorne was a minor poet and miscellaneous writer

---

The Authors of the Monthly Review being determined never to lose sight of truth and candour, are neither to be misled by favour, nor irritated by reproach; neither perverted by prejudice, nor borne down with the current of popular opinion. The books that come under their cognizance will be considered with the same impartiality, whether the Authors be their friends or foes, in plain cloaths or prunella, in power or in prison. They would willingly, indeed, have their censure fall upon books only, without any regard to their Authors; but it is certain that a man may be immoral in his Writings as well as in his Actions, and in that respect he will always be liable to the censure of those, who consider themselves not only as judges in the Republic of Letters, but as members of society, and the servants of their country.

Upon these considerations, in reviewing the works of the learned, we are not only to observe their literary excellencies or defects, not merely to point out their faults or beauties, but to consider their moral tendency; and this more particularly, as it is of greater consequence to society that the heart be mended, than that the mind be entertained. . . .

Had we not then a right to complain, if a person, by profession obliged to discountenance indecency, and expressly commanded by those pure and divine doctrines he teaches, to avoid it; ought we not to have censured such a one, if he introduced obscenity as wit, and encouraged the depravity of young and unfledged vice, by libidinous ideas and indecent allusions?

In reviewing the *Life and Opinions of Tristram Shandy*, we have hitherto had occasion to lament, that, while the Author was exerting his talents to maintain the humour and consistency of his characters, he himself was so much out of character; and we could wish sincerely that we had now no farther reason for complaints of that kind.

The fifth and sixth volumes of this work, indeed, are not so much interlarded with obscenity as the former; yet they are not without their stars and dashes, their hints and whiskers: but, in point of true humour, they are much superior to the third and fourth, if not to the first and second. Some of the characters too are placed in a new light, and the rest are humorously supported. Uncle *Toby* is a considerable gainer by this continuation of his Nephew's Life and Opinions. In the story of *Le Fever* the old Captain appears in a most amiable light; and as this little episode does greater honour to the abilities and disposition of the Author, than any other part of his work, we shall quote it at large, as well for his sake, as for the entertainment of such of our Readers as may not have seen the original. [Quotes the Le Fever episode.]

Since Mr. Sterne published his Sermons, we have been of opinion, that his excellence lay not so much in the humorous as in the pathetic; and in this opinion we have been confirmed by the above story of Le Fever. We appeal to the Heart of every reader whether our judgment is not right?

35. Richard Griffith: Sterne's appeal to pit, box, and gallery

1761–2

Extract from Richard Griffith, preface to *The Triumvirate* (1764), I, xiii–xvii.

Griffith (1704(?)–88) imitated Sterne in 1770 in *The Posthumous Works of a late celebrated Genius*, also known as *The Koran*, a work which some editors accepted as Sterne's own (see No. 61). He states that the preface to *The Triumvirate* 'was wrote in the year sixty-one,' but since he refers to having read volumes V and VI of *Tristram Shandy*, published 21 December 1761, he may or may not have completed it by the New Year. For Griffith's later remarks on Sterne, whom he met and became friends with in 1767, see No. 53d.

In a work like this, designed for the Public at large, there must be something, in allusion to dramatic writings, to entertain the three different classes of auditors; pit, box, and gallery. The stage of Athens, for whence your learned, but ignorant critics, frame their drama, was chaster than ours, because their audience was all of a piece. . . . But modern readers and audiences are in an unhealthful state, and must sometimes be indulged in unwholesome seasonings, to help them to digest proper food.

This then, may seem to have been the design of that anomalous, heteroclite genius, the author of *Tristram Shandy*, whose principal end, I hope and believe, was to inculcate that great *Magna Charta* of mankind, humanity and benevolence.

'A tale may catch him who a sermon flies.'[1]

'Tis true indeed, that he has given us, according to the vulgar phrase,

[1] Cf. George Herbert, 'The Church Porch':
> 'A verse may find him who a sermon flies,
> And turn delight into a sacrifice.'

rather *more sauce than pig*, and this not sufficiently seasoned with
Attic salt,[1] neither. But he seems to have wrote more for the present
age than the future ones; judging like Aurelius, though in a far different sense, that *surviving fame is but oblivion. . . .*[2]

His third part is better, that is, not so bad as his second.[3] There is
a good deal of laughable impertinence in it. He has repeated the same
empty humour there, of an *unlettered* page, and has given us a *carte-
blanche*, in this last.[4] Whatever is neither quite sense, nor absolute
nonsense, is true Shandeic. However, through the whole, there is
some entertainment for a splenetic person, though none at all for a
rational one.

Qui Tristram non odit, amet rhapsodias Rabelais.[5]

But there are some things in that work, which ought to be more
severely reprehended; though it is folly, rather than vice, that tempts
people to speak in a gross manner; while others relish it, in general,
more for want of *taste*, than virtue. It requires genius to be witty,
without being wicked at the same time; but the most *vulgar parts*
may serve for obscenity. 'Tis easier to make one *laugh*, than *smile*;
and when dullness would be witty, it lets fly bawdry, as it does something else, satisfied to raise a laugh, though it does a stink also. Loose
expressions, in a woman, are a double vice, as they offend against
decency, as well as virtue; but in a clergyman, they are treble; because
they hurt religion also.

But to his graver works—His sermons are written professedly,
upon the divine principle of philanthropy. . . . For my part, were I a
bishop, I would not indeed prefer him to a *Cure*, (though I am glad
that he does not want one) because of his *Tristram*, but I would certainly make him my Vicar-general, on account of his *Yoric*.[6]

[1] Griffith continues his gustatory metaphor from the previous paragraph. The phrase 'to
give more sauce than pig' was a colloquialism meaning 'to be very impudent or impertinent ; 'Attic salt' is an allusion to the delicate and refined wit of the Greek classics.
[2] See bk. IV of *The Meditations* of Marcus Aurelius, where this theme is developed.
[3] I.e. vols V and VI are better than vols III and IV.
[4] References to the marbled page in III. 36 and the blank page in VI. 38.
[5] Whoever does not hate Tristram will love the rhapsodies of Rabelais.
[6] I.e. *The Sermons of Mr. Yorick*.

36. A poetic tribute

12–15 February 1762

Mrs [?J. Henrietta] Pye, 'On the Report of the Death of the Reverend Mr. STERNE,' *Lloyd's Evening Post*, x. 158.

This poem, which appeared anonymously, was occasioned by the false report that Sterne had died after arriving in France on his Continental tour. It was reprinted with minor changes in Mrs Pye's *Poems by a Lady* (1767). The report of Sterne's death had been denied a few days before the poem first appeared.

> STERNE! rest for ever, and no longer fear
> The Critic's malice, and the Wittling's sneer;
> The gate of Envy now is clos'd on thee,
> And Fame her hundred doors shall open free;
> Ages unborn shall celebrate the Page,
> Where hap'ly blend the Satirist and Sage;
> While gen'rous hearts shall feel for worth distrest,
> Le Fevre's woes with tears shall be confest;
> O'er Yorick's tomb the brightest eyes shall weep,
> And British genius constant vigils keep;
> Then, sighing, say, to vindicate thy Fame,
> 'Great were his faults, but glorious was his flame.'

37. Sterne and the great humorists

May 1762

Extract from an unsigned notice of Smollett's *Launcelot Greaves*, *Critical Review*, xiii. 427–8.

Instances of the *vis comica*[1] are so rarely exhibited on the stage, or in the productions of our novelists, that one is almost induced to believe wit and humour have taken their flight with public virtue. The poets of these days aim at nothing more than interesting the passions by the intricacy of their plots; if a smile be accidentally raised upon the countenance, it rather proceeds from our finding the characters of the drama in some ridiculous or unexpected situation, than from their having said or done any thing characteristical. In novels especially, the historian thrusts himself too frequently upon the reader. Take a single chapter and it will appear egregiously dull, because the whole joke consists in untying some knot, or unravelling some mystery, and is generally placed in the epigrammatic fashion, in the tail. It is the suspense merely, with respect to the issue, that engages the reader's attention. Characters are distinguished merely by their opposition to some other characters; remove the contrast, and you annihilate the personages, just as little wits in conversation are reduced to mere inanimate figures, when you have taken away the fool who drew forth their talents. How different from this is the ridiculous simplicity of Adams, the absurd vehemence of Western, the boisterous generosity of Bowling, the native humour of Trunnion,[2] and the laughable solemnity of uncle Toby! Each of these characters singly is complete; without relation to any other object they excite mirth; we dip with the highest delight into a chapter, and enjoy it without reflecting upon the contrivance of the piece, or once casting an eye towards the catastrophe. Every sentence, and every action, diverts by its peculiarity; and hence it is that the novels in which those characters are to be found,

[1] Comic power.
[2] These are comic characters, respectively, in Fielding's *Joseph Andrews*, Fielding's *Tom Jones*, Smollett's *Roderick Random*, and Smollett's *Peregrine Pickle*.

will furnish perpetual amusement, while others, which entertain
merely from the nature of the incidents, and the conduct of the fable,[1]
are for ever laid aside after a single perusal: an engaging story will bear
relating but once; a humorous character will bear viewing repeatedly.

38. Sterne's bad example

June 1762

Extract from an unsigned notice of John Hall-Stevenson's *Crazy
Tales, Critical Review*, xiii. 475.

Hall-Stevenson's poems, published anonymously, were thought to
surpass the works of his friend Sterne in both indecency and dullness.

Since the first appearance of those facetious memoirs, written by the
Rev. Mr. Sterne, one would imagine the crazed inhabitants of Moorfields[2] had gained absolute possession of the press, guided the taste of
the public, and poured forth their incoherent rhapsodies, for the entertainment of the good people of England, once reputed so sensible and
judicious. Nothing is relished but what is perfectly whimsical and
altogether extravagant; decency is ridiculed, and the luscious joke
rendered familiar to the ear of the unblushing virgin. As imitators
in general are only qualified to copy the deformities of an original,
so it has happened, that certain high-flavoured strokes, so peculiarly
diverting from the humorous biographer, have degenerated in the hands
of his successors into gross and tasteless obscenity. Such is the rage of
fashion that men of real genius have been seduced into this senseless
mode of writing, only to remain contemptible examples of misapplied talents.

[1] Plot.
[2] That is, the inhabitants of Bethlehem Hospital, the asylum for the insane located in
Moorfields.

39. David Hume on Sterne

November 1762, January 1773

Hume (1711–76), Scottish historian, philosopher, and skeptic, became friends with Sterne in France in 1764.

(a) James Boswell's report of Hume's remarks on *Tristram Shandy* on 4 November 1762 (*Private Papers of James Boswell from Malahide Castle*, ed. Geoffrey Scott i (1928). 127)

Tristram Shandy may perhaps go on a little longer; but we will not follow him. With all his drollery there is a sameness of extravagance which tires us. We have just a succession of Surprise, surprise, surprise.

(b) Extract from a letter to William Strahan, the publisher, 30 January 1773 (*Letters of David Hume*, ed. J. Y. T. Greig (1932), ii. 269)

[England] is so sunk in Stupidity and Barbarism and Faction that you may as well think of Lapland for an Author. The best Book, that has been writ by any Englishman these thirty Years (for Dr Franklyn is an American) is *Tristram Shandy*, bad as it is. A Remark which may astonish you; but which you will find true on Reflection.

40. Sterne's nonsense

December 1762

Extract from an anonymous pamphlet, published in Edinburgh, *Jack and his Whistle . . . [and] A Paper dropt from Tristram Shandy's Pocket-book* (1762), pp. 15–17.

This pamphlet, which satirizes both Sterne and John Home (1722–1808), the Scottish dramatist, rings the changes on Walter Shandy's theory of the auxiliary verbs in volume V of *Tristram Shandy*. In the following extract, Sterne is imagined to be speaking.

Can I write nonsense? Ay, that I can, and with as genteel and pretty a glee, as if into me had transmigrated the merry soul of Dean Jonathan.[1] Here, with your leave, honest Mr Monthly Bookstealer, and not in the pathetic, lies the strength of Tristram.[2] The nicety of your critical scent with reverence profound I admire; and I owe you ceaseless gratitude for that refined policy, by which, while seeming my enemy, you have done me more effectual service, than you could have done, had you openly declared your heart-felt friendship. In words you condemn your friend, but you kindly retail those passages of his lucubrations, which you well know would not fail to recommend him. . . .

Have I ever wrote nonsense? The number of my purchasers, the yet greater number of my readers, the weight of my purse, the admiration of the gay and frolicsome, the contempt of the grave, and the pity of the pious, say, I have. . . .

How long and how often should I write nonsense? How many volumes of it may suffice to edify and improve mankind? None at all. How many to display my genius? One. How many to testify my contempt of the public taste? Ten thousand, if I should live to write them, would not suffice.

[1] A reference to Jonathan Swift, who had said 'Vive la bagatelle' ('Long live trifles'), and who, like Sterne, was often thought too frivolous (and too indecent) in his writings for a clergyman.
[2] An allusion to the *Monthly Review*'s assertion that Sterne's forte lay in the pathetic. See No. 34d.

41. Charles Johnstone: Sterne in the character of a wit

1762

Extracts from Charles Johnstone, *The Reverie; or, a Flight to the Paradise of Fools* (1762), i. 190-1, 199.

Johnstone (1719(?)-1800(?)), author of the popular *Chrysal, or the Adventures of a Guinea*, which has been called 'the best scandalous chronicle of the day,' did not mention Sterne by name in *The Reverie* nor allude to his being a clergyman, but contemporary readers would have understood that Sterne was being described or caricatured. There is no evidence that Johnstone ever met Sterne, but elsewhere in his book he retails several scurrilous anecdotes entirely to Sterne's discredit. Johnstone's attack, combining personal invective with literary criticism, is significant both because it reflects some of the professional jealousy that other writers must have felt at Sterne's success and social triumphs and because it illustrates the way in which estimates of Sterne's character and actions affected estimates of his work. *The Reverie* was reprinted in 1763 and 1767.

Observe that man who stands in yonder coffee-house, pumping his brain for pleasantry, and labouring for wit to entertain the sneering croud around him, whose fulsome compliments and ironical applause pass upon his vanity for a tribute justly due to his merit. He is one of your professed wits, whose good opinion of themselves makes them think every one obliged to admire what they say.

He was raised to this eminent station by the success of a ballad he wrote some time ago, of which it may be difficult to determine whether its merit lay in its oddity, its obscenity, or its profaneness.[1] However, the thing took with the public taste in so extraordinary a manner, that the happy author not only got the price of a new coat

[1] An allusion to *Tristram Shandy*.

149

by the sale of it, but was also admitted to the tables of all those who liked such buffoonery, to entertain them, and their company; where, having an eye to business, he always took the opportunity when they were in high spirits and could refuse nothing, to sollicit subscriptions for a collection of *old saws* which he had picked up and tagg'd some how together, by which artifice he contrived to make a good penny of them also.[1]

Elevated with this success, he thought he had nothing more to do but publish *a second part of the same tune*,[2] to make his fortune at once; but, to his great mortification, he found himself mistaken; for, the novelty that recommended the former being now worn off, there was little or no notice taken of it: beside, he had exhausted the spirit of obscenity and profaneness so thoroughly in the first part, that there remained nothing for him now but dregs, too coarse for the grossest taste, tho' he strove to make up for the quality by the quantity, of which he gave most plentiful measure.

Severe as this disappointment was to him in every respect, he affected not to feel it; but, modestly imputing it to the badness of the public taste, takes the liberty, by way of reprisal, to turn every thing that it approves into ridicule, with a petulance little short of scurrility; and to support the character of a privileged wit, never misses an opportunity of being impertinent to every person he converses with. . . .

But this personal licentiousness, though perhaps the most immediately painful to particulars, is not the worst instance in which this person abuses the talents nature has bestowed upon him with more than common liberality. You see the levity of his looks and behaviour; the same folly infects his writings to the most extravagant excess. In these he is dissipation itself. Starting from one subject to another, he jumbles all together the lightest and most serious, so as to make them appear equally ridiculous, sacrificing every thing to raise a laugh, as if that were the sole end of genius, the sole object of erudition.

Nor is this all; there are some things over which nature herself commands to throw a veil. To lift this up therefore, and make them the subject of wit and pleasantry, even in the almost boundless liberty of discourse, is a great offence; but in writing it is absolutely unpardonable, as that perpetuates the evil, and lays the foundation for debauching generations yet unborn. This is the grossest prostitution of powers given for a better purpose, and is always brought to a severe account.

[1] An allusion to Sterne's *Sermons* and his solicitation of subscriptions for them.
[2] An allusion to the second installment of *Tristram Shandy*, vols III and IV.

42. Sterne's Rabelaisian caricatures

1762

Extract from an unsigned entry on Sterne in *An Historical and Critical Account of the Lives and Writings of the Living Authors of Great-Britain* (1762), p. 20.

With Regard to the Romance of *Tristram Shandy*, tho' it is the Opinion of many good Judges, that it had much greater Success than it deserves, it is by no means destitute of Humour. It is obvious that the Author proposed the extravagant Work of the famous *Rabelais* as his Model, as the Characters approach almost to Caricaturas,[1] and the Drollery of the Stile to Indecency. The four last Volumes are generally thought to fall short of the two first; and indeed it seems somewhat absurd to continue a Work of so ludicrous a Nature so long, even if the Author could constantly keep up to the Humour with which he set out at first; for as *Horace* justly observes,

Nec lusisse pudet, sed non incidere ludum.

'It is not amiss to deviate from Gravity, and to trifle sometimes, but it is wrong to do so always.'[2]

---

[1] The early form of the word 'caricature' when it was first borrowed into English from Italian.
[2] Epistles I, 14: 36.

43. Charles Churchill on Sterne

1762

Extract from *The Ghost*, bk. III, ll. 967–84, quoted from *The Poetical Works of Charles Churchill*, ed. Douglas Grant (1956), p. 131.

Churchill (1731–64), like Sterne, was often censured for producing works not suitable to the character of a clergyman. Churchill's satirical poems were sometimes compared by reviewers to *Tristram Shandy* for their wit, their digressions, and their incoherence. For other remarks of Churchill on Sterne see No. 93a, p. 298, n. 3.

> Could I, whilst *Humour* held the Quill,
> Could I *digress* with half that skill,
> Could I with half that skill return,
> Which we so much admire in STERNE,
> Where each *Digression*, seeming vain,
> And only fit to entertain,
> Is found, on better recollection,
> To have a just and nice Connection,
> To help the whole with wond'rous art,
> Whence it seems idly to depart;
> Then should our readers ne'er accuse
> These wild excursions of the Muse,
> Ne'er backward turn dull Pages o'er
> To recollect what went before;
> Deeply impress'd, and ever new,
> Each Image past should start to view,
> And We to DULLMAN¹ now come in,
> As if we ne'er had absent been.

¹ A dull or stupid person; used humorously as a proper name.

44. A poetic tribute to *Tristram Shandy*

July 1763

Extract from an anonymous 'Elegy on the decease of TRISTRAM
SHANDY,' *St. James's Magazine*, ii. 312–16.

Playfully lamenting the fact that no more volumes of *Tristram
Shandy* have appeared, this anonymous versifier concludes his poem
with an epitaph praising Sterne through the character of Tristram
Shandy.

Know readers all! who know to read aright,
　Beneath this stone doth TRISTRAM SHANDY lie!
In troth he was a most egregious wight,
　He'd make the gravest laugh, the merriest cry.
He gave to misery (all he had) a tear,
　But freely us'd, for sorrow's balm, a joke:
At length he fell, thro' treatment too severe,
　He fell a prey to death's untimely stroke.
His *works*, his failings and his worth disclose,
　And reader! when you see his hobby-horse,
Wish, for the world's advantage and repose,
　No mortal man may ever rise a worse.

45. Sterne's upstart book

1764

Extract from the anonymous *Anecdotes of Polite Literature* (1764), II (pt ii). 25–9.

This book has sometimes been attributed, though incorrectly, to Horace Walpole. The prediction of a decline in Sterne's popularity was also made by David Hume (see No. 39a) and by Richard Farmer, classical tutor at Cambridge, who is reported to have told a group of students in 1765 that 'however much [*Tristram Shandy*] may be talked about at present, ... in the course of twenty years, should any one wish to refer to the book in question, he will be obliged to go to an antiquary to inquire for it' (*New Monthly Magazine*, x (December 1818). 389).

Extremes, however, in composition, as in morals, are ever dangerous, and the author, who, despising all rules, indulges himself in the reveries of romantic inclination, unless he produces a very admirable work indeed, will scarce meet with the lasting applause of those great authors, whose works formed the basis of criticism itself. A piece wrote in a lively manner, which sets all method at defiance, will undoubtedly take vastly with the publick, as a man of any genius may strike out something which has not been hackneyed by the multitude of authors; but a work of this nature, however it may succeed at first, will scarcely obtain a lasting possession of fame. . . .

I apprehend the celebrated romance of *Tristram Shandy* may be ranked in this class of works: never piece made more noise for a time, or occasioned a greater number of imitations. Its success was too lively at first to hold; and ever since the first appearance it has gradually declined in reputation: men of sense and taste now regard it as a trifling book, which contains several very good strokes of wit and humour, and will serve to laugh at for half an hour; but it is not now compared to Don Quixote. The novelty of the performance made many overlook the indecency, which is too often met with in it; but now the merit of

every chapter in it is weighed more justly, and we find, if there are
many very laughable strokes in it, there are also many other indecent,
and some even heavy; in a word, it is one of those upstart books which
blaze a while and then are forgot; and I am fully persuaded that a few
years will bury Tristram Shandy in oblivion.

46. Sterne no fit ambassador from hell

1764

Extract from *The Anti-Times* (1764), anonymous poem addressed
to Charles Churchill, pp. 6–8.

A council in hell has met to choose a representative to 'sow dissen-
tion' in England.

> ASMODEUS[1] next, (amidst lascivious leers,)
> Address'd the conclave of infernal peers:
> If I have any skill, in mischief's trade,
> St-rne is the man, shou'd be our Legate made;
> A Ch-rch buffoon, a sac-rd-tal ape,
> A Merry-Andrew, dress'd in decent crape.
> His volumes, full of innuendoes nice;
> Are great provocatives to carnal vice.
> His chesnuts, STARS, and BLANKS, and NOSES are
> So many traps, to catch th' unwary Fair.
> Much of the jargon lumber of his book,
> May well be deem'd an Asmodean hook.
> 'Twas I at first inspir'd my Tristram's soul,
> To write the SLAWKENBERGIAN STARRY scrole;
> I sent the lustful vapours to his brain,
> And made concupiscence th' ascendant gain:

[1] An evil demon who appears in later Jewish tradition as 'king of demons' and is sometimes identified with Beelzebub or Apollyon.

Then his opinions he produc'd to view;
From whence great gain will to our state accrue. . . .
    Now fraudful BELIAL[1] cut Asmodeus short,
And rising, thus address'd the list'ning court:
That St-rne is one of Vice's champions bold,
Is high in Pandemonium's list inroll'd,
All this I grant: but beg Asmodeus' leave,
Reasons against this CANDIDATE to give.
Tho' SLAWKENBERGIUS makes young sinners smile,
And STARS, and BLANKS, and NOSES, may beguile;
Tho' what he writes, almost the greatest part,
May tend to stain with sin the humane heart,
Flashes of wit, and sense, break radiant forth!
And shew the man has much internal worth.
No spleen, nor malice rank, first-born of Hell,
Nor sland'rous thoughts within his bosom dwell.
He's guilty of a most religious book;
A fault, which we can never overlook.
Rakes, bucks, and bloods, and ev'n girls of night,
Conn'd Yorick's pages o'er with vast delight:
The courtiers, statesmen, beaus, and men of trade,
All read the sermons, which poor Y-rick made:
I fear some lines flash'd veng'ance in their face,
And kindled up a quenchless flame of grace.
This MERRY way may work our state a spite;
Perhaps he'll JEST them into realms of light.
Some latent sparks of grace within him dwell,
He lashes faults, and hobby-horses well;
Therefore no fit ambassador from Hell.

[1] A name meaning 'worthlessness'; also sometimes identified with Satan, though a separate character in Milton's *Paradise Lost*.

47. The composition of *Tristram Shandy*, vols VII, VIII

1762–5

(a) Extract from Sterne's letter, 9 November 1762, to Robert Foley, his Parisian banker (*Letters*, p. 189)

I am got pretty well, and sport much with my uncle Toby in the volume I am now fabricating for the laughing part of the world—for the melancholy part of it, I have nothing but my prayers—so God help them.

(b) Extract from Sterne's letter, ? June 1764, to Mrs Elizabeth Montagu, his wife's cousin (*Letters*, p. 216)

I am going down to write a world of Nonsense—if possible like a man of *Sense*—but there is the *Rub*.[1] Would Apollo, or the fates, or any body else, had planted me within a League of Mrs Mountague this Summer, I could have taken my horse & gone & fetch'd Wit & Wisdome as I wanted them—as for nonsense—I am pretty well provided myself both by nature & Travel.

[1] *Hamlet*, act 3, sc. 1, l. 65.

(c) Extract from Sterne's letter, 11 November 1764, to Robert Foley (*Letters*, p. 231)

I will contrive to send you these 2 new Vol[s] of *Tristram*, as soon as ever I get them from the press—You will read as odd a Tour thro' france, as ever was projected or executed by traveller or travell Writer, since the world began—

—tis a laughing good temperd Satyr against Traveling (as puppies travel).

(d) Extract from *Tristram Shandy*, VIII. 31, p. 584, published 23 January 1765

For my hobby-horse, if you recollect a little, is no way a vicious beast; . . . 'Tis the sporting little filly-folly[1] which carries you out for the present hour—a maggot, a butterfly, a picture, a fiddle-stick—an uncle *Toby*'s siege—or an *any thing*, which a man makes a shift to get a stride on, to canter it away from the cares and solicitudes of life— 'Tis as useful a beast as is in the whole creation—nor do I really see how the world could do without it— (p. 131)

[1] Foolish or ridiculous notion; foolish hobby.

48. Reviews of *Tristram Shandy*, vols VII and VIII

January–April 1765

(a) Extract from an unsigned notice in the *Universal Museum and Complete Magazine of Knowledge and Pleasure*, i (January 1765). 36

The reader is not now to be informed of the degree of popularity with which *Tristram Shandy* was once received; whether the real merit of the work, or the novelty of its manner, produced this universal ardor in its favour, we cannot tell; however, the public seems now to be awakened from its delirium, and Tristram tells his tale, as the play-house phrase is, *to empty benches*. In fact, we are ever ready to encourage merit, but must be excused, if we cannot be brought to regard ribbaldry and incoherent stupidity as the genuine characteristics of humour. The kindness of the public, however, has abated with every renewed publication of this writer; and we are apt to suppose the seventh and eighth volumes of *Tristram Shandy* will add but little to the reputation of those preceding.

(b) Extract from an unsigned notice in the *Critical Review*, xix (January 1765). 65–6

The Spectator somewhere observes, that an author may print a joke but he cannot print a face, which is often the best part of a joke. The principal part of the work before us is its manner, which is either above or below criticism; for if it is level with it, it becomes a kind of an impassive object, upon which the artillery of criticism must be discharged in vain. We have already done justice to all that was justifiable in the preceding volumes of this work, and wish that the author . . . had, in the two volumes before us, afforded the least field for the only pleasing part of our task, that of approbation.

The seventh volume contains an unconnected, unmeaning, account of our author's journey to France.—Well, says my uncle Toby, Corporal, did you see that same cock—Cock, cock, said my father—what cock?—Here my mother took a large pinch of snuff—Why, the invisible cock, said my uncle Toby—Did you pay for seeing it, said my father? (gaping over the table)—Yes, and please your honour, that I did—and where was he? said my mother (taking up a stitch in my father's stockings)—Why in a box, and please you, madam (replied the corporal)—And you really saw him, said uncle Toby (taking the pipe out of his mouth, and shaking out the ashes)—Lord bless your honour's soul (said the corporal) how could I see him, did not I tell you he was invisible?—Did the man tell you so before you paid the money, said my father, knitting his brows!—Yes, yes, replied the corporal—Then, Trim, said my father, you was not cheated; for if you paid your money for an invisible thing, how couldst thou see it? Aristotle treats upon this subject in his chapter of cocks.—Here my mother took another large pinch of snuff.[1]

We are afraid the purchasers of these two volumes are pretty much in the corporal's situation. The author has pretended, from his commencement of authorship, neither to wit, taste, sense, nor argument, —*Videri vult et est*.[2] His purchasers have bought the sight of his invisible cock, without being cheated; for they have been beforehand told he is invisible.

To be serious, (if it is possible to be so with the writer of *Tristram Shandy*) we advise him most heartily to consider the case of uncle Toby's red breeches. They were worn so long, that they became thin, threadbare, and rotten, and the corporal could not find a taylor who could turn them, so as to make a decent appearance in his approaches to the widow Wadman. Indeed, Tristram, your wit and humour, we are afraid, will very soon be in the same predicament with uncle Toby's red breeches.—So we remain, with our love to widow Wadman,

Your humble servants,
THE REVIEWERS of BREECHES.[3]

[1] There is no episode exactly like this in vol. VII of *Tristram Shandy*.
[2] He wishes to be in the public eye and is.
[3] See *Tristram Shandy*, VII. 32, p. 524.

(c) Extract from Ralph Griffiths's unsigned review in the *Monthly Review*, xxxii (February, 1765). 120–39. Griffiths (1720–1803), founder and conductor of the *Monthly Review*, accompanies Sterne on his journey to France and engages in dialogue with him, commenting on the new installment chapter by chapter

REVIEWER. HOLLO! Mr. Shandy! Won't you stay and take company? you are for Calais, are you not?

SHANDY. Who the D— are you? What! my old friend the Reviewer! But you see I am in a d— hurry: So if you are going my way you must make confounded haste I can tell you. . . .

REV. When d'ye come out again? the gentlemen of our *corps* long to have another touch with ye.

SH. Do they? poor devils! Well, every man that's born with a mouth, has a right to eat, that's certain—but *you're* an honest fellow—and had no concern with the other hungry curs in knawing my jerkin so confoundedly. . . .[1]

REV. *reading*.] 'Chap. V. CALAIS, *Calatium, Calusium, Calesium*. This town if we may trust its archives, the authority of which I see no reason to call in question, was *once* a small village, &c. &c. &c. hum****** hum ****** hum ****** [*to the end of the chapter*.

SH. Well!—what will your brother Critics say to *that*, think ye?

REV. Say! why—but, first do you give me full liberty both of thought and speech: for we are now in France?

SH. Free-thinking, free-writing, and free-speaking for ever!

REV. Huzza!—then, to deal plainly with you, I fear my brethren will say, that, notwithstanding you imagine yourself to be very arch and witty upon travel-writers, and 'Addison with his satchel of school-books hanging at his a— and galling his beast's crupper at every stroke,'[2] they will pronounce you to have been, here, *out* of humour; and perhaps, charge you with having poorly had recourse to a dull expedient for filling up half a score pages:—Though you did not *actually* copy the siege of Calais from Rapin.—[3]

[1] See Nos 27a, 28a.
[2] See *Tristram Shandy*, VII. 4.
[3] Paul de Rapin (1661–1725), French historian, treated the siege of Calais briefly in his *L'Histoire d'Angleterre*. For the reference to Rapin and the quotation in the next speech, see *Tristram Shandy*, VII. 5–6.

SH. 'No—! by that all-powerful fire which warms the visionary
brain, and lights the spirits through unworldly tracts! ere I would take
advantage of the helpless reader, and make him pay, poor soul! for
fifty pages which I have no right to sell him,—naked as I am, I would
browse upon the mountains, and smile that the north wind brought
me neither my tent nor my supper.'

REV. Nobly said!—that flight to the mountain's top was lofty
indeed! Perfectly Fingalian![1]

SH. Put on, my brave boy, and make the best of thy way to *Montreuil*.

REV. From Montreuil to Abbeville, and from Abbeville to Amiens
in so short a time! Why, Sir! neither Death nor the Devil himself can
overtake you, at this rate!

SH. Tell me not of Death now. A *lovelier* object has engrossed my
attention. Oh! that innkeeper's daughter at Montreuil! Did you not
observe how the cunning gipsey, knitting her long, taper, white
thread stocking, pinned it to her knee, to shew that 'twas her own, and
fitted her exactly?—That nature should have told this creature a word
about a *Statue's thumb!*

REV. Your hand, Mr. Shandy!—had you unfortunately written
twenty descriptions of Calais, I would forgive you every one of 'em,
for the sake of that delicate stroke of the *Statue's thumb!* . . .

REV. Your droll *uncertainty*—which side of the way the people
walk on, in the streets of this vast metropolis:[2] *that* was excellent.—
But don't put into your book that queer reflection[3] on the coachman's
talking bawdy to his lean horses—you are certainly out, Mr. S—, in
your judgment of the public taste. Obscenity is not in high vogue now,
as it was in the time of Charles the Second; when, like an impudent
strumpet, it stared poor decency out of countenance, and banished her
the realm.

SH. But it *is* in high vogue with *me*. A fig for the taste of the public!
I *live*, Sir! and I *write*, Sir! to my own taste—Perhaps you will also
condemn my story of the abbess of Andoüillets and the fair Margarita
—Read it—but, approve or not approve, it *shall* go in.

REV. Well! let's read it, however, 'Chap. XXI. The Abbess of
Andoüillet's ********* being in danger of an *anchilosis*, or stiff joint

---

[1] An allusion to *Fingal*, the 'ancient epic poem' forged by James Macpherson (1736–96).
[2] The reviewer has now arrived at vol. VII, ch. 17.
[3] It is difficult to see why the reviewer takes such offense at Sterne's 'reflection,' which is
not expressed obscenely. See *Tristram Shandy*, VII. 17.

*********** [*and so on, to the end of the chapter.*—Why, really now, Mr. S—, you had better let Janatone have this paper, to singe the next fowl she claps down before her father's kitchin-grate. Don't insert it—'tis a low—poor—hackney'd joke; picked out of the common Parisian jest-books.

SH. And is not mine as arrant a jest-book as any of them?—Why not import a joke or two from the continent, as well as other French commodities? though it be a little stale here, it will be new and fresh in London. Beside, have I not cook'd it up, and season'd it to the *haut gout*,[1] with Margarita's finger, the Abbess's virginity, and the liquorish Muleteer? By ***! it shall go.—

REV. By all that's decent and discreet! it is unpardonable to print such stuff! I grant you, there's humour in your manner of dressing this mess; but it is *such* humour as *ought* to please none but coachmen and grooms. Why, the duce! will you prohibit every modest woman in the three kingdoms from reading your book?

SH. Prohibit the modest women! ha! ha! ha! Prithee, Critic, let's look at your feet—Aye! *square toes*[2]—I thought so! . . .

REV. I tell you again, Sir! this same bawdy, and these bawdyisms, will be the ruin of you! What is this, here, Ch. XXIX. p. 106? Why you might as well write *broad Rochester*[3] as set down all these obscene asterisms!—setting the reader's imagination to work, and officiating as pimp to every lewd idea excited by your own creative and abominable ambiguity. Why don't you speak out, and let us know the worst you would say?

SH. And so draw up my own indenture for a three year's apprenticeship to a hemp-beater in Clerkenwell-college![4] very pretty advice, indeed! no, I will stick to my *stars*—and defy the B***** of G********.[5] There is no act in force for the punishment of astronomy. They cannot serve me as the Venetians served Gallileo.—[6]

REV. Hold! it is downright prophanation to mention that excellent man on this vile occasion. I perceive your libidinous imagination is too far gone, to afford even the smallest hope for a cure. But, be

[1] I.e. made it spicy.
[2] A square toes is an old-fashioned person; one having strict ideas of conduct.
[3] See No. 11a, p. 65, n. 1.
[4] That is, 'and so lay myself open to legal prosecution.' Prisoners in Clerkenwell prison (jocularly referred to as a college) were required to beat the rotten stems of hemp, detaching the fibers. Cf. No. 121, p. 368.
[5] Bishop of Gloucester, William Warburton. See No. 16.
[6] Galileo Galilei (1564–1642), pioneer astronomer and physicist who was tried for heresy, lived briefly at Venice.

intreated!—do, in respect to our *wives* and *daughters*, be as decent as *you can*. Here, take the pen, and strike out all that Jenny whisper'd in your ear.

SH. No—'I never blot out—never cancel—RESOLUTION'S the word!'

REV. OBSTINACY's the fact—I could give it a worse name—

SH. Thank you for your tenderness—you Reviewers are, indeed, the very flower of courtesy—But, hang it—let's not quarrel about our wives and daughters. . . .

REV. You have had many adventures at Lyons, I think; but that with the ass pleases me much; even more, if possible, than your notable contest with his Most Christian Majesty's commissary—But you have not yet told me how you came to leave your father and uncle Toby behind, at Auxerre—

SH. There are secrets in all family concerns—But is it possible to please your reverence? Do you really approve my conduct with regard to my long-ear'd friend—

REV. Most heartily! You there shew'd so much benevolence—so much true and delicate humour, that I almost forgive you what lately pass'd about *Jenny*; and will, if I live to return to Old England, particularly desire my brethren of the Review, to recommend, in an especial manner, your twenty-third chapter.—But, what, in the name of common sense, do you mean by the conclusion of it; what is the world to understand by the REVIEWERS OF YOUR BREECHES?[1]

SH. Don't you understand it? ha! ha! ha!—faith, nor I neither! ha! ha! ha!—Pray reach me my fool's cap—ha! ha! ha!

REV. Ha! ha! ha!—If you have the happy art of thus laughing, and making others laugh, at nothing,—What can you not effect when you really mean something? . . .

SH. This *solitary* journey o'er the plain of Languedoc, has proved 'the most fruitful and busy period of my life;—stopping and talking to every soul I met who was not in a full trot—joining all parties before me—waiting for every soul behind—hailing all those who were coming through cross roads—arresting all kinds of beggars, pilgrims, fiddlers, fryars,—not passing by a woman in a mulberry-tree, without commending her legs, and tempting her into a conversation with a

[1] This appears at the end of the thirty-second, not the twenty-third chapter of vol. VII. The phrase appears to carry on the jocular battle with the critics that Sterne began in vol. III with the passage about his jerkin. See (b) above and Nos 27a, 28a.

pinch of snuff.—In short, by seizing every handle, of what size or shape soever, which chance held out to me in this journey—I turned my *plain* into a *city*.—I was always in company, and with great variety too; and as my mule lov'd society as much as myself, and had always some proposals on his part to offer to every beast he met—I am confident we could have pass'd through Pall-mall or St. James's Street[1] for a month together, with fewer adventures—and seen less of human nature.'

REV. Admirable!—Mr. Shandy, you understand the art, the true art of travelling, better than any other mortal I ever knew or heard of! O! what pleasure, what a delightful exercise of benevolence have I lost, by not keeping company with you, all the way from Avignon!

SH. Fun?—banter?—irony?—eh?

REV. Irony!—no,—by this hand! Tristram! thou hast won my heart also—What a social soul! We will never suffer a cross word between us again—. . . .

SH. 'Why could I not live and end my days thus? Just Disposer of our joys and sorrows, cried I, why could not a man sit down in the lap of Content here—and dance, and sing, and say his prayers, and go to heaven with his nut-brown maid? Capriciously did she bend her head on one side, and dance up insiduous—Then 'tis time to dance off, quoth I; so changing only partners and tunes, I danced it away from Lunel to Montpellier.'—

REV. Give me thy hand, dear Shandy! Give me thy heart! —What a delightful scene hast thou drawn! Would we had it upon two yards of REYNOLDS's canvass![2]—How engaging are the natives of these happy plains! for happy they *will* be, in spite of KINGS!—What good humour! What ease! What nature!—In one sense, France alone can be called *the land of* FREEDOM!

SH. Now you grow quite good-natured—I'll shew you the manuscript of my eighth volume; and you shall be introduced to the sweet widow Wadman.

REV. I'm extremely glad we've met with your worthy Father again, and that good soul—your Uncle Toby; with the honest Corporal, and Obadiah—for I've a sincere regard for the whole family—a dog, from Shandy-hall, should always be welcome to me. Is your Uncle quite recover'd yet of the wound in his groin?

---

[1] Busy, fashionable streets in London frequented by people of all classes.
[2] An allusion to Sir Joshua Reynolds (1723–92), English portrait painter noted for the range of characterization in his paintings. Sterne sat to Reynolds three times; the first portrait of Sterne by Reynolds was engraved and used as a frontispiece for the *Sermons of Mr. Yorick* (see No. 17, n. 1).

SH. He will never obtain a perfect cure of that wound.

REV. I'm sorry for it;—because, to tell you the truth, it begins to grow offensive.

SH. Humph!—What, I suppose you want to give it a dressing, and to try your critical scalping-knife upon it—

REV. No—faith! I don't desire to come so near it.—I tell you what, Mr. Shandy—before I do myself the pleasure of perusing this volume, —mind! I tell you before-hand, if I meet with any thing offensive to decency, I must *mark* it:—indeed, my friend—you are amazingly clever in many things—but—you want decency.—Nay, hear me out! —You have great merit, in some respects. Your characters are new, and admirably supported throughout. Your Father's is perfectly new, singular, strongly mark'd, and powerfully sustain'd. Your Uncle too, is an amiable original: and Trim—I've no where met with his fellow. Doctor Slop, likewise, and even Mrs. Susannah, all have their peculiar excellencies:—but, indeed, you do want decency. . . .

[The Reviewer continues with a review of volume VIII, comparing the chapters to flowers. He finds the first chapter 'a poor, scentless, field-daisy,' the second 'a down-right nettle.' Chapter XVI, however, is 'a pretty flower':]

REV. Here is something to compensate for the dulness, or worse than dulness, of the foregoing fifteen chapters. Here Mr. Shandy shews himself a master in the science of *human feelings*, and the art of describing them. Nor is there any thing here to offend the most chaste, or most delicate Reader: Except a light stroke or two, which, had there been nothing worse in the other parts of his performance, nobody would have felt. . . .

[The reviewer continues with high praise for the account of Uncle Toby's courtship of the Widow Wadman, commenting on the passage describing the widow's eye:]

REV. Never was any thing more beautifully simple, more natural, more *touching*! O Tristram! that ever any grosser colours should daub and defile that pencil of thine, so admirably fitted for the production of the most delicate as well as the most masterly pictures of men, manners, and situations!—*Richardson*—the delicate, the circumstantial RICHARDSON himself,[1] never produced any thing equal to the

---

[1] Critics often thought of Samuel Richardson's novels as more 'delicate' and more refined than those of his contemporaries.

amours of Uncle Toby and the Widow Wadman! . . . [In the concluding section of the review, Sterne and the reviewer meet at a tavern:]

SH. Are you not a pretty gentleman, Squire Critic, to keep one
waiting near half an hour beyond the time appointed?

REV. Your pardon, Mr. Shandy! but 'twas your own fault for leaving
your manuscript with me: I could not, for the soul of me, part with
your most worthy, excellent, Uncle Toby, a minute sooner. Here, take
your papers, and success attend your publication—provided you eraze—

SH. Have not I told you, again and again, that I never blot out?
Positively I will not eraze a syllable: So, Critics, do your worst!

REV. Inflexible, indiscreet,—incomparable!—Well, fellow-traveller!
be not angry—if the public will be good-natured enough to over-look
your imperfections—surely I may, who am so much obliged to you for
your patient bearing with all my exceptions, and reprehensions.

SH. Come, Old Boy! Reviewing must be cursed dry work—Excellent Frontiniac![1]—Here's success to the Review! and pray, at your
next meeting at the Crown and Anchor,[2] give my compliments to
every Square-toe belonging to the Corps—and, if you please, tell
them, that if they damn these my seventh and eighth volumes, I'll be
even with them, and *damn them* in my ninth and tenth.

REV. Ah, Mr. Shandy, your *ninth* and *tenth*! that's talking of things
at a great distance! Better take a friend's advice. Stop where you are.
The Public, if I guess right, will have *had enough*, by the time they get to
the end of your eighth volume.—Your health, Mr. Shandy, and hearty
thanks for the entertainment you have given me—but,—excuse me if
I hazard a bold conjecture,—I am inclined to think that, all this while,
you have not sufficiently cultivated your best talents. Give up your
Long Noses, your Quedlinbergs, and your Andoüillets.—Dr. Slop,
indeed, is a *great* character: but, try your strength another way. One of
our gentlemen once remarked, in *print*, Mr. Shandy—that he thought
your excellence lay in the PATHETIC.[3] I think so too. In my opinion,
the little story of Le Fevre has done you more honour than every thing
else you have wrote, except your Sermons. Suppose you were to
strike out a new plan? Give us none but amiable or worthy, or exem-
plary characters; or, if you will, to enliven the drama, throw in the
innocently humorous. Desipere in loco.[4] No objection to Trim, any more

[1] A kind of wine.
[2] A tavern in the Strand famous for its social clubs.
[3] See No. 34d.
[4] To trifle in the appropriate place. See Horace, *Odes*, IV. vii. 28.

than to Slop. Paint Nature in her loveliest dress—her native simplicity. Draw natural scenes, and interesting situations—In fine, Mr. Shandy, do, for surely you can, excite our passions to *laudable* purposes—awake our affections, engage our hearts—arouze, transport, refine, improve us. Let morality, let the cultivation of virtue be your aim—let wit, humour, elegance and pathos be the means; and the grateful applause of mankind will be your reward.

SH. Have ye done?—I'm glad on't! Hark ye—Jenny wants me to give her a whirl in the chaise next *Sunday*—Will you *preach* for me? you have an admirable knack at exhortation!—

(d) **Extract from Jean Baptiste Suard's unsigned notice of volumes VII and VIII**, appearing originally in the *Gazette Littéraire de l'Europe*, as translated and printed in the *London Chronicle*, xvii, no. 1299 (10 April—18 April 1765). 373

This is the continuation of one of the most whimsical productions that ever appeared in any language. It is a sort of jack-pudding[1] romance, in the taste of *Pantagruel* and the *Satyre Menippée*. The author, however, is neither so learned, nor so satyrical as *Rabelais*, tho' he equals him in mirth and in want of decency. It is worth remarking, that the authors of these three singular compositions were three Clergymen.[2]

Mr. STERNE, the historian of *Shandy*, published some years ago his two first volumes, which both amused the public, and exercised its curiosity. They were *supposed* to contain a pleasant and delicate satire, in which a *sage* put on a *fool's cap* to disguise his views. This same sage published soon after four volumes more, which were read with the greatest avidity; their readers, nevertheless, awaked out of their dream, and, to their great surprize, began to perceive, that they did not understand the joke. Their patience, however, was not exhausted; they still expected to be led into the secret; they fondly imagined that there *really was a secret*; and that if they did not perceive the design of the author and the cream of the jest, it was their own fault. Some imagined that they had discovered a *profound meaning* in a scene of buffoonery, where there was no meaning at all. At length the publick

[1] See No. 28c, p. 126, n. 3.
[2] François Rabelais (*c.* 1494–*c.* 1553) was both priest and physician. *La Satire Ménippée*, a sixteenth-century political pamphlet, was produced by a group headed by Jacques Gillot, priest, at whose house the writers met.

began to see clearly that Mr. STERNE had amused himself at their cost, and that his work was a *riddle*, without an *object*.

This adventure is not unlike the famous story of the *man* who, some years ago, informed the public, that he would put himself in a *bottle* before their eyes. The credulous multitude, both great and small, flocked to the theatre to behold this wonder; but the droll carried away their money and left the bottle empty; not however more empty than the two last volumes of the life of *Tristram Shandy*.[1]

49. Mrs Montagu on Sterne

April 1765

Elizabeth Montagu (1720–1800), wife of Edward Montagu, for many years was leader of the literary group known as the Blue-stockings, which met for social evenings of conversation about books. She was a cousin of Sterne's wife. For her remarks on the *Sentimental Journey* after Sterne's death, see No. 58f.

(a) **Extract** from a letter from Elizabeth Montagu to Mrs Sarah Scott, her sister, dated April 1765 (*Mrs. Montagu*, ed. Reginald Blunt (1923), i. 187)

Not knowing what temptations the town of Bath may offer, I have sent you the deepest Divine, the profoundest casuist, the most serious (on paper) the reformed Church affords. I suppose from the description you will guess this grave and sage? personage can be no other

[1] In the original article in the *Gazette Littéraire* the author goes on to say: 'What deserves mention in this work is its amiable and continuing current of philanthropy. There are several strokes of a tender and genuine sensibility which is not usually allied with buffoon-ery; in writing all the nonsense which his imagination provided, the author has not per-mitted himself to engage in personal satire.' For more information on Suard and his wife, see No. 134.

than the Rev^d Mr. Sterne. I will venture to say for him, that whatever he may want in seriousness he makes up in good nature. He is full of the milk of human kindness, harmless as a child, but often a naughty boy, and a little apt to dirty his *frock*. On the whole I recommend him to your acquaintance, and he has talents and qualities that will recommend him to your friendship.

(b) Extract from a letter from Elizabeth Montagu to Mrs Sarah Scott, dated 11 April 1765 (ibid., i. 188–9)

I am glad Tristram gave you some entertainment; I can never send you such another. The extravagant applause that was at first given to his works turn'd his head with vanity. He was received abroad with great distinction which made him still more vain, so that he realy believes his book to be the finest thing the age has produced. The age has graced him, he had disgraced the age. . . . I like Tristram better than his book. He had a world of good nature, he never hurt any one with his witt, he treats asses on two legs as well and gently as he does that four legged one in his book. A man of witts, and such he certainly is with all his oddities, that never makes use of the sharp weapon ever at his side to alarm or to wound his neighbour, deserves much indulgence.

50. *Sermons of Mr. Yorick*, vols III, IV

1765–6

(a) Excerpt from Sterne's letter to his friend Thomas Hesilrige, 5 July 1765 (*Letters*, p. 252)

Have you seen my 7 & 8 graceless Children[1]—but I am doing penance for them, in begetting a couple of more ecclesiastick ones—which are to stand penance (again) in their turns—in Sheets[2] ab^t the middle of Sept^r—they will appear in the Shape of the 3^d & 4 Vol^s of Yorick. These you must know are to keep up a kind of balance, in my shandaic character, & are push'd into the world for that reason by my friends with as splendid & numerous a List of Nobility &c—as ever pranced before a book, since subscriptions came into fashion[3]—

(b) Extract from an unsigned two-part review in the *Critical Review*, xxi (January, February 1766). 49, 99

The author of *Tristram Shandy* is discernible in every page of these discourses. They who have read the former will find in the latter the same acute remarks on the manners of mankind, the same striking characters, the same accurate investigation of the passions, the same delicate strokes of satire, and the same art in moving the tender affections of nature. But the author sometimes forgets the dignity of his character, and the solemnity of a christian congregation, and condescends, on the most interesting topics of religion, to excite a jocular idea, or display a frivolous turn of wit. . . .

Mr. Yorick, as we have seen in our last Review, is no drowzy preacher, no gloomy religionist. He treats every topic with a peculiar

[1] An allusion to vols VII and VIII of *Tristram Shandy*.
[2] Sterne is punning upon the 'sheets' of his forthcoming book and the white sheets that sinners were forced to wear when they did public penance for sexual offenses.
[3] Vols III and IV of Sterne's *Sermons* had 693 subscribers, an impressive, though not unparalleled number, and the list did contain many prominent names of the day.

aid of good-humour; and endeavours not only to improve, but to entertain his readers.

(c) Extract from an unsigned review by William Rose (see No. 13c) in the *Monthly Review*, xxxiv (March 1766). 207-8

Whether all the sermons contained in these two volumes were preached or not, we cannot inform our Readers. We would willingly believe, for the sake of the Author's credit, that they were not: there is an air of levity in some of them, altogether unbecoming the dignity and serious-ness of pulpit-discourses, and which no brilliancy of wit, luxuriance of fancy, nor elegance of composition can atone for. *Propriety* is a rule as necessary to be observed in writing, as decorum is in conduct; and whoever offends against the one, must necessarily incur the just censure of every competent judge, as much as he who offends against the other.

Serious subjects, indeed, seem but little suited to Mr. Sterne's genius; when he attempts them, he seldom succeeds, and makes but an awk-ward appearance. He is possessed, however, of such a fund of good humour, and native pleasantry, and seems, at the same time, to have so large a share of philanthropy, that it is impossible, for us at least, to be long displeased with him.—His sermons, if they must all be called by that name, contain many pertinent and striking observations on human life and manners: every subject, indeed, is treated in such a manner as shews the originality of his genius, and as will, in some measure, soften the severity of censure, in regard to his ill-timed pleasantry and want of discretion.

(d) Extract from a letter from William Cowper, the poet, to his friend Joseph Hill, dated 3 April 1766 (*Correspondence of William Cowper*, ed. Thomas Wright (1904), i. 64-5)

I read a good deal, though I have neither read Colman or Sterne.[1] I agree with you entirely in your judgment of the works of the latter,

[1] Though Cowper states he had not read vols III and IV of the *Sermons*, I have placed his response to the two earlier volumes here since it was occasioned by the appearance of the second installment. Cowper (1731-1800), with his evangelical bent, would not be expected to approve Sterne's sermons.

considered as moral performances, for the two first volumes of his sermons I read in London. He is a great master of the pathetic; and if that or any other species of rhetoric could renew the human heart and turn it from the power of Satan unto God, I know no writer better qualified to make proselytes to the cause of virtue than Sterne. But, alas! my dear Joe, the evil of a corrupt nature is too deeply rooted in us all to be extirpated by the puny efforts of wit or genius. The way which God has appointed must be the true and the only way to virtue, and that is faith in Christ. He who has received that inestimable keeping deep into his heart, has received a principle of virtue that will never fail him. This is the victory that overcometh the world, even our faith, and there is no other. The world by wisdom knew not God, it therefore pleased Him by the foolishness of preaching to save them that believe. To save them from their sinful nature here and from His wrath hereafter, by that plain but despised and rejected remedy, faith in Christ. Therefore it is that though I admire Sterne as a man of genius, I can never admire him as a preacher. For to say the least of him, he mistakes the weapon of his warfare, and fights not with the sword of the Spirit for which only he was ordained a minister of the Gospel, but with that wisdom which shone with as effectual a light before our Saviour came as since, and which therefore cannot be the wisdom which He came to reveal to us.

51. Sterne and a Black admirer

July 1766, June 1778

Ignatius Sancho (1729–80) was born on board a slave ship. John Montagu (1689–1749), second Duke of Montagu, became Sancho's patron, and he spent much of his life in the service of the Montagu family. Sancho also opened a grocer's shop and devoted his spare time to the study of music and literature, becoming acquainted with Johnson, Garrick, and Sterne. In his letters Sancho sometimes imitates the Shandean style; first published in 1782, they reached a fifth edition in 1803.

(a) Sancho's letter to Sterne, dated 21 July 1766 (*Letters of the Late Ignatius Sancho,* 1968 facsimile of the 5th ed. (1803), pp. 70–2)

REVEREND SIR,

It would be an insult on your humanity (or perhaps look like it) to apologize for the liberty I am taking.—I am one of those people whom the vulgar and illiberal call '*Negurs.*'—The first part of my life was rather unlucky, as I was placed in a family who judged ignorance the best and only security for obedience.—A little reading and writing I got by unwearied application.—The latter part of my life has been —thro' God's blessing, truly fortunate, having spent it in the service of one of the best families in the kingdom.—My chief pleasure has been books.—Philanthropy I adore.—How very much, good Sir, am I (amongst millions) indebted to you for the character of your amiable uncle Toby!—I declare, I would walk ten miles in the dog-days, to shake hands with the honest corporal.—Your Sermons have touch'd me to the heart, and I hope have amended it, which brings me to the point.—In your tenth discourse, page seventy-eight, in the second volume—is this very affecting passage—'Consider how great a part of our species—in all ages down to this—have been trod under the feet of cruel and capricious tyrants, who would neither hear their cries, nor pity their distresses.—Consider slavery—what it is—how bitter a draught—and how many millions are made to drink it!'[1]—Of all my favourite authors, not one has drawn a tear in favor of my miserable black brethren—excepting yourself, and the humane author of Sir George Ellison.[2]—I think you will forgive me;—I am sure you will applaud me for beseeching you to give one half-hour's attention to slavery, as it is at this day practised in our West Indies.—That subject, handled in your striking manner, would ease the yoke (perhaps) of many—but if only of one—Gracious God!—what a feast to a benevolent heart!—and, sure I am, you are an epicurean in acts of charity.—You, who are universally read, and as universally admired—you could not fail—Dear Sir, think in me you behold the uplifted hands of thousands of my brother Moors.—Grief (you pathetically observe) is eloquent; —figure to yourself their attitudes;—hear their supplicating addresses! —alas!—you cannot refuse.—Humanity must comply—in which hope I beg permission to subscribe myself,

Reverend Sir, &c.
IGN. Sancho.

(b) Sterne's reply to Sancho, dated 27 July 1766 (*Letters*, pp. 285–6)

There is a strange coincidence, Sancho, in the little events (as well as in the great ones) of this world: for I had been writing a tender tale of the sorrows of a friendless poor negro-girl,[3] and my eyes had scarse done smarting with it, when your Letter of recommendation in behalf of so many of her brethren and sisters, came to me—but why *her brethren*?—or your's, Sancho! any more than mine? It is by the finest tints, and most insensible gradations, that nature descends from the fairest face about St James's,[4] to the sootiest complexion in africa: at which tint of these, is it, that the ties of blood are to cease? and how many shades must we descend lower still in the scale, 'ere Mercy is to vanish with them?—but 'tis no uncommon thing, my good Sancho,

[1] 'Job's Account of the Shortness and Troubles of Life, considered,' first published in vol. II of the *Sermons of Mr. Yorick*. Sancho is quoting from a reprint.
[2] *The History of Sir George Ellison* (1766) was written by Mrs Sarah Robinson Scott, sister of Mrs Elizabeth Montagu (see No. 49).
[3] Cf. *Tristram Shandy*, IX. 6, pp. 606–7. Sterne seems to hint that he may have written a longer version of this 'tender tale' than finally found its way into *Tristram Shandy*.
[4] See No. 14, p. 83, n. 3.

for one half of the world to use the other half of it like brutes, & then endeavour to make 'em so. for my own part, I never look *Westward* (when I am in a pensive mood at least) but I think of the burdens which our Brothers & Sisters are *there* carrying—& could I ease their shoulders from one ounce of 'em, I declare I would set out this hour upon a pilgrimage to Mecca for their sakes—wch by the by, Sancho, exceeds your Walk of ten miles, in about the same proportion, that a Visit of Humanity, should one, of mere form—however if you meant my Uncle Toby, more—he is y^r Debter,[1]

If I can weave the Tale I have wrote into the Work I'm ab^t—tis at the service of the afflicted—and a much greater matter; for in serious truth, it casts a sad Shade upon the World, That so great a part of it, are and have been so long bound in chains of darkness[2] & in Chains of Misery; & I cannot but both respect & felicitate You, that by so much laudable diligence you have broke the one—& that by falling into the hands of so good and merciful a family, Providence has rescued You from the other.

and so, good hearted Sancho! adieu! & believe me, I will not forget y^r Letter. Y^rs

L STERNE

(c) Extracts from a letter from Sancho to an unidentified friend, 10 June 1778, comparing Fielding and Sterne (*Letters of Sancho,* pp. 144–6)

So, my wise critic—blessings on thee—and thanks for thy sagacious discovery!—Sterne, it seems, stole his grand outline of character from Fielding—and whom did Fielding plunder? thou criticizing jack ape! —As to S—, perhaps you may be right—not absolutely right—nor quite so very *altogether* wrong—but that's not my affair.—Fielding and Sterne both copied nature—their palettes stored with proper colours of the brightest dye—these masters were both great originals— their outline correct—bold—and free—Human Nature was their subject—and though their colouring was widely different, yet *here*

---

[1] Sterne originally wrote and crossed out 'the Corporal' before 'my Uncle Toby.' In another version of this letter in Sterne's *Letter Book* he wrote: 'If you meant the Corporal more he is your Debtor.' (*Letters,* pp. 286–7).
[2] II Peter, 2: 4 (in R. V. 'pits' not 'chains').

and *there* some features in each might bear a little resemblance—some faint likeness to each other—as, for example—in your own words—Toby and All-worthy—The external draperies of the two are as wide as the poles—their hearts—perhaps—twins of the same blessed form and principles.—But, for the rest of the Dramatis Personae, you must strain hard, my friend, before you can twist them into likeness sufficient to warrant the censure of copying. . . . Read boy, read—give Tom Jones a second *fair* reading!—Fielding's wit is obvious—his humour poignant—dialogue just—and truly dramatic—colouring quite nature—and keeping chaste.—Sterne equals him in every thing, and in one thing excels him and all mankind—which is the distribution of his lights, which he has so artfully varied throughout his work, that the oftener they are examined the more beautiful they appear.—They were two great masters, who painted for posterity—and, I prophesy, will charm to the end of the English speech.—If Sterne has had any one great master in his eye—it was Swift, his countryman—the first wit of this or any other nation.—But there is this grand difference between them—Swift excels in grave-faced irony—whilst Sterne lashes his whips with jolly laughter. . . . Swift and Sterne were different in this—Sterne was truly a noble philanthropist—Swift was rather cynical. What Swift would fret and fume at—such as the petty accidental *sourings* and *bitters* in life's cup—you plainly may see, Sterne would laugh at—and parry off by a larger humanity, and regular good will to man. I know you will laugh at me—Do—I am content:—if I am an enthusiast in any thing, it is in favor of my Sterne.

TRISTRAM SHANDY

vol. IX (1767)

---

52. *Tristram Shandy*, vol. IX

January–March 1767

(a) Extract from *Tristram Shandy*, IX. 12–13, pp. 614–17, published 29 January 1767

Upon looking back from the end of the last chapter and surveying the texture of what has been wrote, it is necessary, that upon this page and the five following, a good quantity of heterogeneous matter be inserted, to keep up that just balance betwixt wisdom and folly, without which a book would not hold together a single year: nor is it a poor creeping digression (which but for the name of, a man might continue as well going on in the king's highway) which will do the business—no; if it is to be a digression, it must be a good frisky one, and upon a frisky subject too, where neither the horse or his rider are to be caught, but by rebound.

The only difficulty, is raising powers suitable to the nature of the service: FANCY is capricious—WIT must not be searched for—and PLEASANTRY (good-natured slut as she is) will not come in at a call, was an empire to be laid at her feet. . . .

—I never stand conferring with pen and ink one moment; for if a pinch of snuff or a stride or two across the room will not do the business for me—I take a razor at once; and having tried the edge of it upon the palm of my hand, without further ceremony, except that of first lathering my beard, I shave it off; taking care only if I do leave a hair, that it be not a grey one: this done, I change my shirt—put on a better coat—send for my last wig—put my topaz ring[1] upon my

---

[1] In medieval tradition topaz cooled the passions and was a cure for sensuality.

finger; and in a word, dress myself from one end to the other of me, after my best fashion. . . .

[T]he soul and body are joint-sharers in every thing they get: A man cannot dress, but his ideas get cloath'd at the same time; and if he dresses like a gentleman, every one of them stands presented to his imagination, genteelized along with him—so that he has nothing to do, but take his pen, and write like himself.

For this cause, when your honours and reverences[1] would know whether I writ clean and fit to be read, you will be able to judge full as well by looking into my Laundress's bill, as my book: there was one single month in which I can make it appear, that I dirtied one and thirty shirts with clean writing; and after all, was more abus'd, curs'd, criticis'd and confounded, and had more mystic heads shaken at me, for what I had wrote in that one month, than in all the other months of that year put together.

—But their honours and reverences had not seen my *bills*. (pp. 48–57)

(b) Extract from an unsigned notice in the *Critical Review*, xxxiii (February 1767). 138

A critic would prove himself as extravagant as the author affects to be, should he pretend to give a character of this work, whose wit may be termed generical. We wish, however, that it had been a little better accommodated to the ear of innocence, *virginibus puerisque*,[2] but, perhaps of all the authors who have existed since the days of Rabelais, none can with more justice than Tristram put his arms a-kimbo, strut through his room, and say,

None but myself can be my parallel.[3]

[1] See No. 33d, n. 1 for a similar expression.
[2] To maidens and youths.
[3] Cf. Lewis Theobald, *The Double Falsehood*: 'None but himself can be his parallel' and Seneca, *Hercules Furens*, I, l. 84.

STERNE

(c) Extract from an unsigned notice in the *Gentleman's Magazine*, xxxvii (February 1767). 75–6

Of this work there can be neither epitome nor extract. The ninth volume consists of the same whimsical extravagancies that filled the other eight, which, as they owed great part of their effect to novelty, must gradually please less and less, and at last grow tiresome. In questions of taste, however, every one must determine for himself; and what is humour is as much a question of taste, as what is beauty. It is probable that the greatest part of those who have lavishly praised this work, spoke from their feeling; their praise, therefore, being only in proportion to their pleasure, was, with respect to them, just; but it has been censured rather from judgment than feeling, and as its *bad* is an object of judgment, though its *good* is an object of taste, it may certainly be determined how far this censure has been just. It has been charged with gross indecency, and the charge is certainly true; but indecency does no mischief, at least such indecency as is found in *Tristram Shandy*; it will disgust a delicate mind, but it will not sully a chaste one: It tends as little to inflame the passions as *Culpepper's Family Physician*; on the contrary, as nastiness is the strongest antidote to desire, many parts of the work in question, that have been most severely treated by moralists and divines, are less likely to do ill than good, as far as Chastity is immediately concerned. How far he is a friend to society, who lessens the power of the most important of all passions, by connecting disgustful images with its gratifications, is another question: Perhaps he will be found to deserve the thanks of virtue no better than he, who, to prevent gluttony, should prohibit the sale of any food till it had acquired a taste and smell that would substitute nausea for appetite.

He that would keep his relish of pleasure high, should not represent its objects in a ludicrous, much less in a disgusting light; whatever is made lightly familiar to the mind, insensibly loses its power over it, for the same reason that nakedness allures less in *Africa*, than apparel in *Europe*. He therefore that understands pleasure, will, in this respect, keep his conversation as pure as the Philosopher or Saint, which all dablers in bawdry and nastiness would do well to consider.

180

(d) Extract from an unsigned review by Ralph Griffiths (see No. 48c) in the *Monthly Review*, xxxvi (February 1767). 93–102

Several have compared Mr. Sterne, in his humorous capacity, to Cervantes; and others, with more propriety, to Rabelais; but they are all mistaken. The Reviewers have, at length, discovered his *real* proto-type,—HARLEQUIN.[1] Do you see the resemblance, Reader? if you do not, with a single glance of the mind's eye, perceive it, it would be an idle attempt for us to set about *making it out*;—you would, mean while, have a dull time of it: and we might lose our labour at last. To *us*, however, it is a clear case, that the *Reverend Tristram*, does not sound half so well as *Harlequin-Shandy*; and that, after all the scholia, commentaries and glossaries that have appeared, in order to explain the nature and design of these whimsical volumes, and to ascertain the class and order of literary composition to which they belong, we scruple not to affirm, that so motley a performance, taking the whole together, as far as the publication hath hitherto proceeded, can only be denominated the PANTOMIME OF LITERATURE. . . .

The volume opens with a *dedication*, to a great man:—and a *great man* he must be, indeed, who finds out the wit or the humour of this preliminary scrap. But, with this Merry-Andrew of a writer, the jest oftentimes consists only in his setting dull readers to work, in order to *find the jest out*: while he stands by, grinning like a satyr, and enjoying the fun of seeing them busily employed, like the wise men of Gotham, in dragging the fish-pond to get out the moon. . . .[2]

[The reviewer continues to comment on the book chapter by chapter, giving special praise to the apostrophe to Jenny in chapter 8:]

The allusion to the clouds, in the above reflection, is not wholly new; but the passage has something in it excessively striking! There is more poetry in those few lines, than in a dozen of the half-crown productions, miscalled POEMS, with which we are every month obliged to swell the catalogue-part of our Reviews. . . .

[1] See No. 13c, p. 77, n. 2.
[2] According to legend, the 'Wise Men of Gotham,' inhabitants of a village near Notting-ham, gained a reputation for being fools through a stratagem they employed when King John wished to establish a hunting preserve near their village. Foreseeing the ruinous cost of supporting the court, they convinced the king's messengers through their antics that they were all imbeciles and the king decided to have his hunting preserve elsewhere.

[The reviewer continues by pretending bafflement at the chronology of Sterne's story:]

What an intricate knot has this frolicksome Writer tied! There is no such thing as undoing it. The thread of his narrative of uncle Toby's courtship is so perplexingly entangled, by his unlucky transposition of the chapters, that we despair of unravelling it: some detached circumstances, however, may be acceptable to our Readers:—take them, then, zig-zag as they chance to drop out, while we *whir* the leaves backward and forward. . . .

Well! poor uncle Toby, after all, seems to make nothing of his widow. We shall leave him to carry on the siege in his own way; and try what other curiosities we can discover, while we wander through the other parts of this literary wilderness.

What a pretty, whimsical, affecting kind of episode has he introduced, in his chapter entitled INVOCATION! and which he has, with unusual propriety, begun with a very striking *invocation* to—But our Readers shall have the chapter entire, except the abrupt transition in the two last lines, which, in our opinion, serve but to *spoil all*, by an ill-tim'd stroke of levity; like a ludicrous epilogue, or ridiculous farce, unnaturally tagged to the end of a deep tragedy, only as it were, to efface every elevated, generous, or tender sentiment that might before have been excited by the nobler part of the evening's entertainment. . . .

[Quotes The Invocation from chapter 24, omitting the last sentence, and then goes on to comment on Sterne's apology for his two blank chapters:]

Very true! there are millions of folios, quartos, octavos, and duodecimos in the world, which are a thousand times worse than these thy inoffensive spotless pages; and well would it have been for thy reputation S—! had some scores of *thine* too, which are *not* blank, been left in the like state of primaeval innocence! . . .

[The reviewer continues to comment on individual chapters:]

Chap. xxxi. A very interesting conversation between Captain Shandy and Trim; in which the servant gives his master a very important hint, relating to the widow's conduct and views. There is more nature in this chapter, and more art in its composition, and more *delicacy*, than in any other part of the volume; but it would not appear to advantage enough to do justice to the Author, if extracted from the book:

those who have perused and attentively regarded all the preceding occurrences in the course of uncle Toby's courtship, can best judge of its merit.

The remainder of the volume affords nothing to blame, and almost as little to commend; if we except the story of the parish bull, in the last chapter,—which is dull, gross, and vulgar.—O what pity that Nature should thus capriciously have embroidered the choicest flowers of genius, on a paultry groundwork of buffoonry!

(e) Extract from a letter from an unidentified correspondent to *Lloyd's Evening Post*, xx (11–13 March 1767). 241

Nothing sure disgraces the present age more, than to see a Clergyman continuing to give us, without any animadversion, up to the *ninth* volume of a bawdy composition. The same hand, that one day gives us the most *pathetic* Sermons, the next gives us the most feeling compositions, to rouse our sensitive appetites; to inflame with lust, and debauch and corrupt our youth of both sexes. . . . Surely our Spiritual Rulers must *frown* at these things![1] As his own large stock of bawdy now seems to run low, and he has, I suppose, exhausted the new supplies he had brought with him from France and Spain, (where he went to recruit,) he is now, in this ninth volume, reduced to ransack into poor old antiquity; shewing, barefacedly, that he scorns Religion should be any check or restraint upon him. . . .

(f) Extract from the anonymous 'Journal of a Modern Man of Taste,' from *The Adventures of an Author*, in the *Gentleman's Magazine*, xxxvii (March 1767). 116

Oct. 2. Wait upon Lady L—, and find *Tristram Shandy* upon her toilet —She desires me to explain the stars. I excuse myself, by telling her

[1] A similar letter, denouncing Sterne and demanding he be censured, was sent by a group of 'well wishers' to Robert Drummond, Archbishop of York, but apparently nothing came of it. (See *Life*, pp. 423–4; *Letters*, pp. 300–1, 383.)

I have not read it, and ask her what she thinks of *Locke*?—She blushes—is confused—'and is surprised I should put so indecent a question to her.'[1]

53. The composition of *A Sentimental Journey*

1767-8

(a) Excerpt from Sterne's letter to his daughter Lydia, 23 February 1767 (*Letters*, p. 301)

I shall not begin my *Sentimental Journey* till I get to Coxwould[2]—I have laid a plan for something new, quite out of the beaten track.

(b) Excerpt from Sterne's letter to Thomas Becket, his London bookseller, 3 September 1767 (*Letters*, p. 393)

My *Sentimental Journey* goes on well—and some Genius[e]s in the North declare it an Original work, and likely to take in all Kinds of Readers—the proof of the pudding is in the eating.

[1] This brief passage is significant in revealing both the general ignorance of the influence of John Locke upon Sterne and the recognition of that influence by at least one critic.
[2] Sterne is writing to his daughter from London; he returned to Coxwold in late May.

(c) Excerpt from Sterne's letter, probably addressed to Sir William Stanhope, brother of the Earl of Chesterfield, 27 September 1767 (*Letters*, pp. 395–6)

[M]y *Sentimental Journey* will, I dare say, convince you that my feelings are from the heart, and that that heart is not of the worst of molds—praised be God for my sensibility! Though it has often made me wretched, yet I would not exchange it for all the pleasures the grossest sensualist ever felt.

(d) Excerpts from Richard Griffith, *A Series of Genuine Letters between Henry and Frances*, v (1770), all concerned with Griffith's meeting with Sterne in September 1767

Now we talk of Philosophy, the modern Democritus, Tristram Shandy, is here.[1] The Bishop has invited him, and introduced us to each other. He mentioned my Strictures on his Writings[2] to me, and said that they had hurt him a little at first, notwithstanding the fine Qualifications I had thrown in, in Compliment to his moral Character. But upon going through the Work, he confessed that he soon became reconciled to me, was sensible of a strong Sympathy of feeling coming upon him every Chapter, and said to himself, 'This Man, surely, hath no *Inimicability* in his Nature.'

He has communicated a Manuscript to us, that he means soon to publish. It is stiled a *Sentimental Journey through Europe*, by Yoric. It has all the Humour and Address of the best Parts of *Tristram*, and is quite free from the Grossness of the worst. There is but about Half a Volume wrote of it yet. He promises to spin the Idea through several Volumes, in the same chaste Way, and calls it his *Work of Redemption*; for he has but little Superstition to appropriated Expressions.

I think that [a] strong . . . Parallel might be drawn between this Person and one Alain, an antient Author of the thirteenth Century.[3]

[1] Sterne and Griffith were house guests of Dr Jemmett Browne, Bishop of Cork and Ross. Democritus (*c.* 460–*c.* 370 BC) was known as the 'Laughing Philosopher.'
[2] See No. 35. For Griffith's later forgery of Sterne's posthumous works, see No. 61.
[3] Alain de Lille (*c.* 1128–1203) was theologian, philosopher, historian, and poet. Baillet, Griffith's source (see below), erroneously gives 1294 as the date of Alain's death.

. . . I shall give you the Passage I allude to, out of Baillet's Characters of antient Writers, which I happened to bring down with me for Amusement on this Tour. [Griffith quotes with minor changes from Adrien Baillet, *Jugemens des Savans sur les Principaux Ouvrages des Auteurs* (1722), iv. 262–3, which I have translated as follows:] 'Barthius says that [Alain] shone forth almost alone in the midst of the darkness of his century. But he adds that one is still reduced today to asking what he meant to say in his works. One finds in them many stilted thoughts, in which there usually are doubly jumbled meanings, since he not only has failed to convey a meaning to his readers but probably did not understand the meaning himself—it is an almost impenetrable chaos. One can see the work clearly enough, however, to distinguish the character of a true sophist who wished to employ all the scholastic tricks. There are great nothings wrapped in studied obscurities.

His style is consonant with his matter—he has no rule, no method, no uniformity; he is puzzling, obscure, and completely irregular. The affectation of his figures and his flowers, which he doesn't know how to arrange, tries the reader's patience.

But, after all, he has a mind which is lively, bold, discerning, easy, and even agreeable, and which would have performed wonders with a bit more judgment and with the enlightenment of the last two centuries of criticism.'

I should not have sent you this Extract, if it had not been qualified by the first and last Paragraphs, and that the Characters of their Writings were not really so extremely alike. (pp. 83–5)

[In another letter dated 10 September 1767 Griffith describes a jocular compact with Sterne:]

Tristram and *Triglyph*[1] have entered into a League, offensive and defensive, together, against all Opponents in Literature. We have, at the same Time, agreed never to write any more *Tristrams* or *Triglyphs*. I am to stick to *Andrews*,[2] and he to Yoric. (p. 86)

[Writing some time later, Griffith recalled more of his conversations with Sterne at Scarborough:]

I shall take this Occasion of mentioning a Compliment paid me by Sterne. Upon looking through my Manuscripts lately at Scarborough, he collated some Passages out of his Writings and mine which agreed

---

[1] Griffith had used the pseudonym of 'Biograph Triglyph' for his novel *The Triumvirate*.
[2] Andrews is the good young man in Griffith's *The Triumvirate*.

in the same Sentiments, though differently expressed. This, said he, is not extraordinary, where Persons are apt to copy out of the same Original, namely, the humane and feeling heart. (p. 129)

[After Sterne's death Griffith again remembered his visit with Sterne and Sterne's talk of his friendship for Mrs Daniel Draper.][1]

[Sterne] was making every One a Confidant in that Platonic, I suppose, as he did me, on the Second Day of our Acquaintance. But, in truth, there was nothing in the Affair worth making a Secret of—The World that knew of their Correspondence, knew the worst of it, which was merely a simply Folly. Any other Idea of the Matter would be more than the most abandoned Vice could render probable. To intrigue with a Vampire! To sink into the Arms of *Death alive*! (pp. 199–200)

(e) Extract from Sterne's letter to his close friend Mrs William James, 12 November 1767 (*Letters*, pp. 400–1)

My *Sentimental Journey* will please Mrs. J[ames], and my Lydia—I can answer for those two. It is a subject which works well, and suits the frame of mind I have been in for some time past—I told you my design in it was to teach us to love the world and our fellow creatures better than we do—so it runs most upon those gentler passions and affections, which aid so much to it.

---

[1] Sterne met Mrs Daniel Draper (*née* Elizabeth Sclater) (1744–78) during January of 1767 while she was on a visit to England from India. Sterne's wife had elected in 1764 to remain in the south of France after Sterne's second Continental tour. Sterne began a sentimental flirtation with Mrs Draper similar to those he had carried on before with other women; but, worn out in body and spirit, he was pulled more deeply into this friendship with his Eliza (sometimes called his Bramine) than he had ever been before. 'My wife cannot live long . . . and I know not the woman I should like so well for her substitute as yourself,' he wrote two months after meeting Mrs Draper (*Letters*, p. 319). Yet he thought of the relationship at least partly as contributing to his literary projects, and compared Eliza to Swift's Stella and Waller's Sacharissa (see ibid.). After Mrs Draper's return to India in April at her husband's summons, Sterne began a *Journal to Eliza* (not published until 1904), which makes an interesting companion piece to the *Sentimental Journey*, showing in less polished and less controlled form some of the emotions that were refined and subtilized in his travels. Some later critics seized upon Sterne's relationship with Eliza (illustrated through both genuine and forged letters) to attack his moral character, as well as his sentimental philosophy; while other writers, seizing upon the Romantic melancholy of the situation and the delicacy of Sterne's emotions, praised Sterne's sensibility and tried to imitate it. As Griffith insists, the relationship was obviously innocent, though more important to Sterne than a mere flirtation.

(f) Extract from Sterne's letter to a lady identified only as Hannah, 15 November 1767 (*Letters*, p. 401)

—but I have something else for you, which I am fabricating at a great rate, & that is my *Journey*, which shall make you cry as much as ever it made me laugh—or I'll give up the Business of sentimental writing —& write to the Body.

(g) Extract from Sterne's letter to an unidentified nobleman, 28 November 1767 (*Letters*, pp. 402–3)

'Tis with the greatest pleasure I take my pen to thank your Lordship for your letter of enquiry about Yorick—he has worn out both his spirits and body with the *Sentimental Journey*—'tis true that an author must feel himself, or his reader will not—but I have torn my whole frame into pieces by my feelings—I believe the brain stands as much in need of recruiting as the body—therefore I shall set out for town the twentieth of next month, after having recruited myself a week at York.—I might indeed solace myself with my wife, (who is come from France) but in fact I have long been a sentimental being—whatever your Lordship may think to the contrary.—The world has imagined, because I wrote *Tristram Shandy*, that I was myself more Shandean than I really ever was—'tis a good-natured world we live in, and we are often painted in divers colours according to the ideas each one frames in his head. . . .

I hope my book will please you, my Lord, and then my labour will not be totally in vain. If it is not thought a chaste book, mercy on them that read it, for they must have warm imaginations indeed!

(h) Extract from Sterne's letter to Sir George Macartney, 3 December 1767 (*Letters*, p. 405). Sterne had met the young Macartney (1737–1806) in 1762 at Paris before the start of the latter's long and varied career in government and politics

In three weeks I shall kiss your hand—and sooner, if I can finish my *Sentimental Journey*.—The duce take all sentiments! I wish there was not one in the world!—My wife is come to pay me a sentimental visit as far as from Avignon—and the *politesses* arising from such a proof of her urbanity, has robb'd me of a month's writing, or I had been in town now.—I am going to ly-in; being at Christmas at my full reckoning—and unless what I shall bring forth is not *press'd* to death by these devils of printers, I shall have the honour of presenting to you a *couple of as clean brats* as ever chaste brain conceiv'd—they are frolicksome too, *mais cela n'empeche pas*—[1]

(i) Extract from Sterne's letter to a friend who cannot be identified with certainty, (?)17 February 1768 (*Letters*, p. 412)

I will send you a set of my books—they will take with the generality— the women will read this book in the parlour, and *Tristram* in the bed-chamber.[2]

(j) Extract from 'In the Street. Calais,' *A Sentimental Journey*, pp. 114–20

Lord! said I, hearing the town clock strike four, and recollecting that I had been little more than a single hour in Calais—

—What a large volume of adventures may be grasped within this little span of life by him who interests his heart in every thing, and who, having eyes to see,[3] what time and chance are perpetually holding

---

[1] But that is no hindrance.
[2] Cf. No. 2a, p.41, n. 3.
[3] Cf. Matthew, 13: 13; Mark, 8: 18; and Luke, 8: 10. See also Psalms, 115: 4–8; 135: 15–18; Jeremiah, 5: 21; Ezekiel, 12: 2.

out to him as he journeyeth on his way, misses nothing he can *fairly* lay his hands on.—

—If this won't turn out something—another will—no matter— 'tis an assay upon human nature—I get my labour for my pains—'tis enough—the pleasure of the experiment has kept my senses, and the best part of my blood awake, and laid the gross to sleep.

I pity the man who can travel from *Dan* to *Beersheba*,[1] and cry, 'Tis all barren—and so it is; and so is all the world to him who will not cultivate the fruits it offers. I declare, said I, clapping my hands chearily together, that was I in a desart, I would find out wherewith in it to call forth my affections—If I could not do better, I would fasten them upon some sweet myrtle, or seek some melancholy cypress to connect myself to—I would court their shade, and greet them kindly for their protection—I would cut my name upon them, and swear they were the loveliest trees throughout the desert: if their leaves wither'd, I would teach myself to mourn, and when they rejoiced, I would rejoice along with them.

The learned SMELFUNGUS[2] travelled from Boulogne to Paris— from Paris to Rome—and so on—but he set out with the spleen and jaundice, and every object he pass'd by was discoloured or distorted— He wrote an account of them, but 'twas nothing but the account of his miserable feelings.

I met Smelfungus in the grand portico of the Pantheon[3]—he was just coming out of it—'*Tis nothing but a huge cock-pit*,[4] said he—I wish you had said nothing worse of the Venus of Medicis, replied I—for in passing through Florence, I had heard he had fallen foul upon the goddess, and used her worse than a common strumpet, without the least provocation in nature.[5]

I popp'd upon Smelfungus again at Turin, in his return home; and a sad tale of sorrowful adventures had he to tell, 'wherein he spoke of

[1] That is, from one end of a country to the other; Dan was at the northern boundary of the Holy Land, Beersheba at the southern boundary. Cf. Judges, 20: 1; II Samuel, 24: 2; I Chronicles, 21: 2.
[2] Sterne's uncomplimentary name for novelist Tobias Smollett, whose *Travels through France and Italy* (1766) are alluded to in the preceding and following paragraphs.
[3] Sterne probably met Smollett in Montpellier in November 1763, although Smollett had returned to England when Sterne arrived in Italy in November 1765.
[4] Vide S—'s Travels. [Sterne's note.] See Tobias Smollett, *Travels through France and Italy*, ed. Thomas Seccombe (1935), pp. 268–9.
[5] See ibid., pp. 235–6. Smollett saw 'no beauty in the features of Venus' but praised its 'symmetry' and asserted that 'the back parts . . . are executed so happily, as to excite the admiration of the most indifferent spectator.'

moving accidents by flood and field, and of the cannibals which each other eat: the Anthropophagi'—he had been flea'd alive, and be-devil'd, and used worse than St. Bartholomew, at every stage he had come at—[1]

—I'll tell it, cried Smelfungus, to the world. You had better tell it, said I, to your physician.

Mundungus,[2] with an immense fortune, made the whole tour; going on from Rome to Naples—from Naples to Venice—from Venice to Vienna—to Dresden, to Berlin, without one generous connection or pleasurable anecdote to tell of; but he had travell'd straight on looking neither to his right hand or his left, lest Love or Pity should seduce him out of his road.

Peace be to them! if it is to be found; but heaven itself, was it possible to get there with such tempers, would want objects to give it—every gentle spirit would come flying upon the wings of Love to hail their arrival—Nothing would the souls of Smelfungus and Mundungus hear of, but fresh anthems of joy, fresh raptures of love, and fresh congratulations of their common felicity—I heartily pity them: they have brought up no faculties for this work; and was the happiest mansion in heaven to be allotted to Smelfungus and Mundungus, they would be so far from being happy, that the souls of Smelfungus and Mundungus would do penance there to all eternity. (Vol. I, pp. 83–9)

(k) Excerpt from 'The Passport. Versailles,' *A Sentimental Journey*, pp. 216–19

The Count led the discourse: we talk'd of indifferent things;—of books and politicks, and men—and then of women—God bless them all! said I, after much discourse about them—there is not a man upon earth who loves them so much as I do: after all the foibles I have seen, and all the satires I have read against them, still I love them; being

[1] Sterne satirizes Smollett's account of his difficulties in traveling from Turin to Nice (ibid., pp. 315ff.) by paraphrasing *Othello*, act 1, sc. 3, ll. 134–45. St Bartholomew, one of the twelve apostles, according to tradition was flayed alive and crucified in Armenia.

[2] Mundungus was identified by Cross (*Life*, p. 461) as Dr Samuel Sharp (1700(?)–78), author of *Letters from Italy* (1766); but Stout (*A Sentimental Journey*, p. 119 n.) thinks the identification unlikely. The important point, of course, is the contrast in views of traveling between Mundungus and Sterne rather than any specific satire.

firmly persuaded that a man who has not a sort of an affection for the whole sex, is incapable of ever loving a single one as he ought.

Hèh bien! Monsieur l'Anglois,[1] said the Count, gaily—You are not come to spy the nakedness of the land[2]—I believe you—*ni encore*,[3] I dare say, *that* of our women—But permit me to conjecture—if, *par hazard*,[4] they fell in your way—that the prospect would not affect you.

I have something within me which cannot bear the shock of the least indecent insinuation: in the sportability of chit-chat I have often endeavoured to conquer it, and with infinite pain have hazarded a thousand things to a dozen of the sex together—the least of which I could not venture to a single one, to gain heaven.

Excuse me, Monsieur Le Count, said I—as for the nakedness of your land, if I saw it, I should cast my eyes over it with tears in them—and for that of your women (blushing at the idea he had excited in me) I am so evangelical in this, and have such a fellow-feeling for what ever is *weak* about them, that I would cover it with a garment, if I knew how to throw it on—But I could wish, continued I, to spy the *nakedness* of their hearts, and through the different disguises of customs, climates, and religion, find out what is good in them, to fashion my own by— and therefore am I come.

It is for this reason, Monsieur le Compte, continued I, that I have not seen the Palais royal[5]—nor the Luxembourg—nor the Façade of the Louvre—nor have attempted to swell the catalogues we have of pictures, statues, and churches—I conceive every fair being as a temple, and would rather enter in, and see the original drawings and loose sketches hung up in it, than the transfiguration of Raphael itself.[6]

The thirst of this, continued I, as impatient as that which inflames the breast of the connoisseur, has led me from my own home into France—and from France will lead me through Italy—'tis a quiet journey of the heart in pursuit of NATURE, and those affections which rise out of her, which make us love each other—and the world, better than we do. (Vol. II, pp. 64–8)

[1] Well, my English friend.
[2] Cf. Genesis, 42: 9.
[3] Nor.
[4] By chance.
[5] Sterne mentions buildings and collections of art that the visitor to Paris would be expected to see.
[6] Raphael's 'The Transfiguration,' in the Vatican, has sometimes been called the greatest picture in the world.

54. John Hall-Stevenson on Sterne

January 1768

'Fable IV. The Black Bird,' from *Makarony Fables* (1768), 2nd ed., pp. 16–18.

Hall-Stevenson (1718–85), the Eugenius of *Tristram Shandy*, was owner of Skelton Castle, which had a library of rare and curious lore, available to Sterne. Hall-Stevenson was also host to the Demoniacs, a convivial group to which Sterne belonged. In the fable below, Sterne is, of course, the black bird who fights gloom, hypocrisy, and authoritarianism.

In concert with the curfew bell,
An Owl was chaunting Vespers in his cell;
Upon the outside of the wall,
A Black Bird, famous in that age;
From a bow window in the hall,
Hung dangling in a wicker cage;
Instead of psalmody and pray'rs,
Like those good children of St. Francis;
He secularized all his airs,
And took delight in Wanton Fancies.
Whilst the bell toll'd, and the Owl chaunted,
Every thing was calm and still;
All nature seem'd rapp'd and enchanted,
Except the querelous, unthankful rill;
Unawed by this imposing scene,
Our Black Bird the enchantment broke;
Flourish'd a sprightly air between,
And whistled the Black Joke.
This lively unexpected motion,
Set nature in a gayer light;
Quite over-turn'd the Monks devotion,
    And scatter'd all the gloom of night.

I have been taught in early youth,
By an expert Metaphysician;
That ridicule's the test of truth,
And only match for superstition.
Imposing rogues, with looks demure,
At Rome keep all the world in awe;
Wit is profane, learning impure,
And reasoning against the Law;
Between two tapers and a book,
Upon a dresser clean and neat,
Behold a sacerdotal Cook,
Cooking a dish of heavenly meat!
How fine he curtsies! Make your bow,
Thump your breast soundly, beat your poll;
Lo! he has toss'd up a Ragout,
To fill the belly of your soul.
Even here there are some holy men,
Would fain lead people by the nose;
Did not a Black Bird now and then,
         Benevolently interpose.
My good Lord Bishop, Mr. Dean,
You shall get nothing by your spite;
Tristram shall whistle at your spleen,
And put Hypocrisy to flight.

55. Sterne and an American admirer

1767–8

(a) Letter, undated, from Dr John Eustace, a physician in Wilmington, North Carolina, to Sterne, accompanying the present of a 'shandean' walking stick (*Letters*, pp. 403–4)

Sir,—When I assure you, that I am a very great admirer of Tristram Shandy, and have been, ever since his introduction to the world, one of his most zealous defenders against the repeated assaults of prejudice and misapprehension, I hope you will not treat my unexpected appearance in his company as an intrusion. You know it is an observation as remarkable for its truth as its antiquity, that a similitude of sentiments is the general parent of friendship.[1] It cannot be wondered at, that I should conceive an esteem for a person whom nature had most indulgently enabled to frisk and curvet with ease through all the intricacies of sentiment, which, from irrisistible propensity, she had compelled me to trudge through without merit or distinction.

The only reason that gave rise to this adress to you, is my accidentally having met with a piece of shandean statuary—I mean, according to the vulgar opinion; for, to such judges, both appear equally destitute of regularity or design. It was made by a very ingenious gentleman of this province, and presented to the late Governor Dobbs;[2] after his death, Mrs. Dobbs gave it to me. Its singularity made many very desirious of procuring it, but I had resolved, at first, not to part with it, till, upon reflection, I thought it would be a very proper, and probably not an unacceptable compliment to my favourite author, and, in his hands might prove as ample a field for meditation as a buttonhole or a broomstick.[3]

I am, &c.,
JOHN EUSTACE.

---

[1] Cf. Sallust, *Catilina*, 20, 4.
[2] Arthur Dobbs (1689–1765) was appointed governor of North Carolina in 1754.
[3] See *Tristram Shandy*, IX. 14, p. 617, and Jonathan Swift, 'A Meditation upon a Broom-Stick' (1710).

I this moment received your obliging letter, and *shandean* piece of sculpture along with it; of both which testimonies of your regard I have the justest sense, and return you, dear sir, my best thanks and acknowledgments. Your walking stick is in no sense more *shandaic* than in that of its having *more handles than one*—The parallel breaks only in this, that in using the stick, every one will take the handle which suits his convenience. In *Tristram Shandy*, the handle is taken which suits their passions, their ignorance or sensibility. There is so little true feeling in the *herd* of the *world*, that I wish I could have got an act of parliament, when the books first appear'd, 'that none but wise men should look into them.' It is too much to write books and find heads to understand them. The world, however, seems to come into a better temper about them, the people of genius here being, to a man, on its side, and the reception it has met with in France, Italy and Germany, hath engag'd one part of the world to give it a second reading, and the other part of it, in order to be on the strongest side, have at length agreed to speak well of it too. A few Hypocrites and Tartufe's, whose approbation could do it nothing but dishonor, remain unconverted.

I am very proud, sir, to have had a man, like you, on my side from the beginning; but it is not in the power of any one to taste humor, however he may wish it—'tis the gift of God—and besides, a true feeler always brings half the entertainment along with him. His own ideas are only call'd forth by what he reads, and the vibrations within, so entirely correspond with those excited, 'tis like reading *himself* and not the *book*.

A SENTIMENTAL JOURNEY

(1768)

56. Reviews of the *Sentimental Journey*

Spring 1768

(a) Extract from an unsigned review in the *Critical Review*, xxv (March 1768). 181–5

Our Sentimentalist having lately made a journey to that country *from whose bourne no traveller returns*,[1] his memory claims at least as much indulgence as our duty to the public permitted us to allow him when alive. —*De mortuis nil nisi bonum*,[2] said the traveller, when the landlord asked his opinion of his dead small-beer; and if substituting immorality, impudence, and dulness, in the room of virtue, decency, and wit, can recommend a publication, that before us is respectable.[3] What a pity it was that Yorick with his health lost that spirit which rendered him a favourite with thoughtless insipidity, and the dictator of lewdness and dissipation! What a pity it is that he survived his art of imposing upon his countrymen *whim* for *sentiment*, and *caprice* for *humour*! In short, we must do that justice to his memory to say, that he has not left his fellow behind him; and we shall not be at all surprized, if some honest bacchanals should form themselves into a society of Shandyists, and out-rival the lodges of the Bloods, Bucks, and other choice spirits.

Mr. Yorick has, in imitation of some celebrated authors, distinguished his chapters under particular titles, which form their chief contents. His first is termed *Calais*, where all we understand is, that he became the ideal king of France by the help of a bottle of Burgundy.

---

[1] *Hamlet*, act 3, sc. 1, ll. 79–80.
[2] Speak nothing but good of the dead.
[3] Though Smollett's connection with the *Critical* had long since ceased, the savageness of this review is probably due in part to Sterne's attack on Smelfungus (see No. 53 j).

The three or four following chapters have the title of *The Monk*, in which he has taken great pains to draw the figure of a monk who had come to beg charity of him for his convent, but received nothing from our author's benevolence. Half of the first volume has whimsical titles of the same kind prefixed to the chapters; from all of which we only learn, that the author hired a post-chaise, and set out in a delirium, which appears never to have left him to the end of his journey; a fatal symptom of his approaching dissolution. It had, however, the happy temporary effect of making the sufferings of others the objects of his mirth, and not only rendering him insensible to the feelings of humanity, but superior to every regard for taste, truth, observation, or reflection.

[The reviewer goes on to quote from the passage in which La Fleur is hired: 'Montriul,' *Sentimental Journey*, pp. 121–7.]

Who does not see that this character of La Fleur is pieced out with shreds which Mr. Yorick has barbarously cut out and unskilfully put together from other novels?

Having thus given the most intelligible and commendable specimen which these travels afford, we should trespass upon the reader's patience, as well as the decency we owe towards the public, should we follow our Sentimentalist through the rest of his journey, which is calculated to instruct young travellers in what the author meant for the *bon ton* of pleasure and licentiousness.

(b) Extract from an unsigned notice in the *London Magazine*, xxxvii (March 1768). 163

This is the beginning of a work which death has commanded never to be finished—The author's great talents notwithstanding his disregard of order, are universally known, and though some illiberal pen has meanly endeavoured to injure his reputation, by hinting his want of wisdom,[1] still we may say in his own words at the conclusion of Lefevre's story, that if the accusing spirit flies up to heaven's chancery with his indiscretions, it will blush to give them in, and we doubt not, but the recording angel in writing them down will drop a tear upon each, and wash it away for ever.

[1] See No. 58c.

(c) Extract from Ralph Griffiths's unsigned, two-part review in the *Monthly Review*, xxxviii (March, April 1768). 174–85, 309–19

Of all the various productions of the press, none are so eagerly received by us Reviewers, and other people who stay at home and mind our business, as the writings of travellers;—over whom, by the way, we readers have prodigious advantage; for *they* undergo the fatigue, inconvenience, and expence, while *we*, in all the plenitude of leisure and an elbow-chair, enjoy the pleasure and the profit, at so small a charge as—the price of the book. Why here, now, we have many dozens of shrewd observations and choice sentiments, the *ground*work of which must have cost our friend Yorick many a bright glittering guinea. . . .

The journey of our sentimental traveller commences with his voyage to Calais; where his portmanteau, containing half a dozen shirts and 'a black pair of silk breeches,' furnishes occasion for some pathetic reflections on the *droits d'aubaine*:[1]—by the way, though, cousin Yorick, a 'black pair'—is not quite so accurately expressed;—not that we should have minded it, if you had not repeated the slip, more than once: and talked, moreover, of a lady's 'black pair of silk gloves.'—But now, while the *fescue* is pointed at this slip, we would just hint another correction, equally *important*—were we but sure you would not mistake the matter, and suppose we intended any thing like a criticism. You smile! thank you, Dear Coz. for the obliging *sentiment* implied in that smile. Without further hesitation, then, take it:—Why will you deign to adopt the vulgarisms of a city *news-writer*? 'I *laid* at their mercy;' laid *what*, an egg or a wager? 'a man who values a good night's rest will not *lay* down [what? his pipe or his spectacles?] with enmity in his heart—.' 'But Maria should *lay* in my bosom:'[2] our Readers may possibly conclude that Maria was the name of a favourite *pullet*; and the mistake may be excusable: for how can they suppose it possible for one of our first-rate pens to write such English?—But, away with these pitiful *minutiae*!—Behold a nobler object. What an affecting, touching, masterly picture is here! 'Tis The *monk-scene,*—Calais. . . .

Now, Reader, did we not tell thee, in a former Review,[3] (somewhat

[1] The right under French law of the French king to seize all the possessions of a foreigner who died in France.
[2] The passages referred to are on pp. 216, 244, and 275 of Stout's edition.
[3] See No. 48c, Griffiths's review of vols VII and VIII of *Tristram Shandy*; cf. No. 34d, Langhorne's review of vols V and VI.

less than half a century ago) that the highest excellence of this genuine, this legitimate son of humour, lies not in his humorous but in his pathetic vein?—If we have not already given proofs and specimens enough, in support of this opinion, from his *Shandy*, his *Sermons*, and these *Travels*, we could produce more from the little volume before us. . . .

[The following excerpts are from the April issue; the March article was written before Sterne's death.]

'Alas poor Yorick!—a fellow of infinite jest; of most excellent fancy;—Where be your gibes now? your gambols? your songs? your flashes of merriment that were wont to set the table in a roar?'[1] Poor Yorick! Little did we imagine, while lately indulging the play of fancy, in a review of thy Sentimental Journey, that thou wert then setting out on thy last journey, to that far country from whose bourn no traveller returns![2] Little did we think that in those very moments, so grateful, so pleasant to us, thou thyself wert expiring on the bed of mortal pain,— breathing out thy once mirthful soul, and resigning all thy jocund faculties to the ruthless tyrant with whom *there is no* JESTING:—alas, poor Yorick!

But it is not our present purpose to attempt the elegy of this deceased, this lamented son of HUMOUR.—We stand engaged for an account of the second volume of his sentimental rambles,—his last, in our judgment, his best production:—though not, perhaps, the most admired of his works. . . .

[Griffiths begins his account of volume II by quoting 'The Fille de Chambre. Paris,' pp. 187–91.]

What delicacy of feeling, what tenderness of sentiment, yet what simplicity of expression are here! Is it *possible* that a man of *gross ideas* could ever *write* in a strain so pure, so refined from the dross of sensuality! . . .

Travellers in ordinary, or *ordinary travellers*, would have told us how many statues and pictures they met with in their visit to the capital of France; and who chizel'd the one, and pencil'd the other: but the genius of Yorick was superior to such uninteresting details. . . .

In these slight but natural traits, the agreeable though unsubstantial characteristics of the French, may be seen in a truer light, than in the

[1] *Hamlet*, act 5, sc. 1
[2] See No. 56a, p. 197, n. 1.

laboured drawings of more serious travellers.—In the next extract we have a striking picture of human nature, in a simpler garb, and more primitive appearance: it exhibits a scene which occurred in Yorick's journey from France to Italy. . . .

[Griffiths quotes 'The Supper' and 'The Grace,' pp. 280–4.]

There is something in the *grace* of these good people of the mountain, which to the less lively piety of a saturnine Englishman, may perhaps prove rather offensive than edifying; but to the native happy complexion of a truly innocent and virtuous mind, cherished and warmed in the sunshine of a more chearful climate, such natural modes of expressing the grateful hilarity of a good heart, may be far from disagreeable.—O! that there were nothing more justly reprehensible in the effusions of this extraordinary pen! But so it is, and so it ever was with poor Yorick; who could never take leave of his readers without some pleasantry of the *lower species*. Thus the volume before us concludes with a dash of *somewhat* bordering rather on sensuality than sentiment. Another widow is introduced, and another *fille de chambre*; and the Author abruptly breaks off in the middle of a night-scene at an inn in the road to Turin.—A ludicrous *hiatus* ends the book; which the whimsical Writer had scarce closed before the fatal *hiatus* of DEATH put at once a final period to the ramblings and the writings of the inimitable LAURENCE STERNE;—to whom we must now bid eternal adieu!—Farewell, then, admirable Yorick! Be thy wit, thy benevolence, and every blameless part of thy *life* and thy *works*, remembered:—but, on the imperfections of *both*, 'MAY THE RECORDING ANGEL DROP A TEAR, AND BLOT THEM OUT FOR EVER!'

(d) Unsigned notice in the *Political Register*, ii (May 1768). 383

Justly esteemed the best of the late Mr. Sterne's ingenious performances. To that original vein of humour which was so natural to him, and which constitutes the chief merit of his works, he has here added the moral and the pathetic; so that even while he is entertaining (as he always is) we are agreeably instructed, and our passions are sometimes touched with the strongest sensations of pity and tenderness.

57. Some private opinions of the *Sentimental Journey*

Spring 1768

(a) Extract from a letter from Horace Walpole to the poet Thomas Gray, 8 March 1768 (*Horace Walpole's Correspondence with Thomas Gray*, ed. W. S. Lewis, George L. Lam, and Charles H. Bennett (1948), ii. 183)

I think you will like Sterne's sentimental travels, which though often tiresome, are exceedingly good-natured and picturesque.

(b) Extract from a letter from Horace Walpole to George Montagu, 12 March 1768 (*Horace Walpole's Correspondence with George Montagu*, ed. W. S. Lewis and Ralph S. Brown, Jr (1941), ii. 255)

Sterne has published two little volumes, called, *Sentimental Travels*. They are very pleasing, though too much dilated, and infinitely preferable to his tiresome *Tristram Shandy*, of which I never could get through three volumes.[1] In these there is great good nature and strokes of delicacy.

(c) Extract from a letter from Joseph Cockfield to the Reverend Weeden Butler, 19 March 1768 (quoted in John Nichols, *Illustrations of the Literary History of the Eighteenth Century* (1817–58), v (1828). 780)

I have seen the reverend Prebendary's new publication; in his former writings I saw evident marks of his genius and benevolence, but who

[1] See No. 8.

that indulges serious reflection can read his obscenity and ill-applied passages of Holy Scripture, without horror![1]

(d) Extract from a letter from Elizabeth Carter to Mrs Elizabeth Vesey, 19 April 1768 (*A Series of Letters between Mrs. Elizabeth Carter and Miss Catherine Talbot*, ed. the Reverend Montagu Pennington (1809), iii. 334–5)

I thought the tone of one paragraph in your Letter did not seem your own, even before you gave me an intimation that it belonged to the Sentimental Traveller, whom I neither have read nor probably ever shall; for indeed there is something shocking in whatever I have heard either of the author, or of his writings. It is the fashion, I find, to extol him for his benevolence, a word so wretchedly misapplied, and so often put as a substitute for virtue, that one is quite sick of hearing it repeated either by those who have no ideas at all, or by those who have none but such as confound all differences of right and wrong. Merely to be struck by a sudden impulse of compassion at the view of an object of distress, is no more benevolence than it is a fit of the gout, and indeed has a nearer relation to the last than the first. Real benevolence would never suffer a husband and a father to neglect and injure those whom the ties of nature, the order of Providence, and the general sense of mankind have entitled to his first regards. Yet this unhappy man, by his carelessness and extravagance, has left a wife and child to starve, or to subsist on the precarious bounty of others.[2]

[1] Butler (1742–1823) was the amanuensis of William Dodd, the notorious fashionable preacher who was hanged for forgery in 1777.
[2] Misconceptions about Sterne's treatment of his wife and daughter persisted until the publication of Mrs Medalle's edition of her father's letters in 1775 and even until Percy Fitzgerald's *Life of Sterne* in 1864. Elizabeth Carter (1717–1806), poetess, Greek scholar, and letter-writer, was the friend of such notables as Johnson, Burke, Reynolds, Richardson, and Walpole. Mrs Vesey (1715(?)–91), one of the Bluestocking coterie, was famous for her London literary parties.

(e) Remarks of Mrs Elizabeth Burney, Fanny Burney's step-mother, and Mrs Fanny Greville, wife of (Richard) Fulke Greville, MP and man about town, and godmother to Fanny Burney, probably during the spring of 1768, as reported by Fanny Burney, Mme D'Arblay (Frances Burney D'Arblay, *Memoirs of Doctor Burney* (1832), i. 201)

Mrs. Greville, as was peculiarly in her power, took the lead, and bore the burthen of the conversation; which chiefly turned upon Sterne's *Sentimental Journey*, at that time the reigning reading in vogue: but when the new Mrs. Burney recited, with animated encomiums, various passages of Sterne's seducing sensibility, Mrs. Greville, shrugging her shoulders, exclaimed: 'A feeling heart is certainly a right heart; nobody will contest that: but when a man chooses to walk about the world with a cambrick handkerchief always in his hand, that he may always be ready to weep, either with man or beast,—he only turns me sick.'

58. Comments and tributes on Sterne's death

1768

(a) 'On the Death of Yorick,' by an anonymous versifier, dated 25 March 1768 and contributed to the *London Magazine*, xxxvii (June 1768). 323

With wit and genuine humour to dispel,
From the desponding bosom, glooming care,
And bid the gushing tear, at the sad tale
Of hapless love or filial grief, to flow,
From the full sympathising heart, were thine

These pow'rs, O Sterne! But now thy fate demands
(No plumage nodding o'er the emblazon'd hearse,
Proclaiming honours, where no virtue shone)
But the sad tribute of the heart felt sigh.
What, though no taper cast its deadly ray,
Or the full choir sing requiems o'er thy tomb,
The humbler grief of friendship is not mute.
And poor Maria, with her faithful kid,
Her auburn tresses carelessly entwin'd
With olive foliage, at the close of day
Shall chant her plaintive vespers at thy grave.
Thy shade too, gentle monk, 'mid awful night,
Shall pour libations from its friendly eye;
For erst his sweet benevolence bestow'd
Its generous pity, and bedew'd with tears
The sod, which rested on thy aged breast.[1]

(b) Extract from a letter from William Warburton to Charles
Yorke, 4 April 1768 (*Letters from . . . Dr. Warburton . . . to the Hon.
Charles Yorke* (1812), p. 89)

Poor Sterne, whom the papers tell us is just dead, was the idol of the
higher mob. . . . He found a strong disposition in the many to laugh
away life; and . . . he chose the office of common jester to the many.
But what is hard, he never will obtain the frivolous end he aimed at, the
reputation of a wit, though at the expence of his character, as a man, a
scholar, and a clergyman. . . . He chose Swift for his model: but
Swift was either luckier or wiser, who so managed his wit, that he will
never pass with posterity for a buffoon; while Sterne gave such a loose
to his buffoonery, that he will never pass for a wit.[2]

---

[1] This poem was reprinted in Mrs Medalle's edition of her father's *Letters* in 1775 and often
thereafter in editions of Sterne's *Works*.
[2] For Warburton's earlier remarks, see No. 16.

(c) Anonymous 'Lines on the Death of YORICK' quoted in the
Gentleman's Magazine, xxxviii (April 1768). 191

Wit, humour, genius, thou hadst, all agree;
One grain of *Wisdom* had been worth all three.[1]

(d) Extract from the anonymous pamphlet 'The Fig Leaf—Veni,
Vidi, Vici, Ivi; or, He's Gone! Who? Yorick! Grim Death
Appears!', listed in the *Monthly Review* for April 1768, pp. 5–6

Yorick dead! which part of him pray—his buckram jerkin—or the
lining of sarsenet?—It must be the jerkin: the other can never die—His
fame for odity will survive the dissolution of time into eternity. . . .
   [B]eing dead, he is praised by those who condemned him living,
and dispraised by those who were his professed admirers.[2]

(e) Extract from the anonymous poem 'Occasional Verses on the
Death of Mr. Sterne,' listed in the *Monthly Review* for August 1768

He felt for man—nor dropt a fruitless tear,
But kindly strove the drooping heart to chear;
For this, the flowers by SHILOH'S brook that blow,
He wove with those that round LYCAEUM grow;[3]
For this, EUPHROSYNE'S[4] heart-easing draught
He stole, and ting'd with wit and pleasing thought;

---

[1] The anonymous correspondent who quoted these lines went on to write an earnest set
of verses to refute them.
[2] This rambling, irreverent twenty-one page pamphlet ends by drawing the character of
Yorick according to the twelve signs of the zodiac. For Sterne's reference to his jerkin
see No. 27a.
[3] In other words, Sterne united the Biblical and classical traditions, blending sentiment and
reason. Shiloh means 'tranquility' and was a place identified with worship and religious
contemplation. The writer may also be thinking of the waters of Shiloah, a soft flowing
stream. Lycaeum was the place where Aristotle taught.
[4] Joy, one of the three graces, goddesses of charm and beauty.

For this, with Humour's necromantic charm,
Death saw him Sorrow, Spleen, and Care disarm:
With dread he saw—th' associates of his might
Foil'd and expell'd the regions of the light;
'If so,' he cry'd, and seiz'd his sharpest dart,
'My reign may end,'—then wing'd it at his heart.

    If faults he had—for none exempt we find,
They, like his virtues, were of gentlest kind;
Such as arise from genius in excess,
Passions too fine, that wound—ev'n while they bless!
Such as a form so captivating wear,
If faults, we doubt—and, to call crimes—we fear;
Such as, let Envy sift, let Malice fan,
Will only shew that YORICK was a MAN.

(f) Extract from a letter written by Mrs Elizabeth Montagu, probably in 1768 (*Letters*, pp. 440-1)

Poor Tristram Shandy had an appearance of philanthropy that pleased one, and made one forgive in some degree his errors. However, as I think, there is but one way of a mans proving his philanthropy to be real and genuine, and that is by making every part of his conduct of good example to mankind in general and of good effect towards those with whom he is connected. If Tristram gave an ill example to the Clergy, if he rendered his wife and daughter unhappy, we must mistake good humour for good nature. By many humble addresses, he forced me to take some kind of civil notice of him; I assure you his witt never attoned with me for the indecency of his writings, nor could the quintessence of all the witt extracted from all the most celebrated beaux esprits that ever existed, make amends for one obscure period. There are but two kinds of people that I think myself at liberty to hate and despise, the first is of the class of soi disant philosophers, who by sophistry would cheat the less acute out of their principles of religion, the only firm basis of moral virtue; the second are witts who ridicule whatsoever things are lovely, whatsoever things are of good report.[1] The lowest animal in society is a Buffoon. He willingly degrades himself in the rank of rational Being, assumes

[1] Philippians, 4:8.

a voluntary inferiority of soul, defaces the Divine image in his mind to put on the monkey and the ape, and is guilty of spiritual bestiality. Poor Tristrams last performance was the best, his sentimental journey would not have misbecome a young Ensign. I cannot say it was suitable to his serious profession. I used to talk in this severe manner to him, and he would shed penetent tears, which seem'd to shew he erred from levity, not malice, and the great who encourage such writings are most to blame, for they seduce the frail witt to be guilty of these offences, but we are now a Nation of Sybarites who promise rewards only to such as invent some new pleasure.[1]

(g) David Garrick, 'Epitaph on Laurence Sterne,' probably composed in 1768 (*The Poetical Works of David Garrick* (1785), ii. 484)

> Shall pride a heap of sculptur'd marble raise,
> Some worthless, unmourn'd titled fool to praise;
> And shall we not by one poor grave-stone learn
> Where genius, wit, and humour sleep with *Sterne?*[2]

[1] For Mrs Montagu's earlier remarks, see No. 49.
[2] Sterne's grave remained unmarked for more than a year. See No. 59. Garrick's epitaph was reprinted in 1775 in Mrs Medalle's edition of her father's *Letters*. For Sterne's reference to Garrick in *Tristram Shandy*, see No. 27b.

59. Sterne's headstone

1769

Inscription placed on a stone near Sterne's grave, St George's Church, Hanover Square, by two unidentified freemasons, and printed in the *Literary Register* (November 1769), i. 285. The inscription mistakenly gives the date of Sterne's death as 13 September 1769, perhaps the date when the stone was erected.

If a sound head, warm heart, and breast humane,
Unsullied worth, and soul without a stain;
If mental powers could ever justly claim
The well won tribute of immortal fame,
Sterne was *the Man*, who, with gigantick stride,
Mowed down luxuriant follies far and wide.
Yet what, though keenest knowledge of mankind
Unsealed to him the springs that move the mind;
What did it cost him? ridicul'd, abus'd,
By fools insulted, and by prudes accused.
In his, mild reader, view thy future state,
Like him despise, what 'twere a sin to hate.

This monumental stone was erected to the memory of the deceased by two brother masons; for, although he did not live to be a member of their society, yet all his incomparable performances evidently prove him to have acted by the rule and square: They rejoice in this opportunity of perpetuating his high and irreproachable character to after ages.

60. John Trumbull on Sterne

1769, 1773

Trumbull (1750–1831), one of the 'Connecticut Wits,' might have been expected to enjoy Sterne's gaiety, but apparently was put off by his double meanings and his sentimentality. Trumbull wrote the lines in (a) while still studying at Yale.

(a) 'On t[he] Philanthropy of the Author of *Tristram Shandy*. 1769' (Alexander Cowie, *John Trumbull, Connecticut Wit* (1936), pp. 47–8)

When *Sterne*, who could melt at the death of a Fly,
    Declar'd he was *sorry the Devil was damn'd*;[1]
All his maudlin Admirers remurmur'd the sigh
    And the Vot'ries of soft Sentimentals exclaim'd,
'Ah! of *sweet Sensibility* this is the crown!
    What Philanthropy warm in this tender reflection![']
Not *Philanthropy*, Friends—But I'm ready to own,
    'Tis a striking example of *Filial Affection*.

(b) Extract from *The Progress of Dulness* (1773) (bk. II. ll. 231–8, 329–32. Reprinted here from *The Satiric Poems of John Trumbull*, ed. Edwin T. Bowden (1962))

Yet Learning too shall lend its aid,
To fill the Coxcomb's spongy head,
And studious oft he shall peruse
The labours of the Modern Muse.

---

[1] Actually, it was Uncle Toby who was 'sorry' (*Tristram Shandy*, III, 11, p. 179).

From endless loads of Novels gain
Soft, simpring tales of am'rous pain,
With double meanings, neat and handy,
From *Rochester* and *Tristram Shandy*.

Thus 'twixt the Tailor and the Player,
And *Hume*, and *Tristram* and *Voltaire*,
Complete in modern trim array'd,
The Clockwork-Gentleman is made.

61. Richard Griffith and Sterne's 'posthumous works'

1770, 1772

Drawing upon his acquaintance with Sterne and his works (see No. 53d), Griffith presented to the public in 1770 his own forgeries as Sterne's posthumous works, posing as an anonymous editor. *The Posthumous Works of a Late Celebrated Genius* (also known as *The Koran*) has been accepted as genuine by some editors and has appeared in more than one edition of Sterne's collected works, although Griffith revealed the imposition two years later in another anonymous work, *Something New*. In the first selection below (a), Griffith is speaking as editor; the second selection (b) Griffith presented as Sterne's own words. The third selection (c) is Griffith's comment from the later book.

(a) Excerpt from 'The Editor to the Reader,' *The Posthumous Works of a Late Celebrated Genius* (1770), i. v

I here present the public with the remains of an author, who has long entertained and amused them, and who has been the subject both of applause and censure—himself equally regardless of both.—He was a second Democritus,[1] who sported his opinions freely, just as his philosophy, or his fancy led the way: and as he instilled no profligate principle, nor solicited any loose desire, the worst that **could possibly** be said, of the very worst part of his writings, might be only, that they were as indecent, but as innocent, at the same time, as the sprawling of an infant on the floor.[2]

[1] See No. 53d, p. 185 n. 1.
[2] Scott later quoted this defense of Sterne (see No. 123a).

(b) Excerpt from chapter xxxviii, *The Posthumous Works of a Late Celebrated Genius* (1770), i. 170–3

The oddness and novelty of the first volumes [of *Tristram Shandy*] caught hold of the capricious taste of the public.—I was applauded and abused, censured and defended, through many a page.—However, as there were more readers than judges, the edition had sufficient vogue for a sale.—This encouraged me—I went on still with the same kind of *no meaning*; singing, at the end of every chapter, this line from *Midas*, to my *ass-eared* audience,

> Round about the *may-pole* how they trot—

with a parody on the text; where, instead of *brown ale*, you are to read only *small beer*.—[1]

But what entertained me the most, was to find a number of my most penetrating readers had conceived some deep laid scheme or design to be couched under these vagrancies or vagaries, which they fancied and affirmed would unfold itself toward the conclusion of the work.—

Nay some, more *riddle-witted* than the rest, have pretended to be able to trace my clue, through every volume, without losing once sight of the connection.—A fine spirit of enthusiasm this! . . .

However, I must have the *modesty* to admit, that there were, here and there, some striking passages interspersed throughout those volumes,—*In sterquilinio margaritam reperit.*[2]—There are many foibles ridiculed, and much charity and benevolence instilled and recommended.—One saunters out, sometimes, into the fields and highways, without any other purpose than to take the benefit of a little air and exercise;—an object of distress occurs, and draws forth our charity and compassion.

After this careless manner did I ramble through my pages, in mere idleness and sport—till some occurrence of humanity laid hold of me,

---

[1] The allusion is to Kane O'Hara's *Midas; an English Burletta* (1764), p. 18:

> All around the maypole how they trot,
>> Hot
>> Pot,
> And good ale have got.

In the play Midas is changed into an ass and goes about the stage braying as the curtain falls.

[2] He found a pearl in a dunghill.

by the breast, and pulled me aside.—Here lies my only *fort.*—What we strongest feel, we can best express.—And upon such subjects as these, one must be capable of a double energy, who, while he is *pleading for others,* is also *relieving himself.*

(c) Excerpt from *Something New,* 2nd ed. [1772], i. 141–2

Such enthusiasts would have cherished all the plagues of Egypt, in their bosom, and have deemed it an impiety to have destroyed one of their frogs, their caterpillars, their locusts, their grasshoppers, or any of their other vermin.[1]

Under the prejudice of such a sentiment, uncle Toby's handing a fly out of the window, saying, *there is room enough in the world, both for thee and me,* makes a most shining figure, among the *faux-brillants*[2] of morals, to those whose shallow philosophy has never led them to reflect upon the numberless animals, on earth, in air, and in the water, whose instinct directs them to the destruction of others, as necessary to their own preservation; which being certainly the first law of nature, takes place of every other, except in man; whose virtue indeed ought to set the moral obligations above the natural ones.

[1] See Exodus, 8, 10.
[2] False gems.

62. Thomas Jefferson on Sterne

1771, 1787

(a) Extract from a letter to Robert Skipwith, 3 August 1771, 'with a List of Books for a Private Library' (*The Papers of Thomas Jefferson*, ed. Julian P. Boyd (1950), i. 76–7)

A little attention . . . to the nature of the human mind evinces that the entertainments of fiction are useful as well as pleasant. That they are pleasant when well written, every person feels who reads. But wherein is it's utility, asks the reverend sage, big with the notion that nothing can be useful but the learned lumber of Greek and Roman reading with which his head is stored? I answer, every thing is useful which contributes to fix us in the principles and practice of virtue. When any signal act of charity or of gratitude, for instance, is presented either to our sight or imagination, we are deeply impressed with it's beauty and feel a strong desire in ourselves of doing charitable and grateful acts also. On the contrary when we see or read of any atrocious deed, we are disgusted with it's deformity and conceive an abhorrence of vice. Now every emotion of this kind is an exercise of our virtuous dispositions; and dispositions of the mind, like limbs of the body, acquire strength by exercise. But exercise produces habit; and in the instance of which we speak, the exercise being of the moral feelings, produces a habit of thinking and acting virtuously. We never reflect whether the story we read be truth or fiction. If the painting be lively, and a tolerable picture of nature, we are thrown into a reverie, from which if we awaken it is the fault of the writer. . . . We neither know nor care whether Lawrence Sterne really went to France, whether he was there accosted by the poor Franciscan, at first rebuked him unkindly, and then gave him a peace offering; or whether the whole be not a fiction. In either case we are equally sorrowful at the rebuke, and secretly resolve *we* will never do so: we are pleased with the subsequent atonement, and view with emulation a soul candidly acknowleging it's fault, and making a just reparation.

(b) Extract from a letter to Peter Carr, 10 August 1787 (*Writings of Thomas Jefferson*, ed. Lipscomb and Bergh (1903), vi. 258)

The writings of Sterne, particularly, form the best course of morality that ever was written.

63. Richard Cumberland on Sterne

1771, 1806

Cumberland (1732–1811), the author of sentimental comedies, is also remembered for the glimpses of famous people to be found in his *Memoirs*.

(a) Extract from Cumberland's play *The West Indian* (1771), act 2, sc. 1

DUDLEY.
Mr. Fulmer, I have borrow'd a book from your shop; 'tis the sixth volume of my deceased friend Tristram: he is a flattering writer to us poor soldiers; and the divine story of Le Fevre, which makes part of this book, in my opinion of it, does honour not to its author only, but to human nature.

FULMER.
He is an author I keep in the way of trade, but one I never relish'd; he is much too loose and profligate for my taste.

DUDLEY.
That's being too severe: I hold him to be a moralist in the noblest sense; he plays indeed with the fancy, and sometimes perhaps too

wantonly; but while he thus designedly masks his main attack, he comes at once upon the heart; refines, amends it, softens it; beats down each selfish barrier from about it, and opens every sluice of pity and benevolence.

(b) Extract from *Memoirs of Richard Cumberland. Written by Himself* (1806), pp. 506–7

I consider *Tristram Shandy* as the most eccentric work of my time. . . .[1]

As for *Tristram Shandy*, whose many plagiarisms are now detected, his want of delicacy is unpardonable, and his tricks have too much of frivolity and buffoonery in them to pass upon the reader; but his real merit lies not only in his general conception of characters, but in the address, with which he marks them out by those minute, yet striking, touches of his pencil, that make his descriptions pictures, and his pictures life: in the pathetic he excels, as his story of Lefevre witnesses, but he seems to have mistaken his powers, and capriciously to have misapplied his genius.

[1] Cumberland has previously praised Henderson's readings from Sterne (pp. 453–4); see No. 73.

64. Samuel Johnson on Sterne

1773, 1776, 1781

Johnson and Sterne, men of nearly opposite personalities and talents, might well be called the two most influential writers of the latter half of the eighteenth century. (See No. 89.) It was perhaps inevitable that Johnson should disapprove of Sterne. His antipathy arose in part from a different set of critical principles, perhaps in part from Sterne's Whig politics. But his disapproval of Sterne as a clergyman probably contributed most to his attitude. Johnson admitted reading Sterne's *Sermons* in a stagecoach but said, 'I should not have even deigned to have looked at them, had I been at large' (Joseph Cradock, *Literary and Miscellaneous Memoirs* (1826), i. 208), and felt they contained only 'the froth from the surface' of the cup of salvation (*Johnsonian Miscellanies*, ed. George B. Hill (1897), ii. 429). The brevity of his recorded comments on Sterne is itself an indication that he failed to think of Sterne as a serious literary artist. (For an earlier comment attributed to Johnson see No. 34a.)

(a) A conversation with Goldsmith on 15 April 1773 reported in *Boswell's Life of Johnson*, ed. George B. Hill and L. F. Powell (1934–50), ii. 222

It having been observed that there was little hospitality in London; JOHNSON. 'Nay, Sir, any man who has a name, or who has the power of pleasing, will be very generally invited in London. The man, Sterne, I have been told, has had engagements for three months.' GOLDSMITH. 'And a very dull fellow.' JOHNSON. 'Why no, Sir.'

(b) A conversation with Boswell on 20 March 1776 reported in
Boswell's Life of Johnson, ii. 449

I censured some ludicrous fantastick dialogues between two coach-
horses, and other such stuff, which Baretti had lately published.[1] He
joined with me, and said, 'Nothing odd will do long. *Tristram Shandy*
did not last.'

(c) A conversation with Mary Monckton (later Countess of Cork)
in May 1781 reported in *Boswell's Life of Johnson*, iv. 108–9

Johnson was prevailed with to come sometimes into these circles
[i.e. Bluestocking Clubs], and did not think himself too grave even for
the lively Miss Monckton . . . who used to have the finest *bit of blue*
at the house of her mother, Lady Galway. Her vivacity enchanted the
Sage, and they used to talk together with all imaginable ease. A singular
instance happened one evening, when she insisted that some of Sterne's
writings were very pathetick. Johnson bluntly denied it. 'I am sure
(said she) they have affected *me*.'—'Why (said Johnson, smiling, and
rolling himself about,) that is, because, dearest, you're a dunce.' When
she some time afterwards mentioned this to him, he said with equal
truth and politeness; 'Madam, if I had thought so, I certainly should
not have said it.'

[1] The dialogues appear in *Easy Phraseology for the Use of Young Ladies Who Intend to Learn
. . . Italian* (1775) by Giuseppe Marc Antonio Baretti (1719–89), Italian critic who lived
most of his life in England.

65. George Colman the Elder on Sterne

July 1775

Extract from 'The Gentleman,' no. II (12 July 1775), originally published in the *London Packet* and reprinted here from *Prose on Several Occasions* (1787), i. 172.

Colman (1732–94), dramatist and essayist, uses the device of a fictitious correspondent in the selection below.

In opposition to the contemptible animal, the new-fangled being, that now commonly distinguishes itself by the appellation of *The Gentleman*, I am proud to stile myself *A Blackguard*; a name, Sir, that would do you more credit both as a writer, and a man, than the title you have assumed. Humour, that genuine English production, is not the growth of a frippery age, nor founded on polished manners. It can only be cultivated by bold manly wits, such as Cervantes, Rabelais, Moliere, Swift, Gay, Arbuthnot, Fielding, Sterne, &c. &c. These, and such as these, are the Classicks of the School of Blackguard. In that school I have been bred, and have learnt to despise a delicacy of manners that produces effeminacy, and a nicety of taste that proves the weakness of the stomach. If these are models you disapprove, I here take my leave of you; but if English Virtue, English Sense, and English Humour, are meant to be recommended and encouraged by the Author of *The Gentleman*, he shall now and then, if he pleases, hear farther from one who is proud to own himself a friend to those qualities, and to subscribe himself A BLACKGUARD.

66. Sterne's *Letters*

1775

Lydia Sterne Medalle's edition of her father's *Letters* appeared in October 1775; meanwhile, earlier that year two other small collections had appeared, one (*Letters from Yorick to Eliza*) containing ten of Sterne's letters to Mrs Draper (see No. 53d, p. 187, n. 1), the other (*Sterne's Letters to His Friends on Various Occasions*) containing some genuine letters along with some forgeries by William Combe. Combe (1741(?)–1823), who eked out a precarious living by various means, had met and corresponded with Sterne; he continued throughout his lifetime to imitate Sterne and forge scraps of Sterneana.

The selections below are significant in suggesting the importance critics placed upon assessment of Sterne's private character.

(a) Excerpt from an unsigned review of *Letters from Yorick to Eliza* in the *Gentleman's Magazine*, xlv (April 1775). 188

All of [the letters] are expressive of the most tender and (we trust) sentimental friendship. But, between married persons, such cicesbeism is always unsafe, and generally suspicious; and, to virtue, prudence, and even sensibility, must give abundantly more pain than pleasure.

(b) Excerpt from an unsigned review of *Sterne's Letters to His Friends on Various Occasions* in the *London Review*, i (June 1775). 497–501

There was something so extremely singular and problematical in Mr. Sterne's literary character, that it is very difficult to judge of his character as a man by that of his writings. If from these it may be gathered at all, it is most likely to be deduced, with any degree of certainty, from his familiar letters; written, as we may suppose, without any view either to amuse or to recommend himself to the public. . . .

On the whole of this specimen of our Author's epistolary correspondence, it should seem that he was a man who possessed a more considerable share of sentiment than force of reasoning; and that he preserved a tenderness for the sex, most actuated by sentiment, even after the warmth of passion must have subsided.

(c) Excerpt from Ralph Griffiths's unsigned review of *Letters of the Rev. Mr. Sterne, to His Most Intimate Friends* (ed. Lydia Sterne Medalle) in the *Monthly Review*, liii (November 1775). 403–4

The Letters of Sterne . . . will reflect no disgrace on his memory. They are genuine, and they will serve to assist us in forming a more competent idea of the character of the celebrated Yorick, than we could with certainty collect from the writings which were published by himself. He seems, in almost every Letter, to have written from the heart. His immediate situations, and feelings, rather than his genius, appear to have always guided the pen of his correspondence; and we see in the recesses of private life, the man who so conspicuously shone in the public capacity of an Author. His Letters, it is true, will be deemed of various and unequal importance, by their different readers. Some will look, perhaps, for finished models of the epistolary form of writing; and by these, the more trivial *billets*, such as always find their way into collections, will be held in no great estimation: while, to those who may think every thing curious that flowed from the inimitable pen which gave us a *Father Shandy*, an uncle *Toby*, a corporal *Trim*, a Doctor *Slop*, a *Le Fevre*, &c. there will not be found, in the volumes before us, an uninteresting page.—For us, we really think ourselves obliged to Mrs. Medalle for the entertainment she has procured us, in the perusal of her collection; and the more especially, since we consider these Letters as furnishing, in some degree, a Supplement to our favourite work, *The Sentimental Journey*: the greatest part of them bearing relation to those travels abroad which gave birth to that most captivating performance.

(d) Extract from a letter, 30 November 1775, from Henry Mackenzie (see No. 86) to his cousin (*Letters to Elizabeth Rose of Kilravock*, ed. Horst W. Drescher (1967), p. 181)

I saw since I received your Letter mentioning them the Letters of Sterne which you had read; also another Publication of his Letters by his Daughter Mrs Medalle; the first, *to Eliza*, are thought to be spurious, the last are undoubtedly genuine. I think neither one nor t'other, so far as I look'd into them of very great Value; the bad Part of his Writing, a quaintness of Phrase, & a labor'd Versatility of Subject is easily imitated by others, & will always appear in himself; but in these Letters I discover little of that Intimacy with the Heart, that delicate Feeling which apply'd itself to the Pulse of Nature & trac'd her thro' her finest Recesses.

67. Courtney Melmoth on Sterne

1775, 1776

Samuel Jackson Pratt (1749–1814), popular poet of the day who wrote under the pseudonym of Courtney Melmoth, was influenced by Sterne and sometimes imitated him.

(a) Excerpt from a prose interlude in Pratt's poem 'The Tears of Genius, Occasioned by the Death of Dr. Goldsmith,' 2nd ed. (1775) (*Miscellanies* (1785), i. 82–4)

And shall I pass thee o'er, thou gentle spi-spirit?—Was there ought in thy propensions—or in thy way of journeying through the windings of this sad world?—Was there ought unfilial in thy feelings?—ought undeserving or forbidding, that should incline me to overlook thee?— Ah; No—no—Trust me, gentle YORICK, I more than lov'd thee— There was a courtesy in thy demeanor—a milky and humane temperature about thy pulses—and a compassion in the turn of thy mind— however excursive—however retrograde—however digressive—that awaken the most tender recollection—A recollection which hurries the blood into the most affectionate extremities.—Gracious God, what a throb was there!—As I live—and as I love thee—and by the soul of thy venerable relation, the tears are bathing my eye-lashes, while I am talking of thee—And could'st thou—(Oh that Death should have made it necessary to cry alas! in a parenthesis)—could'st thou, YORICK, at this moment, lay thy hand upon my heart—the violence of the motion about the center, would confess the mother—and the tumult of the vessels, together with the rebounds of the pulsation, might assure thee, how thou art rank'd in my estimation—Estimation!—hear me, YORICK, there is another Alas for thee—Thou can'st not hear— GENIUS has much to say of thee—Thou wert nothing else—Thy heart, and head, and every delicate appendage, were the constant champions of all the Charities—all the Civilities.—Thou had'st not, indeed any parade—any ostensibility—or religious prudery about

thee—but yet hast thou done more to the cause of Virtue, than if
thou had'st gone scowling through life.—In all thy excursions—and
whimsical meanders—SENSIBILITY took thee by the hand—by the
heart I might have said—and made thee accessible to every tender
entreaty—every soft petition found its way into thy pocket—the thing
was irresistible—PITY seconded the request, SYMPATHY thirded
it—and if thou haply had'st nothing to bestow—why it was an hard
case, and would cost thee a tear—a drop of disappointment—an elixir
to the sorrowing soul—a treasure rising from the fulness of a rich heart,
and it was given without grudging—so would it, had it been chrystal.
—I honour thy sentiments, and I venerate thy memory—thou
would'st not suffer a nettle to grow upon the grave of an enemy—nor
shall GENIUS ever suffer a weed to grow upon thine.—Peace—peace
to thy shade.

(b) Excerpt from *Observations on the Night Thoughts of Dr. Young*
(1776), pp. 71–4

There is, indeed . . . an *appearance* of singularity and affectation in
Sterne, but it is *only* an appearance. . . . All affectation is to be distinguished by comparing *parts* with the *whole*. If the tenor of an
author's stile be throughout the same; if through a variety of volumes,
you trace a similar *mode* of reasoning, and a similar construction of
language, depend upon it, that it is *not* affectation. On the other hand,
if a writer in pursuit of his subject, forgets in the second part the design
projected in the first; if he starts excentrically from an easy, natural
stile, to a conceited, flippant, shewy manner of expression; if *one* part
of a composition is distinguished for its sublimity, and another for its
meanness, *that*, possibly may be affectation. Now Sterne, (as you will
take notice when you come to be more intimate with him) is a very
uniform writer, both in respect of thinking, and expression of thought:
So is Dr. Young. The first, now and then deviated into trifling, and
the latter sometimes degenerated into bombast or obscurity, but still, it
was in both, the error of nature, and not of art. Neither knew the fault
at the time of composing, nor even at the period of polishing; for, had
this been the case, they would certainly have corrected, at least in a
second edition the mistakes of a first. But the ardour of a great genius,
which is generally, if not constantly, accompanied with a glowing

fancy, often hurries a man into absurdities; and such is a writer's partiality for the offspring of his own imagination, that even in reviewing them at a cooler moment, like over fond parents, judgment either *cannot*, or *must* not see clear enough to correct. The mistake, however, was undoubtedly at first Nature's—But . . . *Correctness* is—I had almost said, of as much importance as genius, and . . . what is written warmly and hastily, should be reviewed, coolly and deliberately. Perhaps Mr. Pope owes half, or more than half his reputation, to a zealous adherence to *this rule*. As to *singularity*, it is at all times better than *sameness*; I mean, it is better to write like an original, than a copier. Every *good writer* is possest of some mark of excellence peculiar to himself; and I am afraid that (such is the debility of the wisest mind) every good writer hath likewise a characteristic imperfection.

68. Boswell on Sterne in *The Hypochondriack*

1778, 1780

Excerpts from *The Hypochondriack*, ed. Margery Bailey (1928).

Boswell contributed a series of seventy essays to the *London Magazine* under this title from 1777 to 1783. There are occasional allusions to Sterne as well as the two comments below, which may represent a cooling of Boswell's enthusiasm for Sterne (see No. 14), but more probably merely reflect the character he has adopted for the essays.

(a) Excerpt from 'On Conscience,' April 1778 (i. 153)

That a well-informed conscience should be the chief director of the actions of man, is most certainly true. I say, a well-informed con-science; for whatever pretty theories have been given us of the beauty of virtue—of the natural moral sense—of the sympathetic feeling of morality—a writer of temporary fashionable fame in this age, hath, amidst much levity, and I am afraid much contaminating extravagance of effusion, had the merit of introducing a decent and clear piece of induction, in which by reasoning upon an eminent example in sacred history he hath shewn that conscience needs to be informed.[1] The pretty theories to which I have alluded, though they pretend to be systems of themselves, are only the flowers of fantastical engraftings upon the blessed plant of Revelation.

(b) Excerpt from 'On Imitation,' August 1780 (ii. 11–12)

In literary composition, the faults of celebrated writers are adopted, because they appear the most prominent objects to vulgar and undis-

[1] See *Tristram Shandy*, II. 17.

cerning men, who would fain participate of fame like theirs by imitating their manner. . . .

How many writers have made themselves ridiculous by dull imitation of the sudden sallies of fancy and unconnected breaks of sentiment in Sterne?

69. John Cleland on Sterne

1779

Boswell's record in his journal of a conversation on 13 April 1779 in which Cleland recalled a meeting with Sterne (date unspecified); *Private Papers of James Boswell from Malahide Castle*, ed. Geoffrey Scott and Frederick A. Pottle xiii (1932). 220.

Cleland (1709–89) was the author of *Fanny Hill*, also known as *The Woman of Pleasure*.

TUESDAY 13 APRIL. (With Cleland.) CLELAND. 'Sterne's bawdy [was] too plain. I reproved him, saying, "It gives no sensations." Said he: "You have furnished me a vindication. It can do no harm." "But," (I said,) "if you had a pupil who wrote C—— on a wall, would not you flogg him?" He never forgave me.' FRASER. 'That was a hard knock to Sterne.' BOSWELL. 'A knock against the WALL.'

70. Some attacks during the 1770s

(a) Entry dated 11 February 1772 in *The Journal of John Wesley*, ed. Nehemiah Curnock [1910], v. 445. Wesley (1703–91), the founder of Methodism, might be expected to disapprove of Sterne's indecency but, surprisingly, objects to Sterne on other grounds. He had read *Tristram Shandy* (see *Letters of the Rev. John Wesley*, ed. John Telford (1931), v. 386), although he did not comment on the earlier work

I casually took a volume of what is called *A Sentimental Journey through France and Italy*. *Sentimental!* what is that? It is not English; he might as well say *Continental*. It is not sense. . . . And this nonsensical word (who would believe it?) is become a fashionable one! However, the book agrees full well with the title, for one is as queer as the other. For oddity, uncouthness, and unlikeness to all the world beside, I suppose, the writer is without a rival!

(b) Extract from a letter, dated September 1772, from Jacob Duché (1737–98), a clergyman who took his pseudonym, Tamoc Caspipina, from his position as *The Assistant Minister of Christ Church And St Peter's In Philadelphia In North America*. He first published his *Observations* in the *Pennsylvania Packet*; they were later reprinted in both America and Europe (letter XVII, *Observations on a Variety of Subjects . . . in a Series of Original Letters* (1774), pp. 207–9)

I was not a little surprized the other day when we dined together at the honourable and worthy Mr. H——'s, to hear you launch forth into such high encomiums upon the character and writings of Mr. STERNE. Unwilling to interrupt the chearfulness of the company by introducing any thing that might have the appearance of a serious dispute, I only rallied you a little upon your attachment to this desultory writer, and reminded you of some passages, the gross indelicacy of which is scarcely covered by the flimsy gauze of his fine expression. You replied to me by quoting some of those tender and pathetic strokes, which we meet with here and there throughout his volumes, which bespeak, as you said, a truly benevolent and sympathetic heart, and more than atone for all the indelicate slips of his pen.

I admire those strokes as much as you do: But still I am not quite satisfied, that the feelings he describes are any thing more than those we have in common with the brute creation, at least that there is any thing heavenly in them, 'till they come to be placed under the direction of an heavenly power, and act in subserviency to its inward dictates; otherwise, passion may get the name of virtue, and a finely attempered frame become the only Heaven we would wish for.

(c) Extract from '*Tristram Shandy*' in the anonymous *Joineriana: or the Book of Scraps* (1772), ii. 151–68

We cannot easily divest the man of his character, nor separate the author from his book—could that be done, as I am much fonder of bestowing praise than censure, I should certainly commend a writer, in whom there is much to be commended, and more to be admired—but far, far more, when we come to consider his function, to be condemned.[1]

He wrote to the folly of the age—which it was his duty, as a christian minister, to have checked—not to have encouraged.

A clergyman and a wit!—I had rather he had been a clergyman and a wise man—

It will not be safe, nor adviseable, in my opinion, for any young clergyman to tread in his steps—altho' he was successful. . . .

[S]hould you chance to turn out a hare-brained wit—an irregular humourist—a rambling-scambling genius!—in the name of parochial peace and harmony! what is to become of your poor flock? . . .

I say, how are they to be tended?—while you are capering and prancing, not only thro' this world, but in the WORLD of the MOON—with MERLIN DE COCCAIE, RABELAIS, BERGERAC and TRIS-

---

[1] Though this anonymous literary hack starts off with straightforward criticism, he soon lapses into a style, partly in imitation of Sterne, which suggests that this piece is one of the last of the bantering attacks that began in the spring of 1760.

TRAM SHANDY?[1]—or dangling after stage-managers?—where 'tis more than a hundred to one, you will be left in the lurch. . . .

If TRISTRAM SHANDY was to come to life again—TRISTRAM would gain a thousand pounds in a month, sooner than I am like to gain a thousand pence in a year, at this rate of going on—

The gentlemen would subscribe to TRISTRAM'S works, without any solicitation—he preaches BAWDRY so genteely—nay, elegantly!

The ladies would subscribe to TRISTRAM—the ladies abominate foul-mouthed BAWDRY!—but such BAWDRY as TRISTRAM'S, they are over head-and-ears in love with!—"Tis, surely, the most delicious BAWDRY in the world!—for it makes you laugh at OBSCENITY, without blushing—there's the sweet of it!'

The clergy would subscribe—'How, the clergy subscribe?'—Yes; the young clergy—who know no better.

The bishops would not subscribe—to *his* LIFE *and* OPINIONS— No:—But some of them, *would give in secret, that their* heavenly father, *who sees in secret, may reward them openly!*—[2]

But they would subscribe to his SERMONS—because they made them laugh—

'How, Sermons make people laugh?'

Did not you know that?—Why Sermons and Moral Essays are the most fashionable vehicles for jests—and we seem to be upon the improving hand—

You shall find all sorts of matter in many of them—except matter of COMPOSITION, matter of WISDOM, matter of TRUTH, matter of PIETY.

---

[1] All of these authors mention the 'world of the moon': Teofilo Folengo (1491–1544) was author of *The Macaronic History of Merlin Coccaie* (1517); written in macaronic Latin and imitated by Rabelais; Rabelais speaks of the possibility of a trip to the moon toward the end of books II and III; Cyrano de Bergerac (1619–55) wrote an account of an imaginary voyage to the moon (*Les États et empires de la lune*; written in 1649, published post-humously); and Sterne dedicates part of *Tristram Shandy* to the moon (I. 9). The connection of the moon with 'lunacy' or insanity (brought on by overexposure to its rays) is probably also in the author's mind.

[2] See Matthew, 6: 1–6, 16–18.

(d) Extract from Thomas O'Brien MacMahon, *An Essay on the Depravity and Corruption of Human Nature* (1774), pp. 1–2, 179–80

Great disputes have arisen of late years, between writers on morality, concerning some of the *leading principles*, or most *important conclusions*, of that study. These contests have been carried on with so much heat, and so little candor, that they are become a sort of national, or religious quarrel. Nothing can well be advanced by *Rochefoucault, la Bruiere, Esprit*, and other French authors, which is not immediately contradicted by Mr. *Hume*, Lord *Shaftesbury*, Mr. *Sterne*, or some other British apologist, for the corrupt heart of man.[1] [MacMahon makes much of the need for grace; attacks at length the passage in Sterne's sermon 'The Case of Elijah and the Widow Zarephath Considered,' in which Sterne praises the latent seeds of compassion in Alexander the Great; and expresses a philosophical view in direct opposition to Sterne's:] [F]ear will always oblige [a man] to keep more or less measures with his fellow creatures. For it is to this passion *alone*, and not to each others *philosophy, philanthropy, seeds of compassion*, or the like ridiculously *impotent checks* that mankind are indebted for the peaceable enjoyment of their *lives and properties* in the midst of such *capricious* and *implacable enemies as they are all one to another*.

(e) Extract from Percival Stockdale (1736–1811), *Miscellanies in Prose, and Verse* (1778), pp. 128–30. Stockdale, miscellaneous writer of poems and essays, was the friend of Garrick, Johnson, and Goldsmith

I am much offended with our Reverend Doctor for having vainly attributed sincerity to a compliment payed him by Lord Bathurst,[2] which compliment implied that his Lordship, in making himself acquainted with Sterne, renewed his acquaintance with Swift, and with

---

[1] François de la Rochefoucauld (1613–80), Jean de la Bruyère (1645–96), and Jacques Esprit (1611–78) were all satirists who pointed out man's weaknesses. David Hume (1711–76) (see No. 39) and Anthony Ashley Cooper, third Earl of Shaftesbury (1671–1713) believed in the importance of sympathy and sentiment and in the existence of an inborn moral sense.

[2] See No. 7.

Pope. Sacred be the names of those illustrious persons, who will be immortal, because they were truly great! I bow before their names with the lowest humility, with a tremulous enthusiasm! Nor may I ever be such a dupe to novelty, as to class inferiour genius of our own times, with those celebrated men. Indeed I would place the statue of Rousseau, but not that of Sterne, on a pedestal collateral with theirs. The works of Swift and Pope will be read with admiration, when the names of Yorick and Tristram Shandy will hardly be remembered.

It is not writing in a manner entirely new; it is not adapting our sentiments to the taste of a frivolous, and licentious age; it is not a capricious, and wild rambling; it is not a happy sporting with the double entendre;—Nor is it sallies of wit, nor transient strokes of the pathetic, that will enable an author to walk down, with majesty, to the latest posterity.—Sterne had great knowledge of the world; he had much wit, and humour; he could move the heart: he was not deficient in imagination; but he was deficient in judgement: he had neither a vigorous, nor a comprehensive mind. He seems likewise to have wanted the power of patient, and intense application. Yet these properties are indispensably requisite to form a master in composition, or an immortal author.[1]

(f) Extract from [the Reverend Philip Parsons (1729–1812), a miscellaneous writer] dialogue IV, *Dialogues of the Dead with the Living* (1779), pp. 72–6. Parsons imagines a conversation between Fielding and Courtney Melmoth (see No. 67)

FIELDING. Sterne, fantastic, giddy, and sensible—Sterne delighted in that wild wood-note strain of digressive and irregular writing, which has captivated numberless copyists, and spoiled them all: you, among the rest, have been drawn too far into the vortex of his giddiness, and whirled about with a whimsical, and not unfrequently a disagreeable, irregularity. I make no doubt but you have your reasons to urge for this desultory manner of writing; what will you plead in its defence?

Mr. MELMOTH.

Variety, the soul of writing. I judged that it relieved the mind from a continued attention, by its pleasing digressions and excursive flights.

[1] This selection is placed between two others, both dated 1775.

FIELDING.

Variety is, as you observe, the soul of writing; but repeated digressions, and flights under no restraint of method, perplex the mind, and by engaging it too deeply in pursuit of the almost invisible chain, destroy their own end, and weaken attention into weariness and disgust. Indeed, my young friend, method is essential to good writing; and I *now* may, without the imputation of vanity, recommend the method which I used myself . . . . Though Sterne touches you frequently with beautiful strokes of wit and tenderness, yet does Uncle Toby (amiable as he is) please you like **Allworthy**, or **Adams**, or **Dr. Harrison?**[1]

Mr. MELMOTH.

He does not. The vivid lightning at a distance flashes surprise and pleasure upon the eye; but the animating light of the sun fills it with a very different sensation.

FIELDING.

Your lively similitude shews no less the quickness, than the justice of your apprehension. But let me ask you one question more, and we will then dismiss the subject of Method. Do you not find more reluctance to lay down the book, when engaged in the *History of a Foundling*,[2] than in the *Life and Opinions of Tristram Shandy*?

Mr. MELMOTH.

I do.

FIELDING.

Yes; and the charm which detains you in the one is Method—and it is Irregularity which sets you free in the other. In the one you are led on by an agreeable connection, which, though pleasingly varied, you keep constantly in view; in the other, you are drawn a thousand different ways, to the frequent loss of that necessary chain, which you as frequently pursue: but, alas! it is often imperceptible—and when perceived, the discovery of it does not (indeed no discovery can) compensate for the perplexity and trouble of the pursuit.

[1] Characters, respectively, in Fielding's *Tom Jones*, *Joseph Andrews*, and *Amelia*.
[2] The subtitle for Fielding's *Tom Jones*.

71. Some neutral critics of the 1770s

(a) Excerpts from two poems by Robert Lloyd (1733–64), a close friend of poet Charles Churchill, in *The Poetical Works of Robert Lloyd* (1774), ii. 64 and ii. 83

[from 'The New-River Head' (1764)]

But to return—The tale is old;
Indecent, truly none of mine—
What BEROALDUS[1] gravely told;
I read it in that sound divine.
And for indecency, you know
He had a fashionable turn,
As prim observers clearly shew
In t'other Parson, Doctor STERNE.

[from 'A Familiar Letter of Rhimes To a Lady']

Like TRISTRAM SHANDY, I could write
From morn to noon, from noon to night,
Sometimes obscure, and sometimes leaning
A little sideways to a meaning,
And unfatigu'd myself, pursue
The civil mode of teazing you.

(b) Extract from a letter (1776?) from William Weller Pepys (1740–1825), patron of literature, member of the Bluestocking assemblies (see No. 49), and friend of Johnson, to his young friend and kinsman William Franks (Alice C. C. Gaussen, *A Later Pepys* (1904), i. 219)

The Man who said that *Tristram Shandy* was an absurd book, because there were neither *Premises* or *Conclusion* in it, was deservedly laughed

---

[1] François Béroalde de Verville (1558–1612), author of the licentious *Le Moyen de Parvenir*, was a canon.

at as a Pedant, because he refer'd the matter in question to a wrong standard; but no one can doubt that even such a strange eccentric composition as that is, may yet be tried by rules adapted to the subject, & a judgment pronounc'd upon its merits, in which people of sound taste, will, upon a thorough examination of it, be found to Agree.

(c) Extract from John Noorthouck (c. 1736–1816), prolific author of many reviews in the *Monthly* (see No. 103b), *An Historical and Classical Dictionary* (1776), ii. entry 'Sterne'

In 1760, [Sterne] came up to London, and published two very small volumes of what might be called a novel, if it admitted of any determinate name, intitled *The Life and Opinions of Tristram Shandy*. In this work he displayed a redundancy of wild extravagant humour and wit, great knowledge of human nature, not a little indecency, absurdity, and arrant nonsense; all which were oddly jumbled together without order, and without any discoverable end or aim, beyond that of making the reader laugh and wonder! People did laugh heartily, the author filled his pockets, and fulfilled a promise he intimated of producing two such volumes every year, for four years. At length however the meer charms of novelty gave way to reflection; *Tristram Shandy* was read with more and more composure every year, until at length the public grew tired of being diverted at the expence of sense and decency, and of consequence the author grew weary of writing; accordingly, after publishing a ninth volume only, he desisted from prosecuting a frolicksome work, which could not either be properly said to have been left finished or unfinished. . . .

When . . . we estimate the abilities of such a spirited flighty writer, we may, in tenderness to his memory, so far follow his example as to overlook his profession, which perhaps was not the object of his deliberate choice; it being clearly inconsistent with his natural disposition and turn of mind: and then we may relax our muscles without reserve. . . . *A Sentimental Journey through France and Italy*, . . . though it is of a like desultory irregular complexion with his *Tristram Shandy*, and like it, imperfect, the author dying soon after it appeared; is greatly beyond that work in sterling merit, for the fine strokes of humour, sensibility, and strong characteristical touches, it contains; and for being less debased with nonsensical dross.

72. Some tributes of the 1770s

(a) Extract from Charles Jenner (1736–74), poet and novelist, *The Placid Man* (1770), i. 74

[W]e find even men of genius stretching their imagination to the very verge of folly, for something new and uncommon. Where a writer happens to have a natural and inexhaustible fund of humour, he may very often succeed in his design of making his readers laugh, by some trick or other, which, in another man, would have been insupportable: a black page, a white page, or a marble page, has done it. But this is a talent which is seldom to be met with; and is perhaps the only one which is, strictly speaking, inimitable; such eccentric geniuses move in an orbit of their own, for others to gaze at.

(b) Extract from 'Sterne' in a catalogue of contemporary authors in the anonymous *Letters Concerning the Present State of England* (1772), p. 398

This inimitable writer has the clearest pretensions to *originality*; a point much deserving of attention, in an age so abounding with copiers and imitators. It is true, he sometimes drove his originality into extravagance; but this is no more than saying, that a great genius was guilty of producing faults and blunders; and how few original ones are there that do not produce such: a truth so clear, that one may venture to pronounce a work a tame, spiritless performance, that has not many absurdities in it. The great force of Mr. Sterne's genius was in the pathetic, in which he has left us many strokes of such genuine, tho' refined nature, that no poet exceeds him.

(c) Extract from 'A Shandyan Dialogue,' *Westminster Magazine*, ii (November 1774). 580–1

I told my dear Yorick one evening, as we sat smoking a pipe by the parlour fire, that *I* would become an author too.

'An author!' said he—with the most civil, smiling sneer in the world. I understood the signal perfectly well.

'I'll not interfere with *your* walk, you may depend upon it,' said I.

'It is impossible you should, replied he:—for if you should chance to strike into it (and there are a hundred chances to one against you if you *try* at it, and are not in it, the Lord knows how) I'll take care you shall not jostle me—no—nor touch the hem of my cassock. . . . Now let us hear what you are going to do.'

'Why, Yorick, replied I, I would with a spirit of perfect good temper join the Sons of Moderation, to calm, if possible, the rude tempests of religious controversy, and sweeten the bitter humours of our fierce Church Polemics. What a confounded noise they are making —what a bustle about nothing!'

'I do sincerely believe, answered Yorick, and have often said, that if a man would sit down in his elbow-chair, and attentively weigh matters in the ballance of cool judgment—making allowances for the passions and prejudices of his fellow-creatures—setting down some-thing to the account of party, interest, ignorance, pride, and the various selfish principles which have always had a main hand in religious debates—I do verily believe, that after an impartial scrutiny of this kind, he would be convinced that the champions have in general, as you observe, fought about nothing, or what is next to nothing, and in the scale of *essentials* will really go for nothing:—that they have puzzled their heads, and sent one another pell-mell to the devil, about matters full as trifling as uncle Toby's Hobby-horses; but not having been quite so innocent and harmless, they have made folks weep where they ought rather to have made them laugh; and covered with the shadow of mock-consequence, have done as much mischief as if they had possess'd the real substance.—If I could not have recourse to ridi-cule, (continued he, after a short pause) to give an outlet to my chagrin, when I see so many puny combatants disgracing the hallowed ground, and mocking the very sanctuary of God:—if I could not treat them with the same indifference and placid contempt that uncle Toby did the fly that pitched upon his nose, when he gently took it from a seat never designed for it, and sent it about its business:—if, (continued he, rising from his seat, and looking as chearful and well pleased as if he had been invited to a concert) if, my dear Charistes, I could not put every thing to rights by a hearty laugh about the *anti-types* of pygmies and cranes, and frogs and mice, held in fierce and formal battle,[1] and rub my hands and enjoy the sport, I should be the most splenetic fellow in the world. . . .'

'Oh! Ridicule (catching a spark of Yorick's fire, I could not forbear offering up this *extemporary* address to the idol of his devotion) how much we owe thee! Thou art the kind relief of the mind, tormented with the follies of the Dull, and the fopperies of the Vain. It is thine to turn vexation into merriment;—to open a vent for chagrin and disgust, and thus carry off the foul humours which nonsense and absurdity breed around the heart, by the smile of sportive raillery, or the sneer of pungent satire. Thus thou makest us merry, where otherwise we should be mad or mortified. Deign ever to grant us thy keen eye and smiling face: then, tho' *trifles lead to serious evils*, with those who give them importance they possess not, yet we will extract some *good* out of them, and by thy *alchemy* transmute e'en sticks and straws, and lead and lumber, into gold.'—

'Amen! ['] said Yorick, with all the heartiness of a parish clerk to the Benediction, when he wanted to go to the next ale-house—and let the sons of Dulness with grave countenances, where the greatest share of their wisdom is lodged—let them pore and plod, and bite their nails, and sink *from thought to thought*, for arguments to overthrow the system they are every moment contributing to the support of; yet Wit and Humour will assert their prerogative, and keep equal pace with Reason and Sense to the end of the world.

[1] The opening of bk. III of the *Iliad* has a simile in which a battle between cranes and pygmies figures. The anonymous *Battle of the Frogs and Mice*, probably written about the end of the sixth century BC, was a parody of the Homeric style and manner.

STERNE

(d) Extract from John Ogilvie (1733–1813), clergyman and fellow of the Edinburgh Royal Society, *Philosophical and Critical Observations on the Nature, Characters, and Various Species of Composition* (1774), i. 338–42

The two higher species of fable (the dramatic and epic) we have now considered particularly, as indicating a certain union of the intellectual powers. ... Before we conclude our observations on this branch of the subject, it may be proper to examine with the same view to the faculties of the mind, some kinds of fable, inferior indeed to the former with regard to the *variety* of *talents* required for their production, but demanding an high degree of such as are indispensably necessary for this purpose, and giving occasion to display no inconsiderable proportion of all.

Among the writers who excel in this class, the first rank will undoubtedly be assigned to those who have attempted to follow out the wanderings of the human heart, and to delineate the first impressions made upon a susceptible mind by interesting objects, as well as the manner in which it feels when insensibly familiarized to their appearance. An author who is capable of exhibiting with propriety a character of this kind, who adapts circumstances to the affections which he proposeth to excite, and paints these so happily when excited, as to imitate nature in her most delicate signatures, possesseth an high share of philosophical excellence, and shows that exquisite sensibility as existing in his own mind, which he pourtrays so justly in that of another. Here indeed the imagination displays no sublimity, or exuberance, as the characters are not of that exalted cast which require these to be exerted: but that instantaneous perception of certain attitudes, which discernment ultimately derives from imagination, that correspondence of which every man is sensible betwixt the action and the feeling giving rise to it in one heart, and excited by it in another; these circumstances denominate taste in the most eminent degree, and that deep insight into human nature, which experience may indeed improve, but cannot possibly confer.

In this kind of fable Mariveaux,[1] Crébillon,[2] and we may add, our

[1] Pierre Carlet de Chamblain de Marivaux (1688–1763), novelist and dramatist, is remembered for the delicate psychology and sensibility of his two novels, *La Vie de Marianne* (1731–41) and *Le Paysan parvenu* (1735–6).
[2] Claude Prosper Jolyot de Crébillon (1707–77) (Crébillon *fils*), was the author of light-hearted, licentious novels with loosely structured or inconsequential narrative lines.

late ingenious countryman Sterne, in his Sentimental Journey, excel all other writers whatever, and their excellence (displayed in one sphere only) is altogether peculiar and inimitable. . . . The merit of the English writer, in the work we have referred to, lies in his happy talent of exciting the tenderest and most affecting sensations from the most trifling occurrences. With no uncommon depth or compass of understanding, this author is distinguished by a copious imagination, and an eminent proportion of the qualities of the heart. His discernment, therefore, which as a philosopher is neither extensive nor accurate, yet as a moral painter is exquisite, and, when employed in its proper sphere, never fails to hit upon strokes of nature the most expressive, and upon motives of powerful and irresistible energy.

(e) Three apophthegms by playwright Joseph Cradock (1742–1826), first published in 1774 in *Village Memoirs*, 3rd ed. (1775), pp. 44–5

Sterne will be immortal when Rabelais and Cervantes are forgot—they drew their characters from the particular genius of the times—Sterne confined himself to nature only.

Till my uncle Toby appeared I had used to assert, that no character was ever better drawn than that of Sir Roger de Coverly.

A man may as well give himself the trouble to copy nature as Sterne.

(f) Extract from the anonymous 'The Leveller,' *Westminster Magazine*, iii (January 1775). 19–20

I remember the first time I read *Tristram Shandy*, it was in the company of two very sensible men, who were each entertaining himself with his own reading. I happened to come to the unfortunate rencounter of Dr. Slop and Obadiah, at the short turn of the garden-wall; and the whole scene presented itself so lively to my imagination, that I laughed, as Lord Chesterfield would say, like a most egregious fool. I thought I saw before me the little fat Doctor, mounted on his diminutive poney, that was waddling through the narrow, dirty lane, at every step sinking to the knees in mire: I thought I saw the hasty Obadiah, mounted on a great unruly brute of a coach horse, galloping at his full speed: I thought I saw him, with this tremendous velocity, bounce upon the unsuspecting Doctor at the sudden turn of the garden-wall; I painted to myself the terror and consternation of the Doctor's face; the vain attempts he would make, in the dirt, to turn his poney out of the way of Obadiah's horse; his crossing himself, like a good Roman-Catholic, on the apprehension of inevitable death; his dropping his whip, through hurry and confusion, in crossing himself; his catching most naturally, and as if by instinct, to recover his falling whip; his losing his stirrups in consequence thereof; his falling, like a windmill, with legs and arms extended; and then sticking, when he reached the earth, like a pack of wool in the mud; then the trepidation of Obadiah at the sight of the Doctor's dirty and dangerous state; the trouble he was at to stop his great, hard-mouthed, stiff-necked brute, which he could by no other means effect, than by pulling him round and round the prostrate Doctor, and bespattering him all with mud; the rueful face of Obadiah, and the aukward apologies he would make: All these, I say, with many other additional circumstances, painted themselves so strongly on my imagination, that I laughed most immoderately loud.[1] My friends, with surprize, asked the reason of my mirth; and I made them no other answer than by reading them the passage forthwith. It tickled the fancy of one of them as much as it had mine, and he joined very heartily in the laugh; but it did not touch my other friend so much. He could not see, he said, any thing so very witty in the misfortune of a poor, harmless, inoffensive man-midwife, who was travelling the road on a visit of civility and complaisance; it was cruel and insulting to laugh at his distress: and as for the unlucky rencounter of the poney and coach-horse, the thing was natural and common enough; it might happen in the neighbourhood of London any day of one's life. In short, he was quite out of humour with us, and peevishly pronounced us to be a couple of idiots for being diverted with such silly conceits. I need not tell my readers, that my grave friend, though a man of a good solid understanding, had neither a sprightly imagination, any taste for humour, nor the least turn for the burlesque.

[1] Cf. *Tristram Shandy*, II. 9, pp. 105-6, which does not contain all these details; Sternes' reader has made an imaginative recreation of the scene.

(g) Extract from the anonymous *Yorick's Skull; or, College Oscitations* (1777), pp. 34–6

The writings of YORICK bear visible marks of a great natural genius, seasoned with uncommon humour, and adorned with the most exquisite sensibility.

My opinion may perhaps appear singular; but I cannot help considering *Tristram Shandy* rather as an admirable caricature of history, than an exact portrait of private life: A lucky attempt at 'modestly overstepping the modesty of nature;'[1] and of alluring mankind with flattering deceptions, beyond the bounds of probability. This appears more strongly in those places where he seems desirous to claim attention by pathos or ridicule. Let any one, after reading Le Fevre, ask his own heart, whether Uncle Toby and the Corporal are not too tender and sentimental? And, I think, the justly-admired amours of Widow Wadman never did or will have existence, but in the brain. Yet it is by these means he has exceeded all writers in his knowledge of disposition and character. By carrying us beyond our usual feelings, he has taught us, that the human heart is capable of the greatest improvement; and that nature never feels herself more noble and exalted, than in the exercise of benevolence and humanity.

I am well aware, that imitations of this irregular genius are laughed at, as absurd and trifling. I grant, that to imitate (as many have done) nothing but his careless, parenthesis'd chapters, deserves this censure; for in these he descends to silliness and buffoonery: But in other parts, it is so much the natural language of the heart, that stories and opinions fall more easily into it than into any other kind of writing.

[1] Cf. *Hamlet*, act 3, sc. 2: 'Suit the action to the word, the word to the action; with this special observance, that you o'erstep not the modesty of nature.'

73. John Henderson reads from Sterne

1770-85

Extract from *Letters and Poems by the Late Mr. John Henderson. With Anecdotes of his Life, by John Ireland* (1786), pp. 26–39.

Henderson (1747–85), who was known as 'the Bath Roscius,' has been described as standing 'next to Garrick in public estimation.' His readings from Sterne, which began in the Shandean Society described below and were later continued for other audiences, became famous, and were recalled with pleasure years later in memoirs and pieces in the magazines.

At this time [i.e. 1770] [Henderson] belonged to an evening society, [called the Shandean Society,] consisting of about twelve or fourteen members, who wished to unite to the festivity of Anacreon,[1] the humour of Prior, the harmony of Pope; and, above all, the sensibility and pleasantry of Sterne. . . .

[I]t was ordained in council, that each member should bring with him a volume of his favourite writer, and read such part aloud as he thought would most contribute to the amusement of the society. Henderson produced a volume of Sterne, the god of his idolatry, entered so fully into the spirit of his author, so happily discriminated the characters, and so forcibly exhibited them, that his companions finding more gratification in hearing him than themselves, which I believe will be acknowledged as strong a testimony of approbation as could be given by a society composed of reading men, constituted him reader to the club, and without an act of parliament, confirmed his right to a name which had been given him by a friend a short time before; decreeing that from, and after that time, he should be distinguished by the name of SHANDY, an appellation he retained many years.

The manner in which he read Sterne's works, threw new light upon many passages, and was the source of much information as well as

[1] See No. 141a, p. 424, n. 1.

pleasantry. In the humorous passages it called forth flashes of merriment, and drew tears from every eye in the pathetic. Never shall I forget the effect he gave to the story of Le Fevre. It kindled a flame of admiration, and promoted a proposal to devote a day to the memory of the author, pour a libation over his grave, and speak a requiem to his departed spirit. . . . Shandy was appointed to select what he thought most fit for the occasion, and the next week produced an Ode, on which the candid critic will look with some allowance, when he considers it as the hasty production of a man little more than twenty years of age. . . .

ODE
INTENDED TO HAVE BEEN SPOKEN AT THE TOMB OF THE LATE LAWRENCE STERNE, ON HIS BIRTH DAY

When he from virtue greatest honour drew,
And held philanthropy to public view,

In pleasure, harmless, innocent, and mild,
Warm as a man, forgiving as a child,
Ev'n then they dar'd to violate his page;
In virtue barren, fruitful in their rage,
Vex'd, inly vex'd, that on inspection clear,
They search'd their hearts and found no Toby there.

Thus envy stung, or dullness veil'd his worth,
'Till nature, warm and zealous in his cause,
Snatch'd him at once from this ill-judging earth,
To realms where angels hail'd him with applause.
Cervantes gaily grave, with accent sweet,
And laughing Rabelais led him to his seat;

To us belongs to vindicate his fame,
To pluck the nettle from his sacred grave,
To turn the darts of malice from their aim,
And point his virtues to the good and brave;

Oh! when ye hear his memory defam'd,
His wit misconstrued, or his heart bely'd,
Loud be his warm benevolence proclaim'd,
'Till rage and error blushing turn aside.
Whate'er their motive, ignorance, or whim,
They slander'd nature when they slander'd him.

74. Sterne's *Complete Works*

1780

Extract from the 'advertisement' to *The Works of Laurence Sterne* (1780), i. iii–vi.

This ten-volume edition, published by a group of London book-sellers, was the first authoritative collected edition of Sterne's *Works* and was to remain the standard one (with slight variations in reprintings) for nearly 125 years. I have been unable to identify the editor.

The works of Mr. Sterne, after contending with the prejudices of some, and the ignorance of others, have at length obtained that general approbation which they are entitled to by their various, original, and intrinsic merits. No writer of the present times can lay claim to so many unborrowed excellencies. In none, have wit, humour, fancy, pathos, an unbounded knowledge of mankind, and a correct and ele-gant style, been so happily united. These properties, which render him the delight of every reader of taste, have surmounted all opposition. Even envy, prudery, and hypocrisy are silent.

Time, which allots to each author his due portion of fame, and admits a free discussion of his beauties and faults, without favour and without partiality, hath done ample justice to the superior genius of Mr. Sterne. It hath fixed his reputation as one of the first writers in the English language, on the firmest basis, and advanced him to the rank of a classick. As such, it becomes a debt of gratitude, to collect his scattered performances into a complete edition, with those embellishments usually bestowed on our most distinguished authors. . . .

It would be trespassing on the reader's patience, to detain him any longer from the pleasure which these volumes will afford, by bespeaking his favour either for the author or his works. The former is out of the reach of censure or praise; and the reputation of the latter is too well established to be either supported or shook by panegyric or criticism. To the taste therefore, the feelings, the good sense, and the candour of the public, the present collection of Mr. Sterne's works may be submitted, without the least apprehension that the perusal of any part of them will be followed by consequences unfavourable to the interests of society. The oftener they are read, the stronger will a sense of universal benevolence be impressed on the mind; and the attentive reader will subscribe to the character of the author, given by a comic writer, who declares he held him to be 'a moralist in the noblest sense; he plays indeed with the fancy, and sometimes perhaps too wantonly; but while he thus designedly masks his main attack, he comes at once upon the heart; refines, amends it, softens it; beats down each selfish barrier from about it, and opens every sluice of pity and benevolence.'[1]

[1] The quotation is from Richard Cumberland's *The West Indian*; see No. 63.

75. Sterne's imitators

1781

Extract from Samuel Badcock's unsigned review in the *Monthly Review*, lxv (July 1781). 65–6, of *Letters between two Lovers, and their Friends,* one of the many imitations of Sterne by the same anonymous author who had written *Letters Supposed to Have Been Written by Yorick, and Eliza.* Badcock (1747–88), a dissenting minister, was one of the *Monthly's* most prolific reviewers.

When we passed our censure on this Writer's former publication, we had been so nauseated with the large quantities of that insipid trash, called *Sentimental Letters, Sentimental Effusions,* &c. &c. which had been poured upon us, under the sanction of Yorick's name, or by an affectation of his light and desultory manner of writing, without one grain of his wit and acuteness; that we thought it our duty to attempt to check the progress of this new species of dulness, and to restore that esteem for good sense, learning, and simplicity, which a fondness for those frivolous and idle productions had a tendency to banish from our country. Every coxcomb who was versed in the *small talk* of love, and who had acquired the knack of writing without thinking, fancied himself to be *another* YORICK! and as it was exceedingly easy to *assume* the *virtue* of sentiment, and as easy to adopt its *cant,* the ELIZAS [1] too, were very numerous! Here reclined a swain, so oppressed by his own gentle feelings, that he could only utter the tender tale of his heart in abrupt and broken sentences. There, on some soft bank, beside the murmuring stream, a nymph, half breathless, melting in her own sensibility, sat drooping—expiring in a soft and pathetic *Oh!*—Here old lovers conveyed their wishes in groans, and sentimental old maids (for want of better amusement!) echoed them back in sighs! Now *palsied* passion (feigning itself to be 'tremblingly *alive* all o'er!') shook itself into ★★★★! Then poor sentiment, frittered by use, dwindled away, and was lost in a —!

This was the most compendious method of supplying 'each vacuity

[1] See No. 53d, p. 187, n. 1.

of sense;' and *stars* and *dashes*, which in reality mean nothing, were supposed to mean too much for language to express; and the Writer, swelling with unutterable feelings, and labouring with those *travels of the heart* which had no issue in birth, was compared to the printer of antiquity, who wisely threw a veil over the subject which he was not able to describe.

Time, however, hath in some measure corrected this folly. . . . The poor trick amused for a little while: but it was played so frequently, and by many, who, only taking it up at second-hand, made such bungling work of it, that it became contemptible, and lost all its power of imposition.

76. Sterne a wit, not a genius

1781

Extract from the Reverend Martin Sherlock, *Letters on Several Subjects* (1781), i. 68–73.

Sherlock (1750(?)–97), who was chaplain to the Earl of Bristol, has earlier credited Sterne with some genius since the *Sentimental Journey* was something 'new'; later in the *Letters* he censures Sterne for sometimes substituting 'indecency for wit.'

Wit is compounded of imagination and judgement. So I said genius was. Yet wit and genius are not two similar faculties which differ only in degree; they are very distinct. A sound judgement is equally necessary to both; but the imagination in a man of genius differs not only in magnitude from the same faculty in a man of wit, but seems to me to be almost of a different species. In many respects they resemble each other, but the essential difference which I think separates them is *heat*. Allow me a familiar image, and I'll make my meaning clear. Wit resembles a lively French lap-dog; genius a high-bred English foxhound: genius resembles a conflagration; wit an artificial firework: or if you chuse a higher and perhaps a juster allusion; genius may be compared to a torrent of lava, and wit to a lively limpid rivulet.

The object of wit is to please; the object of genius is to invent. There never was a man of genius who was not a *deep* thinker: people may have wit who never think deeply; witness a hundred women who are full of wit, and who are incapable of deep thinking. Wit is pretty; genius is sublime: that charms; this transports: wit sparkles; genius blazes: that gives pleasure; this gives rapture. We love wit; we revere genius. The lips of wit are dressed in smiles, as were the lips of Sterne and Voltaire; the brow of genius is plowed with wrinkles, as you see in the busts of Newton and Archimedes. Wit's laurels flourish while they are protected by novelty; the bays of genius acquire freshness by the lapse of years. Am I partial, or am I true? Perhaps I deceive myself, but I mean to be just; Shakspeare's reputation increases daily, while Voltaire's fame is hourly decaying. . . .

From all this dissertation on wit and genius, it is pretty evident on which side the superiority lies. But let not the Wit be discontented with his lot; perhaps it is the milder of the two. As works of genius are difficult to be produced, so they are not easy to be estimated. A trait of wit is produced in an instant; an instant is sufficient to determine it's value. The admiration acquired by genius is partial and slow; the success of wit is rapid and universal. Richardson is not yet arrived at the fulness of his glory; Voltaire gained admirers as fast as he got readers. Wit is relished by every class of mankind; while heaven-born genius is tasted but by few. Some months gave Sterne more reputation than Milton acquired in many years.

77. Vicesimus Knox on Sterne

1782, 1788?

Extracts from *Essays Moral and Literary*, 13th ed. (1793) and *Winter Evenings: or Lucubrations on Life and Letters*, 2nd ed. (1790). The first three selections below appeared, with minor variations, for the first time in the 1782 'new' edition of the *Essays*, 1st ed. (1778); I have been unable to locate a copy of the first edition of *Winter Evenings* (1788).

Knox (1752–1821), ordained minister and headmaster of Tonbridge School, gave one of the most extended treatments of Sterne up until this time. His compilation of *Elegant Extracts* in prose (1783) contained several passages—particularly the 'pathetic' ones—from Sterne, and his compilation of *Elegant Epistles* (1790) contained more than fifty of Sterne's letters; both were frequently reprinted.

(a) Extract from 'On the Manner of Writing Voyages and Travels,' *Essays Moral and Literary*, i. 223–4

Who has read the exquisite touches of nature and sensibility in Sterne's Sentimental Journey, without feeling his nerves vibrate with every tender emotion? Sterne has shewn what important effects may be produced by a true simplicity of style, and a faithful adherence to nature. I wish it were possible to give him the praise of morality as well as of genius; but the poison he conveys is subtle, and the more dangerous as it is palatable. I believe no young mind ever perused his books without finding those passions roused and inflamed, which, after all that the novelist can advance in their favour, are the copious sources of all human misery. Many a connection, begun with the fine sentimentality which Sterne has recommended and increased, has terminated in disease, infamy, want, madness, suicide, and a gibbet. Every writer, whatever may be the weakness and folly of his own life, should take the side of virtue in his public writings, and endeavour to restrain the irregularity of those affections, which, under every restraint, are still capable of producing more evil than any other cause throughout the whole system of human affairs.

(b) Extract from 'On the Moral Tendency of the Writings of Sterne,' *Essays Moral and Literary*, iii. 213–18

That Sterne possessed a fine particle of real genius, if our reason were disposed to deny it, our sensations on perusing him will fully evince. It is, I think, an infallible proof of real genius, when a writer possesses the power of shaking the nerves, or of affecting the mind in the most lively manner in a few words, and with the most perfect simplicity of language. Such a power conspicuously marks both a Shakespeare and a Sterne; though Sterne is far below Shakespeare in the scale of genius.

I am ready to allow to Sterne another and a most exalted merit, besides and above the praise of genius. There never was a heathen philosopher, of any age or nation, who has recommended in so affecting a manner, the benignant doctrines of a general philanthropy. He has corrected the acrimony of the heart, smoothed the asperities of natural temper, and taught the milk of human kindness to flow all-cheerily (it is his own expression) in gentle and uninterrupted channels.

To have effected so amiable a purpose is a great praise, a distinguished honour. I lament that the praise is lessened and the honour sullied by many faults and many follies, which render the writings of Sterne justly and greatly reprehensible.

If we consider them as compositions, and are guided in our judgment by the dictates of sound criticism, and by those standards of excellence, the rectitude of which has been decided by the testimony of the politest ages, it will be necessary to pronounce on them a severe sentence. The great critic of antiquity required as the necessary constituents of a legitimate composition, a beginning, a middle, and an end. I believe it will be difficult to find them in the chaotic confusion of *Tristram Shandy*. But, disregarding the tribunal of Aristotle, to which the modern pretenders to genius do not consider themselves as amenable, it will still be true, even by the decisions of reason and common sense, that his writings abound with faults.

Obscurity has always been deemed one of the greatest errors of which a writer can be guilty; and there have been few readers, except those who thought that the acknowledgment would derogate from their reputation for wisdom, who have not complained that *Tristram Shandy* is in many places disgustfully obscure.

The admirers of Sterne extol his wit. But I believe it will be found that his wit is of the lowest kind, and the easiest of invention; for is it not for the most part allusive obscenity? a species of wit to be found in its fullest perfection in the vulgarest and vilest haunts of vice? It is, indeed, easy to attract the notice and the admiration of the youthful and the wanton, by exhibiting loose images under a transparent veil. It is true indeed there is usually a veil, and the decent are therefore tempted to read; but the veil, like the affected modesty of a courtezan, serves only as an artifice to facilitate corruption.

The praise of humour has been lavished on him with peculiar bounty. If quaintness is humour, the praise is all his own, and let Cervantes and Fielding bow their heads to Sterne. They who admire Uncle Toby, Doctor Slop, and Corporal Trim, as natural characters, or as exhibiting true humour in their manners and conversations, are little acquainted with nature, and have no just taste for genuine humour. It is evident enough that the author meant to be humorous and witty, and many of his readers, in the abundance of their good-nature, have taken the will for the deed.

But till obscurity, till obscenity, till quaintness, till impudence, till oddity, and mere wantonness, wildness, and extravagance, are perfections in writing, Tristram Shandy cannot justly claim the rank to which it has been raised by folly and fashion, by caprice, libertinism, and ignorance. . . .

There are, indeed, exquisite touches of the pathetic interspersed throughout all his works. His pathetic stories are greatly admired. The pathetic was the chief excellence of his writings; his admirers will be displeased if one were to add, that it is the only one which admits of unalloyed applause. It is certainly this which chiefly adorns the Sentimental Journey; a work which, whatever are its merits, has had a pernicious influence on the virtue, and consequently on the happiness, of public and private society.

That softness, that affected and excessive sympathy at first sight, that sentimental affection, which is but *lust in disguise*, and which is so strongly inspired by the Sentimental Journey and by Tristram Shandy, have been the ruin of thousands of our countrymen and countrywomen, who fancied, that while they were breaking the laws of God and man, they were actuated by the fine feelings of *sentimental affection*. How much are divorces multiplied since Sterne appeared!

Sterne himself, with all his pretensions, is said to have displayed in private life, a bad and a hard heart; and I shall not hesitate to pronounce him, though many admire him as the first of philosophers, the grand promoter of adultery, and every species of illicit commerce.

(c) Extract from 'On the Advantage which may be Derived to the Tender and Pathetic Style, from Using the Words and Phrases of Scripture,' *Essays Moral and Literary*, iii. 281–4

Sterne, who, though he is justly condemned for his libertinism, possessed an uncommon talent for the pathetic, has availed himself greatly of the scriptural language. In all his most affecting passages, he has imitated the turn, style, manner, and simplicity, of the sacred writers, and in many of them has transcribed whole sentences. He found no language of his own could equal the finely expressive diction of our common translation. There are a thousand instances of his imitating scripture interspersed in all the better parts of his works, and no reader of common observation can pass by them unnoticed. . . .

It is easy to see that the writer of so many tender and simple passages had imitated the delightful book of Ruth. With what pleasure did a man of his feeling read, 'Intreat me not to leave thee, or to return from following after thee; for whither thou goest, I will go; and where thou lodgest, I will lodge; thy people shall be my people, and thy God my God; where thou diest will I die, and there will I be buried.'[1] Sterne stole the very spirit of this passage, and indeed of all the fine strokes of tenderness, and many an one there is, in a book which is often laid aside by polite scholars as absurd and obsolete. The choice which Sterne has made of texts and of citations from the scriptures in his sermons, are proofs that he (who was one of the best judges of the pathetic) was particularly struck with the affecting tenderness and lovely simplicity of scriptural language.

[1] Ruth, 1: 16–17.

(d) Extract from 'On the Affectation of excessive Sensibility,' *Winter Evenings*, i. 469

Belinda was always remarkably fond of pathetic novels, tragedies, and elegies. Sterne's sentimental beauties were her peculiar favourites. She had indeed contracted so great a tenderness of sensibility from such reading, that she often carried the amiable weakness into common life, and would weep and sigh as if her heart were breaking at occurrences which others, by no means deficient in humanity, viewed with indifference. She could not bear the idea of killing animals for food. She detested the sports of fishing and hunting, because of their ineffable cruelty. She was ready to faint if her coachman whipt his horses when they would not draw up hill; and she actually fell down in a fit on a gentleman's treading on her favourite cat's tail as he eagerly stooped to save her child from falling into the fire.

(e) Extract from 'On the Inconsistency of affected Sensibility,' *Winter Evenings*, ii. 159

Bad passions, and bad actions the consequence of them, have always been common, and will continue to be so in the present condition of human nature; but to boast of them as doing honour to the heart, under the name of *lovely and delicate sensibility*, is peculiar to the fashionable of the present age. Mr. Sterne and Mrs. Draper[1] have too many imitators. A goat is a personage of as great sensibility and sentiment as most of them.

[1] For Sterne's relationship with Mrs Draper, see No. 53d, p. 187, n. 1.

78. Sterne anthologized

1782, 1787

Sterne's work was probably most frequently read during the 1780s in a little book, first published in 1782, which had been expanded and reached a seventh edition within a year and a twelfth by 1793. *The Beauties of Sterne* purported to be 'Selected for the Heart of Sensibility' and to contain 'all his Pathetic Tales, & most distinguished Observations on Life.' An alphabetical table of contents guided the reader in his search for Sterne's sentiments on beauty, compassion, charity, defamation, eloquence, and so on. The rage for books of this kind, extending to many other famous authors, was such that in 1786 Hannah More exclaimed: 'No work in substance now is follow'd,/The Chemic Extract only's swallow'd.' (*Florio: a Tale*, p. 9.) Readers of the *Beauties of Sterne* apparently regretted the one-sided selection of the first editions and the tenth edition of 1787 contained more of Sterne's humor. The two selections below are taken from the prefaces to the third and tenth editions respectively. I have been unable to identify with certainty the editor(s) for these books.

(a) Extract from *The Beauties of Sterne*, 3rd ed. (1782), pp. v-vi

A selection of the Beauties of Sterne is what has been looked for by a number of his admirers for some time; well knowing they would form such a Volume as perhaps this, nor any other language, could equal. Indeed it was highly necessary on a particular score to make this selection: the *chaste* lovers of literature were not only deprived themselves of the pleasure and instruction so conspicuous in this magnificent assemblage of Genius, but their rising offspring, whose minds it would polish to the highest perfection were prevented from tasting the enjoyment likewise. The *chaste* part of the world complained so loudly of the obscenity which taints the writings of *Sterne*, (and, indeed, with some reason), that those readers under their immediate inspection were not suffered to penetrate beyond the title-page of his *Tristram Shandy*;—his *Sentimental Journey*, in some degree, escaped the general censure; though that is not entirely free of the fault complained of.

To accommodate those who are strangers to the first of these works, I have, (I hope with some degree of judgment), extracted the most distinguished passages on which the sun of Genius shines so resplendent, that all his competitors, in his manner of writing, are lost in an eclipse of affectation and unnatural rhapsody. I intended to have arranged them alphabetically, till I found the stories of *Le Fever*, the *Monk*, and *Maria*, would be too closely connected for the *feeling reader*, and would wound the bosom of *sensibility* too deeply: I therefore placed them at a proper distance from each other.—I need not explain my motive for introducing the Sermon on the abuses of Conscience, with the effusions of humanity throughout it; every parent and governor, I believe, (unless a bigotted Papist), will thank me.—I wish I could infuse the pleasure that attended me in compiling this little work, into the breast of the reader, yet unacquainted with *Sterne*—as it is, I promise him, the hours he may devote to this great master of nature and the passions, will be marked with more felicity, than any, since genius led him to the love of letters.

(b) Extract from *The Beauties of Sterne*, 10th ed. (1787), pp. v-viii

---

It has been a matter of much general complaint, that the selections hitherto made were of rather too confined a cast,—and that, contrary to the original, the *utile* and the *dulce*[1] were not sufficiently blended, or in equal quantities. That as the work was intended both for the recreation of our riper years, and the improvement of the more juvenile mind, it dragg'd on rather too serious a system of grave morality, unmix'd with those sprightlier sallies of fancy, which the great Original knew so judiciously and equally to scatter in our way.

It has been likewise observed, that the dread of offending the ear of Chastity, so laudable in itself, has, in the present case, been carried to an excess, thereby depriving us of many most laughable scenes, though in themselves totally free from any objections on the score of indelicacy—and that, upon the whole, the past compilers of Sterne,

[1] The useful and the pleasant.

keeping their eye rather upon his *morality*, than his *humour*—upon his *judgment*, than his *wit*, had liken'd the work to his *Cane Chair, deprived of the one of its knobbs*[1] incomplete and ununiform.—Giving us rather those plants which may be found in all climates and in every soil, than those which are more estimable, because more rare, and which have been brought to perfection in but a very few indeed such skilful hands as his.

To obviate in some measure those founded objections, has been the object of the present edition, in which, the reader, whether of a grave or gay complexion, will find an equal attention paid him—the sprightly reader will find, now for the first time, several scenes of such exquisite fancy—such true Shandean coloring, that he will be astonish'd, they could be overlook'd by any who professed to enumerate the 'Beauties of Sterne.'—Such are, Mr. Shandy's Beds of Justice—Dr. Slop and Susannah—Parson Yorick's Horse—and many other pictures of the same tint. . . .[2]

To promote the interests of Virtue by exhibiting her in her most pleasing attitudes—to seduce, if possible, mankind to pursue that road which alone leads to true happiness, is the warmest wish of the Editor's heart; and he firmly believes, there is no mode so effectual, as strewing such flowers as these in their way—for impenetrable must that heart be which cannot be soften'd by so much good sense, enliven'd with so much good humour.

[1] See No. 27c.
[2] See *Tristram Shandy*, VI. 17–18; VI. 3–4; and I. 10 respectively.

79. Hannah More on Sterne

1782, 1808

Hannah More (1745–1833), close friend of Johnson and influential writer in the Evangelical movement at the turn of the century, attacked Sterne briefly in her poem 'Sensibility' (1782), which reached a twenty-fourth edition by 1850, and again in her Evangelical novel, *Coelebs in Search of a Wife* (1808), which reached a sixteenth edition by 1826. *Coelebs*, though published anonymously, was almost immediately attributed to her. In the selection below (b) from her novel, though the remarks are put into the mouth of one of the characters, they obviously represent her own view. For a reply to these strictures, see No. 108.

(a) Extract from 'Sensibility' in *Sacred Dramas* (1782), p. 285

> Oh, bless'd Compassion! Angel Charity!
> More dear one genuine deed perform'd for thee,
> Than all the periods Feeling e'er can turn,
> Than all thy soothing pages, polish'd STERNE!

(b) Extract from *Coelebs in Search of a Wife* (1808), ii. 83–4

'A judicious reformer,' said Sir John, 'will accommodate his remedy to an existing and not an imaginary evil. When the old romances . . . had turned all the young heads in Europe; or when the fury of knight-errantry demanded the powerful rein of Cervantes to check it—it was a duty to attempt to lower the public delirium. When, in our own age and country, Sterne wrote his corrupt, but too popular lesser work, he became the mischievous founder of the school of sentiment. A hundred writers communicated, a hundred thousand readers caught the infection. Sentimentality was the disease which then required to be expelled. The reign of Sterne is past. Sensibility is discarded, and with it the softness which it must be confessed belonged to it. Romance is vanished, and with it the heroic, though somewhat unnatural elevation which accompanied it. We have little to regret in the loss of either: nor have we much cause to rejoice in what we have gained by the exchange. A pervading and substantial selfishness, the striking characteristic of our day, is no great improvement on the wildness of the old romance, or the vapid puling of the sentimental school.'

80. Robert Burns on Sterne

1783, 1787, 1788

Extracts from *The Letters of Robert Burns*, ed. J. DeLancey Ferguson (1931).

(a) Extract from a letter dated 15 January 1783 to John Murdoch, schoolmaster in Staple Inn buildings, London (i. 14–15)

In the matter of books, indeed, I am very profuse. My favorite authors are of the sentim[1] kind, such as Shenstone, particularly his *Elegies*, Thomson, *Man of feeling*, a book I prize next to the Bible, *Man of the World*,[1] Sterne, especially his *Sentimental journey*, Macpherson's *Ossian*, &c. these are the glorious models after which I endeavour to form my conduct, and 'tis incongruous, 'tis absurd to suppose that the man whose mind glows with sentiments lighted up at their sacred flame— the man whose heart distends with benevolence to all the human race—he 'who can soar above this little scene of things'[2] can he descend

[1] Another novel by Henry Mackenzie, similar to his *The Man of Feeling*.
[2] James Thomson, *The Seasons: Autumn*, l. 966.

to mind the paultry conccerns [sic] about which the terrae-filial race fret, and fume, and vex themselves? O how the glorious triumph swells my heart! I forget that I am a poor, insignificant devil, unoticed [sic] and unknown, stalking up and down fairs and markets when I happen to be in them, reading a page or two of mankind, and 'catching the manners living as they rise,'[1] whilst the men of business jostle me on every side, as an idle encumbrance in their way.

(b) Extract from a letter to Mrs Dunlop, 15 April 1787 (i. 83)

There is an affectation of gratitude which I dislike.—The periods of Johnson and the pauses of Sterne may hide a selfish heart.

(c) Extract from a letter to Dr John Moore, 2 August 1787 (i. 111–12)

My life flowed on much in the same tenor till my twenty third year.—Vive l'amour et vive la bagatelle,[2] were my sole principles of action.—The addition of two more Authors to my library gave me great pleasure; Sterne and M^{c}kenzie.—*Tristram Shandy* and the *Man of Feeling* were my bosom favorites.

(d) Extract from a letter to Mrs Dunlop, 7 December 1788 (i. 278–9)

If Miss Georgina M'Kay is still at Dunlop, I beg you will make her my Compliments, & request her in my name to sing you a song at the close of every page, by way of dissipating Ennui; as David (who, by the by, was, baiting the Sex, no bad Prototype of Miss M^c—, for he was not only fam'd for his musical talents, but was also 'ruddy & well favor'd, & more comely than his brethren'[3] playing on his harp chased

[1] Pope, *Essay on Man*, epistle I, l. 14.
[2] Long live love and long live trifles.
[3] See I Samuel, 16: 12, 18; 17: 42.

the Evil Spirit out of Saul.—This Evil Spirit, I take it, was just, long-spun Sermons, & many-pag'd Epistles, & Birth-day Poetry, & patience-vexing Memorials, Remonstrances, Dedications, Resolution-Addresses, &c. &c. &c. while David's harp, I suppose was, mystically speaking, Tristram Shandy, Laugh & be fat, Cauld kail in Aberdeen, Green grows the rashes, & the rest of that inspired & inspiring family.—

81. Clara Reeve on Sterne

1785

Extract from *The Progress of Romance* (1785), ii. 29–31.

Clara Reeve (1729–1807) was the author of the tremendously popular Gothic novel, *The Old English Baron*. *The Progress of Romance* is cast in the form of a series of evening conversations in which Hortenius, Euphrasia, and Sophronia discuss the merits of works of fiction.

Hort. Do you know that you have pass'd by a book more read and talked of than most of those we have reviewed.
Euph. Likely enough, we have not been quite regular in our pro-gress, but pray who is the great personage omitted?
Hort. No less a man than *Tristram Shandy*, Gent.
Euph. I must beg of *you* to decide upon its merits, for it is not a woman's book.
Hort. Indeed I will not allow of your excuse.—You have spoken freely enough of many other writers, and if you are a competent judge of them, why not of *Sterne*?
Euph. You urge me closely,—in verity I have never read this book half through, and yet I have read enough to be ashamed of. Fashion which countenances every folly, induced me to begin it;—but what can I say of it with safety?—That it is a Farrago of wit and humour,

sense and nonsense, incoherency and extravagance.—The Author had the good fortune to make himself and his writings the *ton of the day*, and not to go out of fashion during his life.—What value posterity will set upon them I presume not to give my opinion of, it is time that must decide upon them, and it will certainly do them justice.

Hort. You are very reserved in your judgment of *Tristram*, but what have you to say against his *Sentimental Journey*?

Euph. It is indisputably a work of merit.—Where *Sterne* attempts the Pathos, he is irresistable; the Reviewers have well observed, that though he affected humour and foolery, yet he was greatest in the pathetic style.—His *Maria* and *le Fevre*, and his *Monk*, are charming pictures, and will survive, when all his other writings are forgot.

82. Mrs Piozzi on Sterne

1786, 1791

Hester Lynch Thrale, later Mrs Piozzi (1741–1821), the friend of Samuel Johnson, might well be expected to share Johnson's disapproval of Sterne, but apparently she agreed with Mary Monckton about Sterne's 'pathetic' powers. See No. 64c.

(a) Extract from Hester Lynch Piozzi, *Anecdotes of the Late Samuel Johnson, LL.D.* (1786), pp. 282–3

May [Cervantes's] celebrity procure my pardon for a digression in praise of a writer who, through four volumes of the most exquisite pleasantry and genuine humour, has never been seduced to overstep the limits of propriety, has never called in the wretched auxiliaries of obscenity or profaneness; who trusts to nature and sentiment alone, and never misses of that applause which Voltaire and Sterne labour to produce, while honest merriment bestows her unfading crown upon Cervantes.

(b) Extract from a diary entry, 1 October 1791, in *Thraliana*, ed. Katharine C. Balderston (1942), ii. 823–4

What shall we say about the native Power of Pathos! Is there, or is there not any such *native* Power! did ever Indian or Infant weep at a dismal Story? unless they had been previously taught to consider weeping as a Distinction? I know Children will be affected at a melancholy Tale after as much Cultivation as suffices to make them suppress what I verily believe is the true *natural* Passion, when something sad is related or seen:—namely *genuine uninstructed Laughter*. . . .

I remember many years ago, when Susan & Sophia [Thrale] came home one Time from Kensington School . . . they used to repeat some Stuff in an odd Tone of Voice, & laugh obstreperously at their own Ideas—upon Enquiry we found out that 'twas the pathetic Passages in *Sterne's Maria* that so diverted & tickled their Spleen. . . .

Now I dare say their hearts are no ways different from those of the next Misses in the next School to theirs; & well does my Memory serve me to bring back their eldest Sister Hester Maria Thrale, weeping at four Years old for the Hare in Gay's last Fable,[1] when all the Beasts refuse to save her from the Hounds; tho' I have no Reason to suppose them made of *Sterner Stuff* as Antony calls it,[2] than She is. but Miss Thrale was a *taught* Child; & Nature had no part in the Tenderness— She had learn'd to be pityful as She had learn'd to be pious—Compassion is certainly *no* native Sentiment of the Soul: The Indians are never compassionate.

Religion only can teach Morality,—Religion alone can supply Reasons for being merciful.

[1] Fable L, 'The Hare and Many Friends,' in the first series of John Gay's *Fables* (1727).
[2] *Julius Caesar*, act 3, sc. 2, l. 98.

83. George Gregory on Sterne

1787, 1788, 1809

Gregory (1754–1808), best known as the translator of Bishop Robert Lowth's *Lectures on the Sacred Poetry of the Hebrews*, was an ordained minister.

For Anna Seward's arguments against his judgment of Sterne, see No. 84.

(a) Extract from Gregory's note in his translation of Lowth's *Sacred Poetry of the Hebrews*, first published in 1787 and reprinted here from the third edition (1835), pp. 181–2

The pathetic is so much the prevailing or distinguishing quality of the Hebrew writings, that I do not hesitate to ascribe much of that superiority which the moderns claim in this respect over the Greeks and Romans, to the free use which they have made of scriptural sentiments and expressions. The reader will easily be able to satisfy himself on this subject by a cursory inspection of Milton, Pope, and even some of our best tragic writers. Mr Knox has very judiciously pointed out how greatly Sterne has been indebted to them.[1] That an author, indeed, who has borrowed from others all the tolerable thoughts which are thinly scattered through his writings, should resort to the readiest and most copious source of pathetic imagery, is not surprising. It is only to be lamented, that he has not made the best use of his plagiarisms; that these noble sentiments are so strangely disfigured by the insipid frivolity of his style—a style which no classical ear can possibly endure, and which must be confessed to derive its principal embellishments from what are called the *typographical* figures.

[1] See No. 77c.

(b) Extract from *Sermons*, first published in 1787 and reprinted here from the second edition (1789), p. xxiv

I know no author so likely as Sterne to corrupt the style and taste of his readers; all his writings are full of trick and affectation, (the very opposite of those chaste models of eloquence which antiquity has transmitted to us,) and are at best only calculated to excite the momentary admiration of the unthinking part of mankind.

(c) Extract from *Essays Historical and Moral*, 2nd ed. (1788), pp. 139–40

In LITERATURE we have [little] to boast; and I wish I could even add, that the national *taste* were likely to survive the wreck of *genius*. . . . The flippancy of France is preferred to the grace, the energy, I had almost said the *virtue*, of our native language; a tale of gallantry, or an unconnected farrago of mock pathetic, is preferred to the elegance of Hawkesworth,[1] or the moral of Johnson; and the tinsel of Sterne,[2] to the classic gold of Addison.

(d) Two extracts from *Letters on Literature, Taste, and Composition*, published posthumously and reprinted here from the Philadelphia edition of 1809 (pp. 16, 215)

. . . novelty is so powerful an instrument in the hands of genius, there is nothing in which young and incompetent writers will so much

[1] John Hawkesworth (1715(?)–73), miscellaneous writer, editor of the *Gentleman's Magazine*, and imitator of Johnson's style.
[2] [Gregory's note, added in the second edition.] I am sorry to find, that the admirers of Mr. Sterne have thought their favourite author degraded by this comparison. Let me assure them, in all honest candour, that if it were possible to oblige them, by speaking more favourably of him, it would give me pleasure to satisfy every well-disposed reader; but I must confess myself one of those insensible and incorrigible beings, who can read trite sentiments and mock pathos without being overwhelmed with admiration or melted into tenderness, merely because it is the fashion to be so: I must further own myself of that impatient temper, that I cannot toil through volumes of nonsense to find a wretched quibble, or a filthy double entendre.

expose themselves as in attempting it. Yet some authors of very secondary talents have acquired much temporary and transient fame, by an air of novelty. Among these, I cannot but rank the author of *Tristram Shandy*, the *Sentimental Journey*, &c. In these most unclassical productions, we see all regard to connexion and arrangement thrown aside; the reader is frequently left to help himself to a meaning, or, if there is one, it is such as no two men understand alike; sentiment is strangely mingled with attempts at wit, and both introduced with little apparent design. . . .

The popularity of Sterne is so far passed away, that it seems like insulting the ashes of the dead to criticize him with severity. Under the class of fictitious narrative it seems as if we could only consider his Tristram Shandy; for in what view to regard the Sentimental Journey, whether as truth or fiction, is difficult to determine; nor does it much signify with respect to so contemptible a performance. I heard it once remarked of this work, 'That the author seemed to have acted folly purposely for the sake of recording it.' The first pages of his Tristram Shandy are a manifest theft from the Memoirs of Martinus Scriblerus.[1] Indeed it has been proved that all his best passages are plagiarisms, of which however he made not the best use. I allow him all his merits when I say he had some turn for humour, some taste for the pathetic. But I am convinced that the ephemoral reputation of Tristram Shandy was much increased by the obscene allusions, and not a little by . . . 'typographical figures.'

[1] The Scriblerus Club was first organized in 1714 to undertake various literary projects, among them *The Memoirs of Martinus Scriblerus*, which was to be a satire on the abuses of learning. Members included Alexander Pope, Jonathan Swift, Dr John Arbuthnot, John Gay, Thomas Parnell, and Robert Harley, Earl of Oxford. The group met and worked together sporadically for twenty years, though the *Memoirs* were not published until 1741, when they were included in an edition of Pope's *Works*. They describe the conception, birth, and education of Martinus as well as later incidents in his career.

84. Anna Seward defends Sterne

1787, 1788

Extracts from *Letters of Anna Seward* (1811).

Anna Seward (1747–1809), minor poetess known as the Swan of Lichfield, knew many of the leading literary figures of her time. Spanning the two centuries, she disliked Johnson heartily and admired Scott, who became her literary executor. Her remarks in (a) below are a direct reply to No. 83a.

(a) **Extract** from a letter to the Reverend George Gregory, 5 December 1787 (i. 375–8)

And now, Sir, our day of combat is come.—You deny Sterne originality—and say that no classic ear can endure his style. These assertions more than surprise—they astonish me. What!—that imagination, which I have always thought of such exquisite, such original colouring! —that penetration which seems to have an hundred eyes with which to look into the human heart!—that happy, thrice happy, mixture of the humorous and the pathetic, in which he stands alone amongst all other writers out of the dramatic scale; resembling none, and whom not one, amongst his numerous imitators, have attempted to copy, without proving, by their total failure, the difficulty of acquiring a manner so singularly, so curiously original. Like ether, its spirit is too subtile and volatile to become the vehicle of any other person's ideas. And then that frolic fancy!—that all-atoning wit!—that style which my ear finds so natural, easy, animated, and eloquent!—how could you thus scorn them?

My dear Sir, *who* are they from whom he has borrowed? Some slight, very slight, resemblance perhaps exists between the best sallies of Swift's humour and Sterne's: but Swift has not any of Sterne's pathos, and Sterne has none of the filthiness of Swift,—though too apt to sport licentiously with comic double-meanings. His fault, in that respect, however justly censurable, has no tendency to injure the minds of his readers by inflaming their passions. Swift and Rabelais, whom he is also accused of copying, never interest the affections, while Sterne guides, turns, and precipitates them into any channel he pleases.

I can believe that he took the hint of character for his sub-acid philosopher from the Martinus Scriblerius of Pope, Swift, and Arbuthnot;[1] but there is an immense superiority in the vividness with which he has coloured his Shandy; in the dramatic spirit he has infused into the character; in the variety of situations in which he has placed the hypothesis-monger,—all natural, probable, and exquisitely humorous. We see and hear the little domestic group at Shandy-hall; nor can we help an involuntary conviction, not only that they all existed, but that they had been of our acquaintance; and where may be found even the most shadowy prototype in books, of uncle Toby and his Trim, of Mrs Shandy and Dr Slop?

At last this note of your's in your great work against Sterne—this note,

> At which my very locks have stood on end,
> Like quills upon the fretful porcupine,[2]

Confirms anew an observation of mine, long since made;—that I never knew a man or woman of letters, however ingenious, ingenuous, and judicious, as to their general taste, but there was some one fine writer, at least, to which their 'Lynx's beam became the mole's dim curtain.'[3] Mason, Hayley, and Boothby, are moles to Ossian, Gray was a mole to Rousseau.—Darwin is a mole to Milton, and that you will say is indeed a *molism*. Envy made Johnson a mole to all our best poets, except Dryden and Pope. You are a mole to Sterne.

(b) Extract from a letter to the Reverend George Gregory, 30 October 1788 (ii. 182–8)

I feel impelled to meet you, once more, on the ground of Sterne's pretensions to literary fame. It appears to me, upon the most mature deliberation, that few, if any, of the ancient or modern writers have greater claims to originality.

[1] See No. 83d, p. 267, n. 1.
[2] *Hamlet*, act 1, sc. 5, l. 20.
[3] La Fontaine, *Fables*, bk. I, fable 7.

Passing over the notorious imitations of the Latin poets, with Virgil at their head, of the Greek ones, recollect that Shakespeare borrowed almost all his plots, and the outlines of many of his characters from old novels—that Milton was indebted to the Scriptures for his story in the Paradise Lost, and to Homer, Dante, and Ariosto, for the chief features of his supernatural scenes. Taking designs from others, was never reckoned plagiarism. . . .

I think the *Tristram Shandy*, in natural humour, in dramatic spirit, and in truth of character, superior to the Scribleriad Family, in Pope's *Miscellanies*.

It cannot be denied, that this joint work of Pope, Swift, and Arbuthnot, suggested to Sterne the plan of *Tristram Shandy*;—but how has he drawn it out!—how glow his colours in the vivid tints of Nature! . . .

Neither can we conceive that such a character as Cornelius Scriblerus ever existed, while Shandy's pedantries and systematic absurdities are natural living manners—he is of our acquaintance;—we sit at table with him. Every personage in his family, down to the fat scullion, lives—and they are, by those happy characteristic touches, that mark the hand of genius, brought to our eye, as well as to our ear.

You observe that Toby Shandy is the Commodore Trunnion of Smollett. It is long since I read *Peregrine Pickle*, and it made so little impression, that I have no remembrance of the Commodore. It is impossible that I should ever, even after the slightest perusal, have forgotten the warm-hearted, honest, generous Toby Shandy, by whose absurdities, so happily mingling with his kindness, and with his virtues, we are betrayed at once into the tears of admiration, and into the convulsions of laughter.

Then the Corporal!—how finely are the traits of his disposition and manners, though of the same complexion, kept apart from those of his master!—What mutual and beautiful light do they throw upon each other! besides affording an admirable moral lesson, concerning the duty of that indulgent kindness, which lightens and sweetens servitude, and of that reverence to which a good master has a claim from his dependents!

Then Slop!—you must allow me to say inimitable Slop! Where will you shew me his prototype?—and O! the acute angle of the garden-wall! Obadiah! the coach horse! the mud! the doctor! and his poney! That story alone, so originally conceived, so happily told, outweighs, in my opinion, all the writings of Smollett, in the scale of genius.

Then for the simply pathetic, shew me the equal of Le Fevre, and his duteous boy!—Ah! my friend, can I learn to think these thrilling recollections the prejudices of girlism, and the echo of other people's opinions?

Surely there is no shadow of resemblance between the Dorothea of Cervantes,[1] and the Maria of Sterne, except in their itinerancy, and in the perfidy of their lovers. Nothing can be more unlike than their characters. The soft shades of insanity thrown over the woes of Maria, render her little mournful sallies a million of times more touching than the studied and minute circumlocution with which Dorothea relates her story.

The wild, yet slow air, which Maria plays to the virgin—her pathetic address to the dog, which she has in a string—'*Thou* shalt not leave me Sylvio!' alluding at once, in those few words, to the desertion of her lover, and to the death of her father;—ah! surely these traits, with many resembling ones, are in the genuine hues of tender sorrow! Strange does it appear to me, when such hearts as Mr Gregory's refuse to recognise, with the thrill of admiration, their pathos, and their truth! More do they interest me for the fair bereaved, than I could ever be interested for a bushel of such indistinct personages of the imagination as Dorothea. We are told that she weeps, but she says nothing that inclines us to weep with her. She yielded to her lover, not through affection, but interest, nor deigns she to bestow one regret on the parents she has deserted. Nature and probability are outraged, when such a character is held up to us as amiable; and surely justice is not less violated, when it is pronounced the prototype of the forsaken, gentle, duteous, tender, and simply-eloquent Maria. . . .

Forgive this second struggle for the fame of Sterne. With less honour for your judgment I had not molested your disapprobation. If your dislike is invincible, we will mention him no more—since, were I to become your proselyte on this subject, it must be at the expence of my gratitude, for many an hour that has been softened by his pathos, and gilded by his wit.

[1] See *Don Quixote*, pt. II, bk. I, chs 1, 2.

85. Johnson's biographer on Sterne

1787

Extract from Sir John Hawkins, *The Life of Samuel Johnson* (1787), p. 218.

Hawkins (1719–89), magistrate and antiquary, was a member of Johnson's circle.

Laurence Sterne, a clergyman and a dignitary of the cathedral church of York, was remarkable for a wild and eccentric genius, resembling in many respects that of Rabelais. The work that made him first known as a writer, was, *The life and opinions of Tristram Shandy*, a whimsical rhapsody, but abounding in wit and humour of the licentious kind. He too was a sentimentalist, and wrote sentimental journies and sentimental letters in abundance, by which both he and the booksellers got considerably. Of the writers of this class or sect it may be observed, that being in general men of loose principles, bad oeconomists, living without foresight, it is their endeavour to commute for their failings by professions of greater love to mankind, more tender affections and finer feelings than they will allow men of more regular lives, whom they deem formalists, to possess. Their generous notions supersede all obligation: they are a law to themselves, and having good hearts and abounding in the milk of human kindness, are above those considerations that bind men to that rule of conduct which is founded in a sense of duty. Of this new school of morality, Fielding, Rousseau, and Sterne are the principal teachers, and great is the mischief they have done by their documents.

86. Henry Mackenzie on Sterne

1788, c. 1825–31

Mackenzie (1745–1831), author of the popular novel, *The Man of Feeling* (1771), and often called a disciple of Sterne, was frequently compared to Sterne (see Nos 119, 123). Perhaps surprisingly, he has recorded no extended panegyric on Sterne; but see his brief earlier remarks on Sterne's *Letters* (No. 66d). Though he notices the importance of Sterne's influence on German sentimental literature of the 1770s in the first selection below, in the second, written sometime near the end of his life, he repudiates Sterne's lighter side.

(a) Extract from 'Account of the German Theatre,' read to the Royal Society of Edinburgh, 21 April 1788, and published in the society's *Transactions*, ii (1790). 158

About this period, the taste for sentimental and pathetic writing began to be wonderfully prevalent in Germany. The works of STERNE, and several other English authors of the same class, were read with the greatest avidity. I remember to have been told of a club or society, instituted at some town in Germany, whose name was taken from the *Snuff-box*, which forms a striking incident in the celebrated story of the monk in the *Sentimental Journey*.[1] The Poems of WIELAND, GESNER, WEISSE,[2] &c. are full of the most refined sentiment and sensibility; and the celebrated *Sorrows of* WERTER of *Goethe* carries those qualities to that enthusiastic height, which has so much captivated the young and the romantic of every country it has reached. This prevalence of highly refined sentiment seems commonly the attendant of newly-introduced literature, when letters are the property of a few secluded

[1] See No. 144.
[2] Salomon Gessner (1730–88), Swiss pastoral poet, and Christian Felix Weisse (1726–1804), poet and writer of children's books, were both known for their 'sentimental' poetry. For Wieland, see No. 141.

men, and have not yet allied themselves to the employments or the feelings of society. The same thing took place at the revival of letters in Europe after the long night of the middle ages. The Platonic love of the ancient romance, and of the poetical dialogue of the *Provencals*, was the produce of the same high-wrought and metaphysical sentiment, which is the natural result of fancy and feeling, untutored by a knowledge of the world, or the intercourse of ordinary life.

(b) Extract from *The Anecdotes and Egotisms of Henry Mackenzie*, ed. Harold W. Thompson (1927), p. 182

Sterne often wants the dignity of wit. I do not speak of his licentiousness, but he often is on the very verge of buffoonery, which is the bathos of wit, and the fool's coat is half upon him.

87. Sterne and the first American novel

1789

Extract from William Hill Brown, *The Power of Sympathy* (1789), i. 62–5.

Brown (1765–93) has been established as the author of this 'first American novel,' which was often attributed to Sarah Morton.

A considerable silence ensued, which *Worthy* first broke, by asking Mrs. *Bourn* what book she had in her hand. Every one's attention was alarmed at this important enquiry. Mrs. *Bourn*, with little difficulty, found the title page, and began to read, '*A Sentimental Journey through France and Italy, by Mr. Yorick.*'

'I do not like the *title*,' said Miss *Bourn*.

'Why, my dear!' apostrophized the mother, 'you are mistaken—it is a very famous book.'

'Why, my dear!' retorted the daughter, 'It is sentimental—I abominate every thing that is sentimental—it is so unfashionable too.'

'I never knew before,' said Mr. *Holmes*, 'that wit was subject to the caprice of fashion.'

'Why 'Squire *Billy*,' returned Miss, 'who is just arrived from the centre of politeness and fashion, says the bettermost genii never read any sentimental books—so you see sentiment is out of date.'

The company rose to go out.—

'Sentiment out of date!' cries *Worthy*, repeating the words of Miss *Bourn*, and taking the book from her mother, as she walked towards the door—'Sentiment out of date—alas! poor *Yorick*—may thy pages never be soiled by the fingers of prejudice.' He continued his address to the book, as they went out, in the same *Shandean* tone—'These anti-sentimentalists would banish thee from the society of all books! Unto what a pitiful size are the race of *readers* dwindled! Surely these *antis* have no more to do with thee, than the gods of the *Canaanites*—In character and understanding they are alike—eyes have *they*, but they see not—ears have *they*, but they hear not, neither is there any knowledge to be found in them.'[1] 'It is hardly worth while to beat it into them,' said my father-in-law, 'so let us follow the company.'

[1] See Psalms, 115: 4–8; 135: 15–18; Jeremiah, 5: 21; Ezekiel, 12: 2.

88. Some attacks and defenses of the 1780s

(a) Extract from *Sentimental Excursions to Windsor and other Places* (1781), pp. 60–2, by Leonard MacNally, self-confessed imitator of Sterne and author of a dramatic adaptation of *Tristram Shandy* (1783)

I have always read STERNE with delight, and never read him but I felt him in my heart more than in my head; yet I hope his precepts have improved my understanding in the same proportion they have expanded my humanity. His precepts affect me like *wine*, they make my heart glad,—they affect me like *love*, or rather they affect me like a *conjunction* of *love and wine*, for they make me generous and gay. Imbibing his opinions has sweetened whatever portion of acidity, Nature, Misfortune, and Disappointment have mixed in my composition; and having grafted them upon my heart, it is probable their emanations may produce some pleasing blossoms, some good fruit—Good fruit may be produced by ingrafting upon a *crab*—

If I should exhibit any feature bearing likeness to STERNE I shall be proud of the similarity; but for this happiness I can scarcely hope. The stile of STERNE is peculiar to himself, his art is to please the imagination and improve the mind, with natural, yet elegant simplicity. He is master of that charming enthusiasm inspired by heaven itself for the instruction of its creatures: and in his composition there is a certain incommunicable art of making one part rise gracefully out of another, which is felt by all, though seen only by the critic. His life, his opinions, his sermons, his journey, his letters, and everything he has written, will be read with admiration, will be read with pleasure, and with profit, when the laboured works of labouring philosophers, travellers, historians, politicians, and other *mouseingendering* compilers shall lie sleeping in dust upon the upper shelves of shops and libraries. The works of STERNE will be in the hands, in the heads, and in the hearts of every man, ay, and every woman too, of feeling; when the works of the *Smell-fungusses* and the *Mundungusses*[1] of the age, will be lining trunks and band boxes.

[1] See No. 53j.

(b) Extract from William Creech (1745–1815), Lord Provost of Edinburgh, publisher of Burns, and miscellaneous writer, 'Letter to *Edinburgh Evening Courant*,' 30 August 1783, reprinted in *Edinburgh Fugitive Pieces* (1815), pp. 150–2

Men are, in every respect, like books: . . . Some men say a great deal about nothing at all, and when they have exhausted their strength in speaking to you for a whole evening, you cannot recollect that they have ever said any thing which is worth remembering, or affects the judgment. Some books, too, talk a great deal about it, and about it, and when you come to the *finis,* you wonder what the d—l the author would be at. Such is the case with the greater part of Sterne's celebrated work, where the author, under an air of pretended mystery, endeavours to conceal nothing at all; and when you have finished, you remember that you have been now and then tickled, but you cannot help thinking that there is more real wit and just satire in a very few pages in Swift or Fielding than in the whole book.

(c) Extract from James Beattie, *Dissertations Moral and Critical* (1783), p. 177. Beattie (1735–1803) was Professor of Moral Philosophy and Logic at the University of Aberdeen. His censure of Sterne is interesting in that he pairs him with Smollett and does not include him with Rabelais. Beattie makes no mention of Sterne in his more famous work *On Fable and Romance*

If, in [an author's] comick scenes, he attempt to raise laughter by unnatural exaggeration; which is sometimes done by Sterne and Smollett: if, instead of humour, he obtrude upon you indecent buffoonery; which is frequent in Aristophanes and Rabelais: if, where he intends wit, he can only bring forth common-place jokes, or verbal quibbles; of which I am sorry to say that there is an example or two in Milton: or if, with Congreve and Vanburgh, he endeavour to make crimes and misfortunes matter of merriment; we must believe, either that he has no true sense of ridicule, or that he wilfully debases it, to gratify the taste of the times, or the singularity of his own temper.

(d) Extract from the dedication 'to Mr. Yorick, in the Elysian Fields' of the anonymous *Unfortunate Sensibility* (1784), pp. vii–viii

[Your] *gaieté de coeur*[1] but ill became the sable vestment.—Can you tell me, Yorick, by what strange mistake you were condemned to so grave a garb, together with all the formal solemnities which wait upon that office—What had you to do with such grimace?—All rules prescribed to genius is an affront, even to the gods—This sentiment may not meet the approbation of the earth-born sons of bigotry and superstition—but you, whose crystal mind contained a million of celestial laws engraven by the golden pen of mighty Jove, must see how mean and trumpery the leaden rules of the poor stupid tyrant custom—You never were created for a priest, unless indeed to be the father of some happy convent—How would thy kind soul have melted at the soft confession of the female penitent, and while the tear of sympathy was mingled with her grief, what tender consolations would have flowed spontaneously from thy benevolent heart!—What easy penance, as the representative of infinite mercy, wouldest thou have enjoined!—Ah! Yorick, thy convent would have been crouded with devotees—this were an employ well suited to thy gentle disposition.

(e) Extract from the anonymous 'On the Imitators of Sterne,' *Westminster Magazine*, xiii (November 1785). 587

For a man to think of accommodating his genius to a manner of writing so peculiar and excentric as that of Sterne's, seems to imply a strange contempt of the great ordinances of Nature, '*Chacun a son talent*'[2] says a French writer, but though every man has some talent, *non omnibus omnia*, no one is equal to all. The genius, or talents of men, nature has marked as variously as their countenances; and if it would be absurd for the whole race of womankind to attempt to alter or adjust their features to the form of any one female face, which they should agree upon as the standard of beauty, and expect to give equal pleasure with the original to those who contemplated their beauty, can it be much less

[1] Wantonness.
[2] Everyone has his own talent.

ridiculous in this herd of scribblers to expect to excite any other
sensation, except that of disgust, by their imitations of a writer, whose
consummate learning, and originality of sentiment, are not his only
recommendations, but who is a like distinguished for the finest satire,
and the most delicate sympathy? Without these latter qualities, which
seldom unite, no writer, I will maintain, can give the faintest imitation
of Sterne.

(f) Extract from *A Chinese Fragment* (1786), pp. 101–3, by Ely
Bates, writer on religious, moral, and political subjects

The *novel* and *romance* has been the species of composition most in
vogue for half a century, and may be justly reckoned among the chief
causes of the general depravity. In China, they are designed to illustrate
some instance of prudence or virtue, and are conducted without any
offence to the strictest decorum; whereas in this Island, they are commonly founded upon the most violent passion in our nature, which
they tend to inflame by an artful series of lewd adventures, and
fascinating descriptions. I have lately seen a *farrago* of this kind; in itself
too low for censure, and which I only notice in relation to the national
character. Under the thin pretext of sentimental refinement, it is calculated, with more effect, to taint the imagination, and corrupt the heart;
and this *novel* is still in fashion. [Sterne] is by some extolled as a philanthropist, and even as a philosopher: For my part, I will venture to pronounce him a *villain* and a *hypocrite*: since, in spite of his effusions of
humanity, he that wantonly stabs the *morals* of his country is a villain;
and he is a hypocrite, if, under such a conduct, he makes pretensions to
benevolence: And how he came to be mistaken for a philosopher, I am
at a loss to determine. Even to have produced such an author, would be
some disgrace to a community; as it could hardly be supposed to have
happened, where morals and decency were had in reputation; but that
he should generally be read and applauded, evinces the profligacy of the
public manners.

(g) Extract from a letter, 7 October 1788, from John Howe, 4th Lord Chedworth (1754–1804) in *Letters from the Late Lord Chedworth to the Rev. Thomas Crampton* (1840), p. 111

Fielding was certainly a very great master of human nature; he ranks very high in my estimate: far, far above Sterne: as a moralist he may be compared with Johnson; I mean for knowledge of the human heart, and I am yet to be convinced that he yields to him; perhaps to few writers in the language.

THE 1790s: PLAGIARISM

89. Charles Dibdin on Sterne and Johnson

1790

Extracts from a history of literature, first published serially in *The By-Stander* in 1789–90, and reprinted here from the collected edition of 1790, pp. 273, 321–2.

Dibdin (1745–1814) had a colorful and stormy career as dramatist, actor, and song-writer. In the second selection, Dibdin refers to Samuel Johnson as 'Oliver,' under the analogy between his literary dictatorship and Oliver Cromwell's political one.

All the would-be lady writers have sprung from RICHARDSON, just as all the would-be gentlemen writers have sprung from STERNE.

If STERNE had been a poet, it is possible that, out of whim, he might have disputed the literary throne with *Oliver*. It is well known he wrote with a view alone to establish a reputation for singularity; for he says himself that when he began *Tristram Shandy*, he did not know what drift he should pursue; and this begets a most curious and severe satire on all those who pretend they saw through his intention from the moment they took the first volume in their hands. But it is not a very uncommon thing for readers to arrogate a knowledge of what an author intended better than he did himself. Oliver, the immaculate Oliver, is not always free from this left-handed gift.

STERNE, with many other merits as a writer, possessed great good sense. He could either surprise or penetrate the heart at will, but he generally chose surprise, because he knew that even a novelty in the mode of making you feel renders the sensation more welcome to you. There was a servility however in this to a great and good mind such as STERNE'S was; but it was the surest chance for popularity, unless, as I hint before, he had fairly entered the lists with Oliver, and contended for the throne.

Had he done this the pretender would have sat in a most uneasy situation.—STERNE had genius enough for any thing, and he knew human nature so well that he had it in his power to have begot the most awkward and clumsy anxiety in Oliver. I have not the smallest doubt that if STERNE had invented a series of dogmas in opposition to those which were daily uttered by Oliver, and credited as gospel by his adherents, an universal laugh would have been raised to the honour of STERNE, and at the expence of the pretender, and perhaps the credit of his pretensions.

90. John Ferriar and Sterne's plagiarism

1791, 1798, 1812

John Ferriar (1761–1815), a medical doctor of wide-ranging literary interests, may have been first drawn to Sterne's work by the obstetrical discussions in the early part of *Tristram Shandy*. His interest in Sterne led him to a continuing study of Sterne's possible literary sources and finally to the conclusion that Sterne had plagiarized widely. Though other writers had hinted at Sterne's lack of originality (see, for example, No. 83a), Ferriar was the first to document Sterne's sources extensively and thus provide solid ammunition for Sterne's detractors. Changes in Ferriar's own attitude can be traced in the selections below: he at first thought that Sterne's originality was not at stake (a), but later concluded, echoing one of the critical clichés about Sterne, that Sterne was a master of the 'pathetic' whose humor, however, was borrowed (b). For some typical reactions to Ferriar's disclosures, see No. 102.

(a) Extract from 'Comments on Sterne,' a paper read before the Literary and Philosophical Society of Manchester on 21 January 1791 and published in the society's *Memoirs*, iv (1793). 45–86

This is almost the only satirical and ethical writer of note, who wants a commentator. The works of Rabelais, Butler, Pope, Swift, and many others, are over-loaded with explanations, while Sterne remains, in many places, unintelligible to the greater number of his readers. . . .

Indeed, there is some danger in attempting to detect the sources, from which Sterne drew his rich singularities. It has been fashionable of late, to decry the analysis of objects of admiration, and those who wish to trace the mysteries of wit and literary pleasure, are held to be profane dissectors, who mangle the carcase of learning, out of spleen and idle curiosity. Besides, the originality of Sterne has scarcely been made a problem; on the contrary, he is considered as the inventor of a new style in our language. I cannot help thinking, however . . . that it imports us little to hear what we do not understand; and though far beneath the dignity of Horace or Pope,[1] who professed to admire nothing, I think it very unphilosophical, to let wonder conquer reason, especially in the closet. . . .

In tracing some of Sterne's ideas to other writers, I do not mean to treat him as a Plagiarist; I wish to illustrate,[2] not to degrade him. If some instances of copying be proved against him, they will detract nothing from his genius, and will only lessen that imposing appearance he sometimes assumed, of erudition which he really wanted.

It is obvious to every one, who considers *Tristram Shandy* as a general Satire, levelled chiefly against the abuse of speculative opinions, that Rabelais furnished Sterne with the general character, and even many particular ideas, of his work. From that copious fountain of learning, wit and whim, our author drew deeply. Rabelais, stored with erudition, poured lavishly out, what Sterne directed and expanded with care, to enrich his pages. And to this appropriation, we owe many of his most pleasing sallies. For being bounded in his literacy acquirements, his imagination had freer play, and more natural graces. He seized the grotesque objects of obsolete erudition, presented by his original, with a vigour untamed by previous labour, and an ardour unabated by familiarity with literary folly. The curious Chapters on Noses afford the strongest proof of this remark. . . .[3]

Perhaps it would do violence to the analogy, to say that the exquisite dialogues, scattered through *Tristram Shandy*, took any colour from those delivered by Rabelais.—At least, it would appear to be refining too far. Yet the contrast and contention of characters and professions so striking in both romances; the strong ridicule thrown upon the love of hypothesis; and the art with which absurdities in every walk of science are exposed, have always impressed me with a general idea of resemblance; and have recalled Pantagruel, Panurge and Epistemon, in many of the Shandean conversations. If there be any degree of imitation in this respect, it is greatly to Sterne's honour. A higher polish was never given to rugged materials. But there can be no doubt respecting Sterne's obligations to another Author, once the favourite of the learned

[1] In a footnote Ferriar quotes Horace, *Epistolae*, I. 6. 1–2: 'To marvel at nothing, Numicius, is almost the one and only thing which can make and keep a man happy'; and Pope, *Essay on Criticism*, part ii, l. 391: 'For fools admire, but men of sense approve.'
[2] Ferriar is using the word 'illustrate' in the sense of 'shed lustre upon' as well as that of 'explain'; the former meaning was still current.
[3] Ferriar quotes parallel passages from Sterne and Rabelais, as well as citing other authors on noses, some of whom Sterne did not know.

and witty, though now unaccountably neglected. I have often wondered at the pains bestowed by Sterne, in ridiculing opinions not
fashionable in his day, and have thought it singular, that he should
produce the portrait of his Sophist, Mr. Shandy, with all the stains and
mouldiness of the last century about him. For the love of scarce and
whimsical books, was no vice of the time when Tristram Shandy
appeared. But I am now convinced, that all the singularities of that
character were drawn from the perusal of *Burton's Anatomy of Melancholy*; not without reference, however, to the peculiarities of Burton's
life, who is alledged to have fallen a victim to his astrological studies.
We are told, accordingly, that Mr. Shandy had faith in astrology.[1]

The *Anatomy of Melancholy*, though written on a regular plan, is so
crouded with quotations, that the reader is apt to mistake it for a book
of commonplaces. The opinions of a multitude of Authors are collected, under every division, without arrangement, and without much
nicety of selection, to undergo a general sentence; for the bulk of the
materials enforces brevity on the writer. In the course of a moderate
folio, Burton has contrived to treat a great variety of topics, that seem
very loosely connected with his subject; and, like Bayle,[2] when he starts
a train of quotations, he does not scruple to let the digression outrun the
principal question. . . . The quaintness of many of his divisions seems
to have given Sterne the hint of his ludicrous titles to several Chapters;[3] and the risible effect resulting from Burton's grave endeavours,
to prove indisputable facts by weighty quotations, he has happily
caught, and sometimes well burlesqued. This was the consequence of
an opinion, prevalent in the last age, . . . that authorities are facts.

But where the force of the subject opens Burton's own vein of Prose,
we discover valuable sense and brilliant expression. The proof of this
will appear in those passages, which Sterne has borrowed from him
without variation. . . . In literature, the springs are commonly more
copious than their derived streams, and are therefore more highly
honoured. But though this applies to Burton, and most of his imitators,
it fails in respect of *Tristram Shandy*, where, though much is directly
drawn from our Author, there are many delightful windings, widely
distant from his influence. I would therefore beware of imitating the
rashness of a Traveller, who should fancy he had discovered the secret

[1] Ferriar makes reference to *Tristram Shandy*, III. 23, p. 206, and V. 28, p. 386.
[2] The reference is to Pierre Bayle (1647–1706), French philosopher famous for his *Historical
and Critical Dictionary*, which contained long notes with many quotations.
[3] The *Tale of a Tub*, and *The Memoirs of Scriblerus* must come in for a share of this influence.
[Ferriar's note]. For *Scriblerus* see No. 83d, p. 267, n. 1.

STERNE

head of a mighty river, while, deceived by imperfect intelligence, he
had only explored the source of an auxiliary stream. . . .[1]
 There is another writer, whose pathetic manner Sterne seems to have
caught; it is Marivaux,—the father of the sentimental style.[2] A careful
perusal of his writings, and of those of the younger Crébillon,[3] might
perhaps elucidate the serious parts of *Tristram Shandy*, and the *Sentimental Journey*. But I must leave this undertaking to those who have
sufficient time to sacrifice to the task. From these Authors, I think,
Sterne learnt to practice what Quintilian had made a precept: Minus
est TOTUM dicere quam OMNIA.[4] With genius enough for the
attempt, one has frequently failed in producing pleasure by the length
of his digressions, and the other by affecting an excessive refinement
and ambiguity in his language. . . . Sterne has seldom indulged these
lapses, for which he was probably indebted to the buoyant force of
Burton's firm Old-English sinews. [Ferriar continues by citing evidence
of influence upon Sterne from Marivaux, Donne, Swift, Montaigne,
and Bishop Hall (the last for Sterne's *Sermons*).]
 What assistance the writings of Voltaire and Rousseau afforded
Sterne, I omit to enquire. The former was the first author of this age,
who introduced the terms and operations of the modern art of war into
works of entertainment; but Sterne's military ardour seems to have
been inspired by the prolix details of honest Tindal.[5] Voltaire himself
reviewed the first volumes of Tristram Shandy, in one of the foreign
Journals, and did not charge their author with the imitation of any
persons but Rabelais and Swift.[6] He was probably not very jealous of
the reputation of a modern English writer.
 Such are the casual notes, with the collection of which I have sometimes diverted a vacant half-hour. They leave Sterne in possession of
every praise but that of curious erudition, to which he had no great
pretence, and of unparelleled originality, which ignorance only can
ascribe to any polished writer. It would be enjoining an impossible task,
to exact much knowledge on subjects frequently treated, and yet to

[1] Ferriar quotes numerous parallel passages of Sterne and Burton, but speaks of Sterne's
'improvements' and asserts Sterne 'has certainly done wonders, whenever he has imitated
or borrowed.'
[2] See No. 72d, p. 240, n. 1.
[3] See No. 72d, p. 240, n. 2.
[4] It is less effective to summarize all that happens than to recount it detail by detail.
(Quintilian, *Institutio oratoria*, 8. 3. 70.)
[5] Nicholas Tindal (1687–1774), author of a translation and continuation of Rapin's *History
of England* (1725–45).
[6] See No. 130b.

prohibit the use of thoughts and expressions rendered familiar by study, merely because they had been occupied by former Authors. There is a kind of imitation which the Ancients encouraged, and which even our Gothic Criticism admits, when acknowledged. But justice cannot permit the Polygraphic Copy to be celebrated at the expence of the Original.

Voltaire has compared the merits of Rabelais and Sterne, as Satirists of the Abuse of Learning,[1] and, I think, has done neither of them justice. This great distinction is obvious; that Rabelais derided absurdities then existing in full force, and intermingled much sterling sense with the grossest parts of his book; Sterne, on the contrary, laughs at many exploded opinions, and abandoned fooleries, and contrives to degrade some of his most solemn passages by a vicious levity. . . .

The talents for so delicate an office as that of a literary Censor, are too great and numerous to be often assembled in one person. Rabelais wanted decency, Sterne learning, and Voltaire fidelity. Lucian alone supported the character properly, in those pieces which appear to be justly ascribed to him. As the narrowness of Party yet infests Philosophy, a writer with his qualifications would still do good service in the Cause of Truth. For wit and good sense united, as in him they eminently were, can attack nothing successfully which ought not to be demolished.

(b) Extracts from *Illustrations of Sterne* (1798). This volume, in which Ferriar amplifies his earlier 'Comments,' opens with an introductory poem, presumably Ferriar's

---

> STERNE, for whose sake I plod thro' miry ways
> Of antic wit, and quibbling mazes drear
> Let not thy shade malignant censure fear,
> Tho' aught of borrow'd mirth my search betrays.
> Long slept that mirth in dust of ancient days,
> (Erewhile to GUISE, or wanton VALOIS dear)[2]

[1] See No. 130b; Voltaire also includes Swift in the comparison.
[2] The House of Valois ruled France from 1328–1589, when it was succeeded by the Bourbon kings. The last Valois, Henry III, was notorious for his scandalous behavior. The Guise family was a dominant influence on the last Valois kings. Ferriar sketches a picture of the culture of the French court at this time (see below).

Till wak'd by thee in SKELTON'S[1] joyous pile,
She flung on TRISTRAM her capricious rays.
But the quick tear, that checks our wond'ring smile,
In sudden pause, or unexpected story,
Owns thy true mast'ry; and *Le Fevre's* woes,
Maria's wand'rings, and the *Pris'ner's* throes
Fix thee conspicuous on the shrine of glory. (p. 2)

When the first volumes of *Tristram Shandy* appeared, they excited almost as much perplexity as admiration. The feeling, the wit, and reading which they displayed were sufficiently relished, but the wild digressions, the abruptness of the narratives and discussions, and the perpetual recurrence to obsolete notions in philosophy, gave them more the air of a collection of fragments, than of a regular work. Most of the writers from whom Sterne drew the general ideas, and many of the peculiarities of his book, were then forgotten. Rabelais was the only French wit of the sixteenth century, who was generally read, and from his obscurity, it would have been vain to have expected any illustration of a modern writer.

Readers are often inclined to regard with veneration, what they do not understand. They suppose a work to be deep, in proportion to its darkness, and give the author credit for recondite learning, in many passages, where his incapacity, or his carelessness, have prevented him from explaining himself with clearness. It was not the business of Sterne to undeceive those, who considered his *Tristram* as a work of unfathomable knowledge.

He had read with avidity the ludicrous writers, who flourished under the last princes of the race of Valois, and the first of the Bourbons. They were at once courtiers, men of wit, and, some of them, profound scholars. They offered to a mind full of sensibility, and alive to every impression of curiosity and voluptuousness, the private history of an age, in which every class of readers feels a deep interest; in which the heroic spirit of chivalry seemed to be tempered by letters, and the continued conflict of powerful and intrepid minds produced memorable changes, in religion, in politics, and philosophy. They shewed, to a keen observer of the passions, the secret movements, which directed the splendid scenes beheld with astonishment by Europe. They exhibited statesmen and heroes drowning their country in blood, for the favours

---

[1] Skelton Castle, the 'Crazy Castle' of Sterne's Eugenius, John Hall-Stevenson. Sterne read many curious and rare books in his friend's library.

of a mistress, or a quarrel at a ball; and veiling under the shew of patriotism, or religious zeal, the meanest and most criminal motives. While he was tempted to imitate their productions, the dormant reputation of most of these authors seemed to invite him to a secret treasure of learning, wit, and ridicule. To the facility of these acquisitions, we probably owe much of the gaiety of Sterne. His imagination, untamed by labour, and unsated by a long acquaintance with literary folly, dwelt with enthusiasm on the grotesque pictures of manners and opinions, displayed in his favourite authors. It may even be suspected, that by this influence he was drawn aside from his natural bias to the pathetic; for in the serious parts of his works, he seems to have depended on his own force, and to have found in his own mind whatever he wished to produce; but in the ludicrous, he is generally a copyist, and sometimes follows his original so closely, that he forgets the changes of manners, which give an appearance of extravagance to what was once correct ridicule. . . . (pp. 4–7)

The establishment of a buffoon, or king's jester, which operated so forcibly on Sterne's imagination, as to make him adopt the name of *Yorick*, furnished an additional motive for the exertions of ludicrous writers, in that age. To jest was the ambition of the best company; and when the progress of civilization is duly weighed, between the period to which I have confined my observations, and the time of Charles II. of this country, it will appear that the value set upon *sheer wit*, as it was then called, was hardly less inconsistent with strict judgment, than was the merriment of the cap and bells with the grave discussions of the furred doctors, or learned ladies of the old French court. . . . (pp. 21–2)

From Rabelais, Sterne seems to have caught the design of writing a general satire on the abuse of speculative opinions. The dreams of Rabelais's commentators have indeed discovered a very different intention in his book, but we have his own authority for rejecting their surmises as groundless. In the dedication of part of his work to Cardinal Chastillon, he mentions the political allusions imputed to him, and disclaims them expressly. He declares, that he wrote for the recreation of persons languishing in sickness, or under the pressure of grief and anxiety, and that his joyous prescription had succeeded with many patients. . . .[1]

The birth and education of *Pantagruel* evidently gave rise to those of

---

[1] See the letter addressed 'To the Most Illustrious Prince and Most Reverend Monseigneur Odet, Cardinal of Châtillon' at the beginning of Rabelais's fourth book.

Martinus Scriblerus,[1] and both were fresh in Sterne's memory, when he composed the first chapters of *Tristram Shandy.*

It must be acknowledged, that the application of the satire is more clear in Rabelais, than in his imitators. Rabelais attacked boldly the scholastic mode of education, in that part of his work; and shewed the superiority of a natural method of instruction, more accommodated to the feelings and capacities of the young. But Sterne, and the authors of Scriblerus, appear to ridicule the folly of some individual; for no public course of education has ever been proposed, similar to that which they exhibit.

Perhaps it was Sterne's purpose, to deride the methods of shortening the business of education, which several ingenious men have amused themselves by contriving. . . .[2] (pp. 24–6)

Sterne has generally concealed the sources of his curious trains of investigation, and uncommon opinions, but in one instance he ventured to break through his restraint, by mentioning *Bouchet's Evening Conferences,*[3] among the treasures of Mr. Shandy's library. . . .

The conversations are not, indeed, connected by any narrative, but I entertain little doubt, that from the perusal of this work, Sterne conceived the first precise idea of his *Tristram*, as far as any thing can be called precise, in a desultory book, apparently written with great rapidity. The most ludicrous and extravagant parts of the book seem to have dwelt upon Sterne's mind, and he appears to have frequently recurred to them from memory. . . . (pp. 41–3)

The use which Sterne made of Burton and Hall, and his great familiarity with their works, had considerable influence on his style; it was rendered, by assimilation with their's, more easy, more natural, and more expressive. Every writer of taste and feeling must indeed be invigorated, by drinking at the 'well of English undefiled;'[4] but like the Fountain of Youth, celebrated in the old romances, its waters generally elude the utmost efforts of those who strive to appropriate them. . . . (pp. 98–9)

[Sterne] had obtained a glimpse of the physiognomic doctrines respecting the nose, but he was ignorant of the general systems which had prevailed concerning the art itself. . . . To have completed Mr.

---

[1] See No. 83d, p. 267, n. 1.
[2] Ferriar mentions Swift, Descartes, Lully, and Erasmus in this connection.
[3] The reference is to the *Serées* of Guillaume Bouchet (*c.* 1514–94).
[4] Spenser refers to 'Dan Chaucer, well of English undefiled' in the *Faerie Queene*, bk. IV, canto ii, st. 32.

Shandy's character, he ought to have been a professed physiognomist. Slawkenbergius's treatise would then have taken form and substance, and Sterne would have written one of the most interesting and amusing books that ever appeared.

Perhaps no man possessed so many requisites for producing a good work on physiognomy. His observation of characters was sagacious, minutely accurate, and unwearied. His feeling was ever just, versatile as life itself, and was conveyed to the reader with full effect, because without affectation. But his imagination was ill-regulated, and it had a constant tendency to form combinations on this particular subject, which his taste alone, to say nothing of other motives, should have led him to reject. . . . (pp. 142–3)

Sterne truly resembled Shakespeare's Biron, in the extent of his depredations from other writers, for the supply of *Tristram*:

> His eye begot occasion for his wit:
> For ev'ry object that the one did catch,
> The other turn'd to a mirth-moving jest.[1]

Burton furnished the grand magazine, but many other books, which fell incidentally into his hands, were laid under contribution. . . . (p. 169)

The plan of the *Sentimental Journey* seems to have been taken from the little French pieces, which have had such celebrity; the *Voyage* of Chapelle and Bachaumont,[2] and the *Voyage* of Fontaine,[3] the merit of which consists in making trifles considerable. The only material difference between Sterne's pleasant fragment and these, consists in the want of verse. The French sentimental tours are enlivened by rhymes of great variety, and Sterne would perhaps have imitated them in this respect, if he could have written poetry. . . . (pp. 177–8)

I have thus put the reader in possession of every observation respecting this agreeable author, which it would be important or proper to communicate. If his opinion of Sterne's learning and originality be lessened by the perusal, he must, at least, admire the dexterity and the good

[1] *Love's Labour's Lost*, act 2, sc. 1.
[2] François Le Coigneux de Bachaumont (1624–1702) and Claude Emanuel Luillier (pseud., Chapelle) (1626–86) were co-authors of the *Voyage de Chapelle et de Bachaumont* (1663), a book of light verse and prose describing a journey through the south of France with much wit and occasional satire.
[3] Charles Fontaine (1514–c. 1588) used materials from his travels in France and Italy in some of his poems.

taste with which he has incorporated in his work so many passages, written with very different views by their respective authors. It was evidently Sterne's purpose to make a pleasant, saleable book, *coute que coute*,[1] and after taking his general plan from some of the older French writers, and from Burton, he made prize of all the good thoughts that came in his way. (pp. 181–2)

(c) Extract from *Illustrations of Sterne*, 2nd ed. (1812), i. 129, 143–4

There are some peculiarities in the principal characters of *Tristram Shandy*, which render it probable that Sterne copied them from real life. My enquiries at York have thrown no light on this subject, excepting what regards the personage of Doctor Slop. From some publications which accidentally fell into my hands, I had formed a conjecture, which . . . is supported by tradition, that under this title, Sterne meant to satirize Dr. JOHN BURTON, of York.[2]
[Ferriar continues with speculations that some of Sterne's other characters had originals in life.]

It is impossible to quit this subject, without remarking, once more, what a waste of talents is occasioned by temporary satire. We know hardly any thing of Sterne's objects; those of Rabelais are merely matters of conjecture; the authors satirized by Boileau are only known by his censures; and the heroes of the Dunciad are indebted to Pope for their preservation. . . . Why will men of genius condescend to record their resentment against blockheads?

[1] Whatever the cost.
[2] John Burton, MD (1710–71), able physician and obstetrician, was caricatured by Sterne with a rather heavy hand as Dr Slop. Sterne's antipathy dates back to political battles of the 1740s when he helped his uncle, Dr Jaques Sterne, influential Yorkshire pluralist, in support of the Whigs against the Tories. Burton's extreme Toryism made him suspect of being a Jacobite and a Papist as well, though the suspicions were apparently unjust. For a fuller account of Sterne's relationship with Burton, see Lewis P. Curtis, *The Politicks of Laurence Sterne* (1929).

91. Joseph Dennie on Sterne

1792, 1796

Joseph Dennie (1768–1812), lawyer, lay preacher, and editor, has been described as 'the ablest writer of familiar essays in the United States before Washington Irving.' As editor of the *Port Folio* (see No. 110) from 1801–12, he was one of the chief arbiters of literary taste. A devotee of Sterne, Dennie modeled the style for his *Lay Preacher* after Sterne's sermons. His essays abound with allusions to Sterne although they do not contain extended critical discussions.

(a) Extract from a letter, 17 April 1792, to his father and mother, Mr and Mrs Joseph Dennie Sr (*The Letters of Joseph Dennie*, ed. Laura Green Pedder (1936), *University of Maine Studies*, 2nd ser., No. 36, p. 107)

Upon a careful review of this *Volume* of my correspondence, I plume myself not a little upon its composition. When I subjoin the reason, you will acknowledge I have cause. It has the double honor, of contradicting an assertion of Aristotle's, & of resembling *Tristram Shandy*. Aristotle avers that every legitimate work should have a beginning, a middle and an end[.] this letter was born in lawful wedlock of labor & invention & yet it has neither of the above requisites. Tristram Shandy abounds in digression & is at war with method. In *these* particulars I am as lucky as Sterne. To what a height I have climbed on the literary ladder!! I have overthrown a dogma of philosophy & I emulate the eccentricities of genius.

(b) Extract from *The Lay Preacher*, 1796 (*The Lay Preacher*, ed. Milton Ellis (1943), *Scholars' Facsimiles & Reprints*, p. 68)

From my attachment to simplicity in writing, I read Sterne more attentively than Stackhouse[1] and prefer a story in Genesis to a volume of Gibbon.

92. Isaac D'Israeli on Sterne

1795, 1796, 1840

Isaac D'Israeli (1766–1848), literary critic and historian, was the father of Benjamin Disraeli, first Earl of Beaconsfield. The friend of Southey and Scott, he was also admired by Byron. He spent a lifetime in researching literary curiosities and published several lively books of history and criticism. The third selection below, though not published until 1840, sums up D'Israeli's lifelong views and looks back to Sterne's popularity at the turn of the century.

(a) Extract from *An Essay on the Manners and Genius of the Literary Character* (1795), pp. 148–9

The writer's heart may be as little penetrated by the charms and virtues he describes, as the tragic poet would be incapable of committing the assassinations and massacres he commands in a verse, or details in a scene.

Montagne appears to have been sensible of this fact in the literary

[1] Thomas Stackhouse (1677–1752) was author of a three-volume *New History of the Bible* (1737).

character . . . and I am not yet persuaded that the simplicity of this old and admirable favourite of Europe might not have been a theatrical gesture, as much as the sensibility of Sterne.

(b) Extracts from *Miscellanies; or Literary Recreations* (1796)

Why is Addison still the first of our essayists? he has sometimes been excelled in criticisms more philosophical, in topics more interesting, and in diction more coloured. But there is a pathetic charm in the character he has assumed, in his periodical Miscellanies, which is felt with such a gentle force, that we scarce advert to it. He has painted forth his little humours, his individual feelings, and eternised himself to his readers. Johnson and Hawkesworth[1] we receive with respect, and we dismiss with awe; we come from their writings as from public lectures, and from Addison's as from private conversations.

Sterne perhaps derives a portion of his celebrity from the same influence; he interests us in his minutest motions, for he tells us all he feels. Richardson was sensible of the power with which these minute strokes of description enter the heart, and which are so many fastenings to which the imagination clings. (pp. 11–12)

Dr. Feriar's Essay on the Imitations of Sterne might be considerably augmented; the Englishman may be tracked in many obscure paths. . . . Such are the writers, however, who imitate, but are inimitable! (p. 318)

(c) Extract from 'Of Sterne,' *Miscellanies of Literature*, new ed. (New York, 1841; preface dated London, May 1840), i. 58–60

CERVANTES is immortal—Rabelais and STERNE have passed away to the curious.

These fraternal geniuses alike chose their subjects from their own times. Cervantes, with the innocent design of correcting a temporary folly to his countrymen, so that the very success of the design might have proved fatal to the work itself; for when he had cut off the heads

[1] See No. 83c, n. 1.

of the hydra, an extinct monster might cease to interest the readers of other times, and other manners. But Cervantes, with judgment equal to his invention, and with a cast of genius made for all times, delighted his contemporaries and charms his posterity. He looked to the world and collected other follies than the Spanish ones, and to another age than the administration of the duke of Lerma; with more genuine pleasantry than any writer from the days of Lucian, not a solitary spot has soiled the purity of his page; while there is scarcely a subject in human nature for which we might not find some apposite illustration. . . .

Rabelais and Sterne were not perhaps inferior in genius, and they were read with as much avidity and delight as the Spaniard. 'Le docte Rabelais'[1] had the learning which the Englishman wanted; while unhappily Sterne undertook to satirise false erudition, which requires a knowledge of the true. . . .

In my youth the world doted on Sterne! Martin Sherlock[2] ranks him among 'the luminaries of the century.' Forty years ago, young men, in their most facetious humours, never failed to find the archetype of society in the Shandy family—every good-natured soul was uncle Toby, every humourist was old Shandy, every child of nature was Corporal Trim! It may now be doubted whether Sterne's natural dispositions were the humorous or the pathetic: the pathetic has survived.

There is nothing of a more ambiguous nature than strong humour, and Sterne found it to be so; and latterly, in despair, he asserted that 'the taste for humour is the gift of heaven!'[3] I have frequently observed how humour, like the taste for olives, is even repugnant to some palates, and have witnessed the epicure of humour lose it all by discovering how some have utterly rejected his favourite relish! Even men of wit may not taste humour! . . . Cervantes excels in that sly satire which hides itself under the cloak of gravity, but this is not the sort of humour which so beautifully plays about the delicacy of Addison's page; and both are distinct from the broader and strong humour of Sterne. . . .

[W]hile more than half of the three kingdoms were convulsed with laughter at [Sterne's] humour, the other part were obdurately dull to it. Take, for instance, two very opposite effects produced by Tristram Shandy on a man of strong original humour himself, and a wit who

[1] The 'learned' Rabelais (with a hint of irony).
[2] For Sherlock's more extended views on Sterne, see No. 76.
[3] See No. 55b.

had more delicacy and sarcasm than force and originality. The Rev. Philip Skelton[1] declared that 'after reading *Tristram Shandy*, he could not for two or three days attend seriously to his devotion, it filled him with so many ludicrous ideas.' But Horace Walpole, who found his *Sentimental Journey* very pleasing, declares that of 'his tiresome *Tristram Shandy* he could never get through three volumes.'[2]

93. Jeremiah Newman on Sterne

1796, 1805

Jeremiah Newman (1759–1839), surgeon and medical and miscellaneous writer, published anonymously several editions of his *Lounger's Common-Place Book* between 1792 and 1805. Comparison of the two excerpts below, the first reprinted from the 'new' edition of 1796, the second from the third edition of 1805, will illustrate the harsher attitudes toward Sterne that were developing at the turn of the century, partly as a result of Ferriar's disclosures, partly as a result of the spread of the Evangelical movement.

(a) Excerpt from *The Lounger's Common-Place Book*, new ed. (1796), ii. 199

STERNE, LAURENCE, an English Clergyman, and a popular writer, the founder of a numerous class, to whom the term *Sentimental* has been given, which, strictly speaking, almost every species of writing, beyond a technical syllabus, or a text book, is, or ought to be. It would be no easy task, precisely to define, what a modern reader means by

[1] Philip Skelton (1707–87) was an extremely diligent and charitable divine of the Church of Ireland.
[2] See Nos 8 and 57a, b.

this fashionable latitudinarian expression, unless we are to rest satisfied with what a female writer once replied to this question, and rather in a peevish way, 'It means to write like Sterne.'

To attempt, what I have confessed is difficult, may perhaps appear presumptuous, but he who fails, possesses more merit, than the man who never tries. If the easiness of writing sentimentally, is to be estimated, by the numbers who have taken the field, it should seem to require no very uncommon abilities; yet, and I trust I may speak without offence; Has there yet appeared a second Yorick? The nearest approach, I have sometimes thought, was made by Mr. Pratt,[1] and Mr. Keat,[2] but theirs is an humble distance; besides, I fear, they want that which bursts forth, or *seems* to burst forth so often in Sterne, a heart.

The sentimental writer, then, if we are allowed to draw our rules from his great prototype, the author of *Tristram Shandy*, as the antient critics from Homer, the sentimental writer must, by the force of natural genius, be enabled, from the various, the common, and, to the million, the unimportant occurrences of life, to select materials, calculated in an extraordinary manner, to interest, elevate, and surprize.

Unembarrassed by those fetters of continuity and coherence, which sound criticism expects from common writers, he considers himself as at liberty, to wander discursively, or rather to leap over barren rocks, or uncultivated precipices, and except, when he occasionally stoops to crop a rose, raise a lilly, or drop a sentiment, to gallop without reins, and sometimes without judgment, from Alps to Pyrenees, 'whilst folly claps her hands, and wisdom stares,'[3] and the fatigued reader, in the rapid pantomime of pleasure, pathos, humour, dullness, and obscenity, is alternately pleased, vexed, bewildered, and lost.

—To sketch out affecting and masterly pictures, to raise his reader on the very tiptoe of expectation, and at last to defeat ardent curiosity, by asterisks and dashes; to prophanely tread the borders of impiety and lewdness, that too in the most dangerous mode, without giving the alarm of disgusting language; by powers wonderfully and sublimely pathetic, to reach at times, the inmost recesses of the heart, and with scarcely a page intervening, to irritate, irresistibly to irritate us by

[1] See No. 67.
[2] George Keate (1729–97), poet and miscellaneous writer, was one of Sterne's many imitators.
[3] See Charles Churchill, *The Rosciad*, l. 68, in *Poetical Works*, ed. Douglas Grant (1956), p. 5. Though the poem was published in 1761, this line was added in the seventh edition of 1763. Perhaps Newman remembers that Churchill has referred to Sterne a few lines above as 'too gay' a judge to decide the contest among the actors.

matchless sallies of genuine humour; such strange compound of wit and absurdity, goodness and indecorum, excellence and inanity, delicacy and grossness, such powers, Yorick, were thine!

(b) Excerpt from *The Lounger's Common-Place Book*, 3rd ed. (1805), iii. 234–5

STERNE, LAURENCE, an English clergyman, a popular, but in my opinion, an irritating, a voluptuous, and dangerous writer, whose books I think have done considerable mischief, and for this reason; although acting precisely on the system of Rochester[1] and other licentious writers, he does not give the previous alarm of obscene language.

Sterne is the founder of a numerous class of authors, to whom the term *sentimental* has been given, which, strictly speaking, almost every species of writing, beyond a technical syllabus, or a text book, is, or ought to be. It is not easy to define, what a modern reader means by this once fashionable expression, unless we rest satisfied with what a female writer once replied to this question, and rather in a peevish way, '*It means to write like Sterne.*'

To attempt a description of what I have confessed is difficult, may appear presumptuous, but he who fails, possesses more merit than the man who never tries. Yet, if the easiness of writing sentimentally, is to be estimated by the numbers who have taken the field, it should seem to require no very uncommon abilities.

The sentimental writer, then, if we are allowed to draw our rules from his great prototype, the author of *Tristram Shandy*, the sentimental writer must, by the force of natural genius, be enabled, from the various, the common, and, the unimportant occurrences of life, to select materials, calculated to interest, elevate, and surprize.

Unembarrassed by those fetters of continuity and coherence, which sound criticism expects from other writers, he considers himself at liberty to wander discursively, and, except when he occasionally stoops to crop a rose, raise a lilly, or drop a sentiment, to gallop without reins, and sometimes without judgment, from Alps to Pyrenees, whilst folly claps her hands, and wisdom stares, and the fatigued reader, in the rapid pantomime of pleasure, pathos, humour, dullness, and obscenity, is alternately pleased, vexed, bewildered, and lost.

[1] See No. 11a, p. 65, n. 1.

To sketch out affecting and masterly pictures; to raise his reader on the very tiptoe of expectation, and at last to defeat ardent curiosity, by asterisks and dashes; to tread closely on the borders of impiety and lewdness, without disgusting language; by powers wonderfully and sublimely pathetic, to reach at times, the inmost recesses of the heart; and with scarcely a page intervening, to irritate, irresistibly to irritate us by matchless sallies of genuine humour; such, strange compound of wit and absurdity, goodness and indecorum, excellence and inanity, delicacy and grossness; such powers, Yorick, were thine!

94. William Godwin on Sterne

1797

Excerpts from *The Enquirer* (1797), pt II.

Godwin (1756–1836), social revolutionary writer, is best known as the author of *Political Justice* and of the novel *Caleb Williams*.

Loose conversation, in those persons with whom it becomes a habit, is ordinarily very disgustful. It is singular enough, that the sallies of persons who indulge themselves in this way, are commonly more remarkable for ordure and a repulsive grossness, than for voluptuousness. The censure however against loose conversation, has probably been carried too far. There seems to be no reason why knowledge should not as unreservedly be communicated on the topic here alluded to, as on any other affair of human life. With respect to persons who, like Sterne, may have chosen this subject as the theme of a wit, pleasant, elegant and sportive, it is not easy to decide the exact degree of reprimand that is to be awarded against them. (p. 271)

Fielding's novel of *Tom Jones* is certainly one of the most admirable performances in the world. The structure of the story perhaps has never been equalled; nor is there any work that more frequently or more happily excites emotions of the most elevated and delicious generosity.

The style however is glaringly inferior to the constituent parts of the work. It is feeble, costive and slow. It cannot boast of periods elegantly turned or delicately pointed. The book is interspersed with long discourses of religious or moral instruction; but these have no novelty of conception or impressive sagacity of remark, and are little superior to what any reader might hear at the next parish-church. The general turn of the work is intended to be sarcastic and ironical; but the irony is hard, pedantic and unnatural. Whoever will compare the hide-bound sportiveness of Fielding, with the flowing and graceful hilarity of Sterne, must be struck with the degree in which the national taste was improved, before the latter author could have made his appearance. (pp. 462–3)

95. William Wilberforce on Sterne

1797

Extract from *A Practical View of the Prevailing Religious System of Professed Christians, in the Higher and Middle Classes, Contrasted with Real Christianity*, first published in 1797 and reprinted here from the first American edition (1798), pp. 202–3.

Wilberforce (1759–1833) was the friend of Hannah More (see No. 79) and the leader of a twenty-year struggle in Parliament to abolish the African slave trade. He was also instrumental in founding the *Christian Observer*. The *Practical View*, which has been called the 'manifesto of the evangelical party of the time,' sold 7,500 copies in six months and had reached a fifteenth edition by 1824; there were also twenty-five American editions.

While all are worthy of blame, who, to [sensibility] have assigned a more exalted place than to religious and moral principle; there is one writer who, eminently culpable in this respect, deserves, on another account, still severer reprehension. Really possessed of powers to explore and touch the finest strings of the human heart, and bound by his sacred profession to devote those powers to the service of religion and virtue, he every where discovers a studious solicitude to excite indecent ideas. We turn away our eyes with disgust from open immodesty; but even this is less mischievous than that more measured style, which excites impure images, without shocking us by the grossnesses of the language. Never was delicate sensibility proved to be more distinct from plain practical benevolence, than in the writings of the author to whom I allude. Instead of employing his talents for the benefit of his fellow-creatures, they were applied to the pernicious purposes of corrupting the national taste, and of lowering the standard of manners and morals. The tendency of his writings is to vitiate that purity of mind, intended by Providence as the companion and preservative of youthful virtue; and to produce, if the expression may be permitted, a morbid sensibility in the perception of indecency. An imagination exercised in this discipline is never clean, but seeks for and discovers something indelicate in the most common phrases and actions of ordinary life. If the general style of writing and conversation were to be formed on that model, to which Sterne used his utmost endeavours to conciliate the minds of men, there is no estimating the effects which would soon be produced on the manners and morals of the age.

96. The *Encyclopaedia Britannica* on Sterne

1797

Excerpt from 'Sterne,' *Encyclopaedia Britannica* (1797), xvii. 795.

George Gleig was the editor of this volume of the *Britannica*, but the article on Sterne, which remained unchanged until the seventh edition in 1842, is unsigned. Sterne had not been included in the *Britannica* editions of 1773 and 1778–83.

The works of Sterne are very generally read. . . . In every serious page, and in many of much levity, the author writes in praise of benevolence, and declares that no one who knew him could suppose him one of those wretches who heap misfortune upon misfortune: But we have heard anecdotes of him extremely well authenticated, which proved that it was easier for him to praise this virtue than to practise it. His wit is universally allowed; but many readers have persuaded themselves that they found wit in his blank pages, while it is probable that he intended nothing but to amuse himself with the idea of the sage conjectures to which these pages would give occasion. Even his originality is not such as is generally supposed by those fond admirers of the Shandean manner, who have presumed to compare him with Swift, Arbuthnot, and Butler.[1] He has borrowed both matter and manner from various authors, as every reader may be convinced by the learned, elegant, and candid comments on his works published by Dr Farrier. . . .

[1] Swift, Dr John Arbuthnot (1667–1735) and Samuel Butler (1612–80), author of *Hudibras* (1663–78), were all satirists, though with rather different styles or 'manners.' Arbuthnot and Swift were both associated with the Scriblerus Club (see No. 83d, p. 267, n. 1).

97. Nathan Drake: Sterne and the pathetic

1798, 1804

Excerpts from *Literary Hours*, 3rd ed. (1804).

Drake (1766–1836) was a medical doctor and miscellaneous writer. The first selection appeared in 1798; the second was added in 1804.

Those writers who have touched the finest chords of pity, who, mingling the tenderest simplicity with the strongest emotions of the heart, speak the pure language of nature, have elegantly drawn the effects of music on the mind; the Fonrose of Marmontelle, the Maria of Sterne, and the Julia de Roubigné of Mackenzie, but more especially the Minstrel of Beattie,[1] sweetly evince this delightful and bewitching melancholy which so blandly steals upon the children of sorrow. (i. 76)

In the annexed Ode to Pity, of which STERNE forms the most conspicuous figure, an appeal is made, not to the life, but to the *pathetic* writings of that eccentric Genius. His *ludicrous* productions, a compound of quaintness and obscene allusion, and, as it has lately appeared, possessing but little originality, I consider as forming no part of the basis, on which his literary reputation rests; and his personal conduct I understand to have been accompanied with a levity, very inconsistent with the profession he had chosen to exercise. It is to Sterne, merely as the author of *Le Fevre*, *Maria* and the *Monk*, compositions which breathe the purest morality, and display the most touching simplicity, both in sentiment and style, that the following lines are addressed. . . . (iii. 16)

[1] The references are to 'La Bergère des Alpes,' a sentimental tale in *Contes Moraux* by Jean François Marmontel (1723–99), in which the hero, Fonrose, woos the heroine with music on the oboe; Sterne's Maria as she appears both in *Tristram Shandy* (IX. 24, p. 629, where, Sterne says, she played 'the sweetest notes I ever heard') and the *Sentimental Journey* ('Maria,' p. 274, where she 'took her pipe, and play'd her service to the Virgin'); *Julia de Roubigné* (1777), sentimental novel by Henry Mackenzie (see No. 86), in which the heroine plays 'heavenly' music on the organ just before her death; and 'The Minstrel,' by James Beattie (see No. 88c), long narrative poem in which the hero sings and plays the harp.

[Drake's rather uneven ode follows, in which Sterne is grouped with Petrarch, Rousseau, Otway, Collins, and Shakespeare, since all are masters of 'pity.']

98. Walpoliana: 'a dead ass and a living mother'

1799

Excerpt from *Walpoliana* (1799), i. 133–4.

John Pinkerton (1758–1826), Scottish antiquary and historian, had known Horace Walpole. After Walpole's death, Pinkerton published anonymously a collection of Walpole's letters and remarks, first in the *Monthly Magazine* in May 1799 and then in two volumes under the title *Walpoliana*. Byron later echoed this passage (see No. 113). The aspersion on Sterne was based on false information; it is impossible to determine whether Walpole ever made the comment, although rumors about Sterne's alleged mistreatment of his mother had started to circulate by the seventies if not earlier. For refutation of the charges see *Letters*, pp. 32–44.

What is called sentimental writing, though it be understood to appeal solely to the heart, may be the product of a bad one. One would imagine that Sterne had been a man of a very tender heart—yet I know, from indubitable authority, that his mother, who kept a school, having run in debt, on account of an extravagant daughter, would have rotted in jail, if the parents of her scholars had not raised a subscription for her. Her son had too much sentiment to have any feeling. A dead ass was more important to him than a living mother.

99. Robert Southey on Sterne

1799, 1834

Southey (1774–1843) was a lifelong admirer of Sterne and made frequent allusions to his works, although he did not record any extended critical comments. His *The Doctor* had, in his own words, 'something of *Tristram Shandy*' in it.

(a) Extract from a letter to C. W. William Wynn, 5 April 1799, comparing Sterne and Kotzebue (*Selections from the Letters of Robert Southey*, ed. John Wood Warter (1856), i. 68)

The German plays have always something ridiculous, yet Kotzebue[1] seems to me possessed of unsurpassed and unsurpassable genius. . . . There is a very good comedy of his lately translated, the 'Reconciliation,' full of those quick strokes of feeling that, like Sterne, surprise you into a tear before you have finished a smile.

(b) Extract from a passage in *The Doctor* (1834) discussing a 'magic word' (*The Doctor &c.*, ed. John Wood Warter, new ed. (1849), p. 385)

But by no such means can the knowledge of my profounder mystery be attained. I will tell thee, however, good Reader, that the word itself, apart from all considerations of its mystical meaning, serves me for the same purpose to which the old tune of Lilliburlero was applied by our dear Uncle Toby,—*our* dear Uncle I say, for is he not *your* Uncle Toby, gentle Reader? yours as well as mine, if you are worthy to hold him in such relationship; and so by that relationship, you and I are Cousins.

[1] August von Kotzebue (1761–1819) was the prolific author of both novels and sentimental bourgeois plays, some of which were very popular in England. He was sometimes said to imitate Sterne.

100. American attacks of the 1790s on Sterne's morality

(a) Extract from anonymous 'Remarks on some of the Writings of Sterne,' *Massachussetts Magazine*, ii (June 1790). 329–30

There are herds of novelists whose representations of life and manners tend to mislead the unwary youth of both sexes. Many of the writings of these, and of some other authors, are too well calculated to add new encouragements to licentiousness and new difficulties to virtue. But scarce any writer has more admirers, or a greater number of humble imitators, than Sterne. And not to admire him for his exquisite touches of nature, for his benevolent attempts to encrease and diffuse *the milk of human kindness,* and to pour oil and wine into the wounds of the afflicted, would justly stigmatize one as destitute of sentiment, genius or benevolence. But to admire him for every thing, would betray the want of true judgment and taste, and of a pure and delicate mind. . . . It is in vain for Sterne, or any of his admirers to pretend, that the words and intentions of the writer are innocent, and all the fault is in the mind or heart of the reader, since he knew what ideas and images his allusions and insinuations would convey to the mind, and made use of them for that very purpose. *Double entendre,* and indelicate allusions, as well as immodest expressions, have never been considered as evidences of re-finement or good breeding.

That Sterne possessed a large share of wit and humour, and had a peculiar faculty of exciting laughter, is felt by the most gloomy and morose of his readers. But then his wit and humour is of the lower and grosser kind, and far inferiour to that refined and delicate humour in which Addison abounded, and for which he is so justly admired. Im-partial and well educated judges would despise the man as a buffoon, or as low and ill bred, who should, in conversation, constantly use such wit and humour as Tristram Shandy's, for their entertainment.

The sensibility and sentimentalism of Sterne were truly amiable, had they been properly regulated and directed. But should a man give way to such a softness of nature, so as to fall in love with every woman he saw, and to feel a greater tenderness for other men's wives than for his own, such sensibility and sentimentalism would soon destroy the peace of families and the order and happiness of societies; and good were it for *poor human nature* if such sentimentalists had never been born. Great were the talents of Sterne as a feeling and descriptive writer; and great were his abilities to make his fellow creatures virtuous and happy. And lamentable it is, that such abilities should in any instance be perverted. But happy for him if the interceding and *recording angel* shall be more prevalent in obliterating his faults, and the restraining angel in preventing their ill effects, than the *accusing angel* in proclaiming and perpetuating them for his condemnation.

(b) Extract from anonymous 'On Sensibility, or, Feeling, as Opposed to Principle,' *American Museum*, x (August 1791). 92. The author has just described a seduction

---

This is the work of an *unprincipled man of feeling*, whose nerves with peculiar irritability, can tremble every hour at the touch of joy or woe; whose finely-fibred heart would thrill perhaps with horror at the sufferings of—a fly. Nevertheless many a fair advocate will plead for him; and is not female eloquence irresistible? Are we not in love with sensibility when we behold in *her* the attachments of endearing friendship, transports of overwhelming joy, and the sympathies of romantic affliction? While she bends, dissolved in tenderness, over the 'bosom-soothing page,' must we not venerate the works of a Sterne, though blended with trash and obscenity? . . .

Such, alas! is the weakness of the human heart and the seduction of the senses, that, in perusing the writings of many modern *sentimentalists*, we thus catch the contagion of romance, and feel ourselves affected by passions, which, if too much indulged, will enervate all the noblest powers of the mind, and lead us insensibly to the vicinage of destruction.

(c) Extract from the Reverend John Bennett, *Letters to a Young Lady* (1791), ii. 64–5

I rejoice to find you disgusted with *Tristram Shandy*. I never thought these writings fit for a lady.

Let me candidly ask our modern fair ones? could they bear to hear such *conversations*, without blushing, or expressing their contempt? And should not then the eye be as chaste, as the ear? The first, indeed, can be gratified in private. But can that delicacy be very exquisite, which can regale, when alone, on sentiments and descriptions, from which, in *public*, it *affects* to turn away with indignation and abhorrence?

I have always, in private lamented, that Sterne was a clergyman. He might be a lively, humorous companion, but he had too much *levity* for this profession. It is true, he had talents, but what is *ungoverned* genius, but a violent flame, which burns, instead of warming, and dazzles, where it should enlighten and direct?

This writer has done inexpressible mischief. He has opened wide the flood-gates of indecency, and an overwhelming torrent has poured on the land. He has conveyed *indelicate* ideas into the minds of young people, under the specious vehicle of sentiment, and he has dignified *eventual* criminality with the false, insidious title of *involuntary* attachment. The corrupted and unblushing fair has gloried in her shame. She has appealed for her justification, from the *grossness* of passion, to secret and *irresistible* feelings of the heart.

It is a just compliment to the present age, that the best writers preserve more decorum.

(d) Extract from Hannah Webster Foster (1759–1840), minor American novelist, *The Boarding School* (1798), pp. 204–5

Since I wrote you last, I have made an agreeable visit to my good friend, Sylvia Star. After rambling in the fields and gardens till we were fatigued, we went into her brother's library. He was in a studious attitude, but gave us a polite reception. We are come to solicit a portion of your repast, Amintor, said I. Be so kind as to furnish us with some instructive page, which combines entertainment and utility; and while it informs the mind, delights the imagination. I am not happy enough to know your taste respecting books, said he; and, therefore, may not make a proper selection. Here, however, is an author highly spoken of by a lady, who has lately added to the numbers of literary publications; handing me Sterne's *Sentimental Journey*. I closed and returned the book. You have indeed mistaken my taste, said I. Wit, blended with indelicacy, never meets my approbation. While the fancy is allured, and the passions awakened, by this pathetic humourist, the foundations of virtue are insidiously undermined, and modest dignity insensibly betrayed. Well, said he, smiling, perhaps you are seriously inclined. If so, this volume of sermons may possibly please you. Still less, rejoined I. The serious mind must turn with disgust from the levity which pervades these discourses, and from the indecent flow of mirth and humour, which converts even the sacred writings, and the most solemn subjects of religion, into frolic and buffoonery. Since such is your opinion of this celebrated writer, said he, I will not insult your feelings by offering you his *Tristram Shandy*. But here is another wit, famous for his '*purity*.' Yes, said I, if obscene and vulgar ideas, if ill-natured remarks and filthy allusions be purity, Swift undoubtedly bears the palm from all his contemporaries. As far as grammatical correctness and simplicity of language can deserve the epithet, his advocates may enjoy their sentiments unmolested; but, in any other sense of the word, he has certainly no claim to '*purity*.' I conceive his works, notwithstanding, to be much less pernicious in their tendency, than those of Sterne. They are not so enchanting in their nature, nor so subtle in their effects. In the one, the noxious insinuations of licentious wit are concealed under the artful blandishments of sympathetic sensibility; while we at once recoil from the rude assault which is made upon our delicacy, by the roughness and vulgarity of the other.

Choose then, said Amintor, for yourself.

101. Some tributes of the 1790s

(a) Extract from an account of a visit to Sterne's grave by George Moutard Woodward (1760(?)–1809), caricaturist and miscellaneous writer (*Eccentric Excursions* (1796), pp. 17–18)

To one who has experienc'd the effects of the magic powers of Sterne, what will be his sensations, when he stands on the very spot, where the heart and hand which evinced such exquisite sensibility are now mingled with the dust?

Such a man will fancy he beholds Tristram's amiable and benevolent Uncle Toby bending over the stone, and behind him (at a respectful distance) he will perceive the honest corporal, divided in which to participate, the grief of his master alone, or the general sorrow for him, from whom they imbibed spirit and animation. At his side the venerable Monk supports the grief-worn *Maria*, while the shades of his beloved *Eliza*,[1] and the worthy Le Fevre flutter over the grave, upborne by the Recording Angel.

It is to be regretted that *Shakespear's expressive line* to which Sterne was so partial, was not engraven on his tomb; for then, according to his own words 'Ten times a day would Yorick's Ghost have the consolation to hear his monumental inscription read over with a variety of plaintive tones, and each, as he walked on, would sighing exclaim,

"ALAS! POOR YORICK!" '

(b) Extract from Jenkin Jones, *Hobby Horses* [1797], pp. 15–17

At gay fifteen the lively Romp disclaims
Frocks, schools, tasks, rods, wax dolls, and skittish games,
Directs her aim to pleasures more refin'd,
And only seeks amusement for the mind.

[1] See 53d, p. 187, n. 1.

New schemes of happiness her thoughts employ
And Reading proves the source of all her joy.
Th'Arabian Nights, the Fairy Tales, Gil Blas,
Clarissa, Grandison, and Pamela,
In turns the damsel for her fav'rite owns,
At length she deigns to venture on Tom Jones.
This ramble proves more pleasing than the rest,
Sterne's *Sentimental Journey* then seems best,
'Till now exalted o'er those narrow lines
Where prejudice her sickly slave confines,
She frames her course to Shandy's bolder height,
And soars above the reach of vulgar flight,
Too little understood! too seldom read!
Where is the gen'rous taste of letters fled?
Shall some light faults, ye captious critics say,
A mighty load of massy worth outweigh?
Is there no medium in the candid mind,
Can moderation no fair balance find?
When ye the merits of a work would learn,
Why do ye thus all rules of justice spurn?
Indeed ye fall on very honest means,
To try *one heart*—a jury of *twelve spleens*.

In Yorick's heart meek Mercy rear'd her throne;
On him the softest beams of feeling shone;
Nature to all he wrote asserts her claim,
And glows with pride at her Le Fever's name.
'Twas she that gave his Shandy manly sense,
Science and satire, wit and eloquence:
At her kind bosom was his Toby nurs'd;
The milk of human kindness quench'd his thirst;
And the redundant streams that dropp'd from him
Foster'd the generous heart of faithful Trim.

(c) Extract from Sterne's imitator, William Combe (1741(?)– 1823) (see No. 66), 'Address to the Shade of Yorick,' *Fragments: in the Manner of Sterne* (1797), pp. 7–8

BELOVED YORICK!—if, in reading thee, I learned to feel,—and, in feeling, to admire thee!—is it not one of the simplest movements of Nature—in admiring—I attempt to imitate thee?—Thus shelt'ring myself behind NATURE, (whom thou lovedst as tenderly as young Le Fevre loved his father)—I pray thy Spirit not to cast its gentle eye upon me, as on PRESUMPTION—but rather as one—who, in imitating thee, is but seeking to cultivate a closer knowledge—with the sources of thy feelings.

[After this preface, Combe brings the characters at Shandy Hall to life again to discuss various topics of the day. This was one of the few imitations of Sterne to win critical acclaim from the reviews. For the establishment of Combe's authorship see Lewis P. Curtis, 'Forged Letters of Laurence Sterne,' *PMLA* (December 1935), l. 1104–5.]

102. Some comments of the 1790s on Sterne's plagiarism

(a) Extract from a communication from 'Eboracensis' to the *Gentleman's Magazine*, lxiv (May 1794). pt. I. 406

How are the mighty fallen! The works whose fancied originality, in spite of their lewdness and libertinism, procured them 'an envied place' in the pocket of every young lady who was able to read them, and in the library of the collegiate, are debased to the level of the lowest of all literary larcenies; they are found to shine with reflected light, to strut in borrowed plumes.

(b) Extract from a correspondent signing himself 'R.F.,' to the *Gentleman's Magazine*, lxviii (June 1798). pt. I. 471

The plagiarisms of Sterne have of late engrossed the attention and research of the Learned World; and, by the labour of Dr. Ferriar and others, that fascinating writer has been stript of many of his borrowed plumes. His far-famed originality and wit have shrunk from the test of enquiry; and the sorry reputation of a servile imitator is almost all that remains of that once celebrated author.

(c) Extract from a reply to (b) by 'M.N.,' *Gentleman's Magazine*, lxviii (August 1798). pt II. 674. This correspondent suggests some possible sources for passages in Sterne and continues

---

The passages, indeed, which I have adduced, do not detract, in my opinion, from Sterne's merit, he has improved on them . . . and he may rather be considered as a fair imitator than a servile plagiarist. Those which Dr. Ferriar has brought before the publick are of a different cast, and prove him a literary pilferer. Yet, however culpable in that respect he may be, we ought not to withhold our admiration of his ingenuity in so nicely blending the sentiments of other writers, though differing in style and character, with his own. His phraseology and humour commonly struck his readers as equally original, peculiar, appropriate, and uniform: and though, in many instances, we can no longer insist on the first quality, we can hardly deny him the credit of preserving the others, even in those places he has most servilely copied, by the introduction of some slight, but characteristic, touches.

(d) Extract from William Jackson of Exeter (1730–1803), famous musician and composer, 'On Literary Thievery,' *The Four Ages* (1798), pp. 244, 257

Instances have been given of Sterne's borrowing, perhaps, stealing, some thoughts and passages from Burton's *Anatomy of Melancholy*. As I myself never steal, at least, knowingly, it may be expected that I should cry out vehemently against thieves. Whether my principles and practice are, as usual, at variance, or whether that rogue Falstaff has given me medicines to make me love the *vocation* because it was his, I know not; but I am willing to let all such thieves as Sterne escape punishment. . . .

The thievery of a fool is never excused, because no one can return the compliment; but, we pardon a genius, because if he takes, he is qualified to give in return. The great natural possessions of Sterne, Prior, and Voltaire, will afford ample resources to those of their successors who have abilities to make reprisals.

(e) Extract from anonymous review of John Ferriar's *Illustrations of Sterne* (see No. 90b), *Critical Review*, xxvi (June 1799). 152–3

Dr. Ferriar has traced the plagiarisms of Sterne with as much perseverance as Bruce sought the source of the Nile.[1] Few, we believe, would wish to follow the path of either; yet many must be interested by the result of their researches. . . .

Dr. Ferriar is of opinion, that Sterne caught from Rabelais the idea of satirising the abuse of speculative opinions. From . . . a long list of neglected authors, he fertilised his fancy, as the husbandman enriches his fields with the refuse of the stable; and the flowers of Sterne sometimes savour of the dunghill from which they were produced. But Burton's *Anatomie of Melancholy* is the mine from which he extracted the greatest treasures. These authors, however, have not suffered from the disingenuity of Sterne. If he had referred to them, there would

[1] James Bruce (1730–94), African traveler, spent several years and suffered extreme hardships while searching for the source of the Nile.

have been little inducement to turn to the passage quoted; but the book from which Yorick pilfered becomes an object of research and value.

103. Some comments of the 1790s on Sterne's style and substance

(a) Extract from the anonymous 'Sterne's La Fleur,' *European Magazine*, xviii (October 1790). 268

Ignorance formerly delighted to attribute a *profundity* to [Sterne's] works, which surely, if it do exist, must be sought and never found. They are valuable as exact draughts from nature of the *foibles* and *failings* that diminish, the PIETY and PHILANTHROPY that exalt, the moral consequence of MAN.

The levity of Sterne is a lancet that lightly produces a *smart*, which we blush at while we acknowledge it. The ridicule of Voltaire is malevolent merriment, which applies a CAUSTIC to what is *festering*, and enjoys the pain of its corrosion.

They are both excellent satirists; but their fate is utterly dissimilar. One is the favourite of the *gloomy growler* at his species; he who joys at discovered depravity—the other, of that best of men, who can readily find an extenuation for the foibles of other characters, in the FAULTS that he feels with sensibility about his own.

(b) Extract from John Noorthouck's unsigned review of an anonymous minor novel in the *Monthly Review*, 2nd ser., v. (July 1791). 337–8. For Noorthouck's earlier comments on Sterne, see No. 71c

Two of the earliest fabricators of this species of goods, the modern novel, in our country, were Daniel Defoe, and Mrs. Haywood;[1] the success of *Pamela* may be said to have brought it into fashion; and the progress has not been less rapid than the extension of the use of tea, to which a novel is almost as general an attendant, as the bread and butter, especially in a morning. While we are on this subject, it is also to be noted, that nothing is more common than to find hair-powder lodged between the leaves of a novel; which evinces the corresponding attention paid to the inside as well as to the outside of a modern head. Richardson, Fielding, Smollet, and Sterne, were the Wedgwoods[2] of their days; and the imitators that have since started up in the same line, exceed all power of calculation!

(c) Excerpt from Henry James Pye (1745–1813), poetaster and poet laureate, *A Commentary Illustrating the Poetic of Aristotle* (1792), p. 165

Perhaps there is not a stronger instance of the difference between manners introduced as secondary to the action, though arising immediately, and necessarily, from it; and their holding the first place, than the novel of *Tom Jones* compared with *Tristram Shandy*.[3] The masterly contrivance of the fable in the former, at once astonishes and delights us; but though we may be struck with the high coloring of the other, we soon perceive it is laid on promiscuously; we are amused, but we are not interested, except in those parts where our passions are

[1] Mrs Eliza Haywood (*c.* 1693–1756), prolific author of minor novels.
[2] Josiah Wedgwood (1730–95) developed processes for producing earthenware which was vastly superior to earlier pottery and became so popular that it was found in nearly every home.
[3] Pye's remarks occur in a note to a sentence in chapter VI of the *Poetics*: 'The professed end of tragedy is to imitate an action, and chiefly by means of that action to shew the qualities of the persons acting.'

engaged by incident, as well as awakened by quality; such as the admirable story of Le Fevre.

(d) Extracts from Dugald Stewart (1753–1828), Professor of Moral Philosophy in the University of Edinburgh, 'Of Imagination,' *Elements of the Philosophy of the Human Mind* (1792) (*Collected Works*, ed. Sir William Hamilton (1854), ii)

[I]t commonly happens that, after a period of great refinement of taste, men begin to gratify their love of variety, by adding superfluous circumstances to the finished models exhibited by their predecessors, or by making other trifling alterations on them, with a view merely of diversifying the effect. These additions and alterations, indifferent, perhaps, or even in some degree offensive, in themselves, acquire soon a borrowed beauty from the connexion in which we see them, or from the influence of fashion: the same cause which at first produced them, continues perpetually to increase their number; and taste returns to barbarism, by almost the same steps which conducted it to perfection.

The truth of these remarks will appear still more striking to those who consider the wonderful effect which a writer of splendid genius, but of incorrect taste, has in misleading the public judgment. The peculiarities of such an author are consecrated by the connexion in which we see them, and even please to a certain degree, when detached from the excellencies of his composition, by recalling to us the agreeable impressions with which they have been formerly associated. How many imitations have we seen of the affectations of Sterne, by men who were unable to copy his beauties? And yet these imitations of his defects, of his abrupt manner, of his minute specification of circumstances, and even of his dashes, produce at first some effect on readers of sensibility, but of uncultivated taste, in consequence of the exquisite strokes of the pathetic, and the singular vein of humour with which they are united in the original. (pp. 324–5)

What we commonly call sensibility, depends, in a great measure, on the power of imagination. Point out to two men, any object of compassion;—a man, for example, reduced by misfortune from easy circumstances to indigence. The one feels merely in proportion to what he perceives by his senses. The other follows, in imagination, the unfortunate man to his dwelling, and partakes with him and his family in their domestic distresses. He listens to their conversation while they recall to remembrance the flattering prospects they once indulged; the circle of friends they had been forced to leave; the liberal plans of education which were begun and interrupted; and pictures out to himself all the various resources which delicacy and pride suggest, to conceal poverty from the world. As he proceeds in the painting, his sensibility increases, and he weeps, not for what he sees, but for what he imagines. It will be said that it was his sensibility which originally roused his imagination; and the observation is undoubtedly true; but it is equally evident, on the other hand, that the warmth of his imagination increases and prolongs his sensibility.

This is beautifully illustrated in the *Sentimental Journey* of Sterne. While engaged in a train of reflections on the state prisons in France, the accidental sight of a starling in a cage suggests to him the idea of a captive in his dungeon. He indulges his imagination, 'and looks through the twilight of the grated door to take the picture.'[1] (p. 452)

(e) Extract from Thomas Wallace, 'An Essay on the Variations of English Prose,' adjudged the Gold Prize Medal when read 18 June 1796 before the Royal Irish Academy and reprinted from *Transactions of the Royal Irish Academy*, vi (1797). 70

In treating of the various styles which have successively appeared from the revolution to the present time I have purposely omitted some which may be thought from their singularity to have deserved notice. Such, for instance, is that of Mr. Sterne. This I have passed over without remark, because, in the first instance, it was merely the style of an individual, and has never been generally adopted by English prose writers; and, in the second place, because it seems to have been the emanation of an eccentric mind, conveying its thoughts in language as capricious, and, perhaps, affected, as the sentiments which suggested them, and as loose as the moral principles by which they were regulated.

[1] 'The Passport. The Hotel at Paris' and 'The Captive. Paris,' *A Sentimental Journey*, pp. 195–203.

(f) Extract from remarks made in 1798 by Mary Berry (1763–1852), friend and editor of Horace Walpole (*Extracts from the Journals and Correspondence of Miss Berry from the Year 1783 to 1852*, ed. Lady Theresa Lewis, 2nd ed. (1866), ii. 80)

Tristram Shandy, while it diverts, always reminds me of a Dutch portrait, in which we admire the accurate representation of all the little disgusting blemishes—the warts, moles, and hairs—of the human form.[1] Even when he affects us, it is by a minute detail of little circumstances which all lead to the weaknesses, and are often connected with the ridicules, that belong to our nature; while Rousseau, on the contrary, like the great masters of the Italian school of painting, gives grace and dignity to every character he brings forward—choosing to represent scenes and situations when every ennobling faculty of our mind is brought into action, and the greatest expression of passion and character is produced without even losing sight of decent grace, or presenting anything disgusting to the imagination.

The one degrades worth, by a thousand little mean circumstances that destroy the respect which it *ought* to inspire; while the other consoles frail human nature with the idea that even great failings are redeemable by virtuous exertion.

(g) Extract from a note (1798) in Thomas J. Mathias (1754(?)–1835), *The Pursuits of Literature*, popular poem published anonymously at the turn of the century which had reached a sixteenth edition by 1812 (*Works of the Author of the Pursuits of Literature* (1799), p. 59)

From these [i.e. Cervantes, Le Sage, Fielding, who 'afford illustration to every event of life'], with great caution, we must pass to later writers. Smollett had much penetration, though he is frequently too vulgar to please; but his knowledge of men and manners is unquestion-

---

[1] The metaphor of the Dutch painting was in vogue. Mrs Barbauld speaks of turning away 'with disgust' from a scene of wretchedness, unless we are pleased 'as we are with a Dutch painting, from its exact imitation of nature' (*Works of Anna Laetitia Barbauld* (1825), ii. 222).

able. Of Sterne and Rousseau it is difficult to speak without being misunderstood; yet it is impossible to deny the praise of wit and originality to Yorick, or of captivating eloquence to the philosopher of vanity. Their imitators are below notice.

(h) Extract from D. Whyte, 'Late Surgeon to English Prisoners in France,' *The Fallacy of French Freedom, and Dangerous Tendency of Sterne's Writings* (1799), pp. 2–14

The system of impiety and corruption of manners was begun by Rabelais, carried on by Bayle,[1] and completed by Voltaire. . . .

In England, the same cause also had its advocates:—there have been Bolingbrokes,[2] and Humes,[3] and Tindals;[4] but their sophistry not being well adapted to the bulk of mankind, their converts have been few.— Sterne, having discovered the mistake of his predecessors, concealed his cloven foot under a flowing tunic, and endeavoured to allure by the gaudy gilding of his nauseous pill. The man, who, as a son of the church, should have endeavoured to support and confirm the authority of the state and the Influence of morality, by whose co-operation the welfare of society and the power and existence of all order so materially depend, has been one of the first and most successful in shaking all those bonds of religion and government, by which man is bound to man. What part of manners is more essential than modesty, and what tie more sacred than marriage?—yet, have not these been the unceasing subject of a raillery, which, with the most unbecoming effrontery, he hath styled *sentimental*?

[Whyte then addresses Sterne.] 'Had you been a man of real gallantry, a *Rochester*,[5] or any such professed debauchee, we might pass over in silent contempt the immoral tendency of your writings; but for you, Sir, an apathist,—can aught be more criminal than to excite voluptuous sensations in others, being entirely unspurred by passion

---

[1] See No. 90a, p. 285, n. 2. Bayle, advocate of religious tolerance and freedom of thought, has been called the founder of eighteenth-century rationalism.

[2] See No. 5, p. 49, n. 2.

[3] See No. 39 and No. 70d, n. 1.

[4] Matthew Tindal (1655–1733), deist and author of 'Christianity as Old as the Creation, or the Gospel a Republication of the Religion of Nature' (1730).

[5] See No. 11a, p. 65, n. 1. Rochester was known for the dissoluteness of his life as well as the indecency of his verse.

yourself? Are our youth too late in being corrupted? or, are they at a loss for the means? Must a clergyman of the Church of England set himself up as a second Satan?—Incapable in partaking of the pleasures he extols,—an apathist,—like the arch apostate, you rejoice but in the consequences of your crime. Although clothed with the sacerdotal character, have you not made a mockery of all that is sacred? . . .

Had you, like Rabelais, proclaimed yourself a deistical rhapsodist, in addition to the general odium of your character, your buffoonery and obscenity would perhaps have been overlooked; but, knowing yourself to be a clergyman of the church of England, you have, in your *Tristram Shandy*, and still more in your much vaunted journey, made strong and frequent professions of all that is moral and humane. But all this is mere pretext: it is, as I said before, the gaudy gilding of a nauseous pill.

Even your claim to sentiment, Sir, I am much inclined to controvert. It seems inconsistent with your mockery of all that is moral and divine.

Had you been a Frenchman, and published your crudities in France, I could have almost forgiven you, as they could scarcely have made Frenchmen worse: they could scarcely have increased the already overflowing tide of corruption. . . .'

Learn, ere the lesson be of no avail—learn that morality is the cornerstone of all establishments, the solid support both of Church and State. We have had warning sufficient; let us beware of immorality and irreligion.—they beget innovations: and of innovations in old establishments, we well know that dreadful are the consequences.

104. Charles Lamb on Sterne

1801, 1822

(a) Extract from a letter, 30 January 1801, to Wordsworth, commenting on the latter's 'The Old Cumberland Beggar' (*The Letters of Charles Lamb*, ed. E. V. Lucas (1935), i. 239)

I will just add that it appears to me a fault in the Beggar, that the instructions conveyed in it are too direct and like a lecture: they don't slide into the mind of the reader, while he is imagining no such matter. An intelligent reader finds a sort of insult in being told, I will teach you how to think upon this subject. This fault, if I am right, is in a ten-thousandth worse degree to be found in Sterne and many many novelists & modern poets, who continually put a sign post up to shew where you are to feel. They set out with assuming their readers to be stupid. Very different from *Robinson Crusoe*, the *Vicar of Wakefield*, *Roderick Random*, and other beautiful bare narratives.

(b) Extract from 'Detached Thoughts on Books and Reading,' first published in the *London Magazine*, July 1822 (*The Life, Letters, and Writings of Charles Lamb*, ed. Percy Fitzgerald (1882), iii. 401)

In some respects the better a book is, the less it demands from binding. Fielding, Smollet, Sterne, and all that class of perpetually self-reproductive volumes—Great Nature's Stereotypes—we see them individually perish with less regret, because we know the copies of them to be 'eterne.'

105. Some American views: Sterne the libertine

1802, 1803, 1822

(a) Extract from anonymous 'Observations on Sterne,' *New England Quarterly Magazine*, iii (1802). 84

I suppose few writers have done more injury to morals than Sterne. By blending sentiments of benevolence and delicacy with immorality and looseness, he induces some people to think that debauchery may be innocent, and adultery meritorious. Since his time, Novel-writers try to corrupt the principle as well as to seduce the imagination. Formerly, if a man felt a passion for the wife or the mistress of his friend, he was conscious at least that, if he persisted in the pursuit, he was acting wrong; and if the Novel-writer invented such a character, it was to hold him out as an object of detestation and punishment. Now this is so varnished over with delicate attachment and generous sensibility, that the most shocking acts of perfidy and seduction are committed not only without remorse, but with self-complacency; for we are always ready to find causes of palliation, for those crimes we are addicted to, and to bend our conscience to our inclination.

(b) Extract from Samuel Miller, *A Brief Retrospect of the Eighteenth Century* (1803), pp. 165–6. Miller (1769–1850) served as associate pastor of the United Presbyterian churches in New York City. Respected as a scholar, he later became Professor of Ecclesiastical History and Church Government at Princeton Theological Seminary

---

To the class of novels, rather than to any other, belongs that remarkable production, the *Life and Opinions of Tristram Shandy*, by the Reverend LAURENCE STERNE. Notwithstanding the often repeated, and well supported charges, brought against this writer, of borrowing without acknowledgment, many of his best thoughts from preceding British and French authors, yet his work is an *unique* in the history of literature. When it first appeared his readers were astonished at the singular farrago of obscurity, whim, indecency, and extravagance which it exhibited. The majority appeared to be at a loss, for a time, what judgment to form of its merits. But some of the friends of the writer, professing to comprehend his meaning, and disposed to place him high in the ranks of wit and humour, gave the signal to admire. The signal was obeyed; and multitudes, to the present day, have continued to mistake his capricious and exceptionable singularities for efforts of a great and original genius. But his genius and writings have certainly been overrated. That he possessed considerable powers, of a certain description, is readily admitted; that the Episodes of *Le Fevre* and *Maria* are almost unrivalled, as specimens of the tender and pathetic, must also be granted; but those parts of his works which deserve this character bear so small a proportion to the rest, and the great mass of what he has written is either so shamefully obscene, so quaintly obscure, or so foolishly unmeaning, that there are very few works more calculated to corrupt both the taste and the morals. That a man who bore the sacred office should employ his talents in recommending a system of libertinism; that he who could so well delineate the pleasures of benevolence and purity, should so grossly offend against both; and that volumes which abound with such professions of exalted philanthropy, should contain so many pages on which a virtuous mind cannot look but with disgust and indignation, are facts more atrociously and disgracefully criminal than the ordinary language of reprobation is able to reach.

(c) Extract from a letter, 22 February 1822, from John Randolph of Roanoke, Virginia (1773–1833), U.S. Congressman, to his nephew, Theodore Dudley (*Letters of John Randolph, to a Young Relative* (1834), p. 245)

Instead of yielding to a morbid sensibility, we must nerve ourselves up to do and to suffer all that duty calls for—in other words, to do our duty in that station in life, 'to which it has pleased God to call us.' What, then, are we to expect from a generation that has been taught to cherish this not 'fair defect' of our perverted nature; to nourish and cultivate, as 'amiable and attractive,' what, at the bottom, is neither more nor less than the grossest selfishness, a little disguised under the romantic epithet of 'sensibility!' This cant (worse than that of 'criticism') has been fashionable since the days of Sterne, a hard-hearted, unprincipled man; a cassocked libertine and 'free thinker;' who introduced it. Heaven be praised! it is now on the decline; and, in a little time, we may consider it, I hope, as entirely *passée*.

106. Sterne's sentimental works

1805

Extract from Hugh Murray, *Morality of Fiction* (1805), pp. 132–4, 142–5.

Murray (1779–1846), was a miscellaneous writer, best known as a geographer.

Nothing is more remarkable in sentimental works than the rambling manner in which they are written, the want of all apparent order and connection, and the frequent breaking off from one subject to another widely remote from it. Unity and consistency, elsewhere thought so essential, are here totally neglected. The writers having dismissed reason, and taken feeling for their sole guide, seem to think themselves absolved from any rules which the former may prescribe. We may observe, however, that the want of order is not altogether so great as at first sight appears. The ideas are connected, not indeed in the ordinary manner, but by certain secret links, not discernible by common readers. Of these links the most general seem to be, either the resemblance, or the contrast, of the sentiments which they tend to inspire. . . .

These authors delight greatly in minute observations upon human nature. A similar tendency has been observed to exist in certain French writers, who, in this particular, excel those of most other nations. There is a striking difference, however, between the two, in the manner of gratifying this propensity. The scrutiny of the latter is of a malignant nature, and consists in laying open those mean and bad motives, which a man would not willingly own to the world, nor even to himself. The object of the former, on the contrary, is to draw forth the amiable propensities which lie concealed under an unpromising outward appearance. Even where they attack failings, there is nothing coarse or insulting in their raillery: it is frequently such as even its object could listen to without pain. . . .

That [Sterne's] writings abound with passages of the most exquisite interest will never be denied by any one qualified to understand or appreciate them. Originality he possesses in an eminent degree, being the creator of a mode of writing almost wholly his own. The way had no doubt been prepared by the degree of refinement to which the age had previously attained. But his being the first to strike out this new path evinces an uncommon strength of genius.

He is distinguished also by wit, and by a very intimate knowledge of human nature. The former, indeed, has been shewn, in many instances, not to be genuine, but collected from out of certain obsolete and long forgotten performances. Nor is he very delicate in his choice. A great proportion of *Tristram Shandy*, in particular, is filled with the lowest and most disgusting buffoonery. It seems not an improbable conjecture, that the feeling and pathetic passages only are the natural product of his own mind, and the rest introduced with the view of suiting his work to the taste of a number of readers, who would have been insensible to more refined beauties.

The *Sentimental journey* bears marks of an improved taste, and is nearly free from this kind of dross. Its example seems to shew, that sentiment may be grafted, with at least equal advantage, upon real, as upon imaginary, incidents. . . .

We frequently find, in poetry, that a writer of great and irregular genius is succeeded by another, distinguished by correct and elegant taste. This is strikingly exemplified in Homer and Virgil, Dryden and Pope. A relation somewhat similar seems to exist between Mackenzie and Sterne. The former, coming later, has not of course the same claim to originality, but is certainly preferable in point of taste and selection. If he be inferior to Sterne in wit and in knowledge of the human heart, in pathetic powers he is fully his equal. He excels particularly in minute imagery, and the affecting detail of little incidents. Nor is his manner of writing quite so rambling and irregular. The narratives, which are carried on in a regular and connected manner, are, I think, those in which he succeeds most completely.

107. Applause and censure

1807

Extract from 'STERNE. Critical Essay on his Writings and Genius,' *Classic Tales*, ed. Leigh Hunt, v (1807). 264–81.

Though Leigh Hunt was the general editor for this anthology, Carew Reynell, printer of *Classic Tales*, or one of his relatives, apparently wrote the essay on Sterne, which preceded excerpts of the stories of Le Fever and Maria and the description of Yorick.

It has fallen to the lot of few writers to attract the applause and censure of the world so largely as STERNE. With the most unequivocal evidences of genius, he mingled in his works so much wit and vulgarity, so much piety and profaneness, so much sentiment and licentiousness, that while the gay and frivolous were inevitably much delighted, the graver classes of society regarded his productions at once with disgust and apprehension. The grand object, however, of his writings, in a moral point of view, appears to have been to put men in good humour with one another, and dispose them not only to those important services which the distresses of life frequently call for in the case of considerable numbers, but to those minute attentions which may be imparted by all in any circumstances, and go far even with the most fortunate individuals, towards supplying that mass of pleasing sensation and reflection for which alone life is desirable. The frank, undisguised, unsuspecting character, is every where in the productions of STERNE exhibited with the charms which naturally attach to it, as conciliating affection, and procuring and bestowing happiness. Its accessibility to imposture is regarded as an inconvenience well compensated by its freedom from the irritation of perpetual distrust; and the smiles occasioned by its simplicity are also an attestation to its inoffensiveness. Yet impulse or sentiment may perhaps be too highly and exclusively extolled. How far it may be permitted to supersede calculation, is still to be determined. . . .

The life and opinions of *Tristram Shandy* displays shrewd observation, ready and genuine wit, and well-drawn character. The pedantries and absurdities of the learned, which are a fair subject for ridicule, are exposed by it without reserve, and pleasantry is ever usefully applied in detaching from philosophy whatever would disgrace it; in separating mere pretension from merit, and discriminating cumbrous learning and supercilious dogmatism, from that well disposed and well stored mind, which, with much knowledge applicable to the real purposes of life, possesses also judgment to controul its excursions into the realms of conjecture; which perceives that it has much to acquire and is never disinclined to learn. . . .

Amidst a number of exquisite sentiments and descriptions, this work must be acknowledged often to fail in interest. The candour, forbearance, and humanity of uncle Toby possess frequently almost a power of fascination. The story of Le Fevre, to borrow a phrase of JOHNSON, finds a mirror in every breast. The death of Yorick, and the prudential exhortations of Eugenius, with various other passages, are truly admirable. But digressions appear to have been as studiousiy sought for by STERNE, as by other writers they are sedulously avoided, are perpetually occurring to impede curiosity, and often substitute nothing but cold or coarse conceits, for the continuance of well compacted narrative. The reader also becomes at length tired of the changes perpetually rung in his ear by uncle Toby of the technical terms of war and fortification. Glacis and ravelins, salient points and counterscarps, cease at length to divert; and the moodiness and incoherence of uncle Toby and his faithful attendant, frequently resemble too strongly the prattling and waywardness of childhood, or the wanderings and tearfulness of dotage. . . .

In the *Sentimental Journey*, bagatelle, obscenity, and sentiment, as in the life of Tristram, are the order of the day. The hints afforded to the traveller by the author are creditable to his temper and feelings, if indeed the conduct of a writer be inferable from his precepts. The spirit of accommodation recommended should ever be displayed, instead of that captious judgment and exasperating dogmatism which render the travels of many one scene of irritation to themselves, and disgust or ridicule to others, tending not to liberalize the mind but to confirm and increase all the prejudices of education. The beauties of this work are great and various. The facility with which the author describes the vivacity and badinage of the French character, is highly interesting. The adventure of the Monk is an admirable lecture on the delicacies of humanity. Le Fleur is an exquisitely painted child of nature. The sorrows of Maria are touched with a pencil as soft and captivating as her own melodious pipe; and in the reflections on the bastile, the starling, and the captive, the charms of liberty are described by one of her own children. A banquet is supplied for the pensive and the gay. Sallies of wit and ejaculations of piety, tragedy and trifles, pun and pathos, are served up with an unsparing hand, and a spirit of humanity and benevolence will find itself cherished by a variety of scenes supplied by the sprightly or the sombre pencil. Amidst so much to excite admiration and delight, it must nevertheless be admitted that the grossest allusions occasionally, although not with so much frequency as in the former work occur, passages in which the author assumes his cap and bells, and appears even solicitous to stimulate passion and defy decorum. To the pure it has been said all things are pure. Yet notwithstanding the high authority for this maxim, there are, perhaps, few parents who would wish their daughters deeply versed in the writings of STERNE, nor are there many husbands who would be delighted to find him the favourite author with their wives, as his works, though well calculated to excite mirth, too often effect it at the expence of decency, and if they can divert spleen can also unfortunately impair modesty.

108. Priscilla Parlante defends Sterne

1810

Extract from the Hon. Mrs M. A. (Jeffreys) Cavendish-Bradshaw, preface to *Ferdinand and Ordella* (1810), i. xxxv–xxxvii.

Mrs Cavendish-Bradshaw, who wrote under the pseudonym of Priscilla Parlante, devotes part of the preface of her novel, which is addressed to 'Mr. Satirist,' to an attack on Hannah More's *Coelebs in Search of a Wife* and a defense of Sterne from her strictures (see No. 79), though she was unaware of Miss More's authorship.

Does . . . the delightful heart-touching sensibility of Sterne, deserve to be thus stigmatised, as the fountain of mental corruption? Is the author of the pathetic tales of Maria and Le Fevre, the delineator of the exquisite characters of Corporal Trim, and my uncle Toby, to be branded by puritanism, as having introduced depravity of morals, and the vapid *pulings* of a sentimental school?—Have, then, Mr. Satirist, the methodistical reformists succeeded in breaking the magic talisman of sensibility? Forbid it, heaven!—Forbid it all ye powers that rule the mind, and govern the best feelings of the heart! . . .

[W]ithout thee, O divine spirit of sensibility, how should we be defended against the insidious poison of bigotted and metaphysical barbarism, whose baleful introduction must extinguish every sentiment of liberality and refinement, levelling in its progress the proud distinctions of intellect and education, and leaving only the sullen daemons of rigid severity to check the errors of mankind, and to divide the empire of our souls.

109. Mrs Barbauld on Sterne

1810

Extract from 'The Origin and Progress of Novel-Writing,' *The British Novelists* (1810), i. 40–2.

Anna Laetitia Barbauld (1743–1825) was the sister of John Aikin (see No. 114) and the editor of Richardson's *Correspondence*. Mrs Barbauld did not reprint either of Sterne's books in *The British Novelists*.

About fifty years ago a very singular work appeared, somewhat in the guise of a novel, which gave a new impulse to writings of this stamp; namely, *The Life and Opinions of Tristram Shandy*, followed by *The Sentimental Journey*, by the rev. Mr. Sterne, a clergyman of York. They exhibit much originality, wit, and beautiful strokes of pathos, but a total want of plan or adventure, being made up of conversations and detached incidents. It is the peculiar characteristic of this writer, that he affects the heart, not by long drawn tales of distress, but by light electric touches which thrill the nerves of the reader who possesses a correspondent sensibility of frame. His characters, in like manner, are struck out by a few masterly touches. He resembles those painters who can give expression to a figure by two or three strokes of bold outline, leaving the imagination to fill up the sketch; the feelings are awakened as really by the story of *Le Fevre*, as by the narrative of *Clarissa*. The indelicacies of these volumes are very reprehensible, and indeed in a clergyman scandalous, particularly in the first publication, which however has the richest vein of humour. The two *Shandys*, *Trim*, *Dr. Slop*, are all drawn with a masterly hand. It is one of the merits of Sterne that he has awakened the attention of his readers to the wrongs of the poor negroes,[1] and certainly a great spirit of tenderness and humanity breathes throughout the work. . . .

It has lately been said that Sterne has been indebted for much of his

---

[1] See No. 51.

wit to *Burton's Anatomy of Melancholy*. He certainly exhibits a good deal of reading in that and many other books out of the common way, but the wit is in the application, and that is his own.

110. The *Port Folio* on Sterne

1810, 1811

The *Port Folio*, which was one of the best-known American periodicals, was published in Philadelphia. It was edited by Joseph Dennie (see No. 91) during this period, though he was in failing health. Matthew Carey (1760–1839), author of the first selection below, was a leading Philadelphia publisher. The second selection is unsigned.

(a) Extract from Matthew Carey, 'Remarks on the Charge of Plagiarism Alleged Against Sterne,' appearing in the *Port Folio*, 3rd ser., iv (October 1810) and reprinted here from Matthew Carey, *Miscellaneous Essays* (1830), pp. 438–46

On a retrospection of those authors, on whose fame a few fleeting years have produced the most injurious effects, I know of none more remarkable than Sterne. This humorous, witty, pathetic, elegant, but licentious writer, was, during his life, and for a considerable period since his death, at the very pinnacle of celebrity. His writings were the standards of fashion. They were read with avidity and delight, as well in the 'gorgeous palaces' of the great, as in the mud-walled huts of the sons and daughters of poverty. Few works, if any, were ever received with more unbounded applause, than the *Sentimental Journey*. Its circulation was immense. It produced a revolution in the public taste. No works carried so sure a passport to fame, and, what to many authors is of more importance, to 'pelf and pudding,' as those in the sentimental style, with which the literary world then actually swarmed.

. . . But alas! . . . From the elevated niche which his bust occupied in the temple of Fame, it has been ignominiously hurled down, and he has now sunk, in the public estimation, into the disgraceful character of a petty thief, who, like the daw in the fable, decorated himself with borrowed plumage. He is regarded as a literary swindler, who has stolen a reputation to which his talents afforded him no claim. He is believed to have palmed upon the world as his own, writings, composed of fragments basely purloined from the most diversified range of writers. . . .

It is about eleven years since Dr. Ferriar, of Manchester, a gentleman of considerable talents and unwearied research, published his 'Illustrations of Sterne,' in which he made a most copious collection of the passages here referred to. This work has been universally esteemed as having ultimately decided the question, and incontestably established the guilt of the culprit. Although I freely acknowledge that the grounds of condemnation are plausible, yet not having been perfectly satisfied with the force of the evidence, I have not been able to subscribe the verdict. I believed from the first perusal of Ferriar's work, that Sterne was innocent. Nay more—I persuaded myself into the opinion, that in the very 'Illustrations,' notwithstanding their plausibility, there was abundant evidence, on a fair and candid examination, to repel the charge. Time, so far from having weakened my opinion on the subject, has fully and completely convinced me that Sterne has been treated with extreme injustice, and that he was innocent of the offence laid to his charge. . . .

In this investigation, I repose with less diffidence on my conclusions, from the circumstance, that how highly soever I admire most of Sterne's writings, the author is by no means a favourite with me. Were I as enthusiastic an admirer of him as some of my friends, I should not feel so confident in the opinions I have formed. . . .

In the 'Illustrations,' Dr. Ferriar relies upon two different kinds of proof. The one consists of a number of passages in Sterne, which bear a strong resemblance to passages to be found in Rabelais, Scarron, Bruscambille, D'Aubigné, Hall, Burton and others. The second is composed of passages, some of them very nearly, and others absolutely, verbatim in his works as they are to be found in books previously published. On the latter class he places his chief reliance. They form his grand phalanx. The others are only adduced as auxiliaries. . . .

I readily admit that the doctor's quotations appear, *prima facie*, to afford evidence of the literary piracy of Sterne. Many intelligent persons, whom I have heard discourse upon the subject, have believed it highly absurd and preposterous to entertain the least doubt upon the validity of the accusation. They regard it as utterly impossible that these passages could have ever appeared in the writings of Sterne, in any other mode than by plagiarism. But it is no novelty for the same fact to afford to different minds diametrically opposite conclusions. This is precisely the case here. From the exact sameness in about a dozen of the striking instances, on which the author of the 'Illustrations' places his chief reliance, principally arises my conviction of the innocence of Sterne. A little reflection will remove the paradoxical appearance of this position.

In every age and in every country contempt has been the fate of the plagiarist. . . .

. . . Let us for a moment suppose that he was a plagiarist in the fullest sense of the word, can we reconcile it with reason, or common sense, or any of the inciting causes that operate upon mankind, that he should have exposed himself to so easy and palpable a detection as he must have been constantly liable to, had he made up his books of shreds and patches, meanly stolen from works, with most of which the literary world was familiar, and hardly any of which were so scarce as to afford a tolerable probability of escape? A detection would have annihilated all his hopes of reputation and all his chances of emolument. This consideration would undoubtedly have been sufficiently powerful to withhold him, however unprincipled he might have been.

. . . I would as soon believe that an artful, loose woman, who was desirous of standing fair with the world, would, in the glare of day, and in the very presence of her most valued friends, march into a brothel with a notorious debauchee, as suppose that Sterne, even admitting his guilt to the fullest extent, would have copied verbatim what he had stolen.

Further. What are those passages said to be stolen? Do they bear such marks of sublimity or excellence, as could have induced Sterne to be guilty of theft for them? By no means. They are generally trite, and many of them not beyond the capacity of an author of very mediocre talents. Some are to the last degree trivial, and would hardly be noticed among the effusions of a ten years old child of precocious talents, by an old gossiping grandmother.

Some of the readers of these lucubrations have by this time become impatient, and are ready with peevishness to ask—Can you believe it possible, that two men shall write ten or twenty lines exactly alike, without any communication with each other? and if not, how can you account for the sameness stated by Ferriar? I hasten to reply, and hope to convince every candid reader that I have not lightly adopted the opinions I advocate.

Every man who has paid attention to the operations of the faculty of memory, must have observed, that when it is of a vigorous character, it so completely possesses itself of the objects submitted to it in reading, as to render it, in many cases, hardly possible, indeed often utterly impossible, at a remote period, to discriminate between sentiments, forms of expression, and images, thus acquired, and those which are the emanations of a man's own intellectual powers. Were it at all necessary, numberless instances might be produced, in support of this hypothesis. But I trust it is self-evident to every person of reflection. Still further. As the doctrine of innate ideas has been long and justly exploded, it is obvious that the great mass of our knowledge must be acquired, and principally from books. And therefore, when we write or converse, we must necessarily, and even to ourselves imperceptibly, derive a large portion of our lucubrations from others. On certain trite and commonplace topics, we can lay claim to very little more as our own than the form and manner of expression. . . .

Let us refer all this to the case of Sterne. His memory must have been very powerful; and his reading, in his early days, when that faculty was in its highest perfection, must have been various and highly miscellaneous. In this course of reading, conformably with the eccentricity of his character, he must have read and been delighted with those comic and satirical writers, whose works he is now charged with having laid so heavily and so unfairly under contribution. . . . They naturally made a strong and inextinguishable impression on his mind. No wonder, therefore, when at a subsequent period of his life, he began himself to write, that his productions should savour so highly of those works, with which his mind was so strongly imbued—no wonder that images, ideas, and forms of expression, so familiar to him, should be constantly obtruding themselves on him—no wonder, in fine, that even whole passages should be presented by his recollection, which he mistook for a tribute offered by his imagination.

. . . I request the reader's attention to another point. After all the tedious hours employed in this research by Ferriar and others, the extent of the alleged thefts is to the last degree insignificant. It would have been like Crœsus robbing a poor widow of her last mite, for so fertile a writer as Sterne to have stolen the passages in question.

Sterne's works are generally published in eight volumes, each averaging about 300 pages. Every page contains about 36 lines, amounting in the whole to above 80,000 lines. And, gentle reader, observe, that on a careful examination of the 'Illustrations,' I can venture to affirm, that the utmost extent of all the thefts adduced against this writer, is not above 300 lines, of which there are not 50, that contain any thing very striking or remarkable. . . .

There is an extraordinary singularity in the case of Sterne. He is now believed to be indebted for a large portion of his works to former authors. And yet some of his writings, in as great a degree as those of any other man that ever lived, possess the most infallible stamp of sterling merit—they are almost inimitable. During his life, and since his death there have been numberless attempts to imitate him, and some of them made by men of considerable talents; not one of which is acknowledged to have approached near to the original.

(b) Extract from 'Critical Comments on Sterne, Smollett, and Fielding,' the *Port Folio*, 3rd ser., vi (November 1811). 415–19

Without maintaining, as before remarked, the universality of the rule, that the page of an author is an evidence of his life and character, we propose to produce some instances where they both shine with correspondent lights. Lawrence Sterne has been unmercifully handled by those who never comprehended his character. His page is replete with the most delicate and tender sentiments, or with obscenity the most odious. At one time it glows with piety; at another it shocks us with its blasphemy; and it is worthy of remark, that whatever character he assumes, his delicacy and obscenity, his piety and his blasphemy, are fascinating still. His impiety, his obscenity are not the impiety and obscenity of a hand inured to the business; they appear not like studied opinions, but involuntary effusions: they are something which we are prepared to expect a moment's meditation will amend.

This anticipating benevolence of the reader results from a slight acquaintance with his page. He has taught us in his first chapter what we are to expect, and that is—disappointment. Conscious as he is that any subject is interesting when handled by him, he delights to present us with the meanest as the more decisive proof of his genius. He follows the irregular impulses of his own sensations, always disappointing and always delighting his reader. We find jocularity in the pulpit and piety in the kitchen. Such contrarieties have given to Sterne the character of a hypocrite, than which nothing can be more unequivocally unjust.

We hope our readers will not believe that we mean to vindicate the exceptionable passages of Sterne, when we pronounce them fascinating. Vice is often fascinating, and on that account the more to be shunned and avoided. But Sterne was no hypocrite. He did express what he felt. It is the frankness and honesty of his character merely, that have given that odious appellation to his name. He was jocose when the occasion demanded gravity, and grave in the season of merriment and whim. Now, that he should give a-loose to his pen, and delineate a train of sensations so entirely opposite and contradictory, may levy a severe tax on his discretion; but it is evidence the most conclusive, that hypocrisy formed no part of his character.

When we consider his life, we shall find it tinged with all these eccentric varieties. He loved the society of his friends, the social glass, and the hospitable table, and would often dash gayety with unseasonable gloom, or enliven gloom with as unseasonable mirth. He always disregarded those forms and ceremonies, consecrated by custom, and followed the impulses of his nature. The very man who could mourn over the body of a dead ass, could abandon the wife of his bosom, and fall desperately in love with another man's.[1]

The reader may perhaps wonder from what deep and recondite motive such anomalies of action can arise. He need not go far—he need not search farther than his own heart to find all those incongruities of character so apparent in the page and in the life of Lawrence Sterne. Startling as this consideration may appear, it is nevertheless literally true. Let him, for instance, disregard all forms and ceremonies, and note down and present to the world his thoughts, as they spontaneously arise, and his page will teem with all the conflicting sensations of this writer's. How often during divine service would his pen reproach him with unseasonable mirth! How often in a ball-room would he be compelled to acknowledge, that the smiles of pleasure on his face played the hypocrite with his heart! How often would he confess that his bosom had been the repository of passions as criminal as Sterne's!

It is this habit to which we have ever been disciplined, of concealing

[1] See No. 53d, p. 187, n. 1. Cf. Nos 98 and 113 making the similar charge that Sterne mourned a dead ass rather than relieving his living mother.

our thoughts from the knowledge of other men, that gives to the page of Sterne that singularity of appearance. Unquestionably it is the duty of every one to restrain his desires, and to put a curb upon his thoughts, and here rests the criminality of Lawrence Sterne. He gave discretion to the winds, he followed the blind and irregular impulses of his passions. While, however, we reprobate a habit so pernicious, let us call things by their proper names, and not charge as hypocrisy that trait in his character founded on qualities directly and irreconcilably hostile to an hypocrite. Thus . . . the page of Lawrence Sterne constitutes his biography.

Some remarks on the style of this writer, though not closely connected with the subject, may not be deemed inadmissible. His wild abruptness, and uniform inconsistency have, we trust, been already accounted for. His wit is altogether of the sportive and harmless kind; it tickles, but never wounds. Probably, there is not to be found in the whole compass of English literature, an example of wit so uniformly sportive, and so perfectly free from the least particle of offence. In addition to this he has a vein of humour, which cannot be denominated wit, although its effects are the same, resulting from an opposition of character, that is constantly preserved. Toby Shandy, and Walter never can be brought to see the same subject in the same point of view; the ludicrous mistakes, and unexpected turns given to the debate, arising from such contrariety of intellects, are productive of many fraternal squabbles, to the inexpressible diversion of the reader. They seem to have entered into a recognizance to misunderstand every syllable they respectively utter.

What further conduces to our entertainment is this: Walter Shandy is a deep and philosophical theorist, and Toby Shandy a man of plain matter of fact common sense. Thus, while Walter is exhausting his intellect in his wild speculations, a simple question or a dry remark from his brother, suddenly stops all further progress, and brings us down to the plain familiar level of common sense. There is much delicate and concealed satire in these parts of the work; they are a sort of practical illustration how false and frivolous such learned speculations are.

Another trait of Sterne is the vivid and distinct descriptions he gives us, not only of the peculiar turns of thinking, but also of the speaker's person, and his peculiar attitudes in speaking. With the exception of the inimitable Cervantes, it will be difficult to find another writer, who, in this branch of composition, exceeds Lawrence Sterne. This always gives to the reader a complete and definite conception of his subject, and answers in a great measure the purpose of painting to his eye. The words are likewise so accurately adjusted to the character speaking, that they cannot, in any one instance, be confounded with any other.

Some critics have thought that Sterne possessed every requisite to have formed a perfect novel; because his conception and delineation of character were so just. They censure his excessive and disconnected mode of writing, and wonder that he did not employ his talents more systematically. We have often had occasion to protest against this mode of determining a literary point; namely, that because a man has done what he did attempt well, he could do something which he never did attempt *much better.* By what process is this fact so soberly ascertained, that Sterne, if he had written more systematically, would not have lost that spritely naïveté that now exhilarates and warms us in every page? Those random and wild effusions so utterly repugnant to every thing like system, would undoubtedly have been lost; and with deference to such critics, they are parts of Sterne that cannot so conveniently be spared. To prescribe system to Sterne really seems to us like teaching a humming-bird to fly according to mathematics; it is his delightful wildness that enables him to rifle every flower of its sweets, and to give his quivering and delicate rainbows to the sun.

Another trait in the composition of our author is, his artless, unstudied, yet sweet and captivating pathos. He finds passion in the most ordinary occurrences, and the reader is led to wonder how incidents so apparently trivial, derive such interest from the pen of Lawrence Sterne. What renders this the more surprising is, that Sterne, when the reader examines his own heart, has told him nothing new. He recollects, or rather believes that he recollects, having experienced the same sensations on similar occasions, and he cannot conceive how Sterne could have given him so faithful a picture of his own mind. This is indeed to hold, as Shakspeare would say, the mirror up to nature,[1] and is the very perfection of writing; namely, to present us with a sentiment or a passion so exactly resembling our own, that we are ourselves deceived so fully, that we believe Sterne has committed plagiarism on us. This we believe to be the only plagiarism of which Sterne has really been guilty, notwithstanding what has been so confidently advanced in opposition, we could heartily wish that his miserable imitators had committed the same kind of plagiarism with their model.

Sterne is not a profound writer: he skims the surface of things, and

[1] See *Hamlet*, act 3, sc. 2.

aims more at interesting the heart than the judgment. He is peculiarly our favourite at those moments when we require something to excite, without laboriously engrossing the attention when excited.

111. William Mudford on Sterne

1811

Extract from 'Critical Observations upon *Tristram Shandy* and the *Sentimental Journey*,' *The British Novelists; comprising every work of acknowledged merit which is usually classed under the denomination of Novels*, iii (1811). i–viii.

Mudford (1782–1848), miscellaneous writer, novelist, and journalist, reprinted both *Tristram Shandy* and the *Sentimental Journey* in his collection of novelists.

The writings of Sterne present, to the critic who sits down to examine them, difficulties which he can hardly find in any other author. Their deviation from all established rules of composition, their fantastic irregularity, and their often foolish attempts to excite surprise or provoke laughter, preclude them from that sober application of criticism which works of more legitimate arrangement would exact. To analyse his volumes may be pronounced impossible: to ascertain, with certainty, their object is, perhaps, no less impossible, and to establish a connexion between them would defy the highest ingenuity of man. . . .

Of a writer so heteroclite and so anomalous as Sterne, it is not easy to speak but with the same incoherency which characterises his own productions. Detached opinions upon detached parts are all that can be attempted. There is no artful intricacy of plot to unfold and commend, no settled purpose of the narrative to disclose, nor many eminently pleasing events or incidents to applaud. All is studied confusion and perplexing abruptness, and the occasional gleams of fancy, wit, and humour, which diversify and adorn this dreary continuity of ruggedness, are like those glimpses of a smiling and beauteous landscape which a traveller sometimes catches as he journies over lonely hills or gloomy desarts of interminable extent. They cheer and refresh his spirits, and lend a transitory lustre which gilds the surrounding barrenness. . . .

His greatest efforts seem to have been employed in the delineation of my *uncle Toby's* character. . . .

Every reader . . . must acknowledge that the character of *Toby* is drawn with some touches that demand the highest commendation. His benevolence, his humanity, and his artlessness, lay hold of the best affections of our nature, which accompany him to the end. His simplicity borders, sometimes, perhaps, upon fatuity; but still, he is so amiable, so kind, and so gentle, that we love the good old soldier with all his weaknesses about him. If I might be allowed to parody a couplet of Pope, I would say,

> If to his share some *human* errors fall,
> Look on his face, and you'll forget them all.[1]

The contemplation of his character, and that of the honest corporal, disposes us to the admission and to the nurture of all those sentiments of compassion, of virtue, and of humanity, in which consist the noblest attributes of man. In him they are displayed with so much attraction, and are made to act with so little artifice, that we feel, instinctively, an awakened desire within us to copy so just a model and a wish to behold more of them in society. Virtue is taught by example, rather than by precept, and robbed of all her austerity. She pleads through him with such gentleness and grace, that every ear is open, and every heart is won. To Sterne certainly belongs the praise of having sought, in this character, to amend mankind, and to purify the passions, by a display of the most endearing qualities that were ever, perhaps, united by the pen of fiction.

With regard to my *uncle Toby's hobby-horse*, I fancy every reader sees him on it too often. We are at first amused, but at last fatigued, with his military operations. There is too much uniformity in them to keep the attention constantly alive. It is wearisome to be constantly introduced to details which few understand, and fewer can relish. When one account is read, all that follow may be easily anticipated. . . .

Mr. *Shandy* appears in a light much less amiable than his brother.

[1] See *The Rape of the Lock*, canto ii, ll. 17–18.

This contrast was intended by Sterne, and he has, in general, very happily supported it. He is petulant and irascible; impatient of the follies of others, and sarcastic in his reprehension of them. In him, if any where, must be sought the object of the work. To ridicule the affectation of obsolete learning, and the belief in absurd theories, *may be* (for I speak with great hesitation) the intention of Sterne, in drawing the character of *Mr. Walter Shandy*. To shew, also, that such belief is prejudicial to human happiness, by teaching us to expect, from secondary and improbable causes, those events which should be referred to, and humbly looked for from the Almighty Disposer of all things, may have been likewise, another part of Sterne's intention: but if it were not, such is the lesson deducible from the character. The satire, however, is much misplaced [because by Sterne's time it was unnecessary]. . . .

[Sterne's] is a brief excellence, for ever spoiled by some weakness. Affectation was, to Sterne, what a quibble was to Shakespeare: 'The fatal *Cleopatra*, for which he lost the world, and was content to lose it. . . .'[1]

The *Sentimental Journey* is more popular than *Tristram Shandy*, because it is a more equal performance, and written with greater attention to the propriety of the subjects that are introduced. There are, in it, more things which will entertain the general reader, delivered in a manner something less incoherent. Still, it is Sterne who writes; and Sterne still endeavours to win his readers by singularity and abruptness. I think, also, that his *sentimental* touches become, at last, irksome. They betray their origin, which was certainly from the head, and not from the heart. He is a sort of knight-errant, who sets forth in quest of adventures, and makes or finds them on all occasions. The emotions which he describes must either have been artificial, or must have sprung from a morbid delicacy of feeling: but the accounts which I have heard of his private life lead me to conclude the former. Kindness for the man, indeed, would teach us to hope so: for what condition of existence could be more wretched than such an organization, than a heart which weeps, and sighs, and bleeds, at every turn of life?

[1] The quotation is from Samuel Johnson's preface to *The Plays of William Shakespeare* (1765).

112. Francis Jeffrey on Sterne in the *Edinburgh*

1813, 1823

Francis Jeffrey (1773–1850), Scottish jurist, co-founder and editor of the *Edinburgh Review,* was a conservative critic who attacked the Romantics. In a letter in 1792 he had praised Sterne as one of 'our best writers' who had 'sometimes' achieved 'a charm in simplicity and naturality of expression' (Lord Cockburn, *Life of Lord Jeffrey* (1852), ii. 9). For Madame de Staël's remarks on Sterne, see No. 136.

(a) Extract from Jeffrey's unsigned review of Mme de Staël's *De la Littérature considérée dans ses rapports avec les institutions sociales,* xxi (February 1813). 46

Mad. de Staël thinks very poorly of our talent for pleasantry; and is not very successful in her delineation of what we call humour. The greater part of the nation, she says, lives either in the serious occupations of business and politics, or in the tranquil circle of family affection. What is called society, therefore, has scarcely any existence among them; and yet it is in that sphere of idleness and frivolity, that taste is matured, and gayety made elegant. They are not at all trained, therefore, to observe the finer shades of character and of ridicule in real life; and consequently neither think of delineating them in their compositions, nor are aware of their merit when delineated by others. We are unwilling to think this perfectly just; and are encouraged to suspect, that the judgment of the ingenious author may not be altogether without appeal on such a subject, by observing, that she represents the paltry flippancy and disgusting affectation of Sterne, as the purest specimen of true English humour; and classes the character of Falstaff along with that of Pistol, as instances of that vulgar caricature from which the English still condescend to receive amusement. It is more just, however, to observe,

344

that the humour, and in general the pleasantry, of our nation, has very frequently a sarcastic and even misanthrophic character, which distinguishes it from the mere playfulness and constitutional gayety of our French neighbours; and that we have not, for the most part, succeeded in our attempts to imitate the graceful pleasantry and agreeable trifling of that people.

(b) Extract from Jeffrey's unsigned review of a group of Scottish novels, xxxix (October 1823). 160–1

[T]here is . . . [a] kind of humour which depends on the combination of great *naïveté*, indolence and occasional absurdity, with natural good sense, and taste and kind feelings in the principal characters—such combinations as Sir Roger De Coverley, the Vicar of Wakefield, and My Uncle Toby, have made familiar to all English readers. . . .

113. Byron: 'that dog Sterne'

1 December 1813

Extract from Byron's journal, 1 December 1813, *Works of Lord Byron*, ii (*Letters and Journals*, ed. Rowland E. Prothero, 1898). 359.

Byron accepted the rumors of Sterne's mistreatment of his mother (see No. 98) which had been circulating for many years. In the selection below he is berating himself for not doing his duty in Parliament. References elsewhere in Byron's works indicate he has read Sterne appreciatively. Byron's journals were not published until 1830.

Ah, I am as bad as that dog Sterne, who preferred whining over 'a dead ass to relieving a living mother'—villain—hypocrite—slave—sycophant! but *I* am no better.

114. John Aikin on Sterne

1814

Extract from 'Laurence Sterne,' in *General Biography* (1814), ix. 243.

Aikin (1747–1822), physician and author, was the brother of Mrs Barbauld (see No. 109). *General Biography*, one of the standard reference works that were produced in increasing numbers in the early nineteenth century, was the joint product of Aikin and William Johnston; Aikin signed the article on Sterne.

This eccentric performance is formed upon the general idea of a kind of self-taught philosopher, in the person of an elderly country-gentleman, full of odd and singular notions, which he displays chiefly in a plan of education laid down for an only son, and commencing from, or rather before, his birth. If in this groundwork a resemblance may be traced to that admirable ridicule of school philosophy and learning, Scriblerus;[1] in the style and filling up, *Tristram Shandy* is wholly original; and the combination of comic delineations of domestic life and characters, exquisite touches of the pathetic, nice observations on the human heart, and whimsical opinions and theories, with much downright extravagance, and a plentiful mixture of indecency, produces a motley whole like nothing that the English language had before presented, and which will probably never be renewed, though attempts have often been made to imitate it. ... [The *Sentimental Journey*] is a desultory narrative of a supposed journey to France and Italy, in the person of Yorick, a favourite character of Tristram Shandy, which, by a number of touching incidents, and strokes of national delineation, is rendered extremely entertaining, and acquired a popularity perhaps more general than that of his former performance, for there are more readers who can feel sentiment and humour, than who can understand wit. It was also freer from impurities than its predecessor, though not entirely unobjectionable in that respect. Its chief fault was an exaggeration of

[1] See No. 83d, p. 267, n. 1.

feeling upon trifling occasions, which, when imitated by inferior writers, degenerated into a kind of cant, highly offensive to taste and good sense.

115. Sterne's characters: goblins and portraits

1814

Extract from the Reverend Edward Mangin, *A View of the Pleasures Arising from a Love of Books* (1814), pp. 82–105.

Mangin (1772–1852), a prebend ordained in the Irish Church, was a miscellaneous writer.

Sterne is perpetually quoted and applauded as excelling in three respects, namely, originality, tenderness and humour.

Dr. Ferriar[1] has proved with great acuteness that he has little or no claim to the title of an *original* author . . . and, indeed, to any attentive reader of Dr. F's ingenious treatise, it is manifest that Sterne's strokes of pleasantry are frequently purloined; of course, there remains of his three alleged excellencies only the power of awakening emotions of tenderness: and that he occasionally has this power in a very eminent degree, cannot be denied. He *describes* also with singular felicity, and displays a very extensive acquaintance with the turnings and windings of the human heart. . . . [Y]et his works, I mean his *Tristram Shandy* and *Sentimental Journey*, are so defiled with impurities of all kinds as to render them repulsive to every admirer of *moral* propriety. . . .

He fails, however, in matters of minor consideration; while he would have his readers suppose that he disdained a regular and methodical narrative, he leaves room for the suspicion that his eccentricity was rather the effect of incapacity than choice. The persons pourtrayed in

[1] See No. 90.

his story of Mr. Shandy, are goblins, not human beings: not individuals selected from the mass of mankind, but formations of his own which he chooses to call men, yet to which he has assigned qualities never found united in any one of our race. The absurd attachment of Mr. Shandy to exploded systems is totally inconsistent with the good sense and neatness of observation he often displays; and the *Captain* at times evinces so sound an understanding, that without supposing him alternately doting and rational, we cannot account for some childish things which he says and does. Don Quixote is not more insane when he mistakes a flock of sheep for a hostile army, than Uncle Toby in his propensity to seeing every subject in a military point of view. His courage, his sensibility, his judicious benevolence, and the experience he has had of life as a soldier, do not accord with such traits of egregious simplicity as the author has thrown into the portrait; and which, had he been announced as a harmless and diverting maniac, would have been perfectly suitable.

Corporal Trim, who is vulgarly conceived to be a *chef-doeuvre* in the ranks of natural character, is, in fact, not so: an old English soldier, and especially one who has held a station of command, may be represented as fond of recollecting and recounting what he has done and suffered in his manly and perilous vocation; and familiarity with his kind-hearted master, who had once been his officer, is most becomingly made a part of the picture; but he too is as inconsistent, as puerile and as visionary as the Captain. . . .

There is a sketch of Sterne's life prefixed to his works, the author of which would willingly vindicate him, and prove him innocent of the indelicacy laid to his charge: he insinuates that Sterne's violations of decorum are not so much in his pages, as in the minds and tastes of his readers. This is poor sophistry, and an affront offered to the common-sense of mankind: were such a mode of argument admissible, as this person uses in his defence of Sterne's ambiguities, there is scarcely any moral obliquity which may not find a similar excuse. If Sterne's manner of writing is so obscure that it requires peculiar discernment to discover its beauties; if these are hidden, and if his indecencies are perceptible at the first glance, the question is decided.

We may be permitted to lament that this accusation is so well founded; and particularly that it should apply to the *Sentimental Journey*; for in it there certainly are many beautiful parts, many of those passages which fill the mind with charming ideas, and make the employment of *reading* so entertaining as it is. . . .

The popularity of the *Journey* has been rather increased than diminished by time; and as before observed, it abounds in those qualifications which characterize books of entertainment; in humour, tenderness, nice developement of the human mind and its various motives; and in fine specimens of what may be called the art of painting with his *pen*, in which the author was a very great master: he exhibits on paper the talents of Carlo Dolce, Vandyke, Teniers and Hogarth,[1] and is often not inferior in composition, colouring and truth to any of them.

His portrait of the forlorn and gentle Maria is complete in all the lines and tints which constitute grace and softness: her form, that of loveliness not impaired but rendered more engaging by feebleness and sorrow, than the beauty of health and happiness can ever be; her ornament, a riband of *pale* green: her attitude, sitting with her elbow in her lap, and her head leaning on *one side* within her hand: her hair streaming loose, and tears trickling down her cheek. The scenic accompaniments are appropriate, and finely in contrast: the season that of the *vintage* in the Bourbonnois, the finest district of France; and the children of labour rejoicing in the prospect of plenty: a description which causes the reader to feel as the traveller says he does: the affections fly out, and kindle with every group; but they are soon recalled by Maria, the poplar and the rivulet. Pity now begins to take her turn; and here, an ordinary describer would suppose that enough had been done; but Sterne was not to be satisfied with any thing less than the utmost precision of finishing, which he accordingly communicates to the piece: YORICK sits down by Maria, and Maria *lets* him wipe away her tears. . . .

It would be wearisome to collect and comment on all the instances which might be produced of Sterne's powers and versatility. His comic exhibitions are often not in any respect inferior to those of a grave or tender cast; nor is it easy to say in which he most excels; but perhaps the general opinion favors the idea that his genius inclined him chiefly to sentiment and pathos. In the 'Journey,' it certainly takes this direction frequently; and when his cheerfulness terminates in something at least

[1] These names suggest the variety of Sterne's talents. Carlo Dolce (1616–86), Italian painter, was popular for his 'highly wrought' pictures; Sir Anthony van Dyck (1599–1641), Flemish painter, was known for the sensitivity of his work and especially for his portraits of women and children; David Teniers the younger (1610–90), Flemish painter, was known for his delicacy of touch, his control of detail, and his striking overall effects; William Hogarth (1697–1764), English illustrator, engraver, and painter, was famous for his satirical portraits. Hogarth did an illustration for *Tristram Shandy* (Work, p. 121).

serious; when, like Milton's 'l'allegro,' it is ennobled by what approaches almost to melancholy, it affects one with the same solemnity of feeling as the view of a mild autumnal evening communicates 'When the faint landscape swims away;'[1] and leaves upon the mind an impression of respect and veneration for the writer, which his wit never does. Had he altogether abstained from the grossness in which he indulges himself, his title to admiration would have been indisputable; as it is, he has forfeited his claim; and though we cannot but regret the circumstance, two thirds of his admirers are laudably ashamed of their idol, and accordingly his works are read by numbers who *dare* not praise them.

It is not possible to speak of the PLEASURES which miscellaneous reading affords, and of the agreeable sensations created by perusing the best efforts of distinguished writers, without taking some notice of the works of *Robert Burns*; the resemblance of his genius to that of the last mentioned author must be obvious to all who are acquainted with the productions of both.

Burns, like Sterne, is a painter: like Sterne he describes admirably; sees every object with a poet's eyes; and exhilarates by his humour, or by his pathetic passages fills the reader's heart with emotions of tenderness; while the happiest sketch of local circumstances generally adorns the story he tells. But, like Sterne, he is sometimes so coarse in his expressions, and so indecorous in his allusions, as to render a *complete* copy of his works inadmissible into any society where good breeding and innocence are cultivated. . . .

Allow me . . . a few observations, in order to point out one of those turns of mind in which he strongly resembles Sterne in his Sentimental Journey; and which, as I have before remarked to you, forms one of the fascinations of that work. Burns frequently adds the greatest imaginable interest to his subject by the introduction of moral reflections: and the force of his moralizing is increased by the reader's surprize on perceiving himself allured, he scarcely knows how, from light and joyous topics, into meditations the most solemn and awful.

This transition from levity to seriousness, produces the finest effect: in his lines, for instance, on turning up a mouse's nest with the plough,[2] the genius of this true poet has given great dignity to what would appear a hopeless subject; and within the limits of a few verses, has

[1] James Thomson, 'Hymn on Solitude,' l. 30.
[2] 'To a Mouse'; the poem bears the subtitle, 'On Turning her up in her Nest with the Plough, November, 1785.'

presented us with samples of nearly all the elements of composition: broad humour, accurate description, the reflections of a sensible mind on social interests, moral deduction, the truest pathos, and that pathos heightened by natural and most affecting references to his own untoward fortunes.

116. Coleridge on Sterne

1818, 1825, 1828, 1833, undated

(a) Extract from Coleridge's MS notes for a lecture on 'Wit and Humour,' delivered at the room of the Philosophical Society in Fetter Lane, 24 February 1818 (*Coleridge's Miscellaneous Criticism*, ed. Thomas Middleton Raysor (1936), pp. 117–26)

The pure unmixed ludicrous or laughable belongs exclusively to the understanding plus the senses of eye and ear; hence to the fancy. Not to the reason or the moral sense. . . .[1]

Hence too, that the laughable is its *own end*. When serious satire commences, or satire that is felt as serious, however comically drest, the free laughter ceases; it becomes sardonic. Felt in Young's satire—not uninstanced in Butler.[2] The truly comic is the *blossom of the nettle*.

In the simply laughable, there is a mere disproportion between a definite act and a definite purpose or end, or a disproportion of the end itself to the rank of the definite person; but when we contemplate a finite in reference to the infinite, consciously or unconsciously, *humor*. So says Jean Paul Richter.

Humorous writers, therefore, as Sterne in particular, delight to end in nothing, or a direct contradiction.

That there is something in this is evident; for you cannot conceive a humorous man who does not give some disproportionate *generality*,

---

[1] Coleridge draws here and elsewhere in his notes on Jean Paul Richter's *Vorschule der Aesthetik* (1804), especially sections 26, 28, 29, 32, 33. For Richter's comments on Sterne, see No. 152.

[2] Coleridge is presumably thinking of Edward Young's *Love of Fame, or the Universal Passion* (1725–8) and Samuel Butler's *Hudibras* (1663–78).

universality, to his hobbyhorse, as Mr. Shandy; or at least [there is] [1] an absence of any interest but what arises from the humor itself, as in Uncle Toby. There is *the idea* of the soul in its undefined capacity and dignity that gives the sting to any absorption of it by any one pursuit, and this not as a member of society for any particular, however mistaken, interest, but as man. Hence in humor the little is made great, and the great little, in order to destroy both, because all is equal in contrast with the infinite.

Hence the tender feeling connected with the *humors* or hobbyhorses of a man.

1. Respect, for there is absence of any interest as the ground-work, tho' the imagination of a[n] *interest* by the humorist may exist, as if a remarkably simple-hearted man should pride himself on his knowledge of the world, and how well he can manage it.

2. Acknowledgement of the hollowness and farce of the world, and its disproportion to the godlike within us.

Hence when particular *acts* have reference to particular *selfish* motives, the humorous bursts into the indignant and abhorring. All follies *not selfish*, it pardons or palliates. The danger of this [is] exemplified in Sterne. . . .

STERNE

A sort of *knowingness*, the wit of which depends, first on the modesty it gives pain to; or secondly, the innocence and innocent ignorance over which it triumphs; or thirdly, on a certain oscillation in the individual's own mind between the remaining good and the encroaching evil of his nature, a sort of dallying with the devil, a fluxionary act of combining courage and cowardice, as when a man snuffs a candle with his fingers for the first time, or better still, perhaps, that tremulous daring with which a child touches a hot tea urn, because it had been forbidden—so that the mind has in its own white and black angel the same or similar amusements as might be supposed to take place between an old debauchee and a prude—[her] resentment from the prudential anxiety to preserve appearances, and have a character, and an inward sympathy with the enemy. We have only to suppose society *innocent*—and [this sort of wit] is equal to a stone that falls in snow; it makes no sound because it excites no resistance. [This accounts] for nine tenths [of its effect]; the remainder rests on its being an offence against the good manners of human nature itself. . . .

[1] All the emendations in this selection are Raysor's.

This source, unworthy as it is, may doubtless be combined with wit, drollery, fancy, and even humour,—and we have only to regret the *mésalliance*; but that the latter are quite distinct from the former may be made evident by abstracting in our imagination the *characters* of Mr. Shandy, my Uncle Toby, and Trim, which are all *antagonists* to this wit, and suppose instead of them two or three callous debauchees, and the result will be pure disgust. Sterne cannot be too severely censured for this, for he makes the best dispositions of our nature the pandars and condiments for the basest.

EXCELLENCES

1. The bringing forward into distinct consciousness those minutiae of thought and feeling which appear trifles, have an importance [only] for the moment, and yet almost every man feels in one way or other. Thus it has the novelty of an individual peculiarity, and yet the interest of a something that belongs to our common nature. In short, to seize happily on those points in which every man is more or less a *humorist*. And the propensity to notice these things does itself constitute a humorist, and the superadded power of so presenting them to men in general gives us the man of humor. Hence the difference of the man of humor, the effect of whose portraits does not depend on the felt presence of himself as a humorist, as Cervantes and Shakespeare, nay, Rabelais— and those in whom the effect is in the humorist's own oddity—Sterne (and *Swift*?).

2. Traits of *human* nature, which so easily assume a particular cast and color from individual character. Hence this, and the pathos connected with it, quickly passes into *humor*, and forms the ground of it—[as in] the story of the Fly. Character [is created] by a delicacy and higher degree of a good quality. [Refers to *Tristram Shandy*, II. 12: 'Go, says he . . . both thee and me' (p. 113).]

3. In Mr. Shandy's character, as of all Mr. Shandys, a craving for sympathy in exact proportion to the oddity and unsympathizability; next to this, [craving] to be at least disputed with, or rather both in one, [to] dispute and yet agree; but [holding] worst of all, to acquiesce without either resistance or sympathy—[all this is] most happily conceived.

Contrasts sometimes increasing the love between the brothers—and always either balanced or remedied.

Drollery in Obadiah

4. No writer so happy as Sterne in the unexaggerated and truly natural representation of that species of slander which consists in gossiping about our neighbours, as *whetstones* of our moral discrimination—as if they were conscience-blocks which we used in our apprenticeship, not to waste such precious materials as our own consciences in the trimming and shaping by self-examination. [Refers to *Tristram Shandy*, I. 18: 'Alas o'day . . . alive at this hour' (p. 45).]

5. When you have secured a man's likings and prejudices in your favor, you may then safely appeal to his impartial judgement. [The following passage is full of] acute sense in ironical wit, but now add *life* to it and *character*—and it becomes *dramatic*. [Refers to *Tristram Shandy*, I. 19: 'I see plainly, Sir . . . of your example' (pp. 50–1).]

6. The physiognomic tact common, in very different degrees indeed, to us all, [is] gratified in Dr. Slop. And in general, [note] all that happiest use of drapery and attitude, which at once gives the *reality* by individualizing, and the vividness by unusual, yet probable combinations. [Refers to *Tristram Shandy*, II. 9: 'Imagine to yourself . . . in the horse-guards. . . . Imagine such a one . . . speed the adverse way' (pp. 104–5).]

7. More humor in the single remark, 'Learned men, Brother Toby, do not write dialogues on long noses for nothing,'[1] than in the whole Slawkenburghian tale that follows, which is oddity interspersed with drollery.

8. The moral *good* of Sterne in the characters of Trim, etc., as contrasted with Jacobinism. [Refers to Trim mourning the death of Bobby, *Tristram Shandy*, V. 7, pp. 359–62.]

9. Each part by right of humoristic universality, a whole. Hence the digressive spirit [is] not wantonness, but the *very form* of his genius. The connection is given by the continuity of the characters.

[1] *Tristram Shandy*, III. 37, p. 229.

(b) Extract from 'On Sensibility,' *Aids to Reflection* (1825) (*Complete Works of Samuel Taylor Coleridge*, ed. W. G. T. Shedd (1853; reprint 1884), i. 137)

All the evil achieved by Hobbes[1] and the whole school of materialists will appear inconsiderable if it be compared with the mischief effected and occasioned by the sentimental philosophy of Sterne, and his numerous imitators. The vilest appetites and the most remorseless inconstancy towards their objects, acquired the titles of the *heart, the irresistible feelings, the too tender sensibility*: and if the frosts of prudence, the icy chains of human law thawed and vanished at the genial warmth of human nature, who could help it? It was an amiable weakness![2]

(c) Extract from a letter, 1828, probably to Alaric Watts, comparing Scott and Sterne (*Unpublished Letters of Samuel Taylor Coleridge*, ed. Earl Leslie Griggs (1933), ii. 420–1)

Of Sir Walter's powers I have as high admiration as you can have, but assuredly polish of style, and that sort of prose which is in fact only another kind of poetry, nay, of metrical composition, the metre *incognito*, such as Sterne's Le Fevre, Maria, Monk, &c., . . .[3] this is not Sir Walter's excellence.

(d) Remarks of 18 August 1833, printed in *Table Talk* (*Coleridge's Miscellaneous Criticism*, pp. 426–7)

I think highly of Sterne—that is, of the first part of *Tristram Shandy*: for as to the latter part about the widow Wadman, it is stupid and dis-

[1] See No. 28a, p. 120, n. 2. Hobbes viewed man mechanically and deterministically.
[2] In one of his contributions to Southey's anonymous *Omniana or Horae Otiosiores* (1812; reprinted with variations from the *Athenaeum*, 1807–8), Coleridge makes the point that love is 'an act of the will' and that if we do not accept that view, either we must 'brutalize our notions' of it or 'we must dissolve and thaw away all bonds of morality by the irresistible shocks of an irresistible sensibility with Sterne' (*Table Talk and Omniana of Samuel Taylor Coleridge*, Oxford ed. (1917), p. 388).
[3] Cf. a similar remark about Sterne in *Biographia Literaria* (1817), ch. XVIII.

gusting;[1] and the *Sentimental Journey* is poor sickly stuff. There is a great deal of affectation in Sterne, to be sure; but still the characters of Trim and the two Shandies[2] are most individual and delightful. Sterne's morals are bad, but I don't think they can do much harm to any one whom they would not find bad enough before. Besides, the oddity and erudite grimaces under which much of his dirt is hidden take away the effect for the most part; although, to be sure, the book is scarcely readable by women.

(e) Marginalia in Coleridge's copy of Shakespeare (*Coleridge's Shakespearean Criticism*, ed. Thomas Middleton Raysor (1930), i. 242)

In Shakespeare and Cervantes it is wit so precious that it becomes wit even to quote or allude to it. Thus Sterne is a secondary wit of this order: and how many a Sterne [there is].

[1] In a letter of 8 April 1820 to Thomas Allsop, Coleridge had said: 'I sincerely trust that Walter Scott's readers would be as little disposed to relish the stupid lechery of the courtship of Widow Wadman, as Scott himself would be capable of presenting it' (*Table Talk and Omniana*, p. 415).
[2] [Hartley N. Coleridge's note.] Mr. Coleridge considered the character of the father, the elder Shandy, as by much the finer delineation of the two. I fear his low opinion of the *Sentimental Journey* will not suit a thorough Sterneist; but I could never get him to modify his criticism. He said, 'The oftener you read Sterne, the more clearly will you perceive the *great* difference between *Tristram Shandy* and the *Sentimental Journey*. There is truth and reality in the one, and little beyond a clever affectation in the other.'

117. Hazlitt on Sterne

1819, 1826

(a) Extracts from *Lectures on the English Comic Writers*, delivered at the Surrey Institution in the winter of 1818–19 and published in 1819 (Lecture I, 'On Wit and Humour,' pp. 14–16; Lecture VI, 'On the English Novelists,' pp. 211–12, 239–41)

There is nothing more powerfully humorous than what is called *keeping* in comic character, as we see it very finely exemplified in Sancho Panza and Don Quixote. The proverbial phlegm and the romantic gravity of these two celebrated persons may be regarded as the height of this kind of excellence. The deep feeling of character strengthens the sense of the ludicrous. Keeping in comic character is consistency in absurdity; a determined and laudable attachment to the incongruous and singular. The regularity completes the contradiction; for the number of instances of deviation from the right line, branching out in all directions, shews the inveteracy of the original bias to any extravagance or folly, the natural improbability, as it were, increasing every time with the multiplication of chances for a return to common sense, and in the end mounting up to an incredible and unaccountably ridiculous height, when we find our expectations as invariably baffled. The most curious problem of all, is this truth of absurdity to itself. That reason and good sense should be consistent, is not wonderful: but that caprice, and whim, and fantastical prejudice, should be uniform and infallible in their results, is the surprising thing. But while this characteristic clue to absurdity helps on the ridicule, it also softens and harmonises its excesses; and the ludicrous is here blended with a certain beauty and decorum, from this very truth of habit and sentiment, or from the principle of similitude in dissimilitude. The devotion to nonsense, and enthusiasm about trifles, is highly affecting as a moral lesson: it is one of the striking weaknesses and greatest happinesses of our nature. That which excites so lively and lasting an interest in itself, even though it should not be wisdom, is not despicable in the sight of reason and humanity. We cannot suppress the smile on the lip; but the tear should also stand ready to start from the eye. The history of hobby-horses is equally instructive and delightful; and after the pair I have just alluded to, My Uncle Toby's is one of the best and gentlest that 'ever lifted leg!' The inconveniences, odd accidents, falls, and bruises, to which they expose their riders, contribute their share to the amusement of the spectators; and the blows and wounds that the Knight of the Sorrowful Countenance received in his many perilous adventures, have applied their healing influence to many a hurt mind.—In what relates to the laughable, as it arises from unforeseen accidents or self-willed scrapes, the pain, the shame, the mortification, and utter helplessness of situation, add to the joke, provided they are momentary, or over-whelming only to the imagination of the sufferer.

The most moral writers, after all, are those who do not pretend to inculcate any moral. The professed moralist almost unavoidably de-generates into the partisan of a system; and the philosopher is too apt to warp the evidence to his own purpose. But the painter of manners gives the facts of human nature, and leaves us to draw the inference: if we are not able to do this, or do it ill, at least it is our own fault.

The first-rate writers in this class, of course, are few; but those few we may reckon among the greatest ornaments and best benefactors of our kind. There is a certain set of them who, as it were, take their rank by the side of reality, and are appealed to as evidence on all questions concerning human nature. The principal of these are Cervantes and Le Sage,[1] who may be considered as having been naturalised among our-selves; and, of native English growth, Fielding, Smollett, Richardson, and Sterne. . . .

It remains to speak of Sterne; and I shall do it in few words. There is more of *mannerism* and affectation in him, and a more immediate refer-ence to preceding authors; but his excellences, where he is excellent, are of the first order. His characters are intellectual and inventive, like Richardson's; but totally opposite in the execution. The one are made out by continuity, and patient repetition of touches: the others, by glancing transitions and graceful apposition. His style is equally different from Richardson's: it is at times the most rapid, the most happy, the most idiomatic of any that is to be found. It is the pure essence of English conversational style. His works consist only of

---

[1] Alain René Lesage (1668–1747), French dramatist and novelist, was best known for his novel *Gil Blas* (1715–35) which gives a panorama of eighteenth-century life.

morceaux[1]—of brilliant passages. I wonder that Goldsmith, who ought
to have known better, should call him 'a dull fellow.'[2] His wit is
poignant, though artificial; and his characters (though the groundwork
of some of them had been laid before) have yet invaluable original
differences; and the spirit of the execution, the master-strokes constantly thrown into them, are not to be surpassed. It is sufficient to name
them;—Yorick, Dr. Slop, Mr. Shandy, My Uncle Toby, Trim,
Susanna, and the Widow Wadman. In these he has contrived to
oppose, with equal felicity and originality, two characters, one of pure
intellect, and the other of pure good nature, in My Father and My
Uncle Toby. There appears to have been in Sterne a vein of dry,
sarcastic humour, and of extreme tenderness of feeling; the latter sometimes carried to affectation, as in the tale of Maria, and the apostrophe to
the recording angel: but at other times pure, and without blemish. The
story of Le Fevre is perhaps the finest in the English language. My Father's
restlessness, both of body and mind, is inimitable. It is the model from
which all those despicable performances against modern philosophy
ought to have been copied, if their authors had known anything of the subject they were writing about. My Uncle Toby is one of the finest compliments ever paid to human nature. He is the most unoffending of God's
creatures; or, as the French express it, *un tel petit bon homme!* Of his bowling green, his sieges, and his amours, who would say or think anything
amiss![3]

(b) Extracts from the *Plain Speaker* (1826), first published anonymously (essay IV, 'On the Conversation of Authors, Continued,'
i. 89–90; essay IX, 'On Novelty and Familiarity,' ii. 248–9)

Lively sallies and connected discourse are very different things. There
are many persons of that impatient and restless turn of mind, that they

[1] 'fragments.' But cf. Hazlitt's statements that in *Tristram Shandy* 'the progress of the
narrative is interrupted by some incident, in a dramatic or humorous shape' (review of
'Sismondi's Literature of the South' in the *Edinburgh Review*, June 1815; *Collected Works of
William Hazlitt*, ed. A. R. Waller and Arnold Glover, ix (1903). 178–9); and that 'Sterne
(thank God!) has neither hero nor heroine, and he does very well without them' ('Why
the Heroes of Romances Are Insipid,' unsigned article in the *New Monthly Magazine* (November 1827), *Collected Works*, xii (1904). 63).
[2] See No. 64a.
[3] These remarks in lecture VI are copied with slight revisions from Hazlitt's review of
Fanny Burney's *The Wanderer* in the *Edinburgh Review* of February 1815.

cannot wait a moment for a conclusion, or follow up the thread of any argument. In the hurry of conversation their ideas are somehow huddled into sense; but in the intervals of thought, leave a great gap between. . . . But there is a method of trying periods on the ear, or weighing them with the scales of the breath, without any articulate sound. Authors, as they write, may be said to 'hear a sound so fine, there's nothing lives 'twixt it and silence.'[1] Even musicians generally compose in their heads. I agree that no style is good, that is not fit to be spoken or read aloud with effect. This holds true not only of emphasis and cadence, but also with regard to natural idiom and colloquial freedom. Sterne's was in this respect the best style that ever was written. You fancy that you hear the people talking.

The true, original master-touches that go to the heart, must come from it. There is neither truth or beauty without nature. Habit may repeat the lesson that is thus learnt, just as a poet may transcribe a fine passage without being affected by it at the time; but he could not have written it in the first instance without feeling the beauty of the object he was describing, or without having been deeply impressed with it in some moment of enthusiasm. It was then that his genius was inspired, his style formed, and the foundation of his fame laid. People tell you that Sterne was hard-hearted; that the author of Waverley[2] is a mere worldling; that Shakespear was a man without passions. Do not believe them. Their passions might have worn themselves out with constant over-excitement, so that they only knew how they formerly felt; or they might have the controul over them; or from their very compass and variety they might have kept one another in check, so that none got very much a-head, and broke out into extravagant and overt acts. But those persons must have experienced the feelings they express, and entered into the situations they describe so finely, at some period or other of their lives: the sacred source from whence the tears trickle down the cheeks of others, was once full; though it may be now dried up; and in all cases where a strong impression of truth and nature is conveyed to the minds of others, it must have previously existed in an equal or greater degree in the mind producing it.

[1] James Sheridan Knowles (1784-1862), *Virginius*, act 5, sc. 2.
[2] I.e. Sir Walter Scott.

(c) Extract from *Notes of a Journey Through France and Italy* (1826), p. 175

As we left Moulins, the crimson clouds of evening streaked the west, and I had time to think of Sterne's *Maria*. The people at the inn, I suspect, had never heard of her. There was no trace of romance about the house. Certainly, mine was not a Sentimental Journey. Is it not provoking to come to a place, that has been consecrated by 'famous poet's pen,' as a breath, a name, a fairy-scene, and find it a dull, dirty town? Let us leave the realities to shift for themselves, and think only of those bright tracts that have been reclaimed for us by the fancy, where the perfume, the sound, the vision, and the joy still linger, like the soft light of evening skies! Is the story of Maria the worse, because I am travelling a dirty road in a rascally Diligence? Or is it an injury done us by the author to have invented for us what we should not have met with in reality? Has it not been read with pleasure by thousands of readers, though the people at the inn had never heard of it? Yet Sterne would have been vexed to find that the fame of his Maria had never reached the little town of Moulins. We are always dissatisfied with the good we have, and always punished for our unreasonableness.

118. John Keats on the Shandean

17 January 1820

Extract from an addition to a letter, 17 January 1820, to Georgina Augusta Keats (*Letters of John Keats*, ed. H. Buxton Forman (1895), pp. 448–9).

In the letter below Keats is comparing three of his friends: James Rice (*d.* before 1833), who has been described as both witty and wise; John Hamilton Reynolds (1794–1852), poet and critic; and Thomas Richards (d. 1831), brother of Keats's publisher.

I know three witty people, all distinct in their excellence—Rice, Reynolds, and Richards. Rice is the wisest, Reynolds the playfullest, Richards the out-o'-the-wayest. The first makes you laugh and think, the second makes you laugh and not think, the third puzzles your head. I admire the first, I enjoy the second, I stare at the third. The first is claret, the second ginger-beer, the third crême de Byrapymdrag.[1] The first is inspired by Minerva, the second by Mercury, the third by Harlequin Epigram, Esq.[2] The first is neat in his dress, the second slovenly, the third uncomfortable. The first speaks adagio, the second allegretto, the third both together. The first is Swiftean, the second Tom Cribean,[3] the third Shandean. And yet these three eans are not three eans but one ean.

[1] Keats has apparently invented this drink.
[2] Minerva was goddess of wisdom; Mercury was the god of wise and clever discourse; for the general character of Harlequin see No. 13c, p. 77, n. 2.
[3] The allusion is to Thomas Moore's *Tom Crib's Memorial to Congress* (1819).

119. Sir Thomas Noon Talfourd on Sterne and Mackenzie

1820

Extract from 'Mackenzie,' first published in the *New Monthly Magazine*, xiii. pt. 1 (1820). 324–5, and reprinted here from *Critical and Miscellaneous Writings of T. Noon Talfourd* (1842), pp. 20–1.

Talfourd (1795–1854), judge, Member of Parliament, and essayist, was Lamb's literary executor and the friend of Lamb, Wordsworth, Coleridge, and Hazlitt.

We think that, on the whole, Mackenzie is the first master of this delicious style. Sterne, doubtless, has deeper touches of humanity in some of his works. But there is no sustained feeling—no continuity of emotion—no extended range of thought, over which the mind can brood in his ingenious and fantastical writings. His spirit is far too mercurial and airy to suffer him tenderly to linger over those images of sweet humanity which he discloses. His cleverness breaks the charm which his feeling spreads, as by magic, around us. His exquisite sensibility is ever counteracted by his perceptions of the ludicrous, and his ambition after the strange. No harmonious feeling breathes from any of his pieces. He sweeps 'that curious instrument, the human heart,' with hurried fingers, calling forth in rapid succession its deepest and its liveliest tones, and making only marvellous discord. His pathos is, indeed, most genuine while it lasts; but the soul is not suffered to cherish the feeling which it awakens. He does not shed, like Mackenzie, one mild light on the path of life; but scatters on it wild coruscations of ever shifting brightness, which, while they sometimes disclose spots of inimitable beauty, often do but fantastically play over objects dreary and revolting. All in Mackenzie is calm, gentle, harmonious. No play of mistimed wit, no flourish of rhetoric, no train of philosophical speculation, for a moment diverts our sympathy. Each of his best works is like one deep thought, and the impression which it leaves, soft, sweet, and undivided as the summer evening's holiest and latest sigh!

120. Sterne and Johnson: 'genius' and 'judgment'

1820

Extract from John Duncan, *An Essay on Genius* (1820), pp. 80–1.

Nothing, in reality, but the blind veneration of what is unknown, and reluctance to dissipate that ignorance which is so congenial to the natural superstition of the human mind, could induce a preference of arbitrary and irregular association, to chastised order and extended connection. The labour, indeed, necessary to purify and render complete any work is generally invisible. But the difference between one which pleases notwithstanding omissions, repetitions and contradictions, and another which contains the whole subject and nothing but the subject, is immense. At the same time, it is apparent that the degree of capacity which is necessary to what is great, is, for the most part, repugnant to that which is pleasant.

A person of a strong mind discovers his abilities rather in pointed sayings and comprehensive axioms, than in flowing eloqence and expanded enumeration; while another of inferior powers mingles facts with arguments, and pursues his way through the course of events, by an instinct which is pleasant because natural. Sterne possessed that lesser excellence and smaller degree of intellect—commonly called genius, if ever man did; for, in him, the admirers of irregularity will find disorder and minuteness in sufficiency, joined with considerable judgment. How many general principles does he give with accuracy; but how much more excellent is he in describing and tracing a train of circumstances, and following nature in her various windings, when conducting events, and displaying the emotions of the heart! But in the pathetic, Sterne is excelled by no writer, ancient or modern. Dr. Johnson, again, in sentiment is awkward, in narration brief and dry; and if he were to be judged of by his art in telling a story, must be pronounced a man of no ability. When he attempts enumeration, he seems to do a thing foreign to his nature; and although its excellence must be admitted, yet his particulars have always a general cast, and, in reality, include many subordinate. In short, he possessed so much judgment as to leave no room in his mind for what is called genius, and was so much abstracted in reasoning as to be incapable of attending to objects alone.

121. Thomas Hood: a burlesque of Sterne

1821

Extract from 'A Sentimental Journey from Islington to Waterloo Bridge,' first published in the *London Magazine* in 1821 and reprinted here from *The Works of Thomas Hood*, ed. Thomas Hood Jr and F. F. Broderip, iv (1871). 357–9.

Hood (1799–1845), friend of Lamb and other leading literary figures, was poet, essayist, and magazine editor. He was known mainly for his comic writings during most of his lifetime, though he is perhaps best remembered today for the social protest of his poem 'The Song of the Shirt.' His own temperament, in its mixture of the serious and the comic, has affinities with Sterne's, and in the passage below he is perhaps ridiculing Sterne's imitators as much as Sterne himself.

A traveller, said I, should have all his wits about him, and so will I. He should let nothing escape him, no more will I. He should extract reflections out of a cabbage stump, like sun-beams squeezed out of cucumbers;[1] so will I, if I can; and he should converse with every and any one, even a fish-woman. Perhaps I will, and perhaps I will not, said I. Who knows but I may make a sentimental journey, as good as Sterne's; but at any rate I can write it, and send it to the London Magazine.

[1] Cf. *Gulliver's Travels*, pt 3, ch. 5.

I had hardly left the threshold of my door, ere I met, as I thought, with an adventure. I had just reached that ancient and grotesque house which is said to have been a summer seat of Queen Elizabeth, though now in the centre of the village, or rather town of Islington, when I observed that the steps which led down to the door, had become the seat, or rather the couch of an unfortunate female. She had, like Sterne's Maria, her *dog*, and her *pipe*, and like her, too, she was evidently beside herself. 'Poor unfortunate and interesting Maria,' said I, as she came into my mind, exactly as Sterne had drawn her. I had touched a string —at the name of Maria, the female for the first time raised her head, and I caught a glance at her uncommon countenance. The rose had not fled from it, nor the bloom, for this was damson, and that was damask; there was a fixedness in her gaze, and although she quickly turned her head away, she could not hide from me that she had a drop in her eye. 'It won't do,' said I, shaking my head, 'Maria found Sterne's handkerchief, and washed it with tears, and dried it in her bosom; but if I lose mine here, it's ten to one if I see it again; and if this Maria should wet it with her eyes, methinks it would dry best again at her nose. There is nothing to sympathise with in her bewilderment—she's rather bewitched than bewitching—she's a dry subject,' and so I left her. My eyes, however, were full charged with the tears, and my bosom with the sighs, which I had expected to mingle with those of the supposed unfortunate. Some sentimentalists would have vented them upon the first dead dog or lame chicken they might meet with, but I held them too valuable to be wasted upon such objects. I hate the weeping-willow set, who will cry over their pug dogs and canaries, till they have no tears to spare for the real children of misfortune and misery; but sensibility is too scarce, and too valuable, not to be often imitated; and these, therefore, are the ways in which they advertise their counterfeit drops. They should be punished like any other imposters, and they might be made of some use to society at the same time; for as other convicts are set to beat hemp, and pick oakum, so I would set these to perform funerals, and to chop onions. These reflections, and the incidents which gave rise to them, I resolved to treasure up, for they would perhaps have their use in some part of my journey.

They will warn me against being too sentimental, said I. In the first place it is ridiculous; secondly, it's useless; and lastly, it's inconvenient: for I just recollect that there's a very large hole in my pocket handkerchief.

122. De Quincey on Sterne and Richter

December 1821

Extract from 'John Paul Frederick Richter,' appearing first pseudonymously in the *London Magazine* (December 1821) and reprinted here from *The Collected Writings of Thomas de Quincey*, ed. David Masson (1890), xi. 264–8.

De Quincey (1785–1859), like Carlyle, saw Sterne's affinity with Richter in the play of his imagination and the joining of seemingly discordant elements (see No. 125). For Richter's own comments on Sterne, see No. 152.

Such, then, being demonstrably the possibility of blending, or fusing, as it were, the elements of pathos and of humour, and composing out of their union a third metal *sui generis* . . . I cannot but consider John Paul Richter as by far the most eminent artist in that way since the time of Shakspere. What! you will say, greater than Sterne? I answer 'Yes, to my thinking'; and I could give some arguments and illustrations in support of this judgment. But I am not anxious to establish my own preference as founded on anything of better authority than my idiosyncrasy, or more permanent, if you choose to think so, than my own caprice.

Second.—Judge as you will on this last point,—that is, on the comparative pretentions of Sterne and Richter to the *spolia opima*[1] in the fields of pathos and of humour,—yet in one pretension he not only leaves Sterne at an infinite distance in the rear, but really, for my part, I cease to ask who it is that he leaves behind him, for I begin to think with myself who it is that he approaches. If a man could reach Venus or Mercury, we should not say he has advanced to a great distance from the earth,—we should say, he is very near to the sun. So also, if in anything a man approaches Shakspere, or does but remind us of him, all other honours are swallowed up in that: a relation of

[1] 'The spoils of honor,' i.e. the arms a victorious general takes on the battlefield from the general he has vanquished.

inferiority to him is a more enviable distinction than all degrees of superiority to others, the rear of *his* splendours a more eminent post than the supreme station in the van of all others. I have already mentioned one *quality* of excellence, viz. the interpenetration of the humorous and the pathetic, common in Shakspere and John Paul; but this, apart from its *quantity* or degree, implies no more of a participation in Shaksperian excellence than the possession of wit, judgment, good sense, &c., which, in some degree or other, must be common to all authors of any merit at all. Thus far I have already said that I would not contest the point of precedence with the admirers of Sterne; but, in the claim I now advance for Richter, which respects a question of *degree*, I cannot allow of any competition at all from that quarter. What, then, is it that I claim? Briefly, an activity of understanding so restless and indefatigable that all attempts to illustrate or express it adequately by images borrowed from the natural world,—from the motions of beasts, birds, insects, &c., from the leaps of tigers or leopards, from the gamboling and tumbling of kittens, the antics of monkeys, or the running of antelopes and ostriches, &c.,—are baffled, confounded, and made ridiculous by the enormous and overmastering superiority of impression left by the thing illustrated. The rapid but uniform motions of the heavenly bodies serve well enough to typify the grand and continuous motions of the Miltonic mind. But the wild, giddy, fantastic, capricious, incalculable, springing, vaulting, tumbling, dancing, waltzing, caprioling, *pirouetting*, sky-rocketing of the chamois, the harlequin,[1] the Vestris,[2] the storm-loving raven—the raven? no, the lark (for often he ascends 'singing up to heaven's gates,'[3] but like the lark he dwells upon the earth),—in short, of the Proteus, the Ariel, the Mercury, the monster,[4] John Paul,—can be compared to nothing in heaven or earth, or the waters under the earth, except to the motions of the same faculty as existing in Shakspere. . . .

[1] See No. 13c, p. 77, n. 2. The harlequin's stage role demanded speed and agility for daring acrobatic tricks and magical effects.
[2] A famous family of ballet dancers known for their grace, originality, and lightness.
[3] See William Shakespeare, sonnet xxix.
[4] De Quincey's last four examples continue to suggest quickness, shifting forms, and forms compounded of diverse elements. Proteus, Greek sea god, had the ability to assume any shape he pleased, often changing rapidly from one to another. Ariel, the airy spirit of Shakespeare's *The Tempest*, combines the quickness and lightness of fire and air in his nature. Mercury, the winged messenger of the gods, was the link between gods and men and between the world of the living and the underworld of the dead. 'Monster' is used in the meaning of an imaginary animal with a form combining human and animal parts or parts from two or more animals.

[T]here cannot be a more valuable endowment to a writer of in-ordinate sensibility than this inordinate agility of the understanding. The active faculty balances the passive; and without such a balance there is great risk of falling into a sickly tone of maudlin sentimentality, —from which Sterne cannot be pronounced wholly free.

123. Scott on Sterne

1823

Extracts from 'Laurence Sterne' and 'Henry Mackenzie,' *Miscellaneous Prose Works of Sir Walter Scott* (1834).

Scott wrote these essays as prefaces for Ballantyne's series of standard novelists (1823). The essays were later reprinted under the title *Lives of the Novelists*.

(a) From essay entitled 'Laurence Sterne,' in *Miscellaneous Prose Works*, iii (i of *Biographical Memoirs*). 289–98

If we consider Sterne's reputation as chiefly founded on *Tristram Shandy*, he must be regarded as liable to two severe charges;—those, namely, of indecency, and of affectation.[1] Upon the first accusation Sterne was himself peculiarly sore, and used to justify the licentiousness of his humour by representing it as a mere breach of decorum, which had no perilous consequence to morals. The following anecdote we have from a sure source:—Soon after *Tristram* had appeared, Sterne asked a Yorkshire lady of fortune and condition whether she had read his book. 'I have not, Mr Sterne,' was the answer; 'and, to be plain with you, I am informed it is not proper for female perusal.'—'My dear good lady,' replied the author, 'do not be gulled by such stories; the

[1] Scott echoes Goldsmith's charges (see No. 19).

book is like your young heir there,' (pointing to a child of three years old, who was rolling on the carpet in his white tunics,) 'he shows at times a good deal that is usually concealed, but it is all in perfect innocence!'[1] This witty excuse may be so far admitted; for it cannot be said that the licentious humour of *Tristram Shandy* is of the kind which applies itself to the passions, or is calculated to corrupt society. But it is a sin against taste, if allowed to be harmless as to morals. A handful of mud is neither a firebrand nor a stone; but to fling it about in sport, argues coarseness of mind, and want of common manners.

Sterne, however, began and ended by braving the censure of the world in this particular. . . .

In like manner, the greatest admirers of Sterne must own, that his style is affected, eminently, and in a degree which even his wit and pathos are inadequate to support. The style of Rabelais, which he assumed for his model, is to the highest excess rambling, excursive, and intermingled with the greatest absurdities. But Rabelais was in some measure compelled to adopt this Harlequin's habit, in order that, like licensed jesters, he might, under the cover of his folly, have permission to vent his satire against church and state. Sterne assumed the manner of his master, only as a mode of attracting attention, and of making the public stare; and, therefore, his extravagancies, like those of a feigned madman, are cold and forced, even in the midst of his most irregular flights. A man may, in the present day, be, with perfect impunity, as wise or as witty, nay, as satirical, as he can, without assuming the cap and bells of the ancient jester as an apology; and that Sterne chose voluntarily to appear under such a disguise, must be set down as mere affectation, and ranked with his unmeaning tricks of black or marbled pages, employed merely *ad captandum vulgus*.[2] All popularity thus founded, carries in it the seeds of decay; for eccentricity in composition, like fantastic modes of dress, however attractive when first introduced, is sure to be caricatured by stupid imitators, to become soon unfashionable, and of course to be neglected.

If we proceed to look more closely into the manner of composition which Sterne thought proper to adopt, we find a sure guide in the ingenious Dr Ferriar of Manchester,[3] who, with most singular patience, has traced our author through the hidden sources whence he borrowed most of his learning, and many of his more striking and peculiar

[1] Cf. No. 61a.
[2] To try to win the public.
[3] See No. 90.

expressions. . . . For proofs of this sweeping charge we must refer the reader to Dr Ferriar's well-known Essay, and *Illustrations*, as he delicately terms them, *of Sterne's Writings*; in which it is clearly shown, that he, whose manner and style were so long thought original, was, in fact, the most unhesitating plagiarist who ever cribbed from his predecessors in order to garnish his own pages. It must be owned, at the same time, that Sterne selects the materials of his mosaic work with so much art, places them so well, and polishes them so highly, that in most cases we are disposed to pardon the want of originality, in consideration of the exquisite talent with which the borrowed materials are wrought up into the new form. . . .

Much has been said about the right of an author to avail himself of his predecessors' labours; and certainly, in a general sense, he that revives the wit and learning of a former age, and puts it into the form likely to captivate his own, confers a benefit on his contemporaries. But to plume himself with the very language and phrases of former writers, and to pass their wit and learning for his own, was the more unworthy in Sterne, as he had enough of original talent, had he chosen to exert it, to have dispensed with all such acts of literary petty larceny.

Tristram Shandy is no narrative, but a collection of scenes, dialogues, and portraits, humorous or affecting, intermixed with much wit, and with much learning, original or borrowed. It resembles the irregularities of a Gothic room, built by some fanciful collector, to contain the miscellaneous remnants of antiquity which his pains have accumulated, and bearing as little proportion in its parts as there is connexion between the pieces of rusty armour with which it is decorated. Viewing it in this light, the principal figure is Mr Shandy the elder, whose character is formed in many respects upon that of Martinus Scriblerus.[1] The history of Martin was designed by the celebrated club of wits, by whom it was commenced, as a satire upon the ordinary pursuits of learning and science. Sterne, on the contrary, had no particular object of ridicule; his business was only to create a person, to whom he could attach the great quantity of extraordinary reading, and antiquated learning, which he had collected. He, therefore, supposed in Mr Shandy a man of an active and metaphysical, but at the same time a whimsical cast of mind, whom too much and too miscellaneous learning had brought within a step or two of madness, and who acted in the ordinary affairs of life upon the absurd theories adopted by the pedants of past ages. He is most admirably contrasted

[1] See No. 83d, p. 267, n. 1.

with his wife, well described as a good lady of the true poco-curante school, who neither obstructed the progress of her husband's *hobby-horse*, to use a phrase which Sterne has rendered classical, nor could be prevailed upon to spare him the least admiration for the grace and dexterity with which he managed it. . . .

Uncle Toby and his faithful squire, the most delightful characters in the work, or perhaps in any other, are drawn with such a pleasing force and discrimination, that they more than entitle the author to a free pardon for his literary peculations, his indecorum, and his affectation; nay authorize him to leave the court of criticism not forgiven only, but applauded and rewarded as one who has exalted and honoured humanity, and impressed upon his readers such a lively picture of kindness and benevolence, blended with courage, gallantry, and simplicity, that their hearts must be warmed whenever it is recalled to memory. Sterne, indeed, might boldly plead in his own behalf, that the passages which he borrowed from others were of little value, in comparison to those which are exclusively original; and that the former might have been written by many persons, while in his own proper line he stands alone and inimitable. Something of extravagance may, perhaps, attach to Uncle Toby's favourite amusements. Yet in England, where men think and act with little regard to ridicule or censure of their neighbours, there is no impossibility, perhaps no great impro-bability in supposing, that a humorist might employ such a mechanical aid as my Uncle's bowling-green, in order to encourage and assist his imagination, in the pleasing but delusive task of castle-building. Men have been called children of larger growth, and among the antic toys and devices with which they are amused, the device of my Uncle, with whose pleasures we are so much disposed to sympathize, does not seem so unnatural upon reflection as it may appear at first sight. . . .

It is needless to dwell longer on a work so generally known. The style employed by Sterne is fancifully ornamented, but at the same time vigorous and masculine, and full of that animation and force which can only be derived by an intimate acquaintance with the early English prose-writers. In the power of approaching and touching the finer feelings of the heart, he has never been excelled, if indeed he has ever been equalled; and may be at once recorded as one of the most affected, and one of the most simple writers,—as one of the greatest plagiarists, and one of the most original geniuses, whom England has produced.

(b) From essay entitled 'Henry Mackenzie,' *Miscellaneous Prose Works*, iv (ii of *Biographical Memoirs*). 10–11

It is needless to point out to the reader the difference between the general character of [Sterne's and Mackenzie's] writings, or how far the chaste, correct, almost studiously decorous manner and style of the works of the author of *The Man of Feeling*, differ from the wild wit, and intrepid contempt at once of decency, and regularity of composition, which distinguish *Tristram Shandy*. It is not in the general conduct or style of their works that they in the slightest degree approach; nay, no two authors in the British language can be more distinct. But even in the particular passages where both had in view to excite the reader's pathetic sympathy, the modes resorted to are different. The pathos of Sterne in some degree resembles his humour, and is seldom attained by simple means; a wild, fanciful, beautiful flight of thought and expression is remarkable in the former, as an extravagant, burlesque, and ludicrous strain of conception and language characterises the latter. The celebrated passage, where the tear of the recording Angel blots the profane oath of Uncle Toby out of the register of heaven, a flight so poetically fanciful as to be stretched to the very verge of extravagance, will illustrate our position. To attain his object—that is, to make us thoroughly sympathize with the excited state of mind which betrays Uncle Toby into the indecorous assertion which forms the groundwork of the whole—the author calls Heaven and Hell into the lists, and represents in a fine poetic frenzy, its effects on the accusing Spirit and registering Angel. Let this be contrasted with the fine tale of *La Roche*,[1] in which Mackenzie has described, with such unexampled delicacy, and powerful effect, the sublime scene of the sorrows and resignation of the bereaved father. This is also painted reflectively; that is, the reader's sympathy is excited by the effect produced on one of the drama, neither angel nor devil, but a philosopher, whose heart remains sensitive, though his studies have misled his mind into the frozen regions of scepticism. To say nothing of the tendency of the two passages, which will scarce, in the mind of the most unthinking, bear any

[1] Mackenzie's 'La Roche,' first contributed to the *Mirror*, a Scottish periodical published in 1779 and 1780 under Mackenzie's editorship, was widely read and was even translated into French and Italian. The character of the father, referred to below, was supposed to be an idealized portrait of Mackenzie's friend David Hume, the famous skeptic philosopher.

comparison, we would only remark, that Mackenzie has given us a moral truth, Sterne a beautiful trope; and that if the one claims the palm of superior brilliancy of imagination, that due to nature and accuracy of human feeling must abide with the Scottish author.

124. Sterne in the *Gentleman's Magazine*

1827-8

Extracts from an anonymous series of essays, 'Some Speculations on Literary Pleasures,' appearing in the *Gentleman's Magazine*, xcvii (sup. July–December 1827). pt. 2. 601–2; xcviii (May 1828). pt. 1. 399–400

The survey of nature in her varieties, the view of her fitness, relations, and harmonies, has naturally a tendency to excite the kindlier feelings. The stern precepts of philosophy, the attenuated chain of scientific inquiry, yields to the philanthropies which often cherish our being with some of its liveliest pleasures. The economy of the visible creation, with its high and exquisite adaptation to its purposes, will often meliorate the powers of the full soul into a review of those who have taken upon them to guide its finer susceptibilities. At the head of such writers has been thought to stand Lawrence Sterne.—And here it may be observed, that poets in every age have addressed a great portion of the embodyings of their minds to the passions; they have consequently proved the instruments of either on the one hand elevating and adding expression and dignity to those excitements of a moral character, which all more or less feel, or of vitiating them to a morbid excrescence. Their influence therefore in society is by no means small. The sentimental novel, likewise popular as it has been for the last age or two, may be thought to have had a more than ordinary share in guiding and directing the tide of moral sentiment amongst certain portions of society which usually impart a fashion to others. For if, as the judicious Lord

Orrery says, 'there is a sort of mode in philosophy, as well as in other things, and Sir Isaac Newton and his notions may hereafter be out of fashion;'[1] the same may with especial propriety be said of those sentimental productions, which, as they spring from the heart, so in these respects they impart a tone to society. But the grand patriarch amongst writers of this class,—the author who for more than half a century has with classical honours (for he has taken his place as a British classic) been thought to have carried pathos and sentiment to the highest chord upon which the sympathies vibrate,—is, in the general suffrage, Lawrence Sterne. . . .

Hobbes,[2] about a century and a half ago and upwards, disseminated a new doctrine in morals, or one at least that has been generally fathered upon him. The philosopher of Malmsbury taught, as is very well known, that every sentiment of the breast, whatever be its complexion, originates remotely in a selfish wish to promote our own gratification; and that no act of virtue was ever performed, for it amounts to this, but with some latent and sinister view of this kind. This theory, finely sophisticated as it is, is at the best equivocal; it teaches that sentiment only centres in itself; but then if this sentiment of self-gratification is found to inhere in a feeling so pure and exalted as to delight in acts of benevolence, it is clear that the author to whom we owe this strange discovery, that man comes into the world in a state of utter hostility to his fellow, teaches either that virtue itself is a selfish and vitiated propensity, or he labours to destroy every incentive to nobleness of thinking, and eradicates every spark of disinterested philanthropy from the breast. Sterne errs in a diametrically opposite direction, by teaching that a diseased and excessive sensibility inheres in the human character. And if the malign and repulsive aspect of the philosophy taught by the author of the 'De Cive,' and the 'Leviathan,' never in this country found its numerous abettors, its fallacies have been exposed from a number of pens. Not so with Sterne, whose false and sicklied sensibility may be thought to have gained immensely more converts among his countrymen. Scarcely has any writer, bearing the rank of critical diplomacy, stepped forward to vindicate propriety, by deciding upon the written *dictum* of authority, whether he was legitimately installed in those honours and that reputation which have

[1] See John Boyle, Earl of Cork and Orrery (1707–62), *Remarks on the Life and Writings of Dr. Jonathan Swift* (1752), letter XII, p. 151. The context is a discussion of pt III of *Gulliver's Travels*.
[2] Coleridge had drawn much the same contrast between Thomas Hobbes (see No. 28a, p. 120, n. 2) and Sterne two years before (No. 116b).

generally circled about his name. We say, then, that Sterne, and it is upon a simple conviction of his desert, has occupied too high a place in the ranks of English literature.

When we read Wordsworth . . . we are not unfrequently reminded that there was a person named Dr. Darwin,[1] who, a few years before him, wrote poetry in a very mediocritous and questionable style of excellence; and that the Della Crusca school of sentiment,[2] which certainly favours Mr. Wordsworth with an occasional archetype, is by no means a safe model for a poet who wishes to reach posterity. . . .

   Wordsworth may in some respects be termed the Sterne of poetry. He has, like his predecessor, endeavoured to extract sentiment where nobody else ever dreamt of looking for it, and has often exalted trifles into a consequence which nature never intended them to occupy; and may therefore be said to have, with Sterne, lent his aid in implanting, in certain literary departments, a tone not always auspicious to true and genuine feeling.

[1] Erasmus Darwin (1731–1802), physician and poet, author of the poems *The Loves of the Plants* (1789) and *The Economy of Vegetation* (1792), and grandfather of naturalist Charles Darwin. Darwin's poems, often ridiculed, were imitations of Pope's style applied to scientific subjects.
[2] The Della Cruscans were a group of insignificant English versifiers who flourished in the 1780s and were satirized in the 1790s for the 'sentimentality' and 'artificiality' of their 'fantastic' and 'insipid' verse.

125. Carlyle on Sterne

1827, 1838

(a) Extract from 'Jean Paul Friedrich Richter,' a review for the *Edinburgh Review* in 1827 (Carlyle's *Complete Works*, Sterling ed. (1885), *Critical and Miscellaneous Essays*, i. 17–19)

It has sometimes been made a wonder that things so discordant should go together; that men of humor are often likewise men of sensibility. But the wonder should rather be to see them divided; to find true genial humor dwelling in a mind that was coarse or callous. The essence of humor is sensibility; warm, tender fellow-feeling with all forms of existence. Nay, we may say that unless seasoned and purified by humor, sensibility is apt to run wild; will readily corrupt into disease, falsehood, or, in one word, sentimentality. Witness Rousseau, Zimmermann, in some points also St. Pierre:[1] to say nothing of living instances; or of the Kotzebues,[2] and other pale hosts of woe-begone mourners, whose wailings, like the howl of an Irish wake, have from time to time cleft the general ear. 'The last perfection of our faculties,' says Schiller with a truth far deeper than it seems, 'is that their activity, without ceasing to be sure and earnest, become *sport*.' True humor is sensibility, in the most catholic and deepest sense; but it is this *sport* of sensibility; wholesome and perfect therefore; as it were, the playful teasing fondness of a mother to her child.[3]

That faculty of irony, of caricature, which often passes by the name of humor, but consists chiefly in a certain superficial distortion or reversal of objects, and ends at best in laughter, bears no resemblance to the humor of Richter. A shallow endowment this; and often more a habit than an endowment. It is but a poor fraction of humor; or rather,

[1] The sentimental side of the work of Jean-Jacques Rousseau (1712–78), and especially his *Confessions*, had an influence on French and German literature somewhat similar to that of Sterne's *Sentimental Journey*. Johann Georg Zimmermann (1728–95), Swiss philosophical writer, was known for the combination of sentimentality, melancholy, and enthusiasm in his character and work. Jacques Henri Bernardin de Saint-Pierre (1737–1814), friend of Rousseau, is best known for his sentimental novel, *Paul et Virginie*.
[2] See 99a, n. 1.
[3] Cf. Carlyle's comparisons of Sterne's humor to the humor of Burns (1828) (*Critical and Miscellaneous Essays*, i. 279–80) and the wit of Voltaire (1829) (ibid., ii. 127).

it is the body to which the soul is wanting; any life it has being false, artificial and irrational. True humor springs not more from the head than from the heart; it is not contempt, its essence is love; it issues not in laughter, but in still smiles, which lie far deeper. It is a sort of inverse sublimity; exalting, as it were, into our affections what is above us. The former is scarcely less precious or heart-affecting than the latter; perhaps it is still rarer, and, as a test of genius, still more decisive. It is, in fact, the bloom and perfume, the purest effluence of a deep, fine and loving nature; a nature in harmony with itself, reconciled to the world and its stintedness and contradiction, nay finding in this very contradiction new elements of beauty as well as goodness. Among our own writers, Shakspeare, in this as in all other provinces, must have his place: yet not the first; his humor is heart-felt, exuberant, warm, but seldom the tenderest or most subtle. Swift inclines more to simple irony: yet he had genuine humor too, and of no unloving sort, though cased, like Ben Jonson's, in a most bitter and caustic rind. Sterne follows next; our last specimen of humor, and, with all his faults, our best; our finest, if not our strongest; for *Yorick* and *Corporal Trim* and *Uncle Toby* have yet no brother but in *Don Quixote*, far as *he* lies above them. Cervantes is indeed the purest of all humorists; so gentle and genial, so full yet so ethereal is his humor, and in such accordance with itself and his whole noble nature. . . .

But of all these men, there is none that, in depth, copiousness and intensity of humor, can be compared with Jean Paul. He alone exists in humor; lives, moves and has his being in it. With him it is not so much united to his other qualities, of intellect, fancy, imagination, moral feeling, as these are united to it; or rather unite themselves to it, and grow under its warmth, as in their proper temperature and climate. Not as if we meant to assert that his humor is in all cases perfectly natural and pure; nay, that it is not often extravagant, untrue, or even absurd: but still, on the whole, the core and life of it are genuine, subtle, spiritual. . . . [W]e look in vain for his parallel. Unite the sportfulness of Rabelais, and the best sensibility of Sterne, with the earnestness, and, even in slight portions, the sublimity of Milton; and let the mosaic brain of old Burton[1] give forth the workings of this strange union, with the pen of Jeremy Bentham.[2]

[1] Robert Burton (1577–1640), whose *Anatomy of Melancholy* (1621) was an important source for Sterne (see No. 90).

[2] Jeremy Bentham (1748–1832), Utilitarian philosopher, demonstrated a terse, clear style in his early writings, but in his later work wrote more eccentrically, coining new words, inserting parentheses, and using complex sentences.

(b) Extract from a lecture of 1 June 1838 (*Lectures on the History of Literature*, ed. J. Reay Greene, 2nd ed. (1892), pp. 170–1)

In [Sterne] there was a great quantity of good struggling through the superficial evil. He terribly failed in the discharge of his duties, still, we must admire in him that sportive kind of geniality and affection, still a son of our common mother, not cased up in buckram formulas as the other writers were, clinging to forms, and not touching realities. And, much as has been said against him, we cannot help feeling his immense love for things around him; so that we may say of him, as of Magdalen, 'much is forgiven him, because he loved much.'[1] A good simple being after all.

[1] See Luke, 7: 36–50.

FRANCE

126. Reviews of *Tristram Shandy* in the *Journal Encyclopédique*

1760–7

(a) Extract from an unsigned review of volumes I and II of *Tristram Shandy*, 15 April 1760, pp. 150–1

This is Horace's monster.[1] Thoughts that are moral, penetrating, delicate, salient, sound, strong, blasphemous, indiscreet, rash: this is what one finds in this book. Freedom of thought is often carried to extremes and appears with all the disorder which usually accompanies it. The author has neither plan nor principles, nor system: he only wishes to talk on and unfortunately one listens to him with pleasure. The vivacity of his imagination, the dazzling quality of his portraits, the distinctive character of his reflections; all please, all interest, all beguile. An Anglican churchman has written this work which Religion has so much to complain of. . . .

Moreover, that irregular progression of ideas, so far removed from the spirit of this age, passes for intentional subtlety. The English find mystery in it and all join in admiring it.

(b) Extract from an unsigned review of volumes III and IV of *Tristram Shandy*, 1 May 1761, p. 131

The third and fourth volumes of the novel *Tristram Shandy*, which were awaited with so much eagerness, have finally appeared. It is hard

[1] Horace begins *Ars Poetica* with the description of monstrous pictures in which a painter joins a human head to the neck of a horse, or the head and torso of a beautiful woman to the ugly tail of a fish. Such pictures, he says, provoke laughter and are like books without a consistent form or shape.

to see how such nonsense could have such a prodigious success: everyone agrees, after reading this little book, that it has no common sense and yet it is in great demand—what an absurdity! To speak at random, to heap buffooneries on buffooneries, obscenities on obscenities, to diffuse over all an original and curious cast of thought: therein lies all the merit of this production. The third volume degenerates in its wit and is nothing but a tissue of obscenities: among other things there is a very boring and very indecent dissertation on long noses. . . . But enough: what we have said will suffice to make clear the nature of this absurdity which is so popular in London.

(c) Extract from an unsigned review of volumes V and VI of *Tristram Shandy*, 1 March 1762, pp. 143–4

The fifth and sixth volumes of this bizarre work, which we have discussed before, have just been published. It is a rhapsody in which the bad far outweighs the good. One finds here the same indecent allusions, the same tedious digressions, the same extravagant sallies which characterized the preceding volumes. The author of *Tristram Shandy* is not nearly so original as the English imagine: Rabelais served as his model. One sees in the French author the same dissertations on the Arts and Sciences; like Shandy, he speaks Hebrew, Greek, Latin, Italian, Spanish, High Dutch, etc. They both make frequent comments on the parts that distinguish the sexes and on the shape that represents *the beast with two backs*.[1] Rabelais, who was a doctor, appears less culpable than his imitator; one pardons more easily his talking to his readers about the disputes *de ventre inspiciendo*,[2] etc. than one can pardon the author of *Tristram Shandy*, who is a York clergyman named Mr. Sterne, for the same offences.

[1] *Othello*, act I, sc. I.
[2] Concerning the examination of the womb.

(d) Extract from an unsigned review of volumes VII and VIII of *Tristram Shandy*, 1 January 1766, p. 137

We do not understand how Mr. Sterne, a clergyman of York, has been able to push this outlandish production so far. We are still more astonished that he finds readers; for it is the most complete delirium of the imagination. At first it was thought there must be some allegory, but in the end one sees only a collection of buffooneries, absurdities, and obscenities that one would not excuse in a soldier, yet the author is a clergyman. The observation has been made in connection with the story of *Tristram Shandy* that we are also indebted to two other ecclesiastics for works of the freest kind, namely Pantagruel and the Menippean Satire,[1] but one must not confuse them with Mr. Sterne's monstrous production.

(e) Unsigned review of volume IX of *Tristram Shandy*, 15 March 1767, p. 145

The same indecency and the same coarseness of thought which characterize the first 8 volumes of this work, which we have reviewed as they appeared, will prevent readers from glancing at this volume which has just appeared.

[1] See No. 48d, p. 168, and n. 2.

127. Denis Diderot on Sterne

7 October 1762

Extract from a letter to Sophie Volland, translated from *Correspondance* (1958), iv. 189.

Diderot (1713–84), Encyclopédiste and friend and admirer of Sterne, has left no extended comments on Sterne, though he imitated *Tristram Shandy* in *Jacques le Fataliste*. For a comparison of these two books much to Sterne's advantage, see No. 135a.

This book so mad, so wise, and so gay is the English Rabelais. It is entitled *The Life, the Memoirs, and the Opinions of Tristram Shandy*. I can't give you a better idea of it than by calling it a universal satire. Mr. Sterne, who is the author, is also a priest.

128. Deyverdun on Sterne's originality

1769

Extract from *Mémoires littéraires de la Grande Bretagne, pour l'an 1768* (1769), pp. 124, 133–4.

Georges Deyverdun (1735–89) and Edward Gibbon, the historian, were joint editors of the *Mémoires littéraires*, while they lived in Switzerland. Though the remarks below, from a review of the *Sentimental Journey*, have been attributed to Deyverdun (see V. P. Helming, 'Edward Gibbon and Georges Deyverdun, Collaborators in the *Mémoires littéraires de la Grande Bretagne*,' *PMLA*, xlvii (1932), 1028–49), he and Gibbon often discussed the articles they were writing and shared and exchanged views.

[*Tristram Shandy*], which was natural, lively, and above all completely original, was extremely well received; but with each installment its lack of form, its indecency, and its obscurity disgusted its readers more, so that they censured it as strongly as they had praised it and professed to see a great difference between the first volumes and the later ones. This difference does not seem so apparent to me—I see in the whole course of the work the beauties and defects which others have found in different installments and if it did not merit the excessive praise which it received at the beginning, it merited even less the treatment it received later. Besides, there is no book in which one does not pay rather dearly for beauties of this sort. . . .

Men of taste cannot mourn enough the loss of an author whose character was original in these times when imitation seems to be snuffing out talent and when the English, denationalizing themselves, are not gaining in elegance and polish what they are losing in force and warmth, while the French move the scene to England and place there characters who are not at home on that stage and who stumble at every step. I have said to actors, I have said to painters, and I repeat to authors —imitation restricts genius: you will never become great through imitation. Was it by imitation that Milton and Shakespeare climbed to the height of Parnassus? If Sterne, walking alone, sometimes lost his way, he also frequently blazed new trails, discovered charming vistas, and found Nature and Sentiment following in his footsteps and holding out their arms to him with a gentle smile.

129. Frénais's translation of the *Sentimental Journey*

1769, 1786

The French edition of the *Sentimental Journey*, the first of Sterne's works to be translated into French, appeared in 1769. Joseph Pierre Frénais (?-c. 1789), the translator, later undertook the translation of *Tristram Shandy* (see Nos 130b, 131). Sterne's *Journey* was understandably popular in France; a second edition was published in 1770 and more than a half dozen reprints appeared before the 'new edition' of 1786, reviewed below in (d).

(a) Extract from J. P. Frénais's translator's preface to the *Sentimental Journey* (1769), pp. i–vi

This little book is the work of Mr. Sterne, prebendary of York, who is famous for that remarkable book, *The Life and Opinions of Tristram Shandy*, a work so extraordinary indeed that it would be nearly impossible to give even a rough idea of it. . . .

Mr. Sterne came to Paris during the last war. When asked if he had found in France no original characters that he could make use of in his history, 'No,' he replied, 'The French resemble old pieces of coin, whose impression is worn out by rubbing.'[1]

---

[1] This anecdote was first reported in the *London Chronicle* (16–18 April 1765), p. 373. Cf. 'Character. Versailles' (*A Sentimental Journey*, p. 232).

But if Mr. Sterne found no strongly expressed character among us, he had the advantage of being able to catch with a great deal of delicacy and feeling the faint shadings which we still have to distinguish us from other people. The work of which we are offering a translation is proof of this. . . . The title, *A Sentimental Journey*, which he has given to his observations, gives a sufficiently clear idea of the book to spare us the trouble of definition. One will find throughout the book an amiable philanthropic nature which never belies itself, and under the cloak of gaiety—and even sometimes of buffoonery—flashes of a tender and true sensibility which draw tears even while one is laughing. No exact French equivalent could be found for the English word 'sentimental' and hence it has been left untranslated. Perhaps the reader will conclude that it deserves to pass into our language.

(b) Extract from an unsigned review of Frénais's translation of the *Sentimental Journey* in the *Journal Encyclopédique*, 1 July 1769, p. 138

This journey is a gay and pleasing painting of French life; but Mr. Sterne's good humor does not prevent him from being touched by everything that wounds humanity and showing the most tender sensibility: this is what has led him to call his work 'sentimental.' Mr. Sterne is known for another book entitled *The Life and Opinions of Tristram Shandy*, which has a most bantering tone and a most lively wit. We hope that the success of the translation of the *Sentimental Journey* will encourage M. Frénais to undertake the translation of *Shandy*.

(c) Extract from an unsigned review of Frénais's translation of the *Sentimental Journey* in the *Mercure de France*, August 1769, pp. 71–4

It is useless to look for order or connection in the productions of Sterne—he loses himself in endless digressions, one leading him to another; he forgets his main objective and often makes his readers forget it while he secures their interest with the strokes of a tender and genuine sensibility which draws their tears. In the present work he recounts his trip to France. He entitles it *A Sentimental Journey*; this title cannot be satisfactorily translated into French. Sterne was sensitive by nature and attempts to describe not so much what he sees as the sensations that objects arouse in him. . . . All in all, it is a pleasant enough trifle with lavish portions of jesting and sentiment.

(d) Extract from an unsigned review of a 'new edition' of Frénais's translation of the *Sentimental Journey* in letter IX, *L'Année Littéraire* (1786), pp. 108–10

The reputation of this work is made, Monsieur; it has even already produced several imitators. It is a remarkable production, in which eccentricity dominates as much as sentiment. It is the account, now comic, now touching, of the various feelings that the author experiences during his journey in France, of the adventures which befall him, of the people he meets. The author has not tried to put any continuity into his story. There are, one may say, so many detached scenes that one can read indiscriminately, without needing to refer to the preceding ones. This *Journey*, in short, is very similar to the opinions of *Tristram Shandy*. . . .

A real excellence of this author is that he has never tried to arouse interest by those romantic and unbelievable adventures, which are almost always false to life. His pictures are chosen from the common ranks of society, conceived with delicacy, and executed with wit and gaiety. He has, in short, the rare talent of arousing our interest by pictures and details that we see every day, and which our Authors, always stilted and affected, pretend to scorn, because they don't know how to present them.

130. Voltaire on Sterne

1771, 1777

Voltaire (1694–1778) read at least part of *Tristram Shandy* in English, long before it was translated into French. In a letter to Count Francesco Algarotti in September 1760 he called *Tristram Shandy* 'a very unaccountable book; an original one. They run mad about it in England,' he continued (*Voltaire's Correspondence*, ed. Theodore Besterman (1959), xliii. 137). In 1764, however, he referred to *Tristram Shandy* as 'more lively than decent' (*Oeuvres complètes*, xxv. 167), but he included a discussion of Sterne's 'Sermon on Conscience' in volume II in the *Dictionnaire Philosophique* in 1771. Later he reviewed anonymously Frénais's translation of the first part of *Tristram Shandy* in 1777.

(a) 'On the Deceptions of Conscience,' *Dictionnaire Philosophique* (1771) (*Oeuvres complètes de Voltaire*, ed. A. J. Q. Beuchot (1877–83), xviii. 237–8).

Perhaps this important question has never been better treated than in the comic novel *Tristram Shandy*, written by a parish priest named Sterne, England's second Rabelais.[1] It resembles those ancient little vases decorated with satyrs which contained precious essences.[2]

Two old retired captains, helped by Dr. Slop, raise the most ridiculous questions. In these questions, French theologians are not spared. They talk particularly about a Dissertation presented at the Sorbonne by a surgeon who asks permission to baptize children in their mother's womb by means of a nozzle on a syringe which he will neatly insert into the uterus without injuring mother or child.

Finally they have a corporal read them an old sermon on conscience, composed by Sterne himself.

[1] England's other Rabelais was Swift, Voltaire indicates elsewhere (see (b) below).
[2] This metaphor of the 'little vase' or gallipot was frequently alluded to. See No. 28c and p. 125, n. 2. See also Nos 131d, 137.

Among several pictures superior to those of Rembrandt and the pencil of Callot,[1] there is one of a gentleman and man of the world, spending his days in the pleasures of eating, gaming, and debauchery, doing nothing for which good company can reproach him and consequently reproaching himself for nothing. His conscience and his honor accompany him to the theatre, to the gaming table, and especially to the rendezvous when he pays generously the girl whom he is keeping. He punishes severely the petty larcenies of the common people when he is in a position of authority; he lives gaily and dies without the least remorse.

Dr. Slop interrupts the reading to say that this would be impossible in the Anglican church—it could happen only among the Papists.[2]

Finally Sterne cites the example of David, who has, he says, at one time a delicate and enlightened conscience, at another a very gross and very benighted conscience. When he could kill his king in a cave, he only cuts off the skirt of his robe: that shows a delicate conscience. But he spends an entire year without the least remorse for his adultery with Bathsheba and the murder of Uriah: that shows the same conscience hardened and deprived of light.

Such are, he says, most men. We must agree with this priest that the great men of the world are often in this position: the torrent of pleasure and business engulfs them and they haven't time to have any conscience—conscience is all right for the common people, though even they have scarcely any conscience when it comes to making money. Thus it is good to awaken often the conscience both of dressmakers and of kings with a moral story that can make an impression on them; but to make an impression, one must talk better than most do today.

---

[1] Jacques Callot (1592–1635), French engraver, was famous for his ability to catch the essence of a character with a few bold strokes.
[2] Here, as elsewhere, Voltaire has not quite understood the English of the novel. Cf. *Tristram Shandy*, II. 17, pp. 128–9.

(b) Extract from a review of Frénais's translation of the first part of *Tristram Shandy* in the *Journal de Politique et de Littérature* (25 April 1777) (*Oeuvres complètes*, xxx. 379–82)

For several years our passion for English novels has been so great that finally a man of letters has given us a free translation of *Tristram Shandy*. We still have, of course, only the first four volumes, which introduce us to *The Life and Opinions of Tristram Shandy*; the hero, who has just been born, is not yet baptized. The whole work is made up of preliminaries and digressions. It is a continual jesting in the fashion of Scarron.[1] The low comedy, which forms the basis of this work, does not, however, mean that there are not some very serious things in it.

The English author was a parish priest named Sterne. He pushed the jest so far as to print in his novel a sermon which he had delivered 'On Conscience'; and, strangely enough, this sermon is one of the best in the annals of English eloquence. It is found in its entirety in the translation.

[Voltaire continues with an approving reference to the article in the *Gazette Littéraire* in 1765 which was translated in the *London Chronicle* (No. 48d).]

This eccentric author, who outwitted all of Great Britain with his pen . . . had, however, some philosophy in his head—and just as much buffoonery.

There are, in Sterne, flashes of superior insight, such as one finds in Shakespeare. And where do we not find them? There is an ample store of ancient authors where everyone can take his fill of inspiration at his ease.

It was to be wished that the preacher had written his comic novel just to teach the English not to let themselves be duped any longer by the charlatanry of novelists, and that he could have corrected the long declining taste of the nation which has abandoned the study of Lockes and Newtons for the most extravagant and frivolous works. But that was not the intention of the author of *Tristram Shandy*. Born poor and gay, he wished to laugh at England's expense and to make some money.

Works like this were not unknown to the English. The famous

[1] Paul Scarron (1610–60), French novelist, dramatist, and burlesque poet, is best remembered for his *Roman comique* (1651–7), a picaresque novel of great vigor and wit.

Dean Swift had written several books in this style. Swift has been called England's Rabelais: but it must be admitted that he was clearly superior to Rabelais. As gay and as pleasant as our priest of Meudon, he wrote in his tongue with much more purity and subtlety than the author of *Gargantua* did in his; and we have verses from him of an elegance and an artlessness worthy of Horace.

If one asks who was the first European author of this jesting and bold style in which Sterne, Swift, and Rabelais wrote, it appears certain that the first to distinguish themselves by traveling this dangerous road were two Germans, born in the fifteenth century, Reuchlin and Hutten.[1] They published the famous *Letters of Obscure Men* long before Rabelais dedicated his *Pantagruel* and his *Gargantua* to Cardinal Odet de Châtillon.

[Voltaire continues to discuss the influence of the two Germans in bringing about the Reformation, as well as other examples of literature which helped to bring about political change.]

Tristram Shandy will not bring about any revolution; but we must be grateful to the translator for having suppressed some rather coarse jokes for which England has sometimes been reproached. . . .

There were even some fairly lengthy passages which Sterne's translator did not dare to put into French, like the formula of excommunication used in the Church of Rochester: our sense of propriety would not allow it.

We believe that the translation of *Tristram Shandy*, like that of Shakespeare, will remain unfinished. We live in a time when the most unusual works are attempted but do not succeed.

[1] Johann Reuchlin (1455–1522) and Ulrich von Hutten (1488–1523) were principal contributors to the *Letters of Obscure Men* (1515–17), which were ironic and satirical attacks on the Catholic establishment by a group of young humanists.

131. Frénais's translation of *Tristram Shandy*

1776, 1777

Impelled by the success of his translation of the *Sentimental Journey*, Frénais began a translation of *Tristram Shandy*, which he was never to finish. The first four volumes appeared in 1776 and were reviewed by Voltaire (see No. 130b). As Frénais's preface makes clear, his translation is a free one, sometimes more nearly an imitation than a translation.

(a) Extract from the preface to Frénais's translation of the first four volumes of *Tristram Shandy* (1776). Frénais begins his preface with a reference to Voltaire's discussion of Sterne in the *Dictionnaire Philosophique* (No. 130a) and his designation of Sterne as 'England's second Rabelais'

Mr. Sterne was indeed influenced by the works of the priest of Meudon: but he by no means imitated his licentiousness. Sterne always paints his subjects with propriety and it would be difficult to paint them with more feeling or more delicacy. . . . Sterne's is one of the most difficult English works to translate; and if a translator might be considered worthy of a place among men of letters, I might aspire to such a place. I might even say, to give myself a stronger claim, that I had to cut out much of the original and replace it with my own invention: I would be merely telling the truth. Actually when Sterne's jests did not always strike me as good ones, I left them where I found them and substituted others. I believe one may take that liberty in the translation of a work whose sole purpose is to amuse, if he does his best not to have his substitutions recognized; and I will be very happy if the reader is unable to detect my presence in the book. . . .

[Frénais continues with a life of Sterne, drawn from various sources, and an account of the reception of Sterne's work.]

Tristram Shandy was to be found in everybody's hands. Many read it and few understood it. Those who were unacquainted with the wit and genius of Rabelais understood it still less. Some readers were stopped by digressions whose meaning they could not fathom; others imagined the book was just a continuing allegory which masked people that the author had not wished to put openly on display. But all agreed that Mr. Sterne was the cleverest, the most delightful writer of his time; that his characters were unusual and striking, his descriptions picturesque, his observations shrewd, and his nature easy.

This work brought him the greatest esteem. He was sought after by the great, the learned, the men of taste, and particularly by all those who tend to ridicule everything that goes on in the world. He enjoyed such a reputation, that people prided themselves on having spent an evening with the author of *Tristram Shandy*; but he experienced the fate of all persons who win fame by their talents. He and his works were torn to pieces in a thousand pamphlets whose titles have even been forgotten; if he had a host of unknown enemies, he had distinguished defenders who avenged him. . . .

His *Sentimental Journey* did not belie his reputation. It was translated into every language almost as soon as it appeared. But his *Tristram Shandy* has so far been translated only into German, and that is not strange: it is a work whose charms cannot easily be put into a foreign tongue. There are even many Englishmen who were bewildered by the appearance of such a book in their own language.

(b) Extract from an unsigned review of Frénais's translation of *Tristram Shandy*, letter I, *L'Année Littéraire* (1776), pp. 3–25

All the flashes of a free and original imagination characterize, Sir, the facetious work which I am announcing to you; a work which, in spite of its outlandish irregularities, sparkles with wit, gaiety, and sound philosophy. The late Mr. Stern, its author, is thought of as the Rabelais of England, and his works do indeed deserve to be placed on the same library shelves with those of the jovial priest of Meudon. . . .

It is not true, however, that all Stern's thoughts degenerate into frivolous flashes of wit: one finds in his work subtle and ingenious allusions, adroit criticism of manners and of false scholarship, accurate and sound observations. Stern, although a philosopher, does not appear to have admired our Encyclopedists very much. He sometimes approaches these sublime thinkers, Diogenes' lantern in his hand; he contemplates them and he soon leaves them with a burst of laughter.

(c) Extract from an unsigned review of Frénais's translation of *Tristram Shandy* in *Mercure de France* (January 1777), pp. 129–36

It would be difficult to give a resumé of this work, let alone a clear definition. It is a sort of potpourri filled with a host of digressions, in which the least trifle often furnishes a subject, and which sometimes even come, as the saying goes, suddenly, without rhyme or reason. . . . All in all, nothing could be more pleasant than most of the threads of the strange fabric which makes up these two initial volumes. One could not scatter more gaiety and charm in a gossiping story, pushed to the verge of caricature. There are picturesque descriptions, subtle and clever observations, and above all singular and striking characters such as Captain Toby Shandy, uncle of the infant hero, and the good Corporal Trim, his servant. . . .

The translator has prefixed to these two volumes an account of Sterne's life, which makes one love this writer whose heart appears as honorable and as sensitive as his character was gay and his wit ingenious and amusing.

(d) Extract from an unsigned review of Frénais's translation of *Tristram Shandy* in the *Journal Encyclopédique* (15 January 1777), pp. 256–65

Sterne's originality developed early: even at college he amused his fellow students with the singularity of his ideas. But it was a reading of Rabelais which stimulated his genius. From that moment he shut himself in, appeared no more in the circles in which he had provided diversion, and worked on his *Tristram Shandy*. . . .[1]

One can see from the ludicrous strokes which characterize Toby what Sterne's manner is, how he manages to attach the comic or the

[1] Needless to say, the notion that Sterne shut himself in to write *Tristram Shandy* as soon as he had read Rabelais is without foundation, although Rabelais was one of his sources of inspiration.

burlesque to the smallest incidents. Voltaire compares *Tristram Shandy* to those ancient little vases decorated with satyrs which contained precious essences, and he adds that several of Sterne's pictures are superior to those of Rembrandt and Callot.[1] He is one of those light-hearted philosophers who have successfully called attention to the foolishness of grave philosophers and have thrown ridicule on the different opinions of the scholastics, the eccentricities of famous men, ignorance, and finally the weaknesses of humanity. Frénais's style might be both more lively and more finished. However, there is every reason to believe that the French translation of *Tristram Shandy* will be as well received as that of the *Sentimental Journey* . . . which has gained distinguished approbation.

[1] See No. 130a, p. 391, n. 1.

132. Continuations of Frénais's *Tristram Shandy*

1785, 1786

Two completions of Frénais's translation of *Tristram Shandy* appeared in 1785, one by Antoine Gilbert Griffet de la Baume (reviewed in (a) and (d) below), the other by Charles François, Marquis de Bonnay (reviewed in (b) and (c) below).

De la Baume (1756–1805) was a magazine writer and translator of both English and German works. De Bonnay (1750–1825), diplomat and general, devoted his leisure hours to literary pursuits. Though de la Baume's translation was in some ways more faithful, it was de Bonnay's which was reprinted, together with Frénais's, as the standard French text for more than fifty years. De Bonnay, like Frénais, sometimes omitted sections of his original and sometimes added incidents of his own.

(a) Excerpt from an unsigned review of de la Baume's translation of Sterne's *New Journey into France* [i.e. *Tristram Shandy*, vol. VII], *Followed by the Story of Le Fevre and a Selection of Familiar Letters* in the *Journal Encyclopédique* (15 May 1785), pp. 71–9

There are pliant and facile geniuses who are formed in part by the prevailing taste and who perhaps would be nothing without it; there are others, in contrast, truly original, who could not be purified by the prevailing taste, who cannot be enslaved by the yoke of rules, and who are from the beginning what they will always be. Such was Sterne. His works bear the stamp of a truly original gaiety. His *Sentimental Journey*, after delighting England, has had great success in France.

(b) Extract from an unsigned review of de Bonnay's translation of *Tristram Shandy* in letter ii, *L'Année Littéraire* (1785), pp. 34–50

Nothing could be more outlandish than this work. No order, no sequence, no plan. Imagine a collection of extravagant ideas which are pleasant and moving; sometimes moral, sometimes licentious—one laughs in one chapter, one is moved to pity in another, one yawns in a third. The scenes are disjointed and do not achieve any unity; one might think the author had written his book on the run and that he changed ideas as he came to a new place; what follows is never the result of what has preceded and one comes to the end of the book without knowing whether he is finishing or beginning it. It is a kind of will-o'-the-wisp which leads you a chase, sometimes in one direction, sometimes in another, but which, nonetheless, is more often pleasing than boring. . . .

A book merits praise when the pungent and the pleasing prevail over the tasteless and the trivial; this book which frequently joins original ideas with genuine sentiment deserves that praise.

(c) Excerpt from an unsigned review of de Bonnay's anonymous translation of *Tristram Shandy* in the *Journal Encyclopédique* (15 January 1786), pp. 268–77

Surely it is no small accomplishment to have made *Tristram Shandy* tolerable in a language and for a people which never dispense with the rules of taste, of order, of continuity, of the connection of ideas, even when one writes only to amuse himself or amuse others. . . .

The English, we are told, laughed from beginning to end over . . . nearly every chapter of *Tristram Shandy*. They loved that vagabond imagination, that crowd of ideas which follow each other without any one of them seeming to take rise from that which precedes it nor being obliged to lead to that which follows it. In the very irregularity of this progression, they see a critic, whose piquancy we cannot fully savor; they recognize manners and characteristics which are alien to us and allusions whose subtlety escapes us. Let us not then be astonished at the great vogue this book has had in England.

(d) Extract from an unsigned review of de la Baume's translation of *Tristram Shandy* (printed together with some miscellaneous works) in the *Journal Encyclopédique* (15 March 1786), pp. 445–53

[T]he novel *Tristram Shandy* is without plot; it is a disorderly gallery of paintings or observations and of scenes which are ludicrous, facetious, critical, philosophical, and sentimental. It is . . . the work of a most roving imagination, although everywhere very expressive; it is a disjointed production, whose various parts are, in a way, independent of each other, though joined under the same title.

133. Two views of the 1780s

1785, 1786

(a) Extract from a review by Mallet du Pan (1748–1800), Swiss publicist and long-time staff member of the *Mercure*, in the *Mercure* (12 November 1785) (Translated here from Francis Brown Barton, *Étude sur l'Influence de Laurence Sterne en France au dix-huitième siècle* (1911), pp. 20, 21.)

No one tells a story with greater interest, nor sketches in details with more truth, nor paints with more feeling than Sterne in these fragments [i.e. the episode of Uncle Toby and the fly, the story of the Abbess of Andoüillets, and especially the stories of Le Fever and Maria]. Sterne is dramatic: he brings the reader onstage with him and one sees the actors and recognizes their voices—even their postures, their gestures, their clothing. There is no blurred stroke of the brush, no affectation nor exaggeration. . . .

One would be mistaken to think of Sterne only as a facetious novelist; he is full of reason and he revives moral lessons, maxims, and old truths.

(b) Extract from an anonymous essay 'On the Mind and Works of Sterne,' *Journal Encyclopédique* (1 August 1786), pp. 524-7

The author of the *Sentimental Journey* is best known for the originality of his manner. Child of nature and of inspiration, he rushes down new paths. No plan, no fetters. He roams capriciously and without restraint; but his wandering extravagances, always acknowledged by taste, intellect, and the graces, often affect the heart and sometimes instruct the reason.

There is no man more keenly, more delicately constituted. He is all spirit, all heart. His tender sensibility enfolds every object. The fineness of his impressions discovers unknown hues. His fertile and lively imagination climbs, sinks, explores every tone, every subject. The most lively and realistic pictures, the subtlest and gayest criticism, the riches of poetry, the seductions of eloquence, the sweetest emanations of morality and feeling flow in turn and without order from his facile, natural, and unconstrained pen.

If you do not savor this author, he will often seem needlessly minute, shallow, absurd, childish; but fathom his genius and you will find a great teacher of men. He shows you everywhere around you what you look for at a distance so laboriously—new sources of interest, of emotions, and of pleasures. He teaches you to look for happiness in a sweet freedom from care, loving mankind, making light of your troubles, substituting for your solemn and burdensome follies, follies which are gay, pleasant, sentimental—as free as your fancies.

Shandeism is a kind of epicureanism; but it is the product of a man who is clever, sensitive, and philanthropic.

If these lessons will not fashion a great statesman, a famous leader, one of those principal cogwheels which move that machine called the world, may they not spread out like oil on the surface of the more solid matter which forms these men, soften that surface and make supple their movements? . . . And must the world have so many heroes? Aren't we nearly all restless children who muddy the work in order to seem to have a hand in it? Wouldn't everything go better for us and for others if we would exchange in favor of a gentle Shandeism that painful importance that we vainly affect? . . .

[In *Tristram Shandy* Sterne] delightfully gives himself up to all the caprices of his humor. The free unconcern of his spirit, the gaiety, the madness, the sublimity, the exquisite subtlety of his thoughts, his taste, his inimitable talent for satire—all guide by turns his pen. He wanders over every subject, he explores without ceasing every tone. This fact, which makes this work the most highly valued by Sterne's aficionados and the most severely criticized by his detractors, also makes it more difficult to translate.

134. Madame Suard on Sterne

June 1786

Extract from Amélie Suard's 'Letter from a Lady on Sterne's *Sentimental Journey*,' appearing originally in the *Journal de Paris* (18–19 June 1786), and translated here from J. B. A. Suard, *Mélanges de littérature*, 2nd ed. (1806), iii. 111–22.

Madame Suard (1750–1830), was the wife of Jean Baptiste Antoine Suard (c. 1733–1817), journalist, translator of numerous English works, and acquaintance of Sterne during his Paris visits. The Suards were married about 1775. For Suard's review of one of the installments of *Tristram Shandy*, see No. 48d.

Among the books which have been brought to us from the country, we have read the *Sentimental Journey*. It is the delight of some people— I am one of these—but for others, the object of the deepest scorn. Mademoiselle de Sommery[1] especially, who, as you know, likes only

[1] Fontette de Sommery (c. 1700–90), whose salon attracted some of the leading scholars and literary men of the time, attacked follies unmercifully in her own writing and was known for the frankness and openness of her character. For a further report of her remarks on Sterne, see No. 137.

wit, who breathes nothing but wit, and who finds none at all in this book, looks at me as if she were quite convinced that I am making fun of her when I talk about the charms of this book. The pleasure, for example, that Sterne found in feeling the finger-tip of the lady with black silk gloves makes her die with laughter. I believe now what she has always told me, that the passions are absolutely foreign to her, for to have experienced them is enough for one to rediscover part of their charm by pressing the hand of an object one loves[1] and to realize that the sweetest memories of love, the moments of its greatest joy, often have no other source than a hand kissed or pressed with tenderness.

But, to return to Sterne, what is this, she keeps saying to me, but a book in which the author tries to interest me in the story of a dead donkey, of the buying of a pair of gloves, of the hiring of a footman, of a poor man who begs alms? These chapters don't seem very promising no doubt, I tell her, but Sterne's merit, it seems to me, lies in having given interest to details which have no interest whatever in themselves, in having seized a thousand slight impressions, a thousand fleeting sentiments which pass through the heart or the imagination of a sensitive man, and presented them in penetrating language, in original images or turns of phrase. Sterne enlarges, so to speak, the human heart by painting his own feelings for us; he seizes upon everything which had been neglected before him as unworthy of being treated by a literary artist, and he adds to the treasury of our delights.

Often, in the midst of a chapter which has no apparent value, one sees emerge the strokes of a sweet and sublime morality, and profound glimpses of the heart, whose most delicate movements he fathoms. And then, he seems so disposed to happiness—he finds it so easily! What pleasure one feels in this surrender of his heart, in this innocent wantonness of his imagination, above all in this feeling of goodness, tolerance, universal kindness which joins him to all men! The interest which he takes in recounting all his feelings, passes into the hearts of his readers. An historian attracts us less by the facts than by the manner in which he tells them, the observations that he derives from them. I admit that the incidents of the *Sentimental Journey* are hardly more than those with which an ordinary man could bore us to tears. But it seems to me, my friend, that the charm of sensitive and passionate persons comes from the way they animate and invest everything with feeling. Have you not often felt that it is less the lack of wit that bores us than that absence of soul and life which brings languor and death to every-

[1] The French has 'animates,' probably a misprint of 'anime' for 'aime.'

thing? Have you not met people who had a reputation for being witty, yet whom you found very boring—and others, on the contrary, who had little reputation for wit, yet whom you found good company? Sterne could almost get along without wit. It is not the most witty chapters that are the most interesting; it is those in which he displays that heart and that imagination so quick to be touched: it is that exquisite sensibility, that quality of gaiety and originality which rivets your attention and compels you to finish the book when you have read the first chapter. He seems to write only for his own pleasure, but it is because he appears happy that he makes his readers happy—at least those who feel as I do.

But his talent and wit are uplifted and ennobled by the nature of the sentiments that he feels and the ideas that occur to him. With what art, what truth, he paints a scene and traces a portrait! Look, I beg you, at that of good Father Lorenzo: he draws him for us with features so clear, so precise, that it seems to me a skillful artist, taking his palette, could paint him for us from the description. . . .

As for Sterne's predisposition to love all women, as I do not run the risk of taking him for a lover, I forgive him for it, since this predisposition makes him happy and adds interest to his work. But I am grateful to him for looking upon love as the safeguard of virtue and the best protection against vice. This proves that he has known real love; for love purifies the heart and perfects all virtues. . . .

[Mme Suard continues to discuss her favorite passages, mentioning La Fleur, Juliet (as Maria is called in the French translation), the starling, and the Captive.]

Thus Sterne, whose sensitive and shifting imagination could recreate so sharply life's sad scenes, was nonetheless more inclined to joy in all the pleasant consolations of nature and society.

[Quotes Sentimental Journey, 'In the Street, Calais,' from '. . . was I in a desart . . .' to '. . . I would rejoice along with them,' pp. 115–16.]

What a pleasant, sweet sensibility is that which associates itself through feeling, with dumb, inanimate beings, and do we not thus partake of the Creator's views of the creation when we submit with joy to the order He has established and to the place that He has marked out for us?

My friend, if you have no liking for Sterne, do not tell me so, for I would be afraid I might love you less.

135. Comments at the turn of the century

(a) Extract from François G. J. S. Andrieux's review of Diderot's *Jacques le Fataliste* in the *Décade Philosophique* (1796), pp. 224-5. Andrieux (1759-1833), dramatist and Professor of Literature at the Collège de France, attempted to maintain the classical tradition in opposition to the growing Romantic school

Do you know Rabelais? Do you know Sterne? If you don't know them, I advise you to read them, especially Sterne. But if you wish to see a very feeble imitation of *Tristram Shandy*, read *Jacques the Fatalist*. . . .

You will not find any of the frank and sustained gaiety of the priest of Meudon[1] which dresses reason in masquerade costume, and has some excellent bits of jesting, sunk in a heap of coarseness and nonsense.

You will find in *Jacques* even less of the charm of the writings of the English clergyman—that pleasant simplicity; that shrewdness of observation; that delicacy of sentiment; that wealth of penetrating, droll, and profound ideas—you will not find learning and morality, the comic and the pathetic, all handled with the same superior touch. Sterne can make you laugh with one eye and cry with the other.

(b) Extract from *Le Reveur sentimental* (1796) by Pierre Blanchard (1772-1856), educator and author of many popular books for children (translated here from Barton, *Étude sur l'Influence de Sterne*, p. 87)

I know of no one like Sterne who can find the picturesque, distinctive trait that you have seen a thousand times but never noticed.

[1] I.e. Rabelais.

(c) Extract from Pierre-Simon Ballanche *fils* (1776–1847), religious and social philosopher, *Du Sentiment considéré dans ses rapports avec la littérature et les arts* (1801), pp. 218–19

The impatient reader is doubtless waiting for me to speak of Sterne, that original and pungent writer who created a new style all his own. He painted the emotions in uncommon situations, in picturesque groupings, in subtle observations of customs. He makes one smile, but it is the smile of the heart; he makes one cry, but the tears are as gentle as dew drops. There is often absurdity in his transitions but it is not the absurdity of Ariosto[1] nor of the famous priest of Meudon. . . .[2] Oh, if I could find somewhere an Uncle Toby with his worthy servant Corporal Trim, I would travel hundreds of miles—I would go to the ends of the earth. I would live with him, we would talk about his wound, about the virtues of the Widow Wadman, about the Siege of Namur. We would walk together, we would stop together. We would not harm any living creature. . . . You who have read this remarkable book, haven't you felt that gaiety of heart which is so close to melancholy and which brings tears to the edge of the eyelid? Haven't you wept in earnest in some passages like the episode of Le Fever or that of poor Maria?

[1] Lodovico Ariosto (1474–1533), famous Italian epic poet, wove many stories together in his *Orlando Furioso* and introduced new characters and situations abruptly.
[2] I.e. Rabelais.

136. Madame de Staël on Sterne

1800, 1810

Madame de Staël (1766–1817), whose 'brilliant personality,' it has been said, 'epitomizes the European culture of her time,' commented on Sterne largely as a representative of English 'humour.' In her *Essai sur les Fictions* (1795) she also referred to the *Sentimental Journey* as one of the few 'successful works of fiction in which the pictures of life are presented in situations not involving love' (*Oeuvres complètes de Mme la Baronne de Staël, publié par son fils* (1820), ii. 192–3).

(a) Extract from chapter XIV, *De la Littérature considérée dans ses rapports avec les institutions sociales* (1800), translated here from the Paris edition of 1845, pp. 367–8

There is . . . a sort of gaiety in some English writings, which has all the characteristics of originality and genuineness. The English language has created a word, 'humour,' to express this gaiety, which is an element of the blood almost as much as of the mind; it is dependent upon the nature of the climate and the customs; it would be quite inimitable wherever the same causes did not develop it. Some works of Fielding and of Swift, *Peregrine Pickle*, and *Roderick Random*, but especially the works of Sterne, give a good idea of the style called *humour*.

There is moodiness, I would say almost sadness, in this gaiety; he who makes you laugh does not participate in the pleasure that he causes. One can see that he writes in a somber mood, and that he would be almost irritated with you because you are amused by him. As an abrupt manner sometimes gives more point to praise, the gaiety of the humour is thrown into relief by the gravity of its author. The English have very rarely permitted on the stage the kind of wit which they call *humour*; its effect would not be at all theatrical.

There is misanthropy in the humour of the English, and sociability in that of the French; the one must be read when a person is alone, the

other is all the more striking the larger the audience. The gaiety of
the English leads almost always to a philosophical or moral result; the
gaiety of the French often has as its end only pleasure itself.

The English paint whimsical characters with great talent because
there are a great many such among them. Society effaces the eccentricities, but rural life preserves them all.

(b) Extract from *De l'Allemagne* (1810), translated here from the
1813 London reprint, ii. 327–8

Serious gaiety which turns nothing into a joke, but amuses without
trying to, and makes one laugh without the author having laughed;
this gaiety that the English call humour, is found also in several German works; but it is almost impossible to translate. When the joke
consists of a philosophical thought happily expressed, like Swift's
Gulliver, the change of language makes no difference; but Sterne's
Tristram Shandy loses almost all its charm in French. Jokes which depend
on words say perhaps a thousand times more to the mind than do ideas,
and yet one cannot transmit to foreigners these impressions which are
stimulated by such delicate nuances and are so vivid.

137. Garat on Sterne

1820

Extract from Dominique-Joseph Garat, *Mémoires historiques sur le XVIIIᵉ siècle et sur M. Suard* (1820), translated here from the second edition (1821), ii. 135–52.

Garat (1749–1833), one of Sterne's warmest admirers, was prominent politically, holding the posts of Minister of Justice and senator.

At almost the same time, another Englishman,[1] who was neither poet nor comedian, who was even a minister of the Anglican church, gave uncommon amusement to the gay spirits of Paris through his racy wit, and gave new emotions to tender souls through the most artless, ready, and touching sensibility: this was Sterne. He had a wife who was really his; he loved Eliza, who was the wife of another; and neither of them could keep him from being smitten continually with a momentary passion for every woman whose charms moved him. It was in loving them all so fleetingly that the minister of the gospel kept the purity of his worship in his heart.[2]

I do not know with certainty whether *Tristram Shandy* and the *Sentimental Journey* were known at Paris before Sterne was, or whether Sterne was known there before his works. But there have never been an author and his works who resembled each other more. To read them or to see and listen to him was nearly the same thing; and that perfect resemblance is what makes it more difficult to draw any other parallel, whether to his works or to the author.

Voltaire, however, has called Sterne 'England's second Rabelais,'[3] Swift being the first. Thus there are three Rabelaises, two in England, one in France. There must have been resemblances among these three writers, since Voltaire perceived them. There is one which anybody may see: buffoonery and philosophy are always very close to each

---

[1] Garat has just been speaking of Garrick.
[2] Cf. Nos 53k, 134. See also No. 53d, p. 187, n. 1.
[3] See No. 130a.

other in their works, and often mingled to the point where they are blended. But Rabelais and Swift make you think while making you laugh and never touch your heart. In Sterne, laughter, profound thoughts, and gentle tears can be found on the same page, and often in the same sentence.

What drama moves us more than the four or five chapters of the history of Lieutenant Le Fever? And that is the story of a sick man who comes to a town where no one knows him and dies twenty-four hours later.

The three Rabelaises delight in amusing both themselves and their readers with the *imbroglio* of their narratives and their opinions; but this art—for there is art in these disorders and in these confusions—is a handicap in some ways for the first two. They have so many threads to untwist and disentangle that these sometimes get lost or break in their hands: they lose their way in the web they have woven. Sterne enters into these labyrinths, he leaves them, he goes back, he sets himself up in them, without your ever worrying either about him or about yourself. When neither you, nor perhaps he, knows any longer where he is, he draws so clearly the things and the people he chances upon, he paints them with colors so life-like, that you forget everything in the enchantment of the portraits and the varied tableaux that he traces. He has the shading and the touch of all the great schools and all the great masters—the pencils and brushes of the Flemish, the Romans, and the French follow each other in the style of an Englishman, too original to be of any school and too filled with all the physical and moral impressions from nature herself not to render them by turns with the most lifelike manners of all the schools.

In the story of *the life and opinions of Tristram Shandy*, Tristram's birth is not completely over by the third volume; in the fourth he is barely in breeches; and one judges from the way that the story and the life proceed that when the story is finished, the life will have scarcely begun. But the story of Tristram is not really that of a man; it is that of human nature in Europe, as Sterne saw it.

Always himself torn between passions and virtues, Sterne paints men as not apparently much in control of their actions and their destinies; but this is neither the terrible and heroic fatalism of the Greeks and their tragic theatre, nor the comic and terrible fatalism of *Candide*.

Under the brush of Sterne, man is not imprisoned; he is tossed about. Among the madmen with which *Tristram Shandy* is peopled,

there are many who are gentle and kind; nearly all have their lucid
moments and then they feel the power of universal reason with a force
which would suffice for the liberty, the stability, and the happiness of
humankind. Corporal Trim and Uncle Toby feel, think, and act
sometimes like veritable Socrates's; but it is because they are good and
not because they have the faculty of reason.

Surrounded everywhere by the truth that nature presents to all
their senses, the characters of *Tristram Shandy* either do not grasp this
truth or let it escape when they have grasped it, never realizing that
they do not have it. In a sort of half-sleep, half-dream, they walk on
the brink of all delusions and crimes like somnambulists walking on
the edges of roofs and precipices. And Sterne apparently is afraid to
wake them fully or too fast, because a sudden and complete waking
might be fatal to somnambulists.

A very witty lady, Mlle. de Sommerie, who has written a book
with maxims worthy of La Rochefoucauld and portraits worthy of
La Bruyère,[1] used to say of Sterne that he only painted so many madmen because he was himself mad: but there are times when he takes
off this mask or drops it entirely. Ah! how reality which he represents
in its true light then appears, under his brushes, either etched with
biting clarity, or touching and luminous!

With what lightness and what grace, filled with gaiety and decency,
in the trip of the Abbess of Andoüillets, he holds up to universal
laughter, better than the poem of Vert-Vert,[2] that petty-mindedness
of the convents which disfigures and cheapens all ideas and impressions
of virtue! How he surpasses Gresset in the much more difficult achievement of having 'b' and 'f' fluttering not from the beak of a parrot
but from the pious lips of a saintly abbess and a young novice!

And in the sermon on conscience, which the reader is so astonished—
or rather so filled with wonder and admiration—to find in a book
which promises only jokes and pranks, how he raises himself above all
the philosophers and preachers in the solution of the most enigmatic
problems of the moral sense!

One can cite the authority of Voltaire, who would not have given
Sterne such a compliment if his conscience had permitted him to give
it to himself. 'Perhaps these important questions have never been

---

[1] For Mlle de Sommery see No. 134, p. 402, n. 1. For La Rochefoucauld and La Bruyère,
see No. 70d, n. 1.
[2] *Vert Vert* (1734) was an anticlerical poem by Jean Baptiste Louis Gresset (1709–77), containing ridicule of nuns.

better treated than in the comic novel *Tristram Shandy*, written by a parish priest named Sterne. It resembles those ancient little vases decorated with satyrs which contained precious essences.'[1] What we know and can surmise about Voltaire's opinions on religion gives still more weight to this authority.

The same stores of wit and sentiment are to be found in both the *Sentimental Journey* and *Tristram Shandy*. The former, for example, is no more a 'journey' than the latter is a 'life.' In both, the connections between one chapter and another, between one paragraph and the next, happen by chance, or appear to. If my manner of writing, says the author, is not the best, it is at least the most religious: 'I begin with writing the first sentence—and trusting to Almighty God for the second.'[2] Would our La Fontaine have said it better? Sterne says it again elsewhere; but here is the way he repeats himself. Judge if this is only repetition: 'I know what I am doing when I write the first sentence, and the first guides me to the last.' To choose well and state clearly that first sentence, men like Locke, Condillac[3] and all the true tutors of the human mind designate as the best method.

In *Tristram Shandy* it is Sterne's head which dominates; in the *Journey*, his heart.

It is in England, Tristram's native land and the land of fogs, of sombre passions and profound thoughts, that Sterne is most the jester and the gayest; it is in France, where one expects to hear all the tinkling little bells of folly, that Sterne experienced and that he gives the most touching impressions. It is perhaps art, since it is surprising; but it is also perhaps the local color of the painter—and a moral truth of the philosopher.

When a Frenchman travels in England, or an Englishman in France, one naturally expects a discussion of all the points of comparison in industry, in power, in genius, in liberty and in glory of the two nations; and if the journey is written by a man endowed with some talent for observation and analysis, it can stimulate progress in the two countries in the arts, in the sciences, in public administration, in the fortune of individuals and groups. Examples of this are rare but there are some. This lofty ambition would not have been beyond the genius and the understanding of Sterne.

[1] See No. 28c, p. 125, n. 2 and 130a.
[2] See *Tristram Shandy*, VIII. 2, p. 540.
[3] Étienne Bonnot de Condillac (1715–80), French philosopher and logician, helped to popularize Locke in France.

But this is not what he is looking for; he is not even looking for anything in particular, for thus he can better find what best suits him. He wanders in his country and other countries, in the midst of things belonging to the life common to all; the life in which there can be grandeur neither in events nor possessions, nor thoughts; the life which has always lacked observers as if it were unworthy of any interest, care, or improvement because it is the life of nearly everyone.

Sterne is always on the broad highways and in front of the post horses, in the streets, in the inns and the shops. ... Something of the soul of Sterne passes into the souls of all those who read him; one learns with him to feel with all his heart, to enjoy this host of good things, scattered by nature along all the paths of life and lost for everyone because all hearts are dried up by misery or by wealth, by meanness or by pride.

What a lesson Sterne gives to philosophic pride in the sadness and remorse which strike Yorick to the heart when by harsh truths he has wounded the poor Franciscan who begs for his convent, the good Father Laurence. ...

[Garat continues with praise for Father Laurence and for the skill with which Sterne moves from thoughts of the Bastille to the starling to the captive.]

Sterne's transitions do not always produce such surprises; they do not always jump and connect distances as immense as that between the cage of a starling and the vast empires of despotism; they do not always end by making the tears which have begun to fall at the bondage of a bird pour out because of the chains of humanity; but, always original and always natural, they join together the little and the great, since they are joined together under the view of Him who created both.[1]

Well, who has not been much more touched than surprised at the story of that unfortunate girl who lost her mind in losing her beloved, whose acquaintance we made in *Tristram* under the name of Maria and whom we find again with so many charms under the name of Juliet[2] in the *Journey*? Neither the madness of Clementine, nor the funeral procession of Clarissa,[3] with all the narrative talents of a great novel and all those of Richardson's genius, opens to greater depths of our souls

[1] Cf. Coleridge's similar remark in No. 116a.
[2] Maria became Juliet in Frénais's translation of *A Sentimental Journey*.
[3] The references are to Clementina della Porretta in Richardson's *The History of Sir Charles Grandison* and to the heroine of his *Clarissa*.

the sources of all tears. It is only a few pages, but one would think them taken from the history of God's chosen people; they prove that God's people are everywhere where there are feeling hearts. That celestial strain, so often found in Sterne, roused in Mr. Suard's breast the memory of all the consoling thoughts from his studies of the Bible in prison on the island of Sainte Marguerite.[1]

[Garat continues with a panegyric on Suard and a discussion of Suard's great fondness for Sterne.]

What convinced [Suard] most strongly that all was true in this Englishman, unique even for the English, was that he was always and everywhere the same; never fixed in his plans, and always carried away by his impressions; in our theatres, in our salons, on our bridges, always a little at the mercy of objects and people, always ready to be amorous or pious, to jest or to exalt. When he had stopped one day before the statue of Henry IV and was soon surrounded by a crowd attracted by his actions, he turned around and said to them: 'Why do you all look at me? Follow my example,' and all fell to their knees, as he had, before the statue. The Englishman forgot that it was the statue of a king of France. A slave would not have paid such tribute to Henry IV.

What then were the attributes, natural and acquired, of this genius whom we love as much as the greatest and who resembles them so little?

Mr. Suard asked Sterne himself that question and he felt certain he received a completely honest reply. Sterne attributed his 'originality' i n the first place to a constitution in which the sacred principle which forms the soul predominated, that immortal flame which nourishes and feeds upon life, which exalts and suddenly changes every sensation, and which is called 'imagination,' or 'sensibility,' according to whether it traces with the brush of the writer scenes or emotions. In the second place, to daily reading of the Old and New Testaments, books which accorded both with his taste and his profession. In the third place, to the study of Locke, which he had begun in his youth and which he continued all during his life, to that philosophy which those who are able to recognize it explicitly and implicitly will discover or sense in all his pages, in all his lines, in the choice of all his expressions; to that philosophy which is too religious to try to explain the miracle of sensation, but which, with the miracle for which it does not have the

---

[1] Suard was imprisoned for more than a year when he was seventeen for refusing to betray a friend who had been involved in a duel.

temerity to ask reason or accounting from God, unfolds all the secrets of the understanding, avoids errors, reaches truths open to all—a holy philosophy without which there could never be a true universal religion on the earth, nor a true morality, nor true power of man over nature.

138. Sterne in the standard reference works

1830, 1836

(a) Extract from Charles-Athanais Walckenaer, *Vies de plusieurs personnages célèbres des temps anciens et modernes* (1830), x. 419–30

Laurence Sterne is one of that small group of writers who have been able to interest and please by initiating us into the ramblings of their minds, the flights of their imaginations, the peculiarities of their characters. Sterne paints mankind while seeming only to try to amuse his readers and to make sport of them and of himself—while seeming occupied solely in studying his feelings, his tastes, his particular bents, in order to get an exact and meticulous understanding of the emotions which he feels and of the chance events which cause them. A more persuasive moralist because he tells a story rather than instructing; a slyer satirist because it is while shaking the jester's bells that he looses his sharpest arrows; a more moving storyteller because he puts more simplicity into his words, and seems to restrain his penetrating sensibility which betrays itself in reticence; a more entertaining buffoon because he does not try to be one, but merely gives in to the jovial temperament which propels him; finally, a more agreeable author because he always chats and never composes formally: such is Sterne, who certainly had no model and should never serve as one, because the style in which he excelled is against both reason and taste, because it is suited only to the genius that created it, and because even he has not been able to show us its advantages without illustrating at the same time its drawbacks and defects. . . .

The originality of [*Tristram Shandy*], the anguish that it gave its readers to guess the design, to discover the sense of certain passages which had none; the mad and often licentious gaiety which seemed to control the author; the pages of genuine pathos, and of deep philosophy; the oddness of the characters; the ridicule poured out on men for whom the gravity of their positions ought to have aroused respect—all combined to give this book an extraordinary success. But, at the same time, this success aroused the severity of the critics and the animosity of members of the clergy, who thought, and with reason, that the author did not show sufficient respect for his clerical character. . . .

The *Sentimental Journey* is incomparably the best of Sterne's works. It is the one that is often reprinted, the one that people like to reread in its entirety.

[Walckenaer quotes from Scott's *Lives of the Novelists* (see No. 123), reporting Scott's view that Sterne is guilty of plagiarism though Walckenaer's judgment is 'wholly different.']

It seems to us that in a work of imagination, a new style, when it is pungent and pleasing, is the principal merit of an author, and gives him claims to originality.

[Walckenaer summarizes Scott's discussion of Sterne's style and particularly Scott's charge that Sterne's style is 'affected.' He quotes Scott's conclusion that Sterne is 'one of the greatest plagiarists, and one of the most original geniuses whom England has produced.']

Such is Mr. Walter Scott's opinion of Sterne. It is true in certain respects; but it is neither exact nor just, because the censure and perhaps also the praise, are exaggerated. Scott's opinion seems to us entirely unjust, if it is applied to the *Sentimental Journey*, the best of Sterne's productions. After all, it is by the most perfect thing that he has left that an author should be judged.

(b) Extract from *Dictionnaire historique ou biographie universelle*, translated here from the eighth edition (1836), xviii. 576–7. The *Dictionnaire historique* was first published in 1781 under the editorship of François Xavier de Feller (1735–1802); the article on Sterne is unsigned

Sterne (Laurence), English priest and preacher, born in Clonmel, Ireland, in the year 1713, died in 1768, had the clowning and irreverent wit of Rabelais. He aroused laughter, not only by his witticisms, but by an odd face, and a manner of dressing more odd even than his face. . . . Two of his works have been translated into French. The first one is entitled a *Sentimental Journey*, . . . full of wit and trifles, and the second, *The Life and Opinions of Tristram Shandy*. . . . It is a continual jesting in the style of Scarron.[1]

[Quotes from the first paragraph of Walckenaer; No. 138a.]

[1] See No. 130b and p. 392, n. 1.

139. Charles Nodier on Sterne

1830

Nodier (1780–1844), an early master of the fantastic story and precursor of the Surrealists, maintained a salon for members of the Romantic school during the 1820s. He imitated Sterne, undertaking to tell the story of the King of Bohemia and his Seven Castles, which Trim and Uncle Toby somehow lost between them (*Tristram Shandy*, vol. VIII).

(a) Extract from *Histoire du Roi de Bohème et de ses sept chateaux* (1830), pp. 74–5

Nevertheless one must admit that of all the extravagances of which the most obscure man has bethought himself, alas! and the most indefatigable of arrangers of sentences (it is he himself who found for sentences the happy comparison with the stringed instrument which resounds only because it is empty), there is none as pitiful as the *History of the King of Bohemia and His Seven Castles*. We doubt in truth that there exists in any language a suitable term to characterize the daring of the bold scribe who was not afraid to mimic awkwardly what talent itself could not imitate, the originality of a writer. For Sterne was unique among writers and will forever remain unique in all ages; if he had been reserved by the providence of Genius for this reasonable, serious and powerful age in which all useful truths can be shown without a mask, he would have flung aside Trim's crutch and Tristram's bells! There was, however, at the bottom of his clever satire an interest in subject, a family, a plot, a novel.

(b) Extract from 'Miscellanées, variétés de philosophie, d'histoire et de littérature' (1830), translated here from *Oeuvres complètes*, v (1832). 16–21

Rabelais and Sterne have frequently been compared and the comparison is not merely one of those frivolous intellectual games which are good for nothing but producing texts for exercises in rhetoric and show-pieces for the Academy. These two great mockers have blazed a trail for modern philosophic thought. The first signals the gaining of religious independence; the second marks the achievement of political independence.

They are remarkable less for their goals than for the very style of their thought, since the man of genius is never entirely separated from the man himself in the character he imprints on his works. Rabelais, born at a time of growth and social ferment when the world seemed to be coming out of chaos a second time, had, himself, a vigorous, creative mind, though he was disposed to see things from that ridiculous aspect which everything on earth shares. Sterne, living in an age in which a decaying society had collapsed (rather than one in which a society was being born), living under the safeguard of a fairly widespread system of good breeding and social decorum, like all old men who try to appear agreeable, was inclined, rather, to treat the melancholy side of people's lives because he could not help but realize that he was living in the last stages of a dying age. The gaiety of Rabelais is that of a boisterous child who breaks his most precious toys in order to lay bare their mechanisms. The gaiety of Sterne is that of a slightly moody old man who amuses himself by pulling the strings of his puppets. In Rabelais the dominant spirit is unbridled laughter—and I know of no other expression to describe it. In Sterne the dominant spirit is a bitter consciousness of the deceptions of the heart, manifested now in laughter, now in tears, beneath which one always senses the poignant tortures of a concealed anguish. If Rabelais were not so incisive and so profound, he would be only the Democritus of his age. If Sterne were not so naturally pleasing, when he is willing to take the trouble to be, one would take him for the Heraclitus of his age.[1]

[1] Democritus, the 'Laughing Philosopher' (see No. 53d, p. 185, n. 1). and Heraclitus of Ephesus (c. 535–c. 475 BC), a pessimistic critic of mankind, were often paired to represent the possible extremes of philosophical positions.

Posterity will believe from reading them (and will not be mistaken) that Rabelais's time was much more ridiculous and Sterne's much sadder; but perhaps the difference does not stem solely from their differing sensibilities: old absurdities become sad.

Sterne's and Rabelais's stories differ at first glance because of the difference between observing society and observing the family. It is obvious that Rabelais set his scene outside the known world so that he could judge that world with complete freedom and thus he borrowed a fantastic tale from the old story-tellers. It is obvious that Sterne sought to achieve distance in the opposite way, by taking refuge in the farthest recesses of the inner life, and thus he restricted himself to unfolding some common domestic anecdotes. Rabelais forces the reader to stray outside of himself, but Sterne enters the reader himself to take him by surprise.

Rabelais lures his reader into the vast labyrinth of our vanities and our follies by the pleasant illusions which make him lose sight of his starting point and scorn the even less certain point where he will end. Sterne shows the reader the same subjects in a space so narrow, on the other hand, that the mind is amazed at having taken so many journeys without moving from one spot. But make no mistake—the mental horizon of the two writers is no broader in the imaginary cosmography of Xenomanes[1] than in Walter Shandy's parlor and Uncle Toby's bowling green. One would think that Rabelais had tried to make the reader excuse the caustic truth of his satire through the attractiveness of his fabrications. One would think that Sterne had tried to make the reader excuse the innocent fabrication of his story through the attractiveness of his truths. Rabelais is also truthful in his pictures but it is the truth of the malicious rough sketch which presents the face only from its bad side—like a caricature—and seizes upon the contours of a man's figure only to bend his noble lines into grotesque attitudes. Sterne, who perhaps did not see our nature from so high a vantage point nor with so much power, saw it, analyzed it, and described it full-face. Rabelais is one of those cynics whose boldness is justified by the institutions of a young and flourishing society and who attack it with their gibes under a sort of privilege, like the public insulters of the triumphs at the Capitol.[2] Sterne is one of those graceful

[1] Xenomanes, 'the great traveler,' guides Pantagruel on his voyages to fantastic countries in Rabelais's bk. IV.
[2] Under Roman custom, the soldiers following their general in a triumphal procession alternately sang songs in his praise and uttered ribald jests at his expense.

moralists who brighten the agony of dying peoples with a solemn smile and who scatter roses on their shroud.

It is not, moreover, for the critic to seek the exact expression of their similarities and their contrasting qualities—it is Sterne himself who alone could express them. The good and discerning Yorick—as Sterne has painted himself—is a wise man with a jovial and ever so slightly caustic spirit, but benevolent and urbane, and in a direct line of descent from a jester.

140. The first German translation of *Tristram Shandy*

1765

Extract from Johann Friedrich Zückert's preface to his translation of the first eight volumes of *Tristram Shandy* (1765).

Zückert (1739–78), who had published a translation of the first six volumes of *Shandy* in 1763, was a physician at Berlin devoting himself to research and study. He apparently was first drawn to Sterne by the discussions of the passions or 'humours' of man. For a review of Bode's later and more successful translation of *Tristram Shandy*, see No. 141b.

Herewith we deliver to the public the continuation of *The Life and Opinions of Mr. Tristram Shandy* in the present seventh and eighth parts which did not appear in London until this year. If the translator had anticipated all the difficulties he would later encounter so frequently in the translation, he would not have attempted such a ticklish book. The author of it, Mr. Sterne of London as we all know, doubtless had the intention to depict in a humorous manner the follies ingrained in his countrymen and, at the same time, to spread among his jests some serious truths. It was believed that some service would be done to the German public by translating this book, however difficult that task might be. The translator could not imagine that with a book of this kind there would be people who would demand of him that he should observe the same kind of precision in translating that is necessary with a classical author, where not a single word can be lost or changed. Tristram's very peculiar and desultory manner of writing—since he now presents things whose elucidation follows much later, now moves

from one thing to another without any connection, now uses disjointed sentences which, because they have not been completed, remain
obscure, now uses provincialisms which are unfamiliar to a German,
and lastly sometimes invents new words which can hardly be translated—and his long and involved sentences and his allusions to certain
persons and events which cannot even be familiar to every Englishman, must suffice to excuse the translator for his imperfect work. . . .
We ask the reader who is competent in English to judge this translation
according to its purpose, which is to cheer and delight the public and to
make a very marvelous genius known to the Germans.

141. Wieland on Sterne

1767, 1774

Christoph Martin Wieland (1733–1813), like Sterne, was known
for his handling of delicate and tender feelings. One of the
best-known poets of the day, he became an early champion of
Sterne both privately and publicly.

(a) Extract from Wieland's letter to J. G. Zimmermann, 13
November 1767, defending Sterne from a critic's attack, translated here from *Ausgewählte Briefe an verschiedene Freunde* (1815),
ii. 286–9

A propos Yorick, I have been not a little peeved lately to see my favorite
author *Tristram Shandy* judged so cold-bloodedly, perfunctorily and
picayunely in the new *Bibliothek der schönen Wissenschaften*. Thank
heavens that I have a very pretty London edition of it!
What poor souls the critics sometimes are! Works written for mere

entertainment, poems in the manner of Anacreon,[1] etc., are reviewed everywhere as important publications, and an extraordinary and admirable work like *The Life and Opinions of Tristram Shandy* they barely deem worthy to be remembered in passing. It is proper, so it is said, that we quote critics of his nation: 'What pity, that Nature should thus capriciously have embroidered the choicest flowers of genius on a [p]aultry Groundwork of bufoonery!'[2] The good critics! Indeed what a pity! that one can be a critic and not be ashamed of revealing so confidently the wrong side of his understanding. —I confess to you, my friend, that Sterne is almost the only author in the world whom I regard with a kind of awed admiration. I shall study his book as long as I live and will still not have studied it enough. I know of nothing else in which there is so much genuine Socratic wisdom, such sensitive feeling for the good and the beautiful, such an amount of new and fine moral observation, so much healthy judgment, combined with so much wit and genius. Who preaches as well as he when he wants to preach? Who can melt our hearts better than he when he wants to be moving? What author has ever developed a character so well as he did Uncle Toby and honorable Trim? And when he paints for us happy scenes of naively beautiful nature, what writer has ever been so much of a Correggio[3] as he? —I only regret that the Germans are familiar with this original work which cannot be compared with any other (to compare it with Rabelais is to judge it superficially) only through a miserable translation that is completely falsified in many places and is sometimes incomprehensible, a translation in which very frequently the finest features of the original are botched and in which nonsense is made of the most beautiful sense.[4]

(b) Extract from Wieland's review of Bode's translation of *Tristram Shandy* in *Der teutsche Merkur*, viii (1774). 247–8

We come too late to advertise or to extol this work—for where is the man of taste and understanding whose soul is sensitive to the caprices

[1] Anacreon, Greek lyric poet of the sixth century BC, was traditionally associated with the praise of wine and love.
[2] See No. 52d, final paragraph.
[3] Antonio Allegri Correggio (*c.* 1494–1534) was known for the vividness of his paintings, the beauty of his forms, and his concern for sentiment.
[4] See No. 140.

of genius, to wit and irony, to Attic and British, Cervantic and Rabelaisian and (to what is finer and more piquant than all of these four types), to Yorickean salt; whose soul is sensitive to everything that ever made a book so tasteful that one reads it, indeed, even prefers to read it, when one is disgusted with all the usual intellectual dishes—where is, I say, such a man who has not already had Bode's[1] *Tristram* in his hands, who would not rather sell all his other books and his coat and collar in addition, if need be, in order to procure this book, unique in its own way, this book with all its own and its author's eccentricities and oddities, this nevertheless invaluable book, in which wisdom deigns to appear as folly in order to please us fools better, this book written so very consciously for edification and instruction, for the correction and comforting of all human beings who have received from the hands of good old Mother Nature human understanding and sympathy and a little wit to boot—and from the moment of his procuring it to make it his favorite book and to read in it so often that all the pages become so torn and worn out that he—to the great pleasure of the publisher—must buy a new copy? If we are then too late to advertise this translation, it is certainly not too late to bestow upon the translator the gratitude he deserves for his work which perhaps he alone among all Germans was capable of, and whose infinite difficulty, after he had so happily overcome it, gives him an indisputable right to a great part of the fame that belongs to the original. This translation by Bode is not only a new one, it is really the only translation of *Tristram Shandy*. It appeases the shade of immortal Yorick; or rather, the spirit of Sterne himself descended upon Bode, filled him with all his caprice, opened to him an understanding of the most subtle beauties of his work, revealed to him everything, or at least almost everything, that was not also puzzling to the most injudicious readers of the original, taught him the secret of mixing the German language in such a way that he could copy the whole original in it with the least possible loss. In short, the spirit helped him to overcome all difficulties and thus we have gained not only an understandable and faithful translation of *Tristram*, a translation in which Sterne's spirit lives and moves, which speaks a language peculiar to him in which his own whimsy, his own air, all his Sterne-likeness prevails completely, but also a book that

[1] Sterne's popularity in Germany led Johann Bode, who had already translated the *Sentimental Journey*, to undertake a rival translation of *Tristram Shandy* to compete with Zückert's (see No. 140). Bode's more skillful translation appeared in 1774. For further information on Bode see No. 143.

considerably enriches our language and helps to develop it. Not to mention the practical aspect that it gives us by appearing just at this critical time when many minds are in danger of going overboard and when *Tristram* is a genuine, perhaps the only remedy which can stop the progress of the vertigo that has reached epidemic proportions.

142. Herder on Sterne

November 1768

Extract from a letter from Johann Gottfried von Herder to Johann Georg Hamann, November 1768, translated here from *Herders Briefe an Johann Georg Hamann* (1889), p. 49.

Herder (1744–1803), critic, philosopher, and Lutheran theologian, holds an important place in the development of German thought.

I cannot devour enough of Sterne's mood. Just at the moment that I am thinking of him, I receive his *Sentimental Journey* to read through, and if my knowledge of English will not prove inadequate, how gladly I will travel with him. I am already partly so accustomed to following his sentiments through their delicate threads all the way into the soft inner marrow of his humanity, that I think I understand his *Tristram* somewhat better than the common people. Therefore his cursed acid remarks and ambiguities which make the work less recommendable than it really deserves to be, irk me all the more.

143. *A Sentimental Journey* in German

1768

Extract from Johann Joachim Christoph Bode's preface in 1768 to his translation of *A Sentimental Journey*, translated here from the second edition (1769), pp. i–iv.

Bode (1730–93), a more skillful translator than Zückert (see No. 140), was responsible for starting the Sterne cult in Germany with his translation of *A Sentimental Journey*. The 'well-known German scholar' and 'friend' of Bode referred to below is Gotthold Ephraim Lessing (1729–81), leading critic and dramatist.

'Gladly,' said a well-known German scholar when I brought him the news of Sterne's death, 'gladly would I have given him five years of my own life, if that could be done, and even if I had known for certain that all that would remain to me were only eight or ten years. . . . With the stipulation however, that he would have had to write. It would make no difference what, life and observations, sermons and travels. . . .' This scholar, out of friendship for me and respect for the tasteful reader, took the effort to read through my translation, but if many errors remain, they are to be accounted to me alone. Just let me say this, however, about the adjective *empfindsam* for the English *sentimental*: At first I had rendered it by *sittlich* and other expressions as well. I also considered circumlocutions; but my friend coined the word *empfindsam*. As far as I am concerned he had a perfect right to do so, for his critical taste is a conscientious assayer. To be sure, he gave his reasons for it, perhaps only to please certain critics whose taste a pioneer translator has seldom met. Here are his own words: 'It is a matter of translating a word for a word, not one word with several. Consider that *sentimental* is a new word. If Sterne was permitted to invent a new word, then his translator is also permitted to do the same. The English had no adjective at all from *sentiment*; we have more than one from *Empfindung*: *empfindlich, empfindbar, empfindungsreich*, but all these say something different. Be bold! Say *empfindsam*! If a difficult journey is

427

a journey with much difficulty, then a sentimental journey can also be a journey with much sentiment. I am not saying that the analogy would be entirely to your advantage. But whatever the reader may not understand by the word at first, he will gradually become accustomed to understand.'

144. The Lorenzo cult

April 1769

Extract from a letter from Johann Georg Jacobi to Johann Wilhelm Ludwig Gleim, 4 April 1769, translated here from Jacobi's *Sämtliche Werke* (1819), pp. 105–9.

Jacobi (1740–1814) and Gleim (1719–1803) were among the group of Anacreontic lyric poets. On 4 April 1769, Jacobi sent Gleim a package containing a snuffbox with the inscription *Pater Lorenzo* on the outside of the cover and *Yorick* on the inside of it. The explanatory letter to Gleim, translated below, was written on the same day and sent under separate cover; it was published shortly thereafter in the *Hamburger-Correspondent*. Immediately after its appearance there was a great demand for Lorenzo snuffboxes. Some merchants took advantage of the situation and were sending such boxes all over German-speaking Europe, as well as to Denmark and Livonia. Soon there were rumors of a Lorenzo Order that had allegedly been founded by a man of great renown. Jacobi was appalled by the falseness of the sentiment and later explained the phenomenon by the fact 'that it was the sentimental period. Yorick had awakened in the better souls many a truly good feeling that lasted in its simplicity and purity; on the other hand, others sought to feel emotions through art which they would have liked to have, but which were not theirs, and still others contented themselves with the mere outward appearance of sentimentality.' (*Sämtliche Werke*, pp. 103–5)

Listen then, my dearest fellow, to the story of the snuffbox! A few days ago I was reading Yorick's journey to my brother, who feels the same about things as I do, and to a circle of unfeeling women. We came to the story of the poor Franciscan Lorenzo who asked Yorick for alms, was sent packing by him, but made the Englishman regret it by his gentle demeanor, and received from him later as a sign of reconciliation a tortoise-shell box, for which he gave him his own of

429

horn, etc. We read how Yorick used this box to conjure up the gentle
patient spirit of its former owner and to keep his own from being lost
in the worldly struggles that had to be fought. 'The good monk had
died; Yorick sat at his grave, pulled the small box out, pulled some
nettles from the head of the grave, and wept.' We looked at each other
in silence; each was happy to find tears in the eyes of the other; we
celebrated the death of the revered old man Lorenzo and of the good-
hearted Englishman. Our hearts said to us: Yorick would have loved
us if he had known us; and the Franciscan, we believed, deserved to
be canonized more than all the saints of the legends. Meekness, contentment with the world, indefatigable patience, forgiveness for the failings
of humanity, these initial virtues he teaches his pupils. How much
better they are than the pious pride of the majority of endowed orders!
How sweet the memory of the sublime monk was to us, and of the
one who learned from him so willingly! Much too sweet not to be
preserved by something palpable. We all bought a snuff box of horn,
upon which we had printed in golden letters the writing which is on
yours. We all took a vow to give something to every Franciscan who
would ask us for a donation because of holy Lorenzo. If one of our
company should become angered, then his friend need only hold out
to him the box and we have too much feeling to resist this memory
even in the greatest anger. Our ladies, who do not use tobacco, must
at least have a box like this standing on the night table; for to them
belong to a higher degree the gentle emotions which we were to
receive from their glances, from their tone, from their judgments. It
was not enough for us to have made this agreement in a small circle;
we also wished that other friends would do the same. To several we
sent the present that you are getting as an insignia of a holy order;
this letter is to impart our thoughts to others. Many readers will feel
nothing thereby, others will not have the courage to pledge themselves
to a struggle with themselves, still others will even be petty enough to
appeal to their wealth which a box of horn seems to them to insult.
The first we pity, of the second we hope for improvement, and the
third do not exist for us. Perhaps in the future I shall have the pleasure
of meeting here and there in strange places a stranger who will hand
me his box of horn with the golden letters. I shall embrace him as
familiarly as a free mason embraces another after receiving the sign.
O how I would rejoice if I could introduce such a dear custom among
my fellow citizens! Then religion would no longer separate them; they
would have a common saint. The Protestant clergyman would call

the Catholic monk his friend, forgive him for wearing a long grey garment; and the monk would learn during his pilgrimages to the chapel in the sylvan glade to love all men because of the godhead who out of love created the glade for all men.

145. Goethe on Sterne

1772, 1820–2, 1826, 1828, 1829, 1830

Johann Wolfgang von Goethe (1749–1832), giant of the German literature of the latter eighteenth and early nineteenth centuries, was a lifelong admirer of Sterne. The selections below include his earliest mention of Sterne and his comments toward the end of his career when he reread Sterne and assessed Sterne's influence upon his early development. In between there were numerous allusions to Sterne in Goethe's letters. All of the selections below are translated from W. R. R. Pinger, *Laurence Sterne and Goethe* (1918), a convenient repository of all Goethe's references to Sterne.

(a) Extract from a review of an imitation of Sterne, *Frankfurter Gelehrte Anzeigen* (3 March 1772)

Alas the [sic] poor Yorick! I visited your grave and I found—as you did upon the grave of your friend Lorenzo—a nettle. . . . Yorick felt, and this fellow sits down to feel. Yorick is moved by his mood, he cried and laughed in a single minute, and through the magic of empathy we laugh and cry along with him. But here one stands and deliberates: How do I laugh and cry?

(b) Extract from *Campagne in Frankreich 1792*, 1820–2, describing the relationship between Goethe's *Werther* and Sterne's work

At its appearance in Germany *Werther* did not in the least excite the sickness, the fever, of which it has been accused; it merely uncovered the sickness that already lay concealed in young dispositions. During a long happy peace a literary-esthetic development had taken place successfully on German soil within the national language; because the emphasis was on the inner being, a certain sentimentality soon joined it, in whose origin and progress one must not fail to recognize the influence of Yorick-Sterne. Even if his spirit did not hover above the Germans, his emotion was communicated all the more vividly. A kind of tenderly passionate asceticism came into being which, since the humorous irony of the Briton had not been bestowed upon us, usually had to degenerate into a tiresome self torture.

(c) Extract from *Über Kunst und Alterthum. Lorenz Sterne*, written 5 January 1826

It usually happens in the swift process of literary as well as human development that we forget to whom we are indebted for our first stimulations, for our primary impressions. . . . It is for this reason that I call attention to a man who initiated and fostered the great epoch of purer knowledge of human nature, of noble toleration, gentle love, in the second half of the previous century.

I am often reminded of this man to whom I owe so much; I also think about him when people speak of errors and truths which fluctuate among men. In a more delicate sense one can add a third word, namely, *peculiarities*. For there are certain human phenomena which one best expresses with this word. They are mistakenly attributed to things outside of man, are truly within him, and when properly regarded are psychologically most important. They are what constitutes the individual; through them the general is particularized and in the most peculiar there is still perceptible some understanding, reason, and good will that attracts and fascinates us.

In this sense Yorick-Sterne, most tenderly uncovering the human in the human being, very graciously called these peculiarities, in so far as they express themselves in action, *ruling passions*. For in truth it is these which drive a person in a particular direction and push him along on a straight track, and, without need of reflection, conviction, purpose or will power, keep him moving along through life. How closely habit is related to these is immediately obvious: for it favors the ease with which our peculiarities like to meander along undisturbed.

(d) Extracts from a series of aphorisms, probably composed in 1828, *Aus Makariens Archiv, Wilhelm Meisters Wanderjahre*, 2nd ed.

Yorick-Sterne was the most beautiful spirit that ever lived; who reads him immediately feels free and beautiful; his humor is inimitable, and not all humor frees the soul. . . .

Even now at this moment every educated person should take Sterne's works in hand so that the 19th century may also learn what we owe him and realize what we can still borrow from him. . . .

A free soul like his runs the risk of becoming impudent if a noble good will does not restore moral equanimity.

Since he was easily stimulated, everything developed from within him; through constant conflict he distinguished the true from the false, held firmly to the former and was ruthless against the latter.

He felt a definite hatred for seriousness because it is didactic and dogmatic and very easily becomes pedantic, qualities which he despised. Thus his antipathy toward terminology.

In the most varied studies and reading he uncovered everywhere the inadequate and the absurd.

He calls Shandeism the impossibility of thinking about a serious subject for two minutes.[1]

This rapid change from seriousness to levity, from involvement to indifference, from sorrow to joy, is said to lie in the Irish character.

Sagacity and penetration are infinite with him.

His cheerfulness, contentment, patience while traveling—wherever these qualities are most severely tried, they will not easily find their equal.

[1] See *Letters*, p. 139.

As much as the sight of a free soul of this sort delights, we are reminded just as much in this case that we cannot assimilate all—perhaps not most—of what delights us.

The element of concupiscence in which he behaves so gracefully and sensibly would suffice to destroy many another.

His relationship with his wife as well as to the world is worthy of note. 'I did not use my misery like a wise man,'[1] he says somewhere.

He jokes very graciously about the contradictions which make his condition ambiguous. . . .

He is a model in nothing and a guide and stimulator in everything.

(e) Extract from *Journal*, 20 December 1829

Effects of Sterne and Goldsmith. The high ironic humor of both, the former inclined toward formlessness, the latter moving freely within the strictest form. Later the Germans were made to believe that the formless was the humorous.

(f) Extract from a letter to C. F. Zelter, 25 December 1829

Recently *The Vicar of Wakefield* came into my hands; I was compelled to reread the little work from the beginning to the end—being not a little touched by the lively memory of how much I had become indebted to its author during the seventies. It would be impossible to reckon how much effect Goldsmith and Sterne had upon me during this main period of my development. This high good-natured irony, this fairness in view of everything, this gentleness in the face of all adversity, this steadfastness in the face of all change, and all related virtues educated me in the most praiseworthy manner, and in the end it is, after all, these sentiments which finally lead us back from all the false steps we take in life.

It is strange that Yorick is inclined more and more toward formlessness and that Goldsmith is all form, to which I also devoted myself, while the worthy Germans had convinced themselves that formlessness was the quality of true humor.

[1] See ibid.

(g) Extract from *Journal*, 1 October 1830

Read much concerning current events. Finally read in *Tristram Shandy* and admired again and again the freedom to which Sterne had risen during his day, understood also his influence upon our youth. He was the first to raise himself and us from pedantry and Philistinism.

(h) Extract from a letter to C. F. Zelter, 5 October 1830

Recently I took another glance at Sterne's *Tristram* which, at the time that I was a miserable student, had caused much sensation in Germany. With the years my admiration has increased and is still increasing; for who in 1759 recognized pedantry and Philistinism so well and described it with such good humor. I still have not met his equal in the broad field of literature.

146. Von Blanckenburg: Sterne as humorist

1774

Extract from Friedrich von Blanckenburg, *Versuch über den Roman* (1774), translated here from the facsimile edition (1965), pp. 191–200.

Von Blanckenburg (1744–96), after retiring from the army when he was forty, devoted his life to literary projects, including translations.

But I do not believe that a humorous character must always have ridiculous and crass eccentricities. The eccentricity itself I gladly grant. It is the main ingredient of humor in general. I feel that one can love such a man completely—and even more than that—one can respect him. Both of these, and especially the latter, are emotions which according to Home[1] one cannot feel for a humorist. I admit that few persons are as close to my heart as Captain Shandy and Corporal Trim. At any rate, I would not care to have as a friend the man who despises them both because their inclinations simply all tend in one direction and are the kind one attributes to the early years of life. They treat everything they come upon as a soldier would and they relate everything they hear to the warrior's frame of reference. But they do it so innocuously, so innocently, and often so nobly, that the preponderance of this inclination, to my mind, does not detract from them. Let it be remembered that it is this very inclination which, in the story of the unfortunate Le Fever, seems so effective, so attractive.

I think that one might in general divide all humorists into two classes. One can be a humorist of the intellect, or of the heart, i.e., by a peculiar way of thinking and regarding everything, or through peculiar emotions and feelings to which one abandons oneself fully and without constraint. In *The Life and Opinions of Tristram* one finds examples of both kinds: Tristram's father for the first and Uncle Toby

[1] The reference is to Henry Home, Lord Kames (1696–1782), author of *Elements of Criticism*, which was translated into German by Meinard in 1763–8 and had some influence on German critical theory.

and Trim for the other. Both kinds can, of course, be united in one character, and to a certain extent both must be united. But I think that if one or the other dominates, one should call the work by that name if one wants to give it a proper designation.

Part of what Home says about humor seems to fit the humorist of the first type. Because he views and judges all external objects from his own peculiar way of thinking, it is only natural that his opinions must be at odds with the opinions of others. . . . Whether this man is worth laughing at or not depends upon the objects he criticizes and he situation in which he criticizes them, as well as whether he observes them from this side or that. But one does the humorist a disservice if one believes that he can regard all things only from a single point of view. He can regard them all more or less seriously and as important according to the tenor of his temperament and his particular situation. But if he were never to change his position, then he would soon become less than individual; he would become monotonous and be a mere skeleton of a character. . . . If the humorist, either by virtue of his temperament or his general viewpoint, concerns himself with insignificant objects and considers them important, or if he sees in important objects only the insignificant, or being full of them, completely fails to observe the truly more important aspects of them, or if he simply sees in each one of these objects what others do not see, and thus judges them as others do not, then this can perhaps detract from the man's stature. Thus we laugh at the ship's Captain Trunnion in *Peregrine Pickle*; also at times at Tristram's father. Matthew Bramble (in *The Expedition of Humphry Clinker*) also belongs with these humorists; but his humor is more serious and even if, in certain incidents, we twist our mouths toward laughter, we still love the man from our whole heart, as soon as we know him better, more for his humanity and mildness. . . .

The second type of humor—which arises when a human being without any regard for others abandons himself almost exclusively to the inclinations of his heart and thus feels that the way in which others think and evaluate is peculiar—must certainly not be projected into a man whose heart is not capable of a noble sentiment and whose inclinations might be directed toward indecent and vile things. I have already named Uncle Shandy and Corporal Trim as very attractive examples. One could also count good Don Quixote here. In the knight Hudibras[1] both kinds are united. He thinks and he acts uniquely, but

[1] See No. 96, n. 1.

the writer has deliberately given him certain eccentricities which make him more than ridiculous. . . .

If a writer wants to prove himself in both kinds of humor, then he must study diligently the writings of the Englishmen, among whom Sterne stands far above the rest.

147. The extremes of sentimentality

1780, 1781

(a) The poem 'Der Empfindsame,' by L. F. G. Goeckingk (1748–1828), satirical poet and politician (translated here from *Gedichte von L. F. G. Goeckingk* (1780), iii. 176–8)

Mr. Mops, whose every third word is sentimentality and who breaks out in a torrent of tears whenever a blade of grass withers, greeted as a 'novel-smith' the author's trade and then me too.

With my wife he is immediately as familiar as a Frenchman. He kept offering her tobacco from a beggar's snuff box with which he made an exchange like Yorick and slept deeply near the fence.

Mocking the unsentimental, he held a funeral sermon for a mosquito in a glass. When a fly buzzed around his nose, he opened the window and said, 'Fly after Uncle Toby's fly!'

Truly my maid is no longer in her right mind because of Mops. His praise has so delighted her that she openly and freely, in a sentimental manner, permits all the spiders to weave their webs in my house.

He stepped upon my dog's leg. Heavens! What lamenting! It could have moved a paving stone to pity. Even the little dog soon wagged his tail in forgiveness.

O little dog, you shame me deeply. For Mops stole three hours of my life from me. How sad, how sad. Will I be able to forgive him that? And the spiders to boot will be the death of me yet.

(b) The novel *Der Empfindsame* (1781–3), by Christian Friedrich Timme (1752–88) satirizes and burlesques Sterne's sentimental side, as well as Goethe's *Werther* and Johann Martin Miller's *Siegwart*, popular sentimental works of the German Storm and Stress movement.

Extract from chapter I (1781), translated here from Harvey Waterman Thayer, *Laurence Sterne in Germany* (1905), p. 169

Every nation, every age has its own doll as a plaything for its children, and sentimentality is ours. Hardly had kindly Sterne mounted his hobbyhorse and paraded it before us, when—as is usual in Germany— all the youngsters gathered around him, forced themselves upon him, or quickly carved an imitation hobbyhorse, or broke sticks from the nearest fence, or tore the first suitable cudgel from a bundle of twigs, mounted it and rode after him with such a vengeance that they produced a whirlwind which carried along like a swift torrent everything that came too close to it. If it had only been limited to the youngsters, it would not have been so bad. Unfortunately men also got a taste for the jolly little game, sprang off their path, and with sticks and daggers and clerical wigs galloped along behind the boys. To be sure, none overtook their master, whom they soon lost sight of. Now they are making the most nonsensical leaps in the world and yet each one of the apes imagines he is riding as beautifully as Yorick.

148. Tieck on Sterne

1795

Extract from Ludwig Tieck, *Peter Lebrecht* (1795), translated here from Tieck's *Schriften* (1829), xv. 18.

Tieck (1773–1853), novelist, dramatist, and miscellaneous writer, was prominent in the Romantic movement.

O, philanthropic Sterne! how dear you have always been to me above all writers because you do not try to excite our indignation toward human follies and weaknesses, because you do not wield the scourge of satire, but you laugh at and pity yourself and your fellow men alike.

149. Lichtenberg on Sterne

1772–5, 1799, 1800

Georg Christoph Lichtenberg (1742–99) has been called the chief German satirist of the eighteenth century and has been compared to Swift. He twice visited England in the 1770s.

(a) Extract from *Aphorisms* (1772–5), translated here from *Georg Christoph Lichtenbergs Aphorismen*, ed. Albert Leitzmann, vol. 131 of *Deutsche Literaturdenkmale des 18. and 19. Jahrhunderts* (1904), p. 135

I would like to have had Swift as my barber, Sterne as my hairdresser, Newton at breakfast, Hume at coffee.

(b) Extract from *Beobachtungen über den Menschen* (1799), translated here from Lichtenberg's *Vermischte Schriften* (1844), i. 184–6

I cannot help rejoicing whenever the good souls who read Sterne with tears of delight in their eyes believe that the man is reflected in his book. The Sternean simplicity of manners, his warm, sensitive heart, his soul that is sympathetic to everything noble and good, and other such phrases, and the sigh 'alas poor Yorick!' which expresses them all simultaneously, have become like proverbs to us Germans. Presumably this was attributed to a man who had more taste than knowledge of the world, without any further investigation. For those who quote Sterne the most are not those who are capable of appreciating an extremely witty, sly, and flexible judge of the world. One can extinguish the impression upon the mind made by ten proverbs more easily than one impression made upon the heart—and recently people have even placed honest Asmus[1] second to him. That is going too far. Is the good soul of this *Wandsbecker*, known not only from his writing but also for his deeds, to be inferior to Sterne because a false mirror reflects a pleasant image of the latter to us, or seems to? One book can reflect the whole soul of its author, but it betrays a great ignorance of the world and the human heart when one believes this of Yorick's writings. Yorick was a creeping parasite, a flatterer of the Great and an unbearable burr on the clothes of those at whose expense he had determined to feast. . . . A learned and very upright Englishman once asked me, 'What do you think of our Yorick in Germany?' I said he was adored by a great number and that critics of this type of writing who did not exactly adore him all considered him nevertheless to be an exceptional and unique man in his way. I did not find that people thought of him like that in England— 'I beg your pardon,' was the answer. 'One thinks of him exactly that way in England. Only because we know him better, the praise is mitigated by the ugliness of his personal character, for he was a man who used his extraordinary talents mainly to play mean tricks.' I know many, perhaps most of my readers will consider this outright slander. 'Is it not a shame,' they will say, 'to plant nettles on the grave of the one who so tenderly tore them from the grave of Lorenzo?' 'But who would not have torn them out,' I would answer, 'had a duke extended an invitation to him, or if pulling out nettles had not sounded so fine to the inimitable pleasant babbler and painter of emotions?' With wit, combined with worldly knowledge, with flexible nerves, and the intention to appear original, strengthened by some interest, much that is strange in the world becomes possible, when one is weak enough to want it, unfamiliar enough with genuine fame to find it pretty, and has time enough to carry it out.

(c) Extract from *Ästhetische Bemerkungen* (1800), translated here from *Vermischte Schriften*, ii. 11–12

There is, as I have often observed, an unfailing sign as to whether the man who wrote a touching scene, really felt as he wrote, or whether he

[1] Pen name for Matthias Claudius (1740–1815), poet who was sentimental and humorous (in the root sense). He published his work in the *Wandsbecker Bote*. For another comparison of Sterne and Asmus, see No. 159.

enticed tears from us through an exact knowledge of the human heart merely by knowing how and by a clever selection of moving characteristics. In the first case he will never suddenly give up his victory over us at the end of the scene. As his passion cools, ours cools also, and he distracts us without our noticing it. In the latter case, on the other hand, he seldom takes the trouble to make use of his victory, but often plunges the reader—more to the credit of his art than his heart—into another kind of mood which costs him nothing of himself but wit, and deprives the reader of everything he had gained before. I think that Sterne belongs to the second case. The expressions with which he seeks to win approval from one seat of judgment are often incompatible with the victory he has just won from the other. . . .

Sterne does not stand on a very high rung, nor walk on the noblest path. Fielding does not stand even quite so high, but walks on a much more noble path. It is the very path that the man will tread who will one day become the greatest writer in the world. Fielding's *Foundling*[1] is truly one of the best works that has ever been written. If he had been able to make his Sophia a little more appealing to us, and if he had often been briefer where we hear only him, then there would perhaps be no work to surpass it.

[1] I.e. *Tom Jones; or, the History of a Foundling.*

150. Novalis on Sterne

1799–1801

Extracts from notes on Sterne and Jean Paul Richter, made between 1799 and 1801, translated here from *Novalis Schriften* (1901), ii. 2, p. 524; ii. 1, p. 221.

Novalis (pseudonym for Friedrich Leopold, Baron von Hardenberg) (1772–1801), poet and philosopher, was a leader in the Romantic movement.

Jean Paul could perhaps be called a humoristic epic writer. He is only a (instinctive) natural, encyclopedic humorist. (Encyclopedism bears a close relationship to philology.)

Character of loquacity. Loquacity of humor. Tristram Shandy; Jean Paul.

151. Friedrich Schlegel on Sterne

1800

Extract from *Gespräch über die Poesie* (1800), translated here from *Sämtliche Werke*, v (1823). 287–91.

Karl Wilhelm Friedrich von Schlegel (1772–1829), poet, philologist, philosopher, and literary critic, gave impetus to the new Romantic criticism which attempted to interpret works in the light of the creative individuality of their authors. The selection below, which first appeared in the leading Romantic periodical, the *Athenäum*, is part of a 'Letter on the Novel' read aloud by one of the characters in a symposium.

On the other hand you will perhaps still remember that there was a time when you loved Sterne, often delighted in assuming his style, partly to imitate and partly to deride. I still have several of your amusing little letters of this kind which I shall carefully preserve. Sterne's humor most certainly did leave its definite impression upon you. Even though it was not an idealistically beautiful one, it was nevertheless a mode, a genial mode which therefore took possession of your imagination; and an impression that remains so distinct, which we can employ and mold for humor and for seriousness, is not wasted. And what can have a more basic value than that which excites or nourishes the play of our imagination in some way?

You feel yourself that your delight in Sterne's humor was pure and entirely different from the excitement of curiosity that a completely bad book can often elicit from us at the very moment we realize that it is bad. Now ask yourself whether your enjoyment was not related to what we often felt while observing that clever game of paintings called arabesques. —In case you cannot liberate yourself from a share of Sterne's sentimentality, I am sending you herewith a book about which I must tell you in advance, however, so that you will be careful of foreigners, that it has the misfortune or fortune of being a little in disrepute. It is Diderot's *Fatalist*. I think you will like it and you will find the abundance of wit in it quite free of sentimental admixtures. It is planned with understanding and executed with a sure hand. I may call it a work of art without exaggeration. To be sure, it is not great literature, but only an arabesque. But for that very reason it has, in my opinion, no small claims. For I consider the arabesque to be a very definite and essential form of literature. . . .

Literature is so deeply rooted in the human being that even among the most unfavorable circumstances it grows at times wild. In the same way that we find traditional among almost all peoples songs, stories in circulation, some sort of plays (even if crude); we also find some individuals (even in our prosaic age), the members of those classes which write prose—I mean the so-called scholars and educated people—who have felt within them a rare originality of imagination and who have expressed it (although they were still quite far from genuine art). The humor of a Swift, of a Sterne, I mean to say, is the natural poetry of the higher classes of our age. . . .

We must not make the demands upon the men of our present era too high in this essay; what has grown up under sickly conditions can obviously be nothing but sickly. I regard this more as an advantage as long as the arabesque is not a work of art but a product of nature, and I place Richter therefore above Sterne because his imagination is far sicklier, that is, far more strange and fantastic. Just read Sterne again. It has been a long time since you have read him, and I think he will strike you differently now than he did then. Compare our German writers with him constantly. He really has more wit, at least for the reader who takes his works that way: for he might easily do an injustice to himself in them. And through this advantage even his sentimentality seems to rise above the sphere of English sentimentalism.

152. Jean Paul Richter on Sterne

1804

Extract from Jean Paul Richter, *Vorschule der Aesthetik* (1804), translated here from the 1813 edition, pp. 218-20.

Jean Paul (or Johann Paul Friedrich Richter) (1763-1825) was Germany's most important humorist. He was frequently compared with Sterne; see, e.g., Nos 122, 125, 150, 154.

Indeed, seriousness proves itself to be a requirement of humor even in individuals. The serious clerical class had the greatest comic writers, Rabelais, Swift, Sterne. . . . This fruitful injection of humor into seriousness can be confirmed even more by going off on tangents. For example, serious nations had the greatest and most profound sense of the comic; not counting the serious British, the Spaniards, who are just as serious, deliver (according to Riccobini)[1] more comedies than the Italians and French put together. . . . If one cites these historical coincidences without assuming them to be sharply decisive, then one can perhaps continue and even add that melancholy Ireland has produced masterful comedians among whom, after Swift and Sterne, also Count Hamilton must be named who, like the famous Parisian Carlin, was so quiet and serious in life.[2]

[1] Luigi Riccobini (*c.* 1674-1753) wrote on comedy and the history of the theatre.
[2] Anthony Hamilton (1646(?)-1720), known as Count Hamilton, though born in Ireland, spent much of his life in France. He was the author of *Mémoires de la vie du Comte de Grammont* (1713), which has a vivacious, often brilliant style, but Hamilton was said to have been 'naturally grave' and displayed 'little readiness of wit in conversation' (DNB). Carlo Bertinazzi (*c.* 1713-83), celebrated mime and Harlequin known as Carlin, suffered from ill health and was often in pain when he performed his comic routines on the stage.

153. Hegel on Sterne

1818–26

Extract from Georg Wilhelm Friedrich Hegel, *Vorlesungen über die Aesthetik* (1835), translated here from *Werke* (1843), x. pt. 2. 228.

Hegel (1770–1831) investigated the relationship of philosophy to history, government, and esthetics. The selection below, though not published until posthumously in 1835, was based on lectures Hegel gave between 1818 and 1826.

For true humor which seeks to avoid these excesses much depth and richness of spirit are therefore required in order that the genuinely expressive may be abstracted from what appears merely subjective and that the substantial may be extracted from its accidental qualities and from mere fancies. The self-abandonment of the author in the course of his discourse must, as with Sterne and Hippel,[1] be an unselfconscious, relaxed, unpretentious nonchalance that in its very insignificance gives the greatest depth; and since we are dealing only with details which bubble up without any order, the inner coherence must lie all the deeper and must produce in the isolated details as such the focal point of the spirit.

[1] Theodor Gottlieb von Hippel (1741–96), satirical and humorous writer, was known for his constant digressions and was frequently compared to Richter and to Sterne, who influenced him significantly.

154. Heine on Sterne and Jean Paul

1830s

Extract from Heinrich Heine, *Die Romantische Schule*, translated
here from *Sämtliche Werke* (n.d.), v. 330–2, 338.

Heine (1797–1856), giant among the German lyric poets, was
working on *Die Romantische Schule* near the beginning of the decade
though the complete German version of the book did not appear
until 1836, following an earlier shorter edition in 1833 and a first
edition in French the same year.

Jean Paul is a great poet and philosopher, but one cannot be more
unartistic in writing and thinking than he. In his novels he has given
birth to genuinely poetic forms, but all these births drag about with
them a foolishly long umbilical cord, and they entangle and choke
themselves with it. Instead of thoughts he actually gives us his thought
process itself; we see the physical activity of his brain. He gives us, as
it were, more brain than thought. His jests hop about in all directions
like the fleas of his heated intellect. He is the most humorous writer
and at the same time the most sentimental. Indeed, his sentimentality
always gets the better of him and his laughter suddenly turns to tears.
He often disguises himself as a rude and beggarly fellow, but then
suddenly, like the prince incognito of the stage, he unbuttons his coarse
overcoat and we then behold the gleaming star.

In this respect Jean Paul closely resembles the great Irishman with
whom he is often compared. The creator of *Tristram Shandy*, having
become lost in the coarsest trivialities, by a sublime transition can
also remind us suddenly of his princely dignity and his equality with
Shakespeare. Like Laurence Sterne, Jean Paul too, has laid bare his
personality in his writings. He has likewise revealed his human foibles,
but with a certain helpless timidity, particularly as far as sex is concerned. Laurence Sterne shows himself to his public completely un-
clothed; he is stark naked. Jean Paul, on the other hand, has only holes
in his trousers. Some critics wrongly believe that Jean Paul possessed

more genuine feeling than Sterne because the latter, as soon as the subject he is treating reaches tragic heights, suddenly switches to the most humorous, chuckling tone; whereas Jean Paul gradually begins to snivel and quietly permits his tear ducts to drain dry whenever his humor becomes the least serious. Nay, Sterne felt perhaps more deeply than Jean Paul, for he is a greater poet. He is, as I have already mentioned, of equal birth with Shakespeare; Laurence Sterne was also raised on Parnassus by the Muses. But as is the way with women, they soon spoiled Sterne with their caressing. He was the darling of the pallid goddess of tragedy. Once during an attack of cruel tenderness she kissed his young heart so violently, so passionately, with such ardent suction, that his heart began to bleed and suddenly understood all the sufferings of this world and was filled with infinite compassion. Poor young poet's heart! But the younger daughter of Mnemosyne, the rosy goddess of humor, quickly ran and took the suffering boy in her arms and tried to cheer him up with laughing and singing, and gave him the comic mask and the jester's little bells to play with, and soothingly kissed his lips and kissed upon them all her frivolity, all her defiant gaiety, all her witty teasing.

And since then Sterne's heart and Sterne's lips have been in strange contradiction. Sometimes when his heart is very tragically moved and he is about to utter the deepest feelings of his bleeding heart, then, to his own astonishment, the most delightfully funny words flutter from his lips. . . .

The author of *Tristram Shandy* reveals to us the remotest recesses of the soul. He tears a rent in the soul, permits us a glance into its abysses, paradises, and dirty corners and immediately lets the curtain fall again before it. We have looked inside that strange theatre from the front; lighting and perspective have not failed in their effects; and after thinking we have looked into the infinite, we have attained a consciousness of the infinite and the poetic.

155. The Dutch translation of *Tristram Shandy*

1777

Extract from an unsigned review of the second part of Bernardus Brunius's translation of volume I of *Tristram Shandy* in *Vaderlandsche Letteroefeningen*.

This selection, as are all those in this section on the Dutch criticism, is reprinted in F. Louise W. M. Buisman-de Savornin Lohman, *Laurence Sterne en der Nederlandse schrijvers van c. 1780–c. 1840* (1939). In each case the page reference in Lohman will be given at the beginning of the passage. The following passage is found in Lohman, p. 58.

This piece, written in the same manner as the previous one, also includes numerous flashes of wit and whimsical humorous inventions that are primarily intended to ridicule many characters and to mock many people's ways of thinking and reasoning. Most writers think for their readers, but the creator of this work can almost be said to write in order to make his readers think.

156. Ockerse on Sterne

c. 1782, 1788, 1819

Willem Antony Ockerse (1760–1826), theologian, critic, and miscellaneous writer, served as pastor of a Reformed church for ten years before being forced by ill health to give up his church in 1795. He held various positions in public life and returned to the ministry in 1810.

(a) Comment, written about 1782, translated here from *Vruchten en Resultaten van een zestigjarig Leven* (1823), iii. 42 (Lohman, pp. 37–8)

After Sterne's *Sentimental Journey* and Blum's *Sentimental Wanderings*,[1] sentiment is so much in vogue that one may assume it as a livery of the lovesick world. The materials are to be obtained in every bookstore, from every riding master of the sentiments, for a moderate price . . . and the sentimentalist's status is so secure that no French droit d'aubaine[2] could seize it from him, living or dying, unless all of tenderhearted Europe were outlawed at the same time.

(b) Extract from *Ontwerp tot een Algemeene Characterkunde* (1788), p. 131 (Lohman, p. 38)

After Sterne, one strikes literary sparks even from a gallows, a rock, or giant bones.

[1] Joachim Christian Blum (1739–90), German miscellaneous writer, published *Spaziergange* in 1774.
[2] See No. 56c, p. 199, n. 1.

(c) Extract from 'Leibnitz en Sterne,' *Rec. ook der Rec.* (1819), xiii. 172 (Lohman, pp. 53–4) attributed to Ockerse [referring to Sterne's self-portrait as Yorick in volume I of *Tristram Shandy*]

This sketch has been made exactly after life, although there are some who claim that Sterne's wit was cruel, his sentiment feigned. But is it possible, without true sentiment, to create a Maria of Moulines, an Uncle Toby, the story of Le Fever, or the sermon on the Good Samaritan (Sterne's masterpiece)?

157. De Perponcher on Sterne

1788

Extract from Willem Emmery, Baron de Perponcher, 'Nadere Gedagten over het Sentimenteele,' *Mengelwerk*, ix (1788) (Lohman, p. 43)

De Perponcher (1740–1819) was poet, moralist, and theologian. The book referred to in the passage below is John Hall-Stevenson's 'continuation' of the *Sentimental Journey*, actually a vulgarized retelling of Sterne's journey, published in 1769.

[Hall-Stevenson's book] showed that from the beginning this sort of writing was susceptible to misuse and unfortunate development and seemed to be a portent of the fruits that could come out of this seed. The true sentimentalist, on the other hand, to be found in Sterne's own journey, by no means set a bad example; but the book gave others the opportunity to travel a road on which they lost their way. Sterne's journey did not have the fault that the passions—intense and ardent perceptions these days so common—were too strongly evoked. In this respect his imitators have deviated from their original—partly because one always wants to go further than his predecessor, partly, maybe, because some, not knowing, as he did, how to play upon the fine strings of the nobler and more delicate sentiments, have tried to improve upon Sterne through stronger strokes of the passions, through giant leaps of the imagination.

158. Willem Kist on Sterne

1823

Extract from *De Ring van Gyges wedergevonden*, 2nd ed. (1823), pt. I, p. 43 (Lohman, p. 52).

Kist (1758–1841) was the author of loosely structured, digressive novels. In the selection below he refers to the ring of Gyges in bk. II of Plato's *Republic*, which could make its wearer invisible.

All my dear brothers (I said, walking uphill to a romantic spot), as Rabelais, Cervantes, Addison, Steele, Le Sage, Rabener,[1] Swift, Sterne, Fielding, Goldsmith, and a hundred others, including anonymous friends and silent laborers in the field of character description, all have lacked this blessed aid—the ring to make one invisible.

Ah! I exclaimed loudly, raising my voice as I descended the hill, had I only their ingenuity, imagination, mellifluous language, enchanting pens! Sterne! Sterne!

[1] Gottlieb Wilhelm Rabener (1714–71), German satiric writer, attacked middle-class follies.

159. Otto Gerhard Heldring on Sterne

1831-3

Extract from *De Natuur en de Mensch* (1831-3), p. 13 (Lohman, p. 60).

Heldring (1804-76), a student of theology and a social pioneer, is comparing Sterne and Asmus. For Asmus, pen name of Matthias Claudius, see No. 149b, p. 442, n. 1.

In their works life is as it appears in reality, not gay, not sad, but expressing itself now in silent, mild joy, now in melancholy—always full of sympathy, always breathing love.[1]

[1] Cf. similar remarks by Carlyle (No. 125).

RUSSIA

160. The Russian Sterne: Karamzin

1790, 1792

Nikolai Mikhailovich Karamzin (1766–1826), sometimes called 'the Russian Sterne,' was the leader of the Russian Sentimental movement at the turn of the century. His *Letters of a Russian Traveler 1789–90* (published 1791–1801; translated and abridged by Florence Jonas, 1957) contain numerous references to Sterne, and he referred to him in the *Moscow Journal* (1791, ii. 51) as 'the original, inimitable, sensitive, kind, clever, beloved Sterne' (quoted in Ernest J. Simmons, *English Literature and Culture in Russia (1553–1840)* (1935), p. 192). In the first selection below, Karamzin shows a detailed and admiring familiarity with the opening section of the *Sentimental Journey*, describing Sterne's experiences in Calais.

(a) Extracts from *Letters of a Russian Traveler* (June 1790, pp. 255–6; July 1790, p. 317)

Calais, midnight

The coach brought us to a posthouse. I at once set out for Monsieur Dessein (whose house is the finest in town). Stopping before his gates, which are covered with a white pavilion, I looked to the right and left.

'What do you wish, sir?' inquired a young officer in a blue uniform.

'The room in which Laurence Sterne lived,' I replied.

'Where he ate French soup for the first time?' asked the officer.

'And fricasseed chicken,' I replied.

'Where he praised the blood of the Bourbons?'

'Where the fire of brotherly love suffused his cheek with a tender glow?'

'Where the heaviest of metals seemed to him lighter than a feather?'

'Where Father Lorenzo came to him with the meekness of a holy man?'

'And where he would not give him a single sou?'

'But where he would have paid twenty livres to an advocate who would undertake to justify Yorick in Yorick's eyes.'

'Sir, this room is on the second floor, directly above us. An old Englishwoman and her daughter now live there.'

Looking up, I saw a pot of roses in the window. Beside it stood a young woman with a book in her hand, most likely *A Sentimental Journey*!

'Thank you, sir,' I said to the garrulous Frenchman. 'But I should like to ask another question.'

'Where is the *remise*,' the officer broke in, 'in which Yorick became acquainted with the charming sister of Count de L—?'

'Where he made his peace with Father Lorenzo and—his own conscience?'

'Where Yorick exchanged his tortoise-shell snuffbox for Father Lorenzo's horn one?'

'But which was dearer to him than any set with gold and diamonds.'

'That *remise* is fifty paces from here, across the street, but it is locked and Monsieur Dessein has the key. He is now at vespers.'

The officer laughed, bowed, and went away.

'Monsieur Dessein is at the theater,' said a passer-by.

'Monsieur Dessein is on watch,' said another. 'He was recently appointed a corporal of the guard.'

'Oh, Yorick! Oh, Yorick!' I thought. 'How changed everything is in France today! Dessein a corporal! Dessein in uniform! Dessein on guard! *Grand Dieu!*'

It was growing dark, so I returned to the inn.

Modern English literature is hardly worth mentioning. Only the most mediocre novels are now being written here, and there is not even one good poet. The line of immortal British writers was concluded with Young, the terror of the happy and comforter of the unhappy, and Sterne, the original painter of sentimentality.

(b) Karamzin's editorial note on Sterne, accompanying a translation of the story of Le Fever from *Tristram Shandy*, first published in the *Moscow Journal* in February 1792, and reprinted in *Izbranie Sochinenia* (1964), ii. 117

Incomparable Sterne! In what distinguished university did you learn such delicacy of feeling? What branch of rhetoric revealed to you the secret of shaking with words the most delicate fibers of our hearts? What musician commands the strings as skillfully as you command our emotions?

How many times have I read the story of Le Fever! And how many times have my tears flowed onto the pages of this history! Perhaps many of the readers of the *Moscow Journal* have already read it in another language; but can one ever read Le Fever without new heartfelt pleasure? The translation is not mine: I have only read and compared it with the English original. Perhaps some of the beauties of the original have been lost; but each reader can restore them with his own sensitivity.

161. Two enthusiasts of the 1790s

(a) Extract from remarks by Michail N. Muraviev (1757–1807), minor lyric poet noted for his cultivation of 'sensibility,' who wrote in Russian periodicals during the 1790s, reprinted in G. Makogonenko, *Nikolai Novikov i russkoe prosvyeshchyenie* (1951), p. 343

[Sterne's] purpose was not to describe the city, the government, agriculture, commerce, the arts; but he wanted to examine people. . . . A single word, a silence, a look, a sensation, hidden in the heart, provided the material for every word in his book.

(b) Extract from Gavriil Petrovich Kamenev (1772–1803), precursor of the Russian Romantics, 'Sofia,' *Muza* (1796), i. 208–9, as quoted in Simmons, pp. 197–8

O beloved Sterne! sensitive philosopher, thou art able to solve such enigmas! Thou art the master who penetrates into the secret recesses of the heart; thou dost know the reason for Sophia's tears!

162. Sterne satirized

1805

Extracts from Prince Alexander Shakhovskoi, *Novi Sterne* (*The New Sterne*) (1805), reprinted in *Komedii, Stikhotvorenia* (1961), pp. 735–52.

Shakhovskoi (1777–1846), who has been described as a 'literary Jack-of-all-trades,' produced adaptations of Shakespearean plays and dramatic versions of some of Scott's novels. His satirical play *The New Sterne*, reflecting a reaction against the excesses of the Sentimental movement, is interesting evidence that Sterne's influence was widespread enough to be a topic for satire.

[Count Pronskoi, the hero, to escape a marriage arranged by his father, sets out with his servant, Ipat, resolving, in the fashion of Sterne, to write an account of his travels. The count's father sends his friend, Sudbin, to try to lure his son back home. In the following scene, Ipat and a group of peasants watch the count, who has just made his first appearance.]

COUNT (on a hill). Oh Nature! Oh Sterne! . . . I am silent and my silence alone is worthy of you.

459

IPAT. Do you hear how it pleases him to be silent?
COUNT (throwing himself on his knees). Creator of the world, an offering for you! A very important one!
KUZMINISHNA [the miller's wife]. Is he worshipping someone, my friend? Or does he believe in pine trees?

(Scene 3, pp. 738–9)

[In the next scene the count laments the loss of his dog, which has been run over. He speaks a long, sentimental soliloquy, followed by a melancholy song as he plays his guitar. The count meets and falls in love with Malana, a peasant girl, though she doesn't understand his sentimental effusions. The peasants eventually conclude that he is crazy. Ipat explains how this has come about.]

IPAT. Decidedly, my master has lost his mind. A pity . . . and he has such an angelic heart. Tearful writers, whining authors! You, you have ruined my fine gentleman; you will have to answer for him. Those little books I brought him from the University bookstore, they have ensnared the poor Count.

[Later, Sudbin, the family friend sent to rescue the count, enters in a fantastic disguise, pretending to be Malana's father.]

SUDBIN. Do you think your master will recognize me?
IPAT. Not a chance. He wouldn't even know his own father. His thoughts, his eyes, all his senses are perpetually at the other end of the world in another realm. I was just saying how sad it is that such a fine gentleman should have for friends writers who have lost their minds. Tell me, sir, where this sentimental devilry came from.
SUDBIN. It was invented in England, corrupted in France, exaggerated in Germany, and came to us in such a pitiful state that . . .
IPAT. That it's enough to make a cat laugh! The trouble is, someone will catch it from us.

(Scene 9, p. 745)

[Sudbin and Ipat agree that everyone has his own 'point of madness.' The count approaches and Sudbin leaves without being seen.]

COUNT. Ignorance! Ignorance! You are the root of all evil; you are the poison of mankind! Oh, enlightenment! When will your beams illuminate my native land? Our Sternes, our Youngs, our Dorats[1]—

[1] Claude Joseph Dorat (1734–80), known as Le Chevalier Dorat, was a French dramatist and sentimental poet. Russian translations of Edward Young's *Night Thoughts* had gone through several editions in the latter part of the century.

when will their seeds bear fruit? Cruel, harsh ignorance! Ah! Ipat, Ipat! It's monstrous!

IPAT. Sir, what has happened to you?

COUNT. All Nature has changed for me. . . . You see these pearly tears . . . do you see them?

(Scene 10, p. 746)

[The count tells Ipat that his tears are for mankind. He has chased Malana through the village to her home, yelling that he wants to be her savior. He has been ejected from her house and afterwards been stared at by the peasants, who have even warned the little children against him. He would like to be a child of Nature, but now when he approaches the peasants, they move away. Later, Sudbin, still in disguise, appears to encourage the count's pursuit of Malana if he will give up his title, since she would merely be laughed at as a 'countess.' The count thinks what his life with her would be like, as Ipat comments in sarcastic asides.]

COUNT. So, so! Destiny has abandoned me. I will become a farmer . . . and make my home in a nearby cabin. There, I will awaken amiably at sunrise . . . and I will till a little corner of the land or watch the fleecy clouds and the flocks of sheep.

IPAT (aside). Not very taxing work.

COUNT. Milk and the fruits of the earth will be my food.

IPAT (aside). A mediocre table.

COUNT. Soft straw for a bed . . .

IPAT (aside). Hardly a first rate bed.

COUNT. Cicero, Sterne, and Young will entertain me; I will read *La Nouvelle Héloïse*.[1]

IPAT (aside). Your loving companion will yawn or feed the swine out of boredom.

COUNT. Ipat, I will be happy!

(Scene 12, p. 749)

[Ipat then tells the count that he intends to marry Malana's sister, build a cabin nearby, and live a comparably idyllic life. The count is somewhat taken aback at this plan in which Ipat not only would be a 'parody' of him but would also be his brother-in-law. In the final scene the count, still determined to have Malana, kneels before Sudbin (who is still disguised as her father) and makes rash promises. Sudbin then drops his disguise and speaks frankly.]

[1] Jean-Jacques Rousseau's novel (1761) extols the beauties of simple country living.

SUDBIN. This very day you must open your eyes. . . . You must sense how much the imagination of a sensitive young man can be inflamed by extravagant writers who may be ruinous for him. A young man with ardent feelings, tender heart, passionate soul. A young man, reading writers who, despite views to the contrary, are gifted with some eloquence, may lose his way for a moment; but the light of reason will bring him back to the true path.

[The count decides to return home.]

COUNT. Ah. Everyone has helped to open my eyes, which were blinded by enticing imagination. I swear to reform and shun forever all the sentimental oddity which gives us nothing either useful or amusing for our pains.

163. Pushkin on Sterne

1822, 1827, undated

Alexander Pushkin (1799–1837), giant of early nineteenth-century Russian literature, was familiar with Sterne's works, and critics have seen resemblances to Sterne in the digressive habit and the play of a variety of emotions in *Eugene Onegin*, Pushkin's novel in verse.

(a) Extract from a letter, 2 January 1822, to Peter Andreevich Vyazemsky (*Letters of Alexander Pushkin*, ed. J. Thomas Shaw (1963), i. 89)

Zhukovsky infuriates me—what has he come to like in this Moore,[1]

[1] Thomas Moore (1779–1852), Irish poet; Vassily Zhukovsky (1783–1852) admired Moore and based his *Peri and the Angel* (1821) on Moore's *Lalla Rookh* (1817).

this prim imitator of deformed Oriental imagination? All of *Lalla Rookh* is not worth ten lines of *Tristram Shandy*; it is time Zhukovsky had his own imagination and were master of his own fancy.

(b) Extract from 'Fragments from Letters, Thoughts, and Notes,' written in 1827 but suppressed by the censor and not published until 1924 (*The Critical Prose of Alexander Pushkin*, ed. and trans. by Carl R. Proffer (1969), p. 49)

Sterne says that the liveliest of our pleasures ends with a shudder which is almost painful. Unbearable observer! He should have kept it to himself; many people wouldn't have noticed it.

(c) Remarks, undated, reported by A. O. Smirnova and printed by B. L. Modzalevski, 'Pushkin i Sterne ,' *Russkii sovremennik* (1924), no. 2, p. 193

[Gogol] will be a Russian Sterne . . . [for] he sees all, he knows how to laugh, but at the same time he is melancholy and makes us weep.

ITALY

164. Foscolo: Sterne's Italian translator

1805

Extract from the preface to the Italian translation of the *Sentimental Journey* by Didimo Chierico (i.e. Ugo Foscolo).

Foscolo (1778–1827), poet, scholar, and patriot, was the first to make Sterne's work generally available to Italian readers, though some had known it through another translation. While serving as a volunteer in the French army, he traversed much of the ground covered by Sterne in his travels. He later went to London, spending the last eleven years of his life there. In addition to reviews for the *Edinburgh* and *Quarterly* during those last years, he is also remembered for his *Letters of Jacopo Ortis* (1798), which has been called 'a species of political Werther.' Foscolo's preface is dated 1805, although it was not published until 1813, when he completed the translation.

Readers of Yorick, and mine. It was the opinion of the reverend Laurence Sterne, parish priest in England, that a smile can add a thread to the too short woof of life;[1] but it seems that he knew, moreover, that every tear teaches mortals a truth. For, taking the name of Yorick, an ancient tragic clown, he attempted with several writings, and especially with the *Sentimental Journey*, to teach us to know others in ourselves, and to sigh at the same time and to smile less proudly at the weaknesses of our neighbor. Therefore I had translated it, many years ago now, for myself; and now that I believe I have profited by

[1] *Tristram Shandy*, epist. dedicat. [Foscolo's note]. Sterne's dedication to Pitt of the second edition of volumes I and II has a slightly different metaphor: '. . . being firmly persuaded that every time a man smiles,—but much more so, when he laughs, that it adds something to this Fragment of Life.'

reading it, I have retranslated it, as much less literally and as much less arbitrarily as I knew how, for you.

But you must realize, Readers, that the author was of a free mind, and of an eccentric spirit, and most sharp-witted, especially against the vanity of the powerful, the hypocrisy of ecclesiastics, and the professorial servility of lettered men; he inclined also to love and to sensuality; but he wished by all means to appear, and perhaps he was, a good man, compassionate and a sincere follower of the gospel which he interpreted to the faithful. Therefore he derides bitterly, and also smiles with indulgent gentleness; and it seems that his eyes sparkling with desire are lowered in shame; and in the animation of joy, he sighs; and while his fancies burst forth all at once, conflicting and highly agitated, suggesting more than they say, and usurping phrases, words and spelling, he nonetheless knows how to order them with the apparent simplicity of a certain apostolic and restful style. Especially into this little book, which he wrote with the avowed presentiment of approaching death, he transfused with more love his own character; as though in abandoning the earth he wanted to leave it some perpetual memory of a soul so different from others. Now you, Readers, pray for peace for the soul of poor Yorick; pray for peace also for me while I live.

165. Sterne's sentimental side

1822

Extracts from Giovanni Ferri di S. Costante, *Lo Spettatore Italiano* (1822).

Ferri (1755–1830), educator and miscellaneous writer, came to France when young and married a woman whose name he added to his own. He served in various political and educational posts until retiring from public life in 1814. Since he fled to England during the French Revolution, it is barely possible that he visited Sterne's grave, though part of the narrative in (c) below Ferri has translated from the *European Magazine* for November 1782, ii. 325–6.

(a) 'Sterne and Marivaux' (*Lo Spettatore*, i. 309–10)

It was Marivaux[1] who gave the first example of the genre of which Sterne was reputed creator, which consists of painting human life with more truth, making visible in the heart of man a great number of rapid movements, so that they can hardly be noticed. The French moralist, in sharpness of intellect and in knowledge of the human heart, is worth not a bit less than the English. Nor in sensitive perception and pathetic description does he suffer a fault. But in that Sterne surpasses him.

(b) 'Sterne's Humor' (*Lo Spettatore*, i. 387)

Whoever should compare [Sterne] in the matter of the jesting style to Cervantes, to Le Sage, to Fielding, would find that his humor is clowning in contrast to the natural gaiety and sharpness of those writers. The characters of his *Shandy* are almost always exaggerated and ridiculous,

[1] See No. 72d, p. 240, n. 1.

and his discourses are extravagant without being comic. To such defects there is added a studied disorder, determined to break all the rules that good judgment imposes; an impenetrable obscurity, certain immodest allusions, and beneath a transparent veil, many licentious expressions.

(c) 'Sterne's Tomb' (*Lo Spettatore*, iv. 410–13)

I arrived early one day at dear Fanny's house to share with her the sad pleasure of visiting Sterne's tomb. . . . In Fanny's way of taking my arm, I saw she was clothed in such a noble and grave reserve, that I had never seen her so in the many other visits we had made together before. To dispel my doubts I stopped to look at her beneath her hat; and for this impulse I was afterwards very happy, since I had never before seen a perturbed sensibility expressed in two eyes resembling hers. In that moment my attention was attracted by the sight of some figures put on display by a print-seller. I saw La Fleur mounted on his pony taking leave of the company that surrounded him at Montreuil and saying goodbye with a smile to his damsels. Their affectionate wishes that God give him good fortune echoed so in my ears that I was drawn out of the sad reflections into which Fanny's melancholy had thrust me. . . .

[They arrive at the tomb.] She rested an arm and leaned her head on the burial stone, and bathed it in tears. 'O! poor Yorick,' she exclaimed with an anguished voice, ' "thou art a little dust which feels nothing." Your heart will no more be kindled with a noble love to hear the bitter fortunes of Maria! No more will it beat with vivid compassion as you tell the sad history of Le Fever! O! the wretched have lost their best friend! Who will be able to arouse, as you did, sweet sympathy in every breast? Who will be able to teach the philanthropy which makes of all men one family? Accept, O good Yorick, the tribute of my lament. The lament of pity was always for you the sweetest and dearest praise.' And she continues in her laments, protesting that benefactors of humanity should be without death, and that Sterne, therefore, will receive immortality from his writings. She prays to have the fortune to succeed at something in the path of such a teacher! 'O good Sterne, I have had no dearer delights, than the works which are daughters of your genius and your heart. O! if only I could have also learned from you to arouse in my fellows the sensibility with which nature has been generous to all! O! if only I could one day earn some little renown among your good imitators!'

166. Sterne, the Italian

1829

Comments on Sterne by Carlo Bini, translated here from 'Lorenzo Sterne,' *Scritti* (1883), pp. 113–14.

Bini (1806–42), patriot and miscellaneous writer, translated works of Byron, Schiller, and Sterne, including portions of *Tristram Shandy*.

If the softness of the Italian sky, and the melody of Italian sounds, and the rejoicing of the amiable land, which in all its forms unveils the thought of a smile, are wonderful and essential expressions of beauty; if the sons of Italy were once endowed with dispositions in harmony with their solemn language, who of us will not easily acknowledge as expressions of beauty all the works of Sterne? And the Irishman created them so beautiful in our manner, that in fancy you would say his thought had been developed in the breezes of our clear skies, and, mixed with his blood, there flowed within him a flame of the Italic sun.

Appendix: Editions of Sterne's work, 1760–1830

The history of the printing of Sterne's works—both singly and in combination or excerpt, both in English and in translation—is an incredibly tangled skein. The purpose of the tabulation below is to give some notion of the extent of Sterne's popularity, rather than to unravel the numerous bibliographical tangles. The tabulation makes no pretense to completeness, and in the majority of cases I have been forced to rely on a bibliographical listing rather than a first-hand inspection of the edition in question; obviously sometimes such listings are ambiguous, incomplete, or inaccurate. In making the tabulation I have not distinguished between reprintings or variant printings and new editions, but have listed each as a separate item. Editions of Sterne's *Works* varied in content: in addition to *Tristram Shandy* and *A Sentimental Journey* they usually contained sermons and letters and sometimes such spurious works as Richard Griffith's fabrication of Sterne's *'Posthumous Works'* (see No. 61). Especially in the case of foreign editions, not all editions represent the complete work. I have listed by country both translations into French and German and English editions issued in those countries; the latter are indicated by 'Eng.'. In the section for the United Kingdom the place of publication is omitted if it was London.

In making the tabulation, I have used the following sources: Francis Brown Barton, *Étude sur l'Influence de Laurence Sterne en France au dix-huitième siècle* (Paris, 1911); *Cambridge Bibliography of English Literature* and supplement; Wilbur L. Cross, *The Life and Times of Laurence Sterne*, 3rd ed. (New Haven, 1929); Clifford K. Shipton and James E. Mooney, *National Index of American Imprints through 1800; the Short-title Evans* (Worcester, Mass., 1969); Henri Fluchère, *Laurence Sterne: de l'Homme à l'Oeuvre* (Paris, 1961); Alan B. Howes, *Yorick and the Critics* (New Haven, 1958, 1971); Kenneth Monkman, 'The bibliography of the early editions of *Tristram Shandy*,' *Library* (March 1970); Kenneth Monkman and J. C. T. Oates, 'Towards a Sterne bibliography,' in A. H. Cash and J. M. Stedmond, eds, *The Winged Skull* (London, 1971); J. C. T. Oates, *Shandyism and Sentiment, 1760–1800* (Cambridge, 1968); C. A. Rochedieu, *Bibliography of French Trans-*

lations of English Works, 1700–1800 (Chicago, 1948); Harvey Waterman Thayer, *Laurence Sterne in Germany* (New York, 1905). In addition I have tabulated the holdings of the following libraries, usually as reported in catalogues or shelf lists: Bibliothèque Nationale, British Museum, Harvard University Library, Library of Congress, Princeton University Library, University of Michigan Library, Yale University Library.

UNITED KINGDOM

Tristram Shandy, serial publication

Vols I, II: 1760 York; 1760 (3 eds plus 'several piracies,' according to Cross, *Life*, p. 216); 1760 Dublin ('third edition': probably first Dublin ed.); 1761; 1763; 1767 (6th ed.); 1768 (vol. I); 1769 (vol. II).
Vols III, IV: 1761 (2 eds); 1761 Dublin; 1768; 1769.
Vols V, VI: 1762; 1767.
Vols VII, VIII: 1765 (2 eds).
Vol IX: 1767; 1767 Dublin.
Vols I–IV: 1765 Dublin.
Vols V–VIII (4 vols in 1): 1765 Dublin.

Tristram Shandy, complete novel

3 vols 1767; 1768; 9 vols 1769; 1770; 3 vols 1774; 1775; 6 vols 1777; 2 vols 1779; 1779 Dublin; 2 vols 1780; 3 vols 1780 Dublin; 9 vols 1781; 1781 (*Novelist's Magazine*); 6 vols 1782; 2 vols 1783; 3 vols 1786; 6 vols 1793 (Cooke's *Select British Novels*); 3 vols 1794; 2 vols [1808] (Cooke's *Select British Novels*); 1811 (Mudford's *British Novelists*); 1817; 1819 (Walker's *Classics*); 3 vols 1823; 2 vols 1823; 1823 (Ballantyne ser., ed. Sir Walter Scott); 2 vols 1823 (together with *A Sentimental Journey*).

A Sentimental Journey

2 vols 1768 (4 eds); 1768 Dublin (2 eds); 4 vols 1769 (with Hall-Stevenson's continuation); 1769; 1769 Dublin; 2 vols 1770; 1771; 2 vols 1773; 1774; 4 vols 1774; 5 vols 1774; 1775; 1776; 2 vols 1778; 2 vols 1780 (2 eds); 1782 (2 eds with Hall-Stevenson's continuation); [1782] (2 eds); 1782 (*Novelist's Magazine*); 1783; 1783 Edinburgh;

1784 (with Hall-Stevenson's continuation); 2 vols in 1 179–(?) (Cooke's *Select British Novels*); 1790; 1790 (with Hall-Stevenson's continuation); 1791; 1791 (with Hall-Stevenson's continuation); 1792; 1794 (Cooke's *Select British Novels*); 1794; [*c.* 1800]; 1800 Liverpool (in *Mirror of Amusement*); 1801; 1803; 1803 Glasgow; 1804; 1805–6 Edinburgh; 1807; 1808; 1809; 1810; 1810 (Mudford's *British Novelists*); 1812 Gainsborough; 1814 Dublin; 1816 Derby; 1817; 1817 (Walker's Classics); 1817 (with *Letters to Eliza*); 1818 (with *Letters to Eliza*); 2 vols 1823 (together with *Tristram Shandy*); 1824.

Works

5 vols [1769]; 5 vols 1773; 1774; 7 vols 1774 Dublin; 8 vols 1774–8 Dublin; 7 vols 1775; 7 vols 1779 Dublin; 8 vols 1779 Dublin; 10 vols 1780; 5 vols 1780; 5 vols 1780 Dublin; 7 vols 1780 Dublin; 10 vols 1783; 7 vols 1783; 8 vols 1784; 10 vols 1788; 10 vols 1790; 8 vols 1790; 5 vols 1790; 10 vols 1793; 5 vols 1793; 8 vols 1794; 7 vols 1794; 8 vols 1795; 10 vols 1798; 8 vols 1799; 8 vols 1799 Edinburgh; 8 vols 1800 Berwick; 7 vols 1802; 8 vols 1803; 4 vols 1803; 8 vols 1803 Edinburgh; 5 vols 1804–5 Harrisburgh; 4 vols 1808; 3 vols 1808; 7 vols 1810; 4 vols 1815; 4 vols 1819; 1819; 6 vols 1823; 4 vols 1823; 1829.

AMERICA

Tristram Shandy

No separate editions during the period.

A Sentimental Journey

2 vols 1768 Boston; 2 vols in 1 1770 Philadelphia; 2 vols in 1 1771 Philadelphia; 1790 Philadelphia; 2 vols 1791 Philadelphia; 1792 Norwich; 2 vols 1793 Worcester; 1795 New York (2 eds); 1796 New York; 4 vols in 1 1828(?) New York, Nurnberg.

Works

6 vols 1774 Philadelphia; 5 vols 1774 Philadelphia; 6 vols 1813–14 New York, Boston.

FRANCE AND FRENCH TRANSLATIONS

Tristram Shandy

2 vols 1776 York, Paris; 2 vols 1777 Neuchâtel; 2 vols in 1 1777 York, Amsterdam; 2 vols 1784 London, Paris; 2 vols 1784 London; 3 vols 1784 London; 4 vols 1784 London; 6 vols 1784 London; 4 vols 1784–5 Paris, London; 1785 Geneva, Paris; 2 vols 1785 York, Paris; 4 vols in 2 1785 York, Paris; 2 vols 1785 London, Paris (2 eds); 2 vols in 1 1785 London, Paris; 2 vols 1786 London, Paris; 4 vols 1787 York, Paris; 6 vols 1828–9 Paris.

A Sentimental Journey

2 vols in 1 1769 Paris, Amsterdam; 2 vols in 1 1770 Liège; 2 vols 1774 Paris, Amsterdam; 1779 Geneva; 1782 Paris, Lausanne; 2 vols 1782 London (2 eds); 1783 Paris (Eng.) (2 eds); 1784 Lausanne; 2 vols in 1 1784 London, Paris (2 eds); 1785 Geneva, Paris; 2 vols 1785 Geneva; 1786 Berne; 1786 Aix (Eng. and Fr.); 2 vols 1786 Geneva, Paris; 2 vols 1786 Paris, Brussels; 2 vols 1786 Lausanne; 1787 Paris; 1788 Amsterdam, Paris; 2 vols 1788 Paris, Toulouse; 2 vols 1789 London; 1790 Strasbourg; 1792 Paris; 1792 Basle (Eng.); 1793 Paris; 1796 Paris; 2 vols 1796 Paris (Eng. and Fr.); 2 vols in 1 1797 Paris; 2 vols in 1 1797 Dijon; 2 vols 1799 Paris (Eng. and Fr.); 3 vols 1799 Paris (Eng. and Fr.) (2 eds); 1800 Lund, Sweden; 1800 Paris (Eng.); 3 vols 1800 Strasbourg (Eng. and Fr.); 3 vols 1801 Paris; 2 vols 1802 Paris (Eng.); 1811 Paris (Eng.); 2 vols 1820 Paris; 1822 Paris (Eng.); 2 vols 1822 Paris; 1825 Paris; 1825 Paris (Eng.); 1827 Paris; 1828 Paris.

Works

6 vols 1787 London, Paris; 6 vols 1797 Paris; 6 vols 1803 Paris; 4 vols 1803 Paris; 4 vols 1818 Paris (2 eds); 6 vols 1818 Paris; 4 vols 1825–7 Paris; 1828 Paris.

GERMANY AND GERMAN TRANSLATIONS

Tristram Shandy

pts 1–6 1763 Berlin, Stralsund; pts 7–8 1763 Berlin, Stralsund; 1769–72 Berlin, Stralsund; 6 vols 1772 Altenburg (Eng.); 2 vols 1774 Berlin; 9 vols in 4 1774 Hamburg; 6 vols 1776 Altenburg (Eng.); 9 pts 1776 Hamburg; 9 pts 1776–7 Hamburg; 9 pts 1777 Hamburg; 9 pts 1778 Hamburg; 9 pts 1778 Berlin; 1792 Basle (Eng.); 2 vols 1792 Gotha (Eng.); 4 vols 1798 Vienna (Eng.); 3 vols 1801 Leipzig; 4 vols 1805–6 Gotha (Eng.); 3 vols 1810 Hanover.

A Sentimental Journey

2 vols in 1 1768 Hamburg, Bremen; 1769 Hamburg, Bremen; 1769 Braunschweig (2 eds); 2 vols in 1 1770 Hamburg, Bremen; 2 vols 1771 Altenburg (Eng.); 4 vols 1771 Hamburg, Bremen; 1772 Hamburg , Bremen; 2 vols 1772 Altenburg (Eng.); 1774 Braunschweig; 2 vols 1776 Altenburg (Eng.); 1776 Hamburg, Bremen; 1777 Hamburg, Bremen; 2 vols 1779 Göttingen (Eng.); 1780 Mannheim; 2 vols 1787 Göttingen (Eng.); 1792 Basle, Gotha (Eng.); 1794 Halle (Eng.); 4 vols 1797 Leipzig; 2 vols 1798 Vienna (Eng.); 2 vols 1801 Leipzig; 1802 Leipzig; 1804 Hamburg, Bremen; 2 pts 1806 Halle (Eng.); 1806 Göttingen (Eng.); 1815 Altenburg, Leipzig (Eng.); 1825 Zwickau; 1826 Leipzig; 1826 Jena (Eng.); 1827 Essen; 1828 Nürnberg (Eng.); 1829 Leipzig; 1830 Schneeberg (Eng.).

Works

9 vols 1798 Vienna.

Select Bibliography

BARTON, Francis Brown, *Étude sur l'Influence de Laurence Sterne en France au dix-huitième siècle* (Paris: Hachette, 1911).

CASH, Arthur H. and STEDMOND, John M., eds, *The Winged Skull* (papers from the Laurence Sterne Bicentenary Conference) (London: Methuen; Kent State University Press, 1971); esp. pt. IV and appendix.

CROSS, Wilbur L., *The Life and Times of Laurence Sterne* (New Haven: Yale University Press, 3rd ed., 1929).

CURTIS, Lewis Perry, *Letters of Laurence Sterne* (Oxford: Clarendon Press, 1935; reprinted 1965).

FABIAN, Bernhard, 'Tristram Shandy and Parson Yorick among some German Greats,' in Cash and Stedmond, *The Winged Skull*, pp. 194–209.

FLUCHÈRE, Henri, *Laurence Sterne: de l'Homme à l'Oeuvre* (Paris: Gallimard, 1961).

HAMMOND, Lansing, *Laurence Sterne's Sermons of Mr. Yorick* (New Haven: Yale University Press, 1948); esp. chs I, IV, V.

HARTLEY, Lodwick, *Laurence Sterne in the Twentieth Century* (Chapel Hill: University of North Carolina Press, 1966).

HARTLEY, Lodwick, 'The Dying Soldier and the Love-born Virgin: notes on Sterne's early reception in America,' in Cash and Stedmond, *The Winged Skull*, pp. 159–69.

HOWES, Alan B., *Yorick and the Critics* (New Haven: Yale University Press, 1958; reprinted Archon Books, 1971).

KIRBY, Paul F., 'Sterne in Italy,' in Cash and Stedmond, *The Winged Skull*, pp. 210–26.

LOHMAN, F. Louise W. M. Buisman-de Savornin, *Laurence Sterne en der Nederlandse schrijvers van c. 1780–c. 1840* (Wageningen, 1939).

OATES, J. C. T., *Shandyism and Sentiment, 1760–1800* (Cambridge Bibliographical Society, 1968).

PRICE, Lawrence Marsden, *English Literature in Germany* (Berkeley: University of California Press, 1953); esp. pp. 193–206.

RABIZZANI, Giovanni, *Sterne in Italia* (Rome: Formiggini, 1920).

SIMMONS, Ernest J., *English Literature and Culture in Russia (1553–1840)*

(Cambridge, Mass.: Harvard University Press, 1935); esp. pp. 189–201.

STOUT, Gardner D., Jr, ed., *A Sentimental Journey Through France and Italy by Mr. Yorick* (Berkeley and Los Angeles: University of California Press, 1967).

THAYER, Harvey Waterman, *Laurence Sterne in Germany* (New York: Macmillan, 1905).

WORK, James A., ed., Laurence Sterne, *The Life and Opinions of Tristram Shandy, Gentleman* (New York: Odyssey, 1940).

Index

III. AN INDEX OF PERIODICALS AND JOURNALS

IV. GENERAL INDEX

This index includes reviewers and critics, diarists and journal writers; letter writers and their correspondents; Sterne's family and friends; and allusions to people, places, and events. (Anonymous works are listed under their titles, but there are no entries for other works, which are merely indexed under their authors. Material in footnotes is indexed if it is substantive. Entries in Index II (writers, books, and painters to whom Sterne is compared) are not repeated in this general index unless there is substantive information in addition to the comparison.)

Paine, Thomas, 18
Pan, Mallet du, 400–1
Parlante, Priscilla, *see* Cavendish-Bradshaw, Hon. Mrs M. A. (Jeffreys)
Parnell, Thomas, 267
Parsons, Rev. Philip, 233
Pearce, Roy Harvey, 34
Pepys, William Weller, 235
Percy, Thomas, 131
Perponcher, Willem Emmery, Baron de, 453–4
Peters, Charles, 59
Phillips, Teresia Constantia, 139
Pinkerton, John, 305
Piozzi, Hester Lynch Thrale, 12, 263–4
Pitt, William, 1st Earl of Chatham, 64, 464
Plato, 125, 454
Plautus, 126
Pope, Alexander, 53, 62, 88, 226, 244, 261, 265, 267, 269, 270, 283, 284, 327, 342, 378
Porter, Katherine Anne, 31
Pottle, Frederick A., 80
Power of Sympathy, see Brown, William Hill
Pratt, Samuel Jackson (pseud. Courtney Melmoth), 11, 224–6, 233–4
Priestley, J. B., 31
Prior, Matthew, 53, 244, 315
Pushkin, Alexander, 25, 462–3
Pye, Henry James, 317
Pye, Mrs [?J. Henrietta], 144

Quintilian, 40, 286

Rabelais, François, 13, 124, 125, 231, 283, 286, 288, 315, 334, 380, 396, 425
Radishchev, Alexander, 25, 35
Ramler, Charles, 23
Randolph, John, 325
Raphael, 192
Rapin, Paul de, 161, 286
Read, Sir Herbert, 30–1
Reeve, Clara, 12, 262–3
'Remarks on some of the Writings of Sterne,' 307–8
Reynell, Carew, 328
Reynolds, John Hamilton, 364
Reynolds, Sir Joshua, 89, 165, 203
Riccobini, Luigi, 447
Rice, James, 364
Richards, Thomas, 364

Richardson, Samuel, 3, 7, 14, 33, 90, 128, 131, 203, 312, 317, 332
Richter, Jean Paul, 16, 353, 369–71, 379–80, 447, 448
Rose, Elizabeth, 223
Rose, William, 77, 172
Rousseau, Jean-Jacques, 21, 26, 269, 272, 286, 321, 379, 461
Rubin, Louis D., Jr, 36
Ruffhead, Owen, 5–6, 77, 119

St James's Park, 83, 175
Saint-Pierre, Jacques Henri Bernardin de, 379
Saintsbury, George, 29–30, 36
Sallust, 49, 195
Sancho, Ignatius, 9, 174–7
Scarron, Paul, 334
Schiller, Johann Christoph Friedrich von, 379, 468
Schlegel, Karl Wilhelm Friedrich von, 23, 445–6
Schopenhauer, Arthur, 23
Scott, Sarah Robinson, 169–70, 175
Scott, Sir Walter, 15–16, 33, 212, 268, 362, 371–6, 416, 459, 470
Scriblerus, see Memoirs of Martin Scriblerus
Seccombe, Thomas, 29–30
Seneca, 179
Seward, Anna, 13, 265, 268–71
Shaftesbury, Anthony Ashley Cooper, 3rd Earl of, 232
Shakespeare, William, 12, 101, 157, 191, 197, 200, 243, 250, 269, 270, 291, 311, 315, 340, 343, 344, 362, 383, 386, 393, 459
Shakhovskoi, Prince Alexander, 25, 459–62
'Shandyan Dialogue,' 238–9
Sharp, Dr Samuel, 191
Shelley, Percy Bysshe, 16
Shenstone, William, 260
Shepperson, Archibald B., 33
Sherlock, Rev. Martin, 249–50, 296
Skelton, Rev. Philip, 297
Skipwith, Robert, 215
Smirnova, A. O., 463
Smollett, Tobias, 10, 131, 145, 190–1, 197, 317, 320, 337
Socrates, 125, 411, 424
'Some Speculations on Literary Pleasures,' 376–8

THE CRITICAL HERITAGE SERIES

GENERAL EDITOR: B. C. SOUTHAM

Volumes published and forthcoming

Continued